GOOD OLD-FASHIONED
YANKEE INGENUITY
UNSUNG TRIUMPHS OF AMERICAN INVENTION

GOOD OLD-FASHIONED
YANKEE INGENUITY

UNSUNG TRIUMPHS OF AMERICAN INVENTION

HARRY HARRIS

Scarborough House/*Publishers*

Scarborough House/Publishers
Chelsea, MI 48118

FIRST PUBLISHED IN 1990

Text design by Terese Bulinkes Platten

Library of Congress Cataloging-in-Publication Data

Harris, Harry, 1918-
    GOOD OLD-FASHIONED YANKEE INGENUITY: Unsung
    Triumphs of American Invention.

    1. United States—Miscellanea. 2. Inventions—United
States—Miscellanea. I. Title. II. Title: American innovations.
E156.H375   1990   973   85-45015
ISBN 0-8128-3142-X
ISBN 0-8128-6262-7 (pbk)

This book is dedicated, with love,
to my talented trinity,
JEAN, TERRI, and BRAM

"When you steal from one author, it's plagiarism;
if you steal from many, it's research."
—Wilson Mizner (1876-1933)

"An 'authority' is only as reliable as his sources."
—Anonymous (?-?)

INTRODUCTION

To gauge fully the impact of America, or at least that portion of the continent allocated to the United States, on the rest of the world is a formidable task that merits the combined services of a battalion of savants with limitless time and resources.

This book is not intended as a definitive checklist. It is an arbitrary, idiosyncratic assemblage of American people, products, and proclivities that have contributed over the years to the delight or dismay of other nations.

Not all the innovators were native born. The Census Bureau confirms that "Americans" constitute—forgive the mixed metaphor—a polyglot melting pot. In 1980, there were 14,079,906 of them born elsewhere, in 155 other countries—the largest number hailing from Mexico, the smallest number from Madagascar.

In this volume we proudly claim the accomplishments of immigrants here and of Americans abroad.

In war and peace; in matters frivolous, functional, and even literally earthshaking, it seems appropriate to paraphrase the slogan boldly ensconced on a Trenton, New Jersey, bridge:

AMERICA MAKES, THE WORLD TAKES

ABSTRACT EXPRESSIONISM: The first American art genre to influence the work of major painters in other countries, also dubbed "action painting" and "the New York school," emerged in New York City during the mid-1940s and attracted worldwide attention during the following decade.

Encompassing a wide palette of individual styles, mostly but not always nonrepresentational, its basic ingredients include a highly personal, freewheeling approach that capitalizes on serendipitous accidents; use of huge canvases; stress on brushstroke technique and texture; and overall, rather than highlighted, focus of attention. Arshile Gorky, initially an acolyte of Picasso, Miro, and surrealism, was a pioneer; but Jackson Pollock, who splattered paint on king-size canvases he spread on the floor, had the most initial impact on an often derisive public.

Pollock, whose seemingly slapdash technique was reviled by many of his colleagues, began his career as a realistic painter. He began to exaggerate elements and subsequently, accentuated distortions by eliminating recognizable subjects. In 1947, when he began to use aluminum and commercial paints, he switched for the first time from painting on easels to "dripping" on floors. One of his admirers, Willem de Kooning, observed, "Every so often, a painter has to destroy painting. Cezanne did it. Picasso did it with cubism. Then Pollock did it. He busted our idea of a picture all to hell. Then there could be new paintings again."

De Kooning had his own highly successful 1948 one-man show, featuring complex abstractions with a series of grotesque depictions of "glamorous" females. Also in the forefront of the movement were Hans Hofmann, Robert Motherwell, Philip Guston, Franz Kline, and Mark Rothko. A similar approach was borrowed, or coincidentally created, by numerous foreign artists, including Wols (A. O. W. Schulze), Jean Fautrier, Henri Michaux, and Jean Dubuffet.

ACADEMY AWARD: American movies' popularity the world over is manifested by the number of countries that eagerly telecast the prolonged festivities in which the American Academy of Motion Picture Arts and Sciences (AMPAS) announces the year's best films, performances, and technical contributions. On March 24, 1986, that number was a record eighty-five, including France for the first time and with the People's Republic of China for the second time. The total audience was estimated at more than one billion people in some three hundred million homes.

AMPAS was formed in 1927 by the U.S. film industry to raise moviemaking's artistic, educational, cultural, and technical standards. It initially consisted of 36 members—top stars and representatives of the major film studios. One of the former, the swashbuckling Douglas Fairbanks, was the organization's first president. Members now number 4,300 and represent all branches of the industry. In 1929, the Academy presented its first awards (*see* OSCAR), eleven in all, for the 1927-28 achievements. *Wings* was the best picture; Brooklyn-born German-speaking superstar Emil Jannings (for *The Last Command* and *The Way of All Flesh*), and Philadelphia-born Janet Gaynor (for *Seventh Heaven, Street Angel*, and *Sunrise*) were the best actors. The actual presentation ceremony, with about two hundred moviemakers in attendance at a Hollywood Roosevelt Hotel banquet, took a mere 4½ minutes. The winners had been announced three months earlier on the back page of the *Academy Bulletin*. There was little local press coverage and none at all by national news services or radio. By 1986, the number of Oscars had proliferated to thirty-five, and the televised proceedings ran three hours, two minutes, a considerable improvement over 1984's almost four-hour tediumthon. Aside from their fondness for the U.S. films produced in Hollywood and on location around the world, other nations often have a rooting interest closer to home. Foreign stars and technicians have been frequent winners; and since 1948, the year after a foreign language film, Italy's *Shoeshine*, won an Oscar, an award for the "best foreign language film" has been presented annually.

ACCESSIBLE UNDERPANTS: American know-how freed underwear-wearing members of the world's male population from the need to engage in major fumbling during bathroom visits. That daily time-saving convenience was provided by the Kenosha Klosed Krotch, an X-shaped overlapping opening that was made part of union suits in 1910 by S. T. Cooper and Sons of Kenosha, Wisconsin. Long underwear went out of vogue after World War I, because army veterans preferred their summer-issue GI shorts. In 1934, Cooper Underwear introduced even shorter shorts, with patented "Y-front construction," inspired by an abbreviated swimsuit spotted on the French Riviera. The cost: 50 cents. The original Style 1001 was replaced by a more streamlined version, Style 1007, alias the Jockey Classic Brief, with the word "Jockey" imprinted around its elastic waistband.

Perhaps the best-known acronym associated with men's underwear is B.V.D. What the letters stand for has caused frequent conjecture. Early guesses were "Boys' Ventilated Drawers" and "Baby's Ventilated Diapers." The three-letter label actually designates the partners who first manufactured the product in 1876—Bradley, Voorhees, and Day. A recent trend in men's underwear that has enlisted designers in the United States and abroad is toward costlier "men's fashion briefs" with distinctive colors and patterns, an especially peculiar status symbol because the designer label is rarely seen. It's estimated that 50 percent are bought by women.

ADDING MACHINE: The first thoroughly reliable adding machine, the comptometer, was invented in 1884 by Dorr Eugene Felt of Chicago, whose immediate goal, at a time when most accountants and clerks relied on pencil and paper, was to devise a machine that would outperform crackerjack counters capable of mentally adding four columns of figures at a time. His first model, built with a jackknife, was housed in a macaroni box and used meat skewers for punch keys, staples for key guides, and elastic bands for springs. Patented in 1887, it remained the only available multiple-order key-driven calculator until 1902. It was preceded by several machines that were granted patents but that prospective buyers shunned as unreliable. The first to employ depressible keys, invented in 1850 by Du Bois D. Parmelee of New Paltz, New York, was dubbed a "calculator." In 1872 Edmund D. Barbour of Boston introduced a "calculating machine" devised to print totals and subtotals.

The first adding machine successfully marketed was the "adding and listing" device invented in St. Louis in 1885 by Auburn, New-York-born William Seward Burroughs (1855-1898) and patented three years later. Manufacturing of the prototype, however, was not financially feasible. With three partners, Burroughs established the American Arithmometer Company and sold one hundred thousand dollars worth of stock to finance additional experimentation. A new model was unable to withstand heavy use, but in 1891, Burroughs produced the first practical adding machine and patented it two years later. According to legend, Burroughs then went to a storeroom where dust covered fifty earlier machines that only he and a salesman who liked to demonstrate his skill in saloons could operate and, one by one, threw them out a window.

In 1905, seven years after Burroughs's death, American Arithmometer was renamed the Burroughs Adding Machine Company. Later it became the Burroughs Corporation and is the worldwide leader in its field.

ADVERTISING AILMENTS: While diligently studying ways in which to increase the sale of their products, American manufacturers and their advertising agencies, without benefit of medical knowledge, have serendipitously discovered a plethora of plagues. "Athlete's foot," a synonym for pedal ringworm, was made part of the general vocabulary in 1928 by the manufacturers of Absorbine Jr. Another of the ailments, real and phony, that have been dinned into the minds of consumers around the world is "B.O.," for body odor, concocted in 1933 to help peddle Lifebuoy soap. Yet another, "halitosis," alias bad breath, was popularized in 1921 by Listerine mouthwash. C. W. Post's all-grain Postum was not only offered as a source of "red blood," presumably making it a no-no for those who yearned to be blue bloods, but also as a cure for a brand new bugaboo, "coffee nerves." Other made-in-America maladies include "jock strap itch," alias "jock itch"; "underarm odor"; "irregularity"; "dishpan hands"; "tired blood"; and "pink toothbrush." One fictional ailment was created just for Japan. When the manufacturers of Vicks cough drops discovered that sales were slow because the Japanese associated the word "cough" with major illness, they began stressing "the Ahems," caused by "the Ahem bug."

ADVICE: This particular commodity has been doled out since the beginning of time. According to Scripture, some of the wrong kind was disseminated in the Garden of Eden. Two American sisters, identical twins born in Sioux City, Iowa, on July 4, 1918, have been serving since 1956 as compassionate surrogate mamas or tsk-tsking Dutch aunts (female Dutch uncles), dispensing advice on an unprecedented scale. Named at birth Esther Pauline Friedman and Pauline Esther Friedman, they became known the world over as, respectively, "Dear Ann Landers" and "Dear Abby." They attended the same schools and Sioux City's Morningside College and on July 2, 1939, the same wedding ceremony. Then Esther, nicknamed "Eppie," and Pauline, nicknamed "Popo," went separate ways with their husbands, Jules W. Lederer and Morton Phillips—the former to Chicago; the latter to Minneapolis; Eau Claire, Wisconsin; and San Francisco.

In the fall of 1954, Esther entered a contest being conducted by the *Chicago Sun-Times* to find a successor to Ruth Crowley, who wrote an advice-to-the-lovelorn column under the pseudonym of "Ann

Landers." Although she was the only nonprofessional applicant, her entry won, and her first column appeared on October 16, 1955. Her sensible, and often witty, advice achieved rapid popularity, first in U.S. newspapers and then in many published abroad.

Pauline denies that her sibling's success prompted her own submission of sample columns to the *San Francisco Chronicle* in the late fall of 1955, but she was hired to dole out advice under the nom de plaint of "Abigail Van Buren." Her first column appeared in January 1956.

In the 1984 version of a Christmas column she updates annually, Ann Landers wrote, "I have been entrusted with the largest reading audience in the world. What an opportunity to educate, to shine a spotlight on ignorance and fear, to comfort the afflicted and afflict the comfortable." Her column, distributed by the Field News Syndicate, has an estimated readership —and frequent writrership—of 85 million via more than one thousand newspapers in the United States, Canada, Europe, Tokyo, Bangkok, and Hong Kong. "Dear Abby," syndicated by the *Los Angeles Times,* has a smaller, but still substantial, constituency.

AEROSOL CAN: The throwaway spray can, now used for products galore, was made possible by Robert H. Abplanalp's invention in 1949, when he was twenty-seven years old. Abplanalp created a crimp-on valve enabling the contents of cans to be squirted out under the pressure of an inert gas. Similar devices were being sought as far back as 1862. The search for conveniently packaged sprays did not become high priority, however, until World War II, when many GIs overseas were afflicted with malaria and other insect-borne ailments.

In 1943, two Department of Agriculture researchers, L. D. Goodhue and W. N. Sullivan, created a small aerosol can pressurized by a liquefied gas. Within months "bug bombs" in grenadelike containers made by welding heavy steel halves together were GI (government issue) for GIs. They became available to the general public in 1947, mostly in the form of insecticide sprays. It took Abplanalp and engineers three months to create a seven-part leakproof valve for cans to be made of lightweight, sturdy aluminum alloy, instead of heavy steel or the more fragile tin.

Abplanalp's invention made the cans a cheap and practical way to dispense assorted liquids, creams, powders, and foams. His Precision Valve Corporation, which earned him well over $100 million, manufactures a billion aerosol cans annually in the United States and an additional half billion in ten other countries.

This wholesale manufacture of spray cans was jeopardized in the mid-1970s, when researchers warned that the fluorocarbons used for the cans could adversely affect the ozone layer that protects humans from the sun's ultraviolet radiations. Abplanalp again came up with a solution: Aerosol II, or "Aquasol," which substitutes water-soluble hydrocarbons as the propellant. Abplanalp once commented, "Edison said genius was 99 percent perspiration and 1 percent inspiration. I say it's 2 percent inspiration, 8 percent work, and 90 percent luck."

AIR BRAKE: Initially called "atmospheric brake," this device, created in 1869 by Central Bridge, New York-born George Westinghouse (1846-1914), provided a practical way to slow and stop a train without requiring a corps of brakemen to clamber from car to car, through corridors on passenger trains and across the roofs on freight cars, setting a series of hand brakes. Hundreds of patents were granted, but only Westinghouse's, relying on compressed air, worked.

An initial demonstration for officials of the Panhandle Railroad was not entirely successful. Because the air took longer to reach the end of the train, each car stopped at a different time. This was corrected by an improvement Westinghouse patented in 1872. He invented an automatic version fifteen years later. Veteran trainmen pooh-poohed the entire idea, doubting that air could replace manpower and reluctant to end the engineer's traditional "down brakes" whistle signal to brakemen when a station was still miles away. Passengers, however, welcomed the innovation. Under the old system, if some brakes were tighter than others, cars bumped against each other. The air brake increased both comfort and safety. It was one of some four hundred-odd Westinghouse patents, the first, when George was nineteen, a small rotary steam engine. Abetted by Nikola Tesla and other brilliant engineers, Westinghouse pioneered in the development of alternating current (AC) electrical power distribution. The Westinghouse Electric Company was founded by him in 1886 to produce the required dynamos, transformers, and motors. The company's electric equipment was used for the Niagara Falls power plant and for the rapid-transit systems in New York City and London.

AIR CONDITIONING: An eighth-century Baghdad caliph stuffed imported snow between his villa's walls. Leonardo da Vinci devised a water-driven fan. When President James Garfield, punctured by a disappointed office seeker's bullet, lay dying in the White House during the summer of 1881, naval engineers improvised a way to lessen his discomfort from the heat and humidity—by making melting ice trickle through dozens of thin layers of terry-cloth cotton and using fans to pump it into the president's bedroom. The temperature dropped twenty degrees and the air was dryer, but the ice required in fifty-eight days totaled more than 500,000 pounds.

The first really feasible system was concocted in 1902 by Willis Haviland Carrier, a twenty-five-year-old employee of the Buffalo, New York, Forge Company, at the request of the Sackett-Williams

Lithographing and Publishing Company, to prevent humidity from snafuing precise color registration in copies of *Judge*, a humor magazine. Carrier's solution stemmed from an observation he had made in a Pittsburgh railroad station on a cold, foggy night. Every metal surface was wet. The water in the air had condensed, as it does on the outside of a frosty beaker of beer. Eureka! Air could be simultaneously cooled and dried! Carrier's system, plus the widespread availability of electricity after Thomas Alva Edison established the first electrical power plant in New York in 1882, made possible air conditioning's eventual spread throughout the world. Carrier installed the first home air conditioner in a Minneapolis millionaire's home in 1914. Although air conditioning made possible such modern miracles as the computer revolution, jet travel, moon landings, and space shuttles, some consider tinkering with natural weather a mixed blessing, blaming it for year-round TV addiction, increased sexual activity, and even obesity.

Ironically, as late as 1983, thirty-three years after Carrier's death, a Carrier factory in Syracuse, New York, was still relying on electric fans during hot summer months.

AIRLINE: The first airline providing scheduled passenger service was the St. Petersburg-Tampa Airboat Line, which on January 1, 1914, began transporting intrepid individuals, one at a time, across twenty-mile-wide Tampa Bay in a Benoist flying boat piloted by Tony Jannus. The five dollar fare saved customers a thirty-six-mile drive around the bay. The pioneer airline, offering two flights a day, lasted only four months.

A considerably larger body of water was leapfrogged when Pan American Airways' Boeing 314 flying boat, the *Yankee Clipper*, completed the first scheduled commercial transatlantic flight between Botwood, Newfoundland, and Southampton, England, on June 28, 1939. The flight took eighteen hours and forty-two minutes, less time than was usually required nine years earlier to fly from San Francisco to Cheyenne, Wyoming. Nineteen passengers were aboard. The posh plane's facilities included separate passenger cabins, a dining salon, a ladies' dressing room, a recreation lounge, sleeping berths, and a bridal suite.

AIRLINE STEWARDESS: Boeing Air Transport, a forerunner of United Airlines, hired as the world's first airline stewardess an Iowa-born registered nurse, Ellen Church, who made her first flight on May 15, 1930, from San Francisco to Cheyenne, Wyoming. Fifteen passengers were aboard the trimotor Boeing 80A, which made four stops before reaching its final destination. Scheduled time for completion of the 950-mile flight was eighteen hours, but it usually required about twenty-four. Miss Church, a private pilot herself, got the job by suggesting in a letter of application that the presence of female cabin attendants could quiet queasy passengers. Not only was she hired, but at the company's request, she recruited seven other nurses to join her as airborne domestics.

Each stewardess had to be no older than twenty-five, no taller than five feet four inches, and no heavier than 115 pounds. Their duties were considerably more strenuous than dispensing drinks, checking seat belts, and distributing earphones. In addition to serving meals (the menu on Miss Church's first flight, and virtually every one thereafter, consisted of fruit cocktail, fried chicken, rolls, and coffee or tea), these women carried luggage, cleaned the plane, punched tickets, bolted down wicker chairs, helped the pilot and ground crew push the plane in and out of its hangar, and held the gas hose during refueling—all for $125 per month. Although the first stewardess's dark green, woolen twill uniforms with capes and shower-cap-like headgear were hardly likely to induce libidinous thoughts in either passengers or crew, pilots' wives vigorously attempted to have the airborne women replaced by men. However, the wives' vetoes were outweighed by the passengers' enthusiastic approval.

Before the advent of the "stews," passengers ranked below airmail and had to fend for themselves. The copilot sometimes poured coffee from a thermos. The first black stewardess was Ruth Carol Taylor, a graduate nurse from Ithaca, New York, who made her first Mohawk Airlines flight on February 11, 1958. Today "flight attendants," numbering more than 125,000, come in both sexes, all colors, and many nationalities.

AIRMAIL: The first official airmail service was authorized by the Post Office Department (now the U.S. Postal Service) on September 23, 1911, when Earle Lewis Ovington, designated "airmail pilot number one," flew the six miles from Garden City, Long Island, to Jamaica, Long Island, in his Blériot monoplane, *Dragonfly*, carrying 640 letters and 1,280 postcards. An experimental route using military planes and pilots was established on May 15, 1918, when two sacks containing 2,457 pieces of mail were flown from Long Island to Philadelphia on one plane and from Philadelphia to Washington, D.C., on another. From takeoff to landing, 218 miles away, required three hours and twenty minutes. A reverse-route inaugural flight from Washington's Potomac Park, with President Woodrow Wilson among the spectators, misfired because pilot George Boyle was unable to start his 150-horsepower Curtiss "Jenny." After almost a half hour of fiddling, mechanics discovered that the fuel tank was empty. Then Boyle headed south, instead of north. When he landed at Waldorf, Maryland, twenty miles away, for directions, he smashed the plane's propeller. His 140 pounds of "airmail" were transported to Philadelphia by truck and then flown on to New York.

Regularly scheduled service between New York and Washington, D.C., utilizing four pilots, began on August 12, 1918. Transcontinental airmail service followed in 1924. Flying the mail was a hazardous assignment. Pilots flew in open cockpits—without radio navigation help, flight instruments, or weather stations. Especially dangerous was the flight from New York to Chicago, over the Allegheny Mountains, "the graveyard run." Of the first forty pilots assigned to that route, thirty-one were killed. One early airmail pilot achieved international fame at twenty-five. In 1926, Charles A. Lindbergh left his job on the St. Louis-Chicago run to compete for the twenty-five thousand dollar prize being offered for a nonstop flight from New York to Paris. He accomplished that feat in the *Spirit of St. Louis*, a modified single-engine monoplane, on May 21, 1927. He was not the first man to fly across the Atlantic but the first to do it without human company.

AIRPLANE: Who built the first heavier-than-air aircraft to make a sustained flight under its own power? Wright? Wrong!

That distinction goes to Roxbury, Massachusetts-born Samuel Pierpont Langley (1834-1906). His unmanned Model 5, tested on the shores of the Potomac on May 6, 1896, flew about three-quarters of a mile after being catapulted from a platform twenty feet up. It remained aloft for a minute and a half before its one horsepower steam engine ran out of fuel. Langley's "aerodrome," with four cambered fourteen-foot single-tier wings, was sixteen feet long and weighed twenty-six pounds. It would be seven years later before brothers Orville and Wilbur Wright made their historic flights at Kitty Hawk, North Carolina.

On December 17, 1903, the Wrights' *Flyer*—consisting of hardwood, cloth, and wire; with a forty-foot wingspan; and powered by a twelve horsepower, four-cylinder engine bolted to an air frame and connected to a pair of propellers—was launched from a monorail after a thirty-five- to forty-foot run. Piloted by Orville, lying on his belly on the lower wing, it made four flights against a twenty-one-mile wind, at an average speed of thirty-one miles per hour. Their first flight was 120 feet, a shorter distance than the 195 feet between the wings of a Boeing 747. A skeptical press did little to alert the public and the army was indifferent to the longest flight, 852 feet, which lasted fifty-nine seconds. Ironically, two years earlier, Wilbur Wright had predicted "Man will not fly for fifty years." It was not until 1907, after the third *Flyer* made a twenty-four-mile nonstop flight and President Theodore Roosevelt induced the army to commission a new kind of Wright biplane, that the world fully realized the significance of the Wright brothers' accomplishment.

The two world wars triggered tremendous aircraft advances. Because World War II required them, American plane-makers concentrated on long-range craft. As a result, when the war ended, the planes dominating the world scene were those made by Douglas, Lockheed, and Boeing. The development of jet engines made possible tremendous speed and minimal turbulence. In 1967, sixty-four years after the Wrights' historic flight, North America's X-15 A-2 rocket-powered test plane flew 4,534 miles per hour.

AIR TRAFFIC CONTROL: Air traffic control in the United States, a principal concern of the Federal Aviation Administration (FAA), dates from the mid-1930s when "air traffic control centers" were opened in Newark, Cleveland, and Chicago. Equipment was rudimentary—maps to check aircraft positions, blackboards to chart their movement, and voice radio contact. The first regulatory code, the Civil Aeronautics Act of 1938, incorporated this basic concept of guidance from the ground, and it continues to be the primary procedure.

The system has become increasingly complex. Incoming planes now contact a tower, identify themselves, and await landing instructions. That includes clearance to enter the traffic pattern, a runway number, a wind reading, and an altimeter setting. A pilot takes off and lands either by visual flight rules (permissible only when there is a ceiling of at least one thousand feet and a visibility of three miles) or instrument flight rules (in virtually any kind of weather).

Pilot aids for "blind" flying include a variety of sensitive electronic instruments. Radio contact keeps the pilot heading in the right direction. As he approaches his destination, he tunes in the instrument-landing system and, keeping two needles centered, follows a radio-projected glide path. On breaking out of the clouds, he must be able to see at least a quarter mile ahead on the runway. If he can't, he is required to seek an alternate landing field. He is tracked by radar scanners from takeoff to landing. He follows an assigned path and an assigned altitude. Air traffic control monitors his airspeed and gives him his final headings.

In 1947, Peruvian International Airways, using General Electric equipment, became the first airline equipped with radar, showing a clear map of the country below. Many U.S. radars are linked to computer systems that warn if a plane is flying too low or is in danger of hitting high ground. The ground-proximity warning system (GPWS) triggers a synthetic shout of "Pull up!" if an "inadvertent landing" is imminent. The first bad-weather landing system for planes was devised by Luis W. Alvarez (1911-   ), a pilot himself, who won a 1968 Nobel Prize for his studies in the physics of subatomic particles and the development of techniques for detecting them.

ALARM CLOCK: Not everyone may consider it an international boon, but the first mechanical dream aborter was too unwieldy to be thrown at a nagging spouse or a yowling cat. Invented in 1787, by Levi Hutchins of Concord, New Hampshire, it was housed in a twenty-nine-inch-high pine case with a mirror in the door. The alarm rang at a fixed, unchangeable time because Hutchins only wanted something to prevent him from sleeping past his usual wake-up hour—4 A.M. He never bothered to patent or manufacture his bell-ringer. Patented efforts by other American inventors to produce a more reliable waker-upper included an 1882 model that dropped a bar in the snoozer's face, striking "a light blow, sufficient to awaken the sleeper, but not heavy enough to cause pain," and a 1907 model in which the alarm activated a flow of water through perforations in a loop of hose twisted around the victim's neck.

ALCOHOLICS ANONYMOUS: The organization dedicated to the voluntary rehabilitation of chronic tipplers by providing support from ex-drunks was formed on June 10, 1935, by Bill Wilson and Dr. Bob Smith, after a momentous meeting at the Akron City Hospital.

Wilson, a New York broker with a longtime drinking problem, had tried numerous "cures" without success. Shortly after he was introduced to the Oxford Movement by a drinking buddy who had achieved sobriety through its religious teachings, he had a spiritual experience in New York's Towns Hospital while recovering from a binge. "Suddenly," he said afterward, "the room lit up with a great white light. I was caught up into an ecstasy." Later, while in Akron on business, Wilson felt a compulsion to talk to another alcoholic, partly to be of help to a fellow imbiber and partly to subdue his own yen for a drink. He established an immediate rapport with Smith, a frequently soused surgeon. After they had swapped supportive words, they went looking for someone else who might be of a mind to quit drinking. That was the spark that ignited Alcoholics Anonymous (A.A.) and its principal precept: "You help yourself while helping someone else."

The New York A.A. units, initially linked with the Oxford groups, broke away in 1937 but incorporated Oxford Movement concepts into their rehabilitative Twelve Steps. One major difference was A.A.'s accent on anonymity. Two years after their meeting, Wilson and Smith compared notes and found that A.A. principles had resulted in forty dehydrations. The Alcoholics Foundation, an A.A. trusteeship, was founded in 1938.

A major source of income was Wilson's 1939 book, *Alcoholics Anonymous*, the A.A. "bible" known to members as the Big Book, which made the organization self-supporting. It is distributed worldwide by Alcoholics Anonymous World Services. Attempts to limit A.A. membership to people of "moral responsibility" were rejected. The organization's only "admission fee" is the willingness to state, "I think I am an alcoholic. I want to try to stop drinking." By 1983, A.A. had spread to 110 other countries.

An offshoot of A.A. is Debtors Anonymous (D.A.), founded in 1976 by a man who had been a member of A.A. for twenty-seven years. Borrowing A.A. principles, it claimed about 4,000 members in 1986, with chapters in the United States and abroad. Other A.A.-inspired groups provide support for impotent males and overeaters.

ALFRED E. NEUMAN: The befreckled, goofy-looking *Mad* magazine mascot, an international celebrity, reportedly had a human counterpart whose photograph appeared in a nineteenth-century medical textbook that discussed his Dumbolike ears. Another claim is that he was in a high school biology book to illustrate lack of iodine. The photograph, accompanied by the phrase, "What, me worry?" was widely distributed on penny-arcade postcards and borrowed for ads selling patent medicines, shoes, and soft drinks. Because of his gap-toothed grin, his visage became an advertising symbol for Painless Romaine, a nineteenth-century Topeka, Kansas, dentist. After being spotted on a poster, the merry moron was adopted in 1954 by *Mad*'s creator and initial editor, Harvey Kurtzman, and christened Melvin Cowznofski, a name credited to humorist Ernie Kovacs.

In 1956, Al Feldstein, Kurtzman's successor as *Mad*'s editor, decided he preferred Alfred E. Neuman, a name that may have come to *Mad* staffers' minds because radio humorist Henry Morgan constantly needled his conductor, a real Alfred Newman. Kurtzman elevated Alfred to cover-boy status. Often drawn for *Mad* by Norman Mingo, who also painted more conventional portraits, Alfred became the standard-bearer for millions of young iconoclasts and the despair of their parents. *Mad*'s right to use and endlessly re-use the familiar face has been challenged in court, but the judge ruled that *Mad* had every right to adopt the loony lad. Numerous entrepreneurs have approached *Mad* about using Alfred's face on merchandise, but their notions have been rejected as insufficiently *Mad*. After the success of a watch emblazoned with the face of a disgraced vice-president of the United States, there was a proposal for an Alfred E. Neuman watch. The proposer envisioned huge sales for a worthy successor to the classic Mickey Mouse watch, but was turned down, because he had in mind an ordinary timepiece, rather than one that did something peculiar, like run backward. *(See also MAD.)*

ALKA-SELTZER: A newspaper editor gave A. H. (Hub) Beardsley, then president of the Dr. Miles Laboratories, the nugget of news that led to the creation of this widely used stomach-settler and hangover-ameliorator. Beardsley wondered why, during a visit to the Elkhart, Indiana, *Truth* in December 1928, not a single member of its staff had been effected by a raging flue epidemic. The daily's employees were so ostentatiously fit that altruistic editor Tom Keene was lending linotypists to a flu-flogged newspaper in a nearby town. Keene attributed his staff's sturdiness to a home remedy for colds that had been made an official office remedy: repeated doses of aspirin and bicarbonate of soda until all symptoms had vanished. Impressed, Beardsley asked his chief chemist, Maurice Treneer, to formulate an effervescent tablet embodying the Keene ingredients. Coughing and sneezing Miles employees tested Treneer's tablets and found them effective. When Beardsley took samples along during a Mediterranean cruise, fellow passengers reported the tablets also helped to alleviate seasickness. During the early 1930s, Alka-Seltzer acquired a reputation as a cure for morning-after megrims. The ending of Prohibition in 1933 triggered an immediate surge in sales.

ALLERGY: The concept of allergies and how antigens or allergens produce them was first expounded, in a letter to the Academy of Sciences in Vienna, by Clemens von Pirquet and his associate Bela Schick in 1903, but Americans made major allergy-controlling contributions before and after. In 1900, Solomon Solis-Cohen, of Philadelphia's Jefferson Medical College, introduced "adrenal substance" (epinephrine) for the treatment of asthma, hay fever, and hives. In 1910, Samuel J. Melzer, of the Rockefeller Institute, established the fact that bronchial asthma was also categorizable as an allergic ailment. Two years later, Oscar M. Schloss, of Cornell Medical College, initiated scratch tests to determine the substances to which individuals were allergic. In 1915, a superior intracutaneous (between the layers of the skin) test was devised by Robert A. Cooke, himself a victim of allergies, while working in a small New York Hospital laboratory. K. K. Chen, who later became director of pharmacologic research for the Eli Lilly Company, and C. F. Schmidt were instrumental in the 1920s in introducing into Western medicine an antiallergy drug that had been used in China for five thousand years: ephedrine—less powerful than epinephrine, but more lasting and more easily administered by mouth.

In 1959 Stephen Daniel Lockey (1905-1985) was credited with the discovery that commonly used food dyes could be a major cause of allergic reactions. His findings triggered a U.S. Food and Drug Administration order that required the listing of all food additives on package labels. Lockey's interest in allergic reactions began when he was six years old and watched a younger brother die in a shock reaction to a diphtheria vaccine. His three sons, all doctors, collaborated with him on a book about allergy and immunology. In general, allergens are divided into five categories: airborne substances, foods, contact substances, drugs, and infectious agents.

ALTERNATING CURRENT: American travelers abroad find that they require adapters for their hair dryers, shavers, and other electrical equipment. That incongruity is, incongruously, the result of a feud between two American inventors. In 1878, a year before he produced the first practical electric light bulb, Thomas Alva Edison was already using proceeds from his stock ticker and phonograph to establish a New York electric-light company. From the start, he contemplated an entire system. By 1882, that system, which included steam-powered generators, transmission circuits, switches, and even use-measuring meters, began selling power to forty-nine customers. It utilized direct current (DC), with electrons flowing continuously in one direction. Six years after introducing his DC bulb, Edison found himself competing for customers with a former employee who had conflicting notions.

Nikola Tesla, a brilliant, if eccentric inventor, emigrated from Serbia in 1884 and, for a few months, worked in Edison's laboratory. Edison and Tesla quarreled, and Tesla subsequently sold, for $1 million, electrical patents scorned by Edison to George Westinghouse, the inventor of the railroad air brake. Westinghouse organized a company to challenge Edison's and utilized Tesla's concept of alternating current (AC), in which electrons keep reversing their flow. Sixty-cycle AC, used in the United States, changes the direction of flow 120 times a second. Other countries use Edison's DC. Tesla realized that high-voltage AC, unlike DC, could be transmitted over hundreds of miles of wire without major power loss, and with the backing of the Westinghouse company, he was able to harness the energy of the Niagara Falls and, in 1903, to start providing AC for distant parts of New York State. Edison, a notoriously poor loser, tried to discredit AC, charging that it was far more dangerous than DC. New York State penal authorities, convinced by his arguments, decided that AC was just the thing for a humane substitute for hanging and commissioned the world's first electric chair, powered by three Westinghouse AC generators. Actually, it was later proved, DC is somewhat more lethal.

("AC-DC" is also a slang term for bisexuality.)

ALUMINUM: Until the advent of aluminum, the word "metal" automatically conjured up the idea of weightiness. Aluminum is the world's most plentiful metal, comprising (in combination) one-twelfth of the earth's surface; but it was virtually unknown a hundred years ago. In 1825, using a chemical process, a Danish scientist, Hans Christian Oersted, produced tiny globs of the light but sturdy stuff. However, the cost of refining the ores and clays containing aluminum was prohibitive. The metal was so rare that Napoleon III used an aluminum table service for guests who merited something more impressive than gold.

In 1886, when he was twenty-two, Thompson, Ohio-born Charles Martin Hall (1863-1914), after a few months of experimentation, solved a problem that had baffled expert chemists for more than sixty years: how to produce pure aluminum in a way that made its commercial use feasible. His simple, cost-paring method called for passing an electric current through a chemical solution. Enlisting the help of a Pittsburgh metallurgist, Hall established the Pittsburgh Reduction Company. Arthur V. Davis, the company's first salesman, suggested teakettles as a possible product and borrowed a mold. However, the first local merchant he approached nixed that notion and ordered two thousand aluminum pots instead. Davis spent several frantic days trying to track down the equipment necessary for this first practical use of aluminum. Other merchants were less sanguine about the new metal and, in 1889, faced with an overdue four thousand dollar note, Hall and his associates went to Andrew W. Mellon's Pittsburgh bank for a loan. Mellon agreed to swap cash for stock. (By the 1920s, Mellon and his brother had increased their portion of the shares from a tenth to a third and controlled the company.) With Mellon participation, Pittsburgh Reduction prospered, moved to bigger quarters, became the first industrial user of Niagara Falls' hydroelectric power, induced makers of numerous metal products to switch to aluminum, and in 1907, changed its name to Alcoa, for Aluminum Company of America. By then aluminum was in worldwide use for buildings, automobiles, boats, kitchen utensils, surgical instruments, electrical transmission wires, and the Wright brothers' airplane. In 1910, a new product was added: aluminum foil.

ANESTHESIA: The word, spelled "anaesthesia" and defined as "a Defect of Sensation, as in Paralytic and blasted (stricken) Persons," appeared in a 1721 English dictionary, but master vocabulary maven Samuel Johnson snubbed it when compiling his own 1755 language list. There are about ten claimants to its initial use, including Dr. Crawford Williamson Long of Jefferson, Georgia. Ether had been brought to Jefferson by an itinerant science lecturer. Daring young Jeffersonians urged Dr. Long to let them try for a high by inhaling the stuff, and he obliged; but then it occurred to him that ether in more potent doses could serve for something other than fun and games. On March 30, 1842, using sulphuric ether under a towel, he removed a half-inch cystic tumor from the back of James M. Venable's neck. His bill totaled $2.25. The two bits was for the ether. Older townspeople suspected him of sorcery and threatened to string him up. End of Dr. Long's contribution.

A dentist, Dr. Horace Wells, of Hartford, Connecticut, discovered the anesthetic potential of nitrous oxide gas, the "laughing gas" used as party entertainment. On December 11, 1844, after the gas had been administered by a traveling showman, Gardner Colton, he had one of his teeth extracted by a colleague, Dr. John M. Riggs. Failing to realize that the gas had to be combined with oxygen, a discovery that didn't occur for another twenty-four years, Wells almost totaled a patient.

On October 16, 1846, William Thomas Green Morton, a "painless dentist" in Boston, who had reduced his patients' ouch! quotient during tooth yanking by having them inhale the sleep-inducing vapor of a "secret" liquid, was invited to go to Massachusetts General Hospital to assist in a jaw tumor operation. The young man with the problem felt no pain during the surgery and no ill effects after it. However, Morton was banned from hospitals because he refused to disclose the ingredients of his "Lethean gas." One of Morton's admirers, physician and author Oliver Wendell Holmes, whose same-named son became an eminent member of the U.S. Supreme Court, suggested use of "anesthesia," a word of Greek origin, to describe a patient's state of unconsciousness.

APGAR SCORE: The Apgar score, an internationally used ten-point checklist for newborn infants, is named for the anesthesiologist Dr. Virginia Apgar, who developed it while at New York's Columbia-Presbyterian Hospital. The baby is observed by a trained scorer one and five minutes after delivery. The infant is accorded grades of 0, 1, or 2 in five categories: heart rate, respiratory rate, muscle tone, cry, and color. If the total score during the initial check is 3 or less, the infant's condition is critical and requires prompt resuscitative action. An Apgar score of 7 to 10 indicates that all is well. The five-minute check correlates positively with the baby's later survival and normalcy. To earn the top score of 10, the new arrival must display a heart rate over 100, good respiration, active motion, vigorous lung power, and good overall color. Among non-Apgar signs considered cause for parental jubilation are immediate urination and an erect penis.

APPENDICITIS: Severe pain in the abdomen, accompanied by nausea, was once subject to diverse diagnoses. It was dubbed "typhlitis," "perityphlitis," and "peritonitis appendicularis localis" until 1886, when the Chelsea, Massachusetts-born pathologist Dr. Reginald Heber Fitz (1843-1913), a Harvard Medical School professor, rechristened the ailment, pairing a Latin noun and a Greek suffix. After studying 466 cases in the wards and on the dissecting tables of Massachusetts General Hospital, where he bore the title of "Microscopist and Curator of the Pathological Cabinet," he concluded that the characteristic inflammation almost invariably stemmed from the appendix.

In a report at an 1886 meeting of the Association of American Physicians, Dr. Fritz listed symptoms and made these recommendations for initial treatment: rest, liquid diet, and sedation with opium. However, if general peritonitis seemed imminent after twenty-four hours, he advised opening the abdomen and removing the offending organ. In 1889, after checking seventy-two more cases, he recommended earlier surgery. His findings markedly affected worldwide treatment of the disease. The first successful appendectomy, however, is credited to a Davenport, Iowa, surgeon, Dr. William West Grant, who excised Mary Gartside's vermiform appendix at St. Luke's Hospital on January 4, 1885. Another claimant to the distinction of performing the first removal of an infected appendix is George Thomas Morton, son of anesthesia pioneer William Morton (*see* ANESTHESIA). His surgery on a twenty-six-year-old man in an acute stage of appendicitis occurred in Philadelphia on April 27, 1887.

Initially, because of the fear of infection, appendectomies were performed only as a last resort, when the patient's appendix had burst and his life was imperiled. In 1888, Dr. Henry B. Sands, of New York, diagnosed and removed an inflamed appendix before perforation had occurred. The following year, Sands's assistant, Charles McBurney, pinpointed the area of the abdomen where tenderness is most likely to be detected. It is now known as "McBurney's point." After 1890, appendectomies became common; but as late as 1936, 16,480 deaths were attributed to faulty diagnosis and delayed surgery.

ARCH SUPPORT: William (Billy) Scholl, one of thirteen children of a LaPorte, Indiana, dairy farmer, became the family's cobbler at fifteen after designing and sewing a 132,000-stitch harness. Completing an apprenticeship with a local shoemaker, he headed for Chicago to work in a shoe store as a salesman and shoe repairer. Close-up views of misshapen feet inspired in him a yen to become foot doctor to the world. He became an expert on podiatry by enrolling concurrently in two medical schools. In 1904, when he was twenty-two, he used the anatomical know-how resulting from his simultaneous studies to design his first arch support, the "Foot Eazer." To acquire retail outlets for his ultracomfortable shoes, he walked from shoe store to shoe store ten hours a day, presumably sparing himself pedal pain by wearing his own product.

His sales approach was rather unorthodox. To get a store manager's attention, he would toss a human skeleton's foot on a table. To make Americans foot-minded, he sponsored walking competitions and, in 1916, a "Cinderella foot" contest that shunned glass slippers. Women were invited to go to the nearest Dr. Scholl's store to have their foot health assessed by Scholl's "Pedo-Graph," a machine designed to spot deviations from ideal foot structure. From thousands of entries, a panel of judges picked America's most perfect foot. The winner's footprint was displayed in newspapers throughout the land—a reward that presumably thrilled her all the way down to her top-rated tootsies.

Dedicated to ridding people everywhere of such afflictions as corns, bunions, blisters, and ingrown toenails, Scholl conducted a worldwide search for sufferers, accumulating a fortune in the process. He held more than three hundred patents for pedal treatments and for the machines that produced, at home and abroad, such international foot aids as Dr. Scholl's corn, callus, and bunion pads. He also manufactured shoes designed to fit every kind of foot, rather than only those considered "normal"—with men's sizes ranging from 5½ to 16, AAA to EEEEEEE, and women's sizes from 2½ to 13, AAAAA to EEEEEEEE. Dr. Scholl's foot products are now a subsidiary of the Schering-Plough conglomerate. In the late sixties, Dr. Scholl's wooden exercise sandal became a national fad for fashion-conscious women.

ARM AND HAMMER BAKING SODA: Introduction of this product in 1867 was helped by the sheer size of one of its salesmen, Colonel Powell, who, at 7 feet 4 inches, would have been a hot basketball prospect. The muscular arm and raised hammer on every package represent Vulcan, the mythological Roman god of fire and metalwork. It was the symbol of the Vulcan Spice Mill in Brooklyn, New York, owned by James A. Church, who retained the symbol after closing the mill and used it when he went into the baking soda business with his father. He thought it was appropriate because the product had the "force" to make bread dough rise. (Long before *Star Wars*, he may have told his kin, "May the force be with you.")

Arm and Hammer baking soda, generically bicarbonate of soda—a home remedy for heartburn, diarrhea, and other maladies—is in millions of kitchens and medicine cabinets throughout the world. Also used as a metal polish and a refrigerator and Kitty Litter odor-absorber, it is manufactured by the Church & Dwight Company, with 80 percent of its stock owned by more than a hundred descendants of the two New Englanders who started the firm in New York, Dr. Austin Church and his wife's uncle, John Dwight.

ARROW SHIRT: "Sanforization," a process used by cotton finishers throughout the world, is the result of the search by Cluett,

30

Peabody and Company, manufacturers of the internationally popular "Arrow shirt," for a method to minimize the shrinkage of shirt collars. The Arrow shirt itself came into existence after Mrs. Orlando Montague, of Troy, New York, plagued by her blacksmith husband's "ring around the collar" problem, devised the detached collar in 1820. Mrs. Montague, tired of spending hour after hour scrubbing and ironing her spouse's shirts, snipped off all the collars, stitched up the edges and neckbands, and attached narrow strips of fabric to prevent slippage. Neighboring housewives enthusiastically borrowed the idea. A retired minster, Ebenezer Brown, began manufacturing detachable collars in the back of his general store. Similar operations began in shops and lofts elsewhere in Troy. One of the most successful became the Cluett Company, which initially produced only starched collars but expanded to add entire shirts. In 1899, it merged with Coon and Company, whose founders, the Coon brothers, owned the Arrow trademark. An enterprising Coon and Company salesman, Frederick F. Peabody, became a partner in the burgeoning company, which by the end of World War I was offering four hundred shirt styles.

When soldiers returning from overseas showed a marked preference for shirts with inseparable soft collars, Arrow, in 1921, began meeting the demand. The new Arrow Trump, however, posed the same old shirt problem: shrinkage. In 1928, Sanford Cluett, then Arrow's vice-president in charge of research, devised a solution, compressing cotton fabric under tension. Cluett, Peabody and Company earns millions of dollars annually by leasing the process.

ARTIFICIAL HEART: The Jarvik-7 artificial heart, intended eventually to end the need for human donors for heart transplants, bears the name of its inventor, Dr. Robert K. Jarvik, of Salt Lake City. It was first implanted by a team of doctors headed by William DeVries at the Utah Medical Center on December 2, 1982. The recipient was Barney Clark, a sixty-two-year-old retired dentist from Seattle, Washington. The mechanical heart—made of polyurethane, Dacron, and Velcro —was substituted for the two lower chambers of Clark's own heart, the ventricles that pump blood to the lungs and force it into the arteries. In a seven-hour operation, the Jarvik-7 was attached to the two upper chambers of Clark's natural heart, the auricles that receive blood from the lungs and veins. Hoses connected it to an external air compressor that simulated heart action, pumping at least eight quarts of blood per minute. The Jarvik-7 "beat" more than thirteen million times while keeping Clark alive for 112 days. It continued to beat even after Clark's death of massive organ and tissue failure. The second recipient at Louisville's Humana Hospital Audubon on November 25, 1984, William J. Schroeder, exceeded Clark's postoperative longevity but developed serious neurological and kidney problems. The first non-American to undergo the procedure was the fourth recipient, Swedish patient Leif Stenberg. The operation was performed at the Karolinska Hospital in Stockholm by a twelve-member implant team headed by a Norwegian surgeon, Dr. Bjarne K. H. Semb. In December 1985, Mary Lund became the first female recipient via a smaller model, because of women's smaller chest cavities. The Jarvik-7's early setbacks led pioneer heart surgeon Michael DeBakey to wonder if the device should be used only as a temporary expedient while awaiting a human heart, but other surgeons noted that open-heart surgery and heart transplants also provided disappointment. A fourteen-member panel, convened by the National Heart, Lung, and Blood Institute in May 1985, urged federal support for development of a fully implanted artificial heart without an external support system—an achievement they estimated would require thirteen years and $73 million. Its potential cost to recipients: $150,000. Nevertheless, the Jarrik heart was recalled by the FDA in 1990.

ARTIFICIAL INTELLIGENCE: Machines that think are engaging the attention of researchers everywhere, despite dire warnings over the years by Norbert Wiener (*see* CYBERNETICS) and other concerned Cassandras. Artificial intelligence (AI), the operable phrase, was coined in the early 1950s by John McCarthy of the Massachusetts Institute of Technology. An international race is now in progress to develop what AI pioneer Edward A. Feigenbaum and Pamela McCorduck, in a 1983 book of that title, dubbed "the fifth generation." The book urged U.S. development of a computer that would mark a fifth major technical advance in that field—after vacuum tubes, transistors, integrated circuits, and very large-scale integrated circuits. On April 14, 1982, the Japanese Ministry of International Trade and Industry (MITI), announced that it was committing $1 billion to develop a "fifth generation" system capable of such functions as reading, talking, and translating Japanese to and from English.

The widespread interest in AI was manifested in August 1980, when the American Association for Artificial Intelligence, expecting several hundred to attend its initial meeting at Stanford University, drew nearly a thousand, including forty reporters and well-heeled individuals eager to invest. AI is already being utilized in "expert systems," containing data-plus "heuristics," or expert guesses, on specific subjects. Tests of INTERNIST-1, conducted in 1983, proved almost as accurate as attending physicians in diagnosing cases selected from the *New England Journal of Medicine.* CADUCEUS provides similar expertise in the fields of physiology and anatomy. DELTA/CATS-1 is used by the General Electric Company, which has, on its staff, only one human expert to help in the maintenance of diesel locomotives. DEBUGGY, which teaches subtraction, has been programmed to figure out and correct the reasons a student keeps making mistakes.

Among computer programs that have been programmed to "learn" is Terry Winograd's SHRDLU (from the compositor's type row, assembling in order of frequency the twelve most-used English letters: ETAOIN SHRDLU). A SHRDLU spin-off, programs that enable a computer to play chess, are not yet capable of defeating the best human players but merit "expert" ranking.

ASPARTAME: The popular low-calorie sweetener, sold under such brand names as NutraSweet and Equal, was created accidentally, in 1965, in the laboratory of the Skokie, Illinois, pharmaceutical firm of G. D. Searle and Company, by a staff scientist testing various substances for their possible usefulness as drugs. Hailed when introduced in 1981 as a less controversial alternative to another mass-manufactured low-calorie sugar substitute (*see* SACCHARIN), it was approved as an additive to soft drinks in July 1983. However, aspartame, too, has become a target for arguable charges of harmful effects.

ASPIRIN TABLET: Aspirin, that most ubiquitous of wonder drugs, has been traced to times that long preceded the discovery of America by Christopher Columbus, Leif Ericsson, or Whomever. Hippocrates, the Greek physician who is considered the father of medicine and whose principles are embodied in the medical profession's idealistic Hippocratic Oath (sometimes cynically redubbed the Hypocritic Oath), prescribed a form of the multipurpose painkiller when he urged patients in distress to chew willow leaves. The bitter bark contains salicin, not unlike aspirin's main ingredient, $C_9H_8O_4$, acetylsalicylic acid—a compound of carbon, hydrogen, and oxygen first synthesized by German chemist Charles Frederick von Gerhardt in 1853. Not until 1899, however, after some unnamed savior realized that the chemical relieved arthritic pain and headaches, did pharmacists begin to dispense powdered aspirin in small envelopes.

The Bayer Company of New York, an offshoot of the parent company in Germany, began manufacturing the powder in 1899, trademarked the product's name, and in 1915, introduced aspirin in round, white five-grain tablet form. The company came under the supervision of the Alien Property Custodian during World War I and was sold at public auction after the war to Sterling Drug, which outbid more than a hundred other companies by offering $5,300,000. When a 1921 court ruling denied Bayer exclusivity on the word "aspirin," the company began stressing the Bayer part of its name, but that right was limited to the United States. During World War II the U.S. Bayer company and the German Bayer company slugged it out for dominance in Mexico and Central and South America. Sterling doubled its sales between 1941 and the end of the war. The company spends an estimated $20 million a year on ads that strive to persuade a skeptical public that the aspirin tablet bearing a crossword cross is somehow worth up to four times the cost of generic, non-Bayer aspirin containing exactly the same ingredients. The ads apparently work, because Bayer aspirin is the best-selling brand in America, where annual consumption of aspirin exceeds twelve thousand tons a year. That comes to about 150 per year per person.

ASSOCIATED PRESS: A cooperative composed of more than 1,300 U.S. newspapers, the Associated Press, more familiarly "the AP," provides news and photographs to more than 10,000 newspapers and radio and TV stations in more than 100 countries. It maintains 40 bureaus in major U.S. cities and 60 foreign offices.

The AP stems from a fierce competition between New York newspapers in the mid-1800s. After purchasing a swift sloop to thwart the efforts of nine other papers to deny him access to ships bringing international news from Europe, David Hale, managing editor of the *Journal of Commerce,* suggested to the *New York Herald*'s James Gordon Bennett that some plan should be worked out for equitably sharing the single telegraph wire available to the city's newspapers. In May 1848, Hale, Bennett, and other newspaper representatives met at the offices of the *New York Sun* and agreed to organize a news-gathering cooperative owned by its member newspapers.

After numerous vicissitudes, the New York Associated Press evolved into the international AP.

ATOM BOMB: The first atom bomb (A-bomb), deriving its explosive force from the release of atomic energy through the fission (splitting) of heavy nuclei, was produced at Los Alamos, New Mexico, as a result of the collaborative effort by a task force of U.S. brain trusters that began shortly after German scientists Otto Hahn and Fritz Strassmann discovered fission in uranium in 1938. It was successfully tested at Alamogordo, New Mexico, in 1945, and added to America's World War II arsenal, with a devastating effect, at Hiroshima, Japan, on August 6, 1945. That bomb was considered the equivalent of 13,000 short tons of TNT. A second bomb, dropped three days later at Nagasaki, was even more powerful. Atomic weapons were subsequently developed in the USSR (1949), Great Britain (1952) and France (1960).

The A-bomb differed from previous military weapons in its contaminative effect. Aside from its immediate explosive impact and the production of intense neutron and gamma radiation that destroyed living tissue, the bomb left lethal aftereffects: radioactive fission products close to the strike site and, because such products were instantly airborne as dust or gas, radioactive fallout many miles away.

The A-bomb was the precursor of an even deadlier weapon, the H-bomb, or hydrogen bomb, created by thermonuclear reaction or fusion, rather than by fission (*see* H-BOMB). Electronic radiation

34

belts circling the earth, which have resulted from such detonations, are expected to persist in measurable form for many years.

On a less solemn note, America's atom bomb tests on Bikini Atoll, in July 1946, resulted in the naming of a scanty two-piece, bare-midriff bathing suit. Because it was tiny, but capable of producing tremendous shock waves, its French designer named the prototype "atome" (atom). A rival designer, taking note of all the furor at the time over what was happening in the Pacific, dubbed his own "explosive" creation "bikini." By the late 1950s, bikinis, at first a Riviera fad, were being worn on beaches everywhere and rarely causing tremors.

ATOMIC ELEMENTS: American scientists have made numerous contributions to the spectrum of atomic elements. One, astatine (symbol: At), discovered in 1940 by Dale Corson, K. R. MacKenzie, and Émilio Segrè, is believed to comprise less than 1 percent of the earth's crust. It is so rare that it has always had to be synthesized when needed for laboratory experiments. Californium (Cf), discovered in 1950 by Albert Ghiorso, Glenn Seaborg, Kenneth Street, Jr., and Stanley Thompson, is the world's most expensive substance. A man-made element used for radiographic marking of mine shafts and pipelines, it is sold by the Atomic Energy Commission for one thousand dollars per microgram. Cost of a pound would be $530 billion. Einsteinium (Es) was accidentally discovered in 1952 by Ghiorso, Seaborg, Thompson, Gary Higgins, and colleagues in the dust collected from the cloud produced by the first hydrogen bomb test. Neptunium (Np), discovered in 1940 by Edwin McMillan and Philip Abelson, was the first artificially produced element. Plutonium (Pu—appropriate?), discovered in 1940 by Seaborg, Joseph Kennedy, McMillan and Arthur Wahl, is the most dangerous man-made element—a potent organic poison and the heart of the atomic bomb. Promethium (Pm), discovered in 1945 by Jacob Marinsky, Lawrence Glendenin, and Charles Coryell, is the low-radiation source of energy for luminescent watch dials.

Other U.S.-discovered elements include americium (Am), berkelium (Bk), curium (Cm), fermium (Fm), lawrencium (Lr), mendelevium (Md), nobelium (No) and, its discovery shared with Italy, technetium (Tc).

AUREOMYCIN: The most frequently prescribed antibiotic, Aureomycin, was isolated by Benjamin M. Duggar, hired as a researcher by the Lederle Laboratories after his retirement as a University of Wisconsin botany professor. Duggar was assigned by the Lederle research director, Yella Pragada Subbarow, a Harvard-educated Hindu who had once planned to become a Buddhist priest, to supervise the lab's search for a tuberculosis antibiotic that would be more effective than streptomycin. Duggar screened soil samples from all over the world. One, from Columbia, Missouri, contained a previously unknown species of actinomycete. Although it did not seem promising and Duggar was urged to turn his attention elsewhere, he persisted. The result of his experiments was an antibiotic that was named Aureomycin, generically chlortetracycline. Tests conducted in 1947 revealed that Aureomycin, brought to the public's attention by Lederle in July 1948, was useful in the treatment of more than one hundred diseases.

AUTOMATIC PILOT: Although attempts were made as early as 1910 to create an automatic control system that would enable a pilot to concentrate on functions other than maintaining his aircraft's direction and stability, the first efficient automatic pilot was designed in 1913 by Cortland, New York-born Elmer Ambrose Sperry (1860-1930). Sperry's system was tested in a Curtiss seaplane in 1914 by his son, Lawrence, who demonstrated its dependability at a Paris air safety show by flying with his hands in the air while a passenger stood on the seaplane's wing. The elder Sperry's experiments with gyroscopes, beginning in 1890, resulted in numerous devices that added to the safety of water and air travel. Awarded more than four hundred patents for his assorted inventions, he organized eight different companies to manufacture and market them. His innovations earned him laurels from the United States, France, Russia, and Japan.

AUTOMATION: The word, now in widespread use, was coined in 1946 by D. S. Harder, executive vice-president of the Ford Motor Company, who felt that new terminology was needed to describe a major improvement in the company's production technique: automatic materials handling. Ford's production lines were already mechanized. An operator fed an auto part into a machine, pushed a button, and the machine completed the task. However, the part had to be moved to and from the machine by separate mechanical and manual controls. Ford's new twist was that an overhead carrier transported each part from one operation to the next and automatically inserted it, eliminating the need for a middleperson. A fully automatic Ford stamping plant went into operation in Buffalo, New York, in September 1950. A fully automated foundry and engine plant opened in Brookpark Village, near Cleveland, the following year. The latter and a second Cleveland engine plant, opened in February 1955, soon were producing more than a million six- and eight-cylinder engines per year. Since then, automation, not necessarily an unmixed blessing, has become worldwide.

AUTOMOBILE: Several countries lay claim to one of the world's most revolutionary inventions, and many individuals have made major contributions to its development. The first U.S. mechanism that qualifies as an automobile was Philadelphian Oliver Evans's 1805 Orukter Amphibolos. Powered by a five-horsepower steam engine, it was a 15½-ton, 30-foot-long amphibious dredge for deepening the city's harbor. It moved, literally on its own steam, from its construction shed to the docks, where its land wheels were replaced by paddle wheels. Evans offered to bet three thousand dollars that he could build a steam-driven land vehicle speedier than any horse, but there were no takers.

In the 1890s, Stanley Steamers, built by identical twins Francis E. and Freelan O. Stanley, "Mr. F. E." and "Mr. F. O.," vied for acceptance with electric cars propelled by limited battery power. The building of light gasoline engines in 1885 by the Germans Gottlieb Daimler and Karl Benz made possible the development of the modern motor car. In the 1890s, French inventors began using such engines to power road vehicles. Springfield, Massachusetts, brothers Charles E. and J. Frank Duryea put gasoline-powered machines on sale in 1895.

The first automobile factory was established in Michigan in 1899 by Ransom Eli Olds, creator of the "merry Oldsmobile." However, significant mass production was first achieved by engineer Henry Ford, who initiated assembly-line techniques that made automobile manufacture quick and cheap. By 1906, 125 U.S. companies were peddling cars, but they were all outstripped by Ford's no-frills Model T, seven-feet high and available, as Ford was fond of saying, in any shade of black. Actually, some were "Brewster green" with red striping. Introduced on October 1, 1908, Ford's "car for the multitude" registered 10,660 sales the first year. Initially, the car familiarly referred to as "the tin lizzy" and "the flivver" was produced by hand, but by 1913 its chassis was being made on a moving assembly line at Ford's Highland Park, Michigan, plant. Within a year, they were being produced at the rate of one every forty seconds. After grinding out more than 15 million, Ford replaced the Model T, in 1927, with the less austere Model A.

AUTOMOBILE HEADLIGHTS: The first automobile to feature headlights was the Autocar in 1906, which added flicker to a flivver by burning kerosene. If that was a dubious plus, a distinct minus was the absence of a steering wheel. Maneuvering required manipulation of a sticklike shaft at the driver's right.

AUTOMOBILE HEATER: The first interior heating system for automobiles that did not require fire was patented by Augusta M. Rogers of Brooklyn. Within a single four-year period this industrious inventress also registered with the U.S. Patent Office an improved auto spark-arrester, a folding chair, and a canopy to protect the user from mosquitoes and other infuriating insects. The first practical automobile heater is credited to Joseph A. Petnel, an Italian immigrant who worked for the Ford Motor Company and the Western Electric Company during his early years in the United States. Petnel, who died in Troy, New York, in November 1983, also created the three-way lightbulb, the dial telephone, and the automobile turn-signal system and held patents for the automobile sun visor; nylon shirts; and improvements in furnaces, washing machines and typewriter ribbons.

AUTOMOBILE RADIO: In May 1922, eighteen-year-old George Frost, president of the radio club at Chicago's Lane High School, attached a radio to the passenger door of his Model T Ford and, thereby, became the possessor of the world's first car radio. The first commercially produced car radio, the Philco Transitone, was introduced by the Philadelphia Storage Battery Company in 1927. About the same time William P. Lear, a design engineer at the Galvin Manufacturing Company in Chicago, invented what has also been touted as the first workable auto radio. Galvin, who had been manufacturing radio chassis, made a fortune from the new product. He changed his company's name to Motorola, derived from "motor" and "victrola." Lear, who also prospered, later invented aerial navigation aids, a miniature automatic pilot, and the eight-passenger, six-hundred-miles-per-hour Lear Jet. By 1933, the number of U.S. cars equipped with radios was estimated at one hundred thousand. In England several companies promptly began installing radios in Rolls Royces.

AVON LADY: Avon, America's top-earning cosmetic company, owns sixteen factories outside the United States and aggressively pushes its products, including perfumes, costume jewelry, and even duds for both women and men, with the help of more than a million doorbell-ringing Avon ladies around the globe. Begetter of all those multitudinous ladies was David H. McConnell, a door-to-door book salesman with an upstate New York territory. In the 1880s, he conceived the notion that a housewife would be more likely to invite him in if he handed her a gift flacon of perfume before beginning his sales pitch. The ploy worked so well that McConnell decided he should forget the books and peddle the perfume. In 1886, he founded the California Perfume Company, hiring only saleswomen. The first, Mrs. P. F. E. Albee, a Winchester, New Hampshire, widow, recruited and trained the rest of the sales staff, establishing not only the company's nation-spanning sales set-up, but also the neighborly Avon lady concept. The company acquired its Avon identity in 1939.

B

BABY AND CHILD CARE: The book of that title by Dr. Benjamin McLane Spock (1903-   ) is the Western world's second all-time best-seller, topped only by the Bible. Since its initial publication in 1946, it has sold some thirty million copies in the United States alone and has been translated into thirty-eight languages. The 1985 fifth edition was the first to carry a dual byline, Spock's name plus that of Dr. Michael Rothenberg, a pediatrician who echoes his parent-progeny policies.

Although it is crammed with advice about infant care, on topics ranging from nutrition to children's fear of nuclear explosions, it is not a gargantuan tome. Thus spake Spock: "We can't ever let the book get so unwieldy that a mother can't hold it in one hand while she's got a screaming baby in the other."

Though both have displayed eminently logical minds, *Dr.* Spock is not to be confused with *Mr.* Spock, the pointy-eared half-human, half-Vulcan first officer of the starship *Enterprise,* portrayed by Leonard Nimoy in NBC's 1966-1969 "Star Trek" series and, since 1979, several movies (*see* "STAR TREK"). The real Spock was born in New Haven, Connecticut, the oldest of six children of a mother he describes as "tyrannical, oppressive, opinionated, and moralistic" but possessed of a love of babies, which he inherited. After acquiring his M.D., he served residencies in pediatrics at one New York City hospital and in psychiatry at another and completed six years of training at the New York Psychoanalytic Institute. He practiced and taught pediatrics before being summoned to active duty during World War II as a psychiatrist in the U.S. Naval Reserve. During his two years of service, he completed *The Common Sense Book of Baby and Child Care,* published in 1946. The title was later pared. He preached kindly tolerance, rather than rigid dominance; stressed children's individuality; and reassured parents, "You know more than you think you know." Years later, Dr. Spock broadened his opinionating to subjects far from the nursery, speaking on behalf of the National Committee for a Sane Nuclear Policy (SANE) and vigorously opposing the Vietnam War.

BABY BEAUTY PAGEANT: Displays of progeny by proud parents are hardly new, but the first deliberate marshaling of tykes to compare and evaluate their attributes occurred in Springfield, Ohio, on October 14, 1854. There were 127 contestants, including a five-month-old twenty-seven-pound infant and one couple's seventeenth offspring. The winner was a ten-month-old entry; the prize, a silver service. One judge presumably would have preferred to label the proceedings a "brat show." He opined that a baby was "an alimentary canal with a loud noise at one end and no sense of responsibility at the other."

BABY CARRIAGE: A notable proof of the Biblical lament about a prophet's profitlessness in his own country is the case of Charles Burton of New York City, who invented the baby carriage in 1848. Did this boon for infants, parents, and nannies earn unqualified praise? No way. There were hoots as well as huzzahs, mostly from pedestrians who complained that they were constantly being poked by the cumbersome conveyances. Irate, Burton skeedaddled to England and opened a "perambulator" factory. Among his satisfied customers were Queen Victoria, Queen Isabella II of Spain, and the pasha of Egypt. A successful U.S. baby carriage factory was launched in Leominster, Massachusetts, ten years after Burton's aborted try, by the firm of F. W. and F. A. Whitney, later the F. A. Whitney Carriage Company. The first year it produced only seventy-five of its two-wheeled vehicles.

BABY FOOD: Gerber Foods, a Fremont, Michigan-based company, was the first canner in the world to sell commercial baby food, and now packs 150 varieties.

When the firm was launched by Frank Gerber in 1901, it canned peas for noninfants, but all that changed in 1927 when Frank's daughter-in-law, Dorothy, flared up at her husband, Dan. Impatient to leave for a social engagement, he chided her about the time it was taking her to strain peas for their baby daughter, Sally. Dorothy promptly invited him to speed things up by doing it himself. The tediousness of the chore and the realization that mothers reluctant to limit their infants to liquids were compelled to repeat the work again and again pointed the way to a surefire new product. Strained foods at that time were available only by prescription at scattered drugstores, for a prohibitive thirty-five cents per can. A survey indicated the existence of a potential huge grocery-store market for fifteen-cent cans.

In 1928, the Gerbers introduced five varieties of strained baby foods: peas, carrots, spinach, prunes, and vegetable soup. A magazine ad offering six 4½-ounce cans for a dollar to housewives submitting their grocer's name and address built up a list of prospective outlets, and within three months, Gerber strained foods were on sale coast-to-coast. By 1935, more than sixty competitive companies were in the field. Gerber needled Heinz, Beech-Nut, and other rivals by proclaiming, "Babies are our business—our *only* business," but had to abandon the slogan when it eventually joined the national trend toward diversification through acquisition.

To strengthen its reputation for nursery know-how, Gerber published a series of parental guides and responded to mamas' queries. When not providing personal answers, Dorothy Gerber wrote a "Bringing Up Baby" newspaper column. Promotional gimmicks included a fleet of Austin minicars with horns that tootled "Rock-a-Bye-Baby" and a corporate airplane, *Sky Baby*, which bore a likeness of "the Gerber baby." That wasn't Sally, the first recipient of Gerber-strained peas, but an imaginary tyke conceived by artist Dorothy Hope Smith in response to a 1928 search for a magazine-ad moppet. Smith's submission was an unfinished charcoal drawing she offered to complete, but Gerber liked it just the way it was.

BABY RUTH: Six years after its introduction in 1920, a log-shaped, peanut-studded chunk of chocolate created in Chicago by Otto Schnering was proclaiming itself "the world's most popular candy," with daily sales exceeding five million.

Achieving a confectionary best-seller followed several years of trial and error. Just before America's entry into World War I, Schnering leased a small room over a plumber's shop as the headquarters for what he dubbed the Curtiss Candy Company. It consisted of four employees, a five-gallon kettle, and a rented stove. Within a few years this tiny Baby Ruth bassinet had elaborate counterparts in five cities. Among ingenious methods used to peddle the product during the 1920s were barnstorming biplanes, bearing the Baby Ruth trademark, that dropped parachute-borne bars.

The candy bar was *not* a salute to the home-run hitter extraordinary George Herman Ruth (1895-1948), who was nicknamed "Babe" after sportswriters referred to the Baltimore Orioles' new nineteen-year-old pitcher as "Jack Dunn's baby." At the time of the candy bar's debut, Ruth had not yet achieved the baseball eminence he was to gain as a member of the New York Yankees. Instead, "Baby Ruth" was a belated tribute (the candy bar was initially dubbed "Kandy Kate") to the first daughter of a former resident of the White House, Grover

Cleveland. As a toddler during her papa's presidency, she had been a national favorite and was still fondly remembered. (Her sister, Esther, was the first child to be born in the White House.) If one Yankee was not the inspiration for a candy bar bearing his name, another slugger was. In 1977 Standard Brands began manufacturing Reggie, a sweet salute to another home-run specialist: Reggie Jackson.

BACKHAND: According to *The Official Encyclopedia of Tennis*, published by the United States Tennis Association, the backhand stroke in tennis was invented in 1886 by a left-handed Philadelphia woman, Bertha Townsend, who, two years later, became the second U.S. women's champion by defeating the first, Ellen Hansell. She successfully defended her title in 1889 but lost in 1890.

Not all authorities agree that Bertha was either a southpaw or an innovator. Frank Phelps, a Norristown, Pennsylvania, tennis historian, notes that the game stems from two European favorites, court tennis and rackets, and that players in both used a backhand stroke. Moreover, he says, a rare off-court photograph indicates that Bertha was right-handed, and contemporary newspaper accounts say nothing to the contrary. Bertha reputedly was difficult to defeat because she played left-handed, but Phelps believes that that notion stemmed from the fact that right-handed players' backhands were once tagged "left-handers." He's willing to concede that at a time when most women tennis players had weak backhands, Bertha was a notable exception.

BACKSTROKE: The backstroke in its present form, credited to the United States, was originally known as the back crawl when Olympian Harry Hebner introduced it in 1912. Initially, it was an inverted breaststroke, combining alternating arm pulls with a frog kick while the swimmer lay on his back. Hebner was almost disqualified the first time he used it, but American officials successfully argued that Olympic rules specified only that the contestant had to remain on his back. Other swimmers soon abandoned the previous backstroke.

Several other swimming strokes have been altered and improved by Americans, including the two-kicks-per-stroke Australian crawl, also known as the freestyle, which became the six-kick American crawl, and the butterfly, a German variation on the breaststroke, which was refined and popularized in 1933 by Henry Meyer, who sparked its acceptance twenty years later as a legitimate stroke in competitions.

BAKED BEANS: A recipe for baked beans is included by Mrs. S. M. Child in her 1829 book, *The Frugal Housewife*. She felt that for most families, a pound of pork and a quart of beans, with molasses as a binder, would be ample. Mid-nineteenth century rural New Englanders enjoyed Saturday night "baked bean festivals." Earthenware pots filled with beans that had been soaked overnight and then seasoned with mustard, salt pork, and blackstrap molasses were wrapped in bright-colored napkins and toted by youngsters to the neighborhood bakery, where they were cooked all day for family feasting that evening.

The beans were first canned in 1875 by the Burnham E. Morrill Company of Portland, Maine, after the men in their fishing fleet keened about how much they missed their Saturday night bean binges. Baked beans in tomato sauce made their debut in 1880 and were canned by Indianapolis's Van Camp Packing Company in 1891. It's the version of choice in England, where baked beans were introduced by Pittsburgh's H. J. Heinz Company in 1905. They were a resounding success, in more ways than one, and British bean-buyers outbuy Americans, two to one. Why more ways than one? Well, to quote a venerable street jingle, "Beans, beans, the musical fruit; the more you eat, the more you toot!"

BAKELITE: This synthetic substance, widely used for many products requiring insulation from electricity and heat, is named for its discoverer, Belgian-born Leo Hendrik Baekeland (1863-1944). Visiting the United States in 1889, he decided to stay. After working with a New York manufacturer of photographic material, he invented a photographic paper that could be developed in artificial light, named it Velox, and organized a company to produce it. His company was purchased in 1899 by George Eastman of the Eastman Kodak Company for about $1 million. Having become wealthy, Baekeland equipped a laboratory and began experimenting with synthetic resins. In 1907, utilizing high temperatures and intense pressures, he chemically combined phenol and formaldehyde, to produce a hard, insoluble, acid-resistant material capable of being molded into any shape and put to many uses. It was not the first plastic (*see* CELLULOID), but it was more versatile than its predecessors and is considered the fuse that detonated the plastics explosion. Together, Bakelite and rayon demonstrated that man-made materials could not only simulate natural substances but even improve on them. Put on the market in 1909 by the Bakelite Corporation, Bakelite has been used as a substitute for hard rubber, amber, and celluloid; as a laminate or surface coating, and in products as varied as kitchenware, machinery gears, radios, phonograph records, jewelry, pipe stems, umbrella handles, buttons, and billiard balls.

Baekeland, an eccentric, had a custom-built Packard with a roof high enough for his top hat, always wore white sneakers, and, at family dinners, ate soup out of a can.

BAND-AID: Several American doctors made progressive contributions toward the development of the handy, stickum-coated bandage. Samuel D. Gross mentioned the usefulness of medicated adhesive plasters for body fractures in an 1830 edition of a Philadelphia medical journal. Fifteen years later, Drs. Horace H. Day and William H. Shecut, of Jersey City, New Jersey, patented an adhesive plaster that had a thin coat of rubber dissolved in a solvent. It was marketed by Dr. Thomas Allcock as Allcock's Porous Plaster. In 1848, Dr. John Parker Maynard, of Dedham, Massachusetts, introduced a plaster using a fluid derived from guncotton dissolved in sulfuric ether. It was brushed on the skin and then covered with cotton strips.

In 1874, Robert W. Johnson and George J. Seabury, a team working in East Orange, New Jersey, developed a medicated adhesive plaster with a rubber base. Twelve years later, Johnson went off on his own to establish the medical aids firm of Johnson and Johnson. A cotton buyer in the company's purchasing department, Earle F. Dickson, had a young bride who kept suffering minor cuts and burns while engaged in household tasks. Dickson kept bandaging her fingers with Johnson and Johnson gauze and adhesive, but the chore seemed endless. What was needed, he decided, was a prepared supply of something easy to apply, which would stay anchored and sterile. Experimenting, he placed a strip of surgical tape, sticky side up, on the dining-room table, topped it with a pad of gauze, and covered tape and gauze with crinoline. Pleased with the result, he made a precautionary batch for his accident-prone spouse and carried a handful to the office. His colleagues applauded; so did his employers. In 1920, the company's president, James W. Johnson, ordered mass production of what quickly became a first-aid staple. The Band-Aid trademark was suggested by a Johnson and Johnson superintendent, W. Johnson Kenyon.

BANKING, AUTOMATED: The first automated teller machine (ATM), enabling bank patrons to make deposits and withdrawals around the clock after inserting a plastic card and punching in an identifying code number, was installed by the Chemical Bank of New York City at its Rockville Center, Long Island, branch in January 1969. The Bank of Commerce in Toronto followed suit later the same year.

A U.S. study indicating that a live-teller transaction that cost a bank 80 cents could be performed by an ATM for 22.5 cents and that a single machine could handle twelve thousand transactions per month, spurred quick utilization of the new technology by banks and other savings institutions. The first nationwide ATM network, permitting a card's use far from home, was established by thirteen U.S. banks in 1982. The Bank of Montreal joined the network two years later.

Customer acceptance was slower, but by the start of 1985, more than two hundred regional ATM networks were serving fifty million cardholders and handling about 180,000,000 transactions each month. The "beeping electronic tellers," which at first had been located outside member banks and in central downtown areas, began to sprout at various sites, including supermarkets, liquor stores, and service stations. The Dallas-based Southland Corporation installed three thousand ATMs in its 7-Eleven stores. In Washington, Internet Machines at supermarkets can be used by customers of 110 banks, savings and loan associations, and credit unions. Some supermarkets, like Florida's Publix chain, established their own ATM networks, billing participating banks. Plans for coast-to-coast VISA and MasterCard ATM networks were altered after banks protested the co-opting of too many of their previous prerogatives.

BANK ROBBERY: The first desperado to heist a bank reportedly was Langdon Moore, who deprived the National Bank of Concord, Massachusetts, of $310,000 in cash and securities in 1865. Numerous crooks in countries around the world subsequently swiped the idea without offering as much as a nickel in royalties.

BARBED WIRE: The first barbed enclosure patent was granted to Lucien B. Smith of Kent, Ohio, in June 1867, for spaced blocks of wood with protruding points that could keep people out or animals in. There is no proof that Smith's barbed blocks were ever offered for sale.

One year later, M. Kelly received a patent for "Kelly's Diamonds," a twisted two-strand wire with diamond-shaped barbs. Some examples still exist. Over fifteen hundred kinds of barbed wire were subsequently produced, to meet the demand of farmers and ranchers. Because of the shortage of timber, barbed wire was essential for the development of the West's vast cattle ranches. Ranchers who preferred open range called it "devil's rope." Some sources say barbed wire was invented by Henry M. Rose, who showed his creation in 1873 at a county fair in De Kalb, Illinois. Among the fairgoers were farmer Joseph Farwell Glidden (1813-1906) and a couple of cronies, Jacob Haish and Isaac L. Ellwood, who all made fortunes by patenting improvements on what Rose had wrought. Glidden's patent, granted in 1874, was for a new way to anchor the barbs securely. In 1885, about four hundred patents were issued for barbed wire, machines to manufacture it, and associated fences. Early advertisers touted barbed wire as "horse high, pig tight, and bull strong." Although his invention was widely used in the conversion of the West's "wide open spaces" to "wide closed spaces," Glidden, a sedentary type who disliked traveling, never displayed any interest in seeing for himself.

Various kinds of barbed wire are prized by collectors, and a Texas Barbed Wire Association has its headquarters in San Angelo.

BARBIE DOLL: Barbie, the world's best-selling doll, was conceived by Ruth Handler, the wife of one of the founders of Mattel, a Hawthorne, California-based toy company, when she realized that her young daughter, Barbie, enjoyed changing the costumes on paper cutouts of teenagers. Designed by Bill Barton, who later lamented that his creation had become a sex symbol, Barbie, now more than twenty-five years old, still has a curvaceous teenager's figure (measurements in inches: 5¼-3-4¾); a vast wardrobe that grows steadily vaster; and an awesome assemblage of accessories, including a house, swimming pool, water bed, flushing john, computer, sports coupe, catamaran, ten-speed bike, horse, dog, and cat. Everything a materialistic little girl could possibly yearn for.

Barbie socializes with a boyfriend named Ken, named for the Handlers' son; has black and Hispanic counterparts, and holds assorted jobs. Her work clothes indicate that she was the first female astronaut, eighteen years before Sally Ride, and has also been employed as doctor, nurse, and fashion editor. She has been a bride, a mortarboard-wearing college graduate, a skier, a backpacker, an Olympic swimmer, a disco dancer—just about everything, so far, but a porno queen. Over the years she has acquired numerous capabilities. She bends her arms and knees. She winks. She talks. She tans. She sleeps. She changes her hair color from red to black. She kisses, puckering up and leaving a lipstick mark. She was the subject of a ten-minute documentary film, *Not Just Another Doll*, which was seen at the 1983 Montreal World Film Festival. An exhibition that toured France in the summer of 1985 had Barbie in togs by sixty-five designers, including Dior, Saint Laurent, Lanvin, Hermes, and Patou. Barbie, a twenty-five million seller in 1984, was greeted with boos when she made her bow at the 1959 New York Toy Fair, flaunting her shapeliness in a zebra-striped one-piece bathing suit. It wasn't the curves that cued the jeering. At 11½ inches, she was considered too petite at a time when small fry seemed to prefer life-size womanikins. She later "grew up"—to a "supersize" eighteen inches.

The first Barbie dolls, extremely rare, are identifiable by the fact that they have a white iris in their eyes instead of eye color (blue eyes were one of the earliest changes) and sharply arched eyebrows. They sold for three dollars. At a 1978 national auction, a mint copy in its original box brought $501.59, but in 1985 the valuation for a first-generation Barbie was placed at between $1,000 and $1,500. Barbie underwent one major facelift in 1967 and another ten years later.

BARGAIN PRICE: "Bargain" prices requiring an assortment of coins were not conceived by sly retailers as a way to con buyers into thinking that an item priced at, say, $4.99 was an "under $5" cash-saver. The practice so prevalent today, at home and abroad, was initiated by a newspaper publisher. In 1876, twenty-eight-year-old Melville E. Stone, who was later to head the Associated Press, decided that what Chicago urgently needed was a one-cent newspaper to compete with those being sold for a nickel. A major drawback, however, was the local paucity of pennies. Stone went door to door, store to store, selling merchants on the idea that to many people ninety-nine cents seems a considerably smaller sum than a dollar. After persuading a considerable number that odd prices would help business, he imported several barrels of coins from the Philadelphia mint. Pennies became plentiful and Stone's *Chicago Daily News* became a success.

BASEBALL: Although Abner Doubleday is credited with drawing the first diagram of a baseball diamond in 1839 at Cooperstown, New York, Doubleday himself never really claimed he invented the game. It probably evolved from England's cricket and rounders and several rather anarchistic American games. Among them was "one-old-cat," which required one base and three players: a pitcher, a catcher, and a batter. The addition of players and bases made it two-old-cat, three-old cat, and so forth. When there were enough players to form sides, it was called rounders, town ball, goal ball, or base ball. All required hitting a ball and running for a goal.

In 1845, Alexander J. Cartwright, specifying a diamond ninety feet square, codified game rules for his Knickerbocker Base Ball Club of New York, the first organized baseball team. The Knickerbockers, a dapper lot, wore blue wool pants, white flannel shirts, and straw hats. After each game they doffed their playing ensembles and changed into formal attire for a victory-celebrating—or loss-bemoaning—dinner. One comeuppance was a 23-1 loss to the New York Nine. During that game, J. W. Davis, position unspecified, was fined for unseemly language. His penalty: six cents.

Cartwright made major changes in the game. The batter, who previously stood a distance away, was moved to home plate. "Plugging," getting a base runner out by hitting him with a thrown ball, was eliminated. Earlier, dangerous four-foot-high stakes as bases had been replaced by sandbags. A rule permitting batters to insist on either high or low pitches was abolished in the 1870s. In 1909, the cork-centered ball was adopted. Previously, balls were of varying sizes and materials. Each team brought its own ball, and the loser's went to the victor. For a time, officiating was performed by two umpires—one chosen by each team—and a referee who adjudicated disputes between them. By 1882, that had been reduced to a single umpire, authorized to make his own judgments instead of consulting players and even, on some earlier occasions, spectators. Only team captains were permitted to talk to the umpire.

Baseball has become an international export, especially popular in Japan, which conducts its own World Series.

BASKETBALL: In 1891, Canadian-born Dr. James A. Naismith (1861-1939) invented basketball, the only major sport unqualifiedly of American origin, when he was teaching physical education at the International Young Men's Christian Association Training School in Springfield, Massachusetts.

Asked to devise an indoor game, Naismith first tried variations of soccer, lacrosse, and football, then opted for elevated goals. He asked the building supervisor for two boxes about eighteen inches square, but only peach baskets were available. Naismith attached them to the balcony at each end of the school gym and told his students to lob a soccer ball at them. When a shot went in, someone perched on a ladder pried the ball out. Boys were later stationed in the balcony for that chore; and still later, a hole was drilled in the bottom of the basket, so a pole could be poked through. The peach baskets were replaced by what looked like wire wastebaskets with a pullcord. In 1893, a year after Naismith promulgated rules for what he initially dubbed "indoor rugby," bottomless cord nets became standard. Subsequent additions included regulation-size basketballs in 1894, backboards in 1895, dribbling in 1900.

Initially, there was no limit on the number of long-pants-wearing players on each side, sometimes as many as fifty. By the time of the first college game, on February 9, 1895, in which Minnesota State School of Mines defeated Hamline College 9-3, not only the score sounded like the outcome of a baseball game; each team had nine players. That number was reduced to seven and then to the present five. By the 1920s, there were few U.S. schools or colleges without basketball teams. In 1934, basketball became a big-league sports attraction when the sportswriter Ned Irish brought the game from college gyms and armories to New York City's Madison Square Garden. Irish added the postseason National Invitational Tournament in 1938. Professional basketball began before the turn of the century. Several other leagues preceded the forming of the National Basketball Association in 1949.

In 1936, basketball, a more popular export than baseball, was added to the list of Olympic events. As of 1985, the United States had lost only one of seventy-eight Olympic basketball games—to the USSR, in disputed 1972 overtime, 51-50.

BATHING BEAUTY CONTEST: Pulchritude pageants galore—Miss Teen USA, Miss USA, Mrs. America, Miss Black America, Miss World, Miss Universe, any day now Miss Galaxy—all stem from the Miss America competition that was conducted in Atlantic City on September 7, 1921 (*see* MISS AMERICA). It was the first in which comely contestants were judged on, among other things, how they shaped up—or stripped down—in bathing suits. It was also the first in which the participants were identified as representatives of specific localities.

Although the Miss America telecast garners huge ratings, the copycat Miss Universe pageant, beamed by satellite to fifty-one countries for some 600 million living-room connoisseurs of curvaceousness, is the world's most-watched entertainment special. The Miss Universe contest was launched in 1951 by the Catalina bathing suit company after Miss America officials nixed the release of photos showing contestants in Catalina swimwear. The Miss America pageant has progressively minimized beauty as a determinant (it no longer records the traditional chest-waist-hip measurements and mulls elimination of the bathing-suit portion of the proceedings) and accentuated IQ and talent. One "Miss America" contestant "performed" by pulling clothes of her design out of a trunk. Still another stood on her head while a plank was held to her feet and proceeded to tapdance *upside down!*

BATHROOM FIXTURES: David Buick, the automaker whose name was bestowed on General Motors' first car, was a plumber by trade who also invented a process for annealing porcelain with iron. That made possible the manufacture of white porcelain bathtubs, which became an international favorite. About 1900, American enamelware bathroom fixtures —including bathtubs, toilet bowls, and washstands—were installed in Buckingham Palace. However, the Royal Family did not refer to them as "bathroom fixtures." In England a toilet was a "lavatory" and toilet paper a "lavatory roll." Other British euphemisms have included W. C. (for water closet), loo, john (perhaps as a salute to Sir John Harrington, who invented an indoor flusher in 1596), and jake, an abbreviation of Jake's house, whoever *he* was. Attention, Jack Klugman, star of the "Quincy" TV series: Because the first White House toilet was installed during the tenancy of President John Quincy Adams, "Quincy" became American slang for "the facilities." So much for toilet terminology!

To return to our theme, early buyers of American-made toiletware included the king of Prussia, the president of Mexico, the government of Venezuela, and a Russian hospital in St. Petersburg. The bathtub was a popular American export. "Bathtub gin," named for its Prohibition-era source, was not.

BATHYSPHERE: The word was coined in 1930 by the Brooklyn-born naturalist Dr. William Beebe (1877-1962), to identify the vehicle he and Otis Barton designed to facilitate the undersea study of animal life. It was a hollow steel sphere weighing about five thousand pounds with an interior diameter of fifty-four inches and walls about an inch and a half thick. Two quartz windows, three inches thick and eight inches in diameter, permitted underwater observation. In 1934, Beebe established a record when he descended 3,028 feet. The experience was recorded in one of his many books, *Half Mile Down*. Beebe's kind of undersea exploration has been continued by Jacques-Yves Cousteau, of France, who invented the Aqua-lung diving apparatus in 1943 and, later, a process facilitating underwater television.

BEAN BOOT: Orders come from all over the world to L. L. Bean's Freeport, Maine, sportsmen's mecca for the all-weather "Maine hunting shoe" designed about 1910 by Leon Leonwood Bean. Though it is unaesthetically bulky and requires lacing through six pairs of holes and around eight pairs of metal knoblets, the Bean boot is an item of footwear that rugged outdoor types swear by, not at. A hybrid—part rubber, part leather—it is the foundation stone of what has become the world's foremost mail-order sporting-goods supply house.

L. L., who began deer hunting at thirteen, was working at his brother Ervin's haberdashery for twelve dollars a week when he devised the boot as a means to keep his own feet warm and dry during animal-offing excursions. All rubber was cold and clumsy; all leather was too heavy, and it cracked and leaked. A rubber-bottom, leather-top prototype felt so good that L. L. had a local cobbler make a hundred pairs and sold them all by describing their virtues in a mailing to prospective customers culled from a hunting-license list. When ninety of the original pairs came apart, L. L. borrowed money, mailed refunds, and asked the United States Rubber Company to produce an improved version. The result was the classic clodhopper that is still the company's "core product." In 1980, L. L. Bean manufactured 175,872 pairs.

The company repairs whatever it sells and makes to order items it doesn't ordinarily sell, such as Maine hunting shoes in size 17 EEE. L. L. gradually added other products he felt would appeal to outdoorsy men and women, beginning with hand-knit stockings and hunting duds. "A chief reason for the success of the business," he opined, "is the fact that I tried, on the trail, practically every article I handle. If I tell you a knife is good for cleaning trout, it is because I found it so." When L. L. died in 1967, at the age of ninety-four, the company received more than fifty thousand letters of condolence, including a sizable number with foreign postmarks. Many of the letters also contained requests for L. L. Bean catalogs. In 1980, more than twenty-six million were mailed.

BEATNIK: The word "beat," as a synonym for physical and mental exhaustion, has been part of the U.S. lexicon since 1834. In the 1950s, it was also applied to "cool" progressive jazz, more laid-back and intellectual than the emotional "hot jazz" of the 1920s. Soon "beat" was being used to describe an entire life-style, reflecting disdain for traditional American values like dollars-and-cents "success" and taboos on drug use and casual sex.

The Beat (with a capital B), often clad in black turtlenecks and jeans, were gypsies, constantly on the move (via motorbike, jalopy, or hitchhiker's thumb), in restless pursuit of the ultimate experience, like surfers in quest of the perfect wave. Among the earliest Beat bards were John Clellon Holmes in his exhortatorily titled 1952 novel, *Go!*; Allan Ginsberg in his lengthy 1955 poem, "Howl"; and Jack Kerouac, who received the most media attention as an exemplar of the itinerant life-style in his 1957 novel, *On the Road*. Kerouac claimed he invented "beat" for "beatific," explaining, "It means you got the beat." "Beatnik," one of numerous words with diminutive "nik" endings that proliferated after the Russians launched the first space satellite, the Sputnik, in October 1957, was coined by Herb Caen, of the *San Francisco Chronicle*. In his April 2, 1958, "Baghdad-by-the-Bay" column, Caen noted that *Look* magazine, readying a picture spread, had hosted a party for "50 Beatniks." "They're only Beat, y'know," he added pejoratively, "when it comes to work." The Beats later begat a groupie-like corps of more colorfully garbed imitators, many of them bored youngsters from affluent families, who were categorized as hippies (*see* HIPPIE). Abetted by overseas counterparts, they helped spread to various corners of the globe a dilettantish variation of the uninhibited, untidy, and mostly unwelcome beatnik point of view.

BEER CAN: Brewers nowadays are busily confining their sudsy product inside more than thirty-five billion cans annually. Aluminum cans, weighing slightly more than a half ounce, can be turned out at the rate of two thousand per minute to provide those billions of beer cans that will produce millions of distended bellies and an uncountable number of burps.

In January 1935, beer was first placed inside a three-ounce steel container by the Krueger Brewery Company in Richmond, Virginia. Initial production was two hundred cans a day. Bottle buffs sneered at the departure from guzzling tradition until World War II, when GIs overseas were given a choice between beer in cans or no beer at all. Beer in cans became increasingly popular but really zoomed when the aluminum can made its debut in 1958. In 1962, Pittsburgh's Iron City beer test marketed the first pull-ring lids. During 1963, the ultra-rapid two-piece can-making process was developed. In 1975, Louisville's Falls City beer introduced the nondetachable can-opening tab.

Collecting beer cans has become a worldwide hobby. The Beer Can Collectors of America (BCCA), formed in 1970, has five thousand members, including some who have accumulated as many as ten thousand cans. To celebrate the fiftieth anniversary of the beer can's birth, a BCCA delegation convened in Richmond for a banquet highlighted by a ritual in which the contents of beer cans from all over the country were poured into a single vat to produce "the great American brew," subsequently quaffed by all present. Collectors and collections aren't confined to America. One assembler of a four thousand-can collection became hooked when he set out to acquire all ten of a series of cans for Tennent, a Scottish beer, adorned with pictures of beautiful women named, like his wife, Ann. Who says beer buyers can't be romantic? High bid at an auction for a couple of cans that once contained Tiger beer and Rosalie Pilsner (Chicago brews in the 1930s) was six thousand. Also esteemed by collectors is Omaha's Strozette beer, which tried to lure female customers in the 1950s by decorating its can with an orchid. Considered a bust is the Billy Beer produced in huge quantities when Billy Carter's brother was in the White House. (*See also* FLIP-TOP CAN.)

"BELIEVE IT OR NOT":

Gap-toothed LeRoy Ripley (1893–1949), who later rechristened himself Robert, was a sports cartoonist for the *New York Globe* in December 1918 when, desperate for material on a day when nothing illustratable was happening on the sports scene, he assembled a batch of sports oddities. He was going to title the feature "Champs and Chumps" but substituted "Believe It or Not." Readers liked the idea, and soon, Ripley switched from solely sports incredibilities to those of all kinds.

The cartoon that brought him national attention and two hundred thousand indignant letters was one in which he asserted that the national hero Charles A. Lindbergh was "the sixty-seventh man to make a nonstop flight over the Atlantic Ocean." It was true. What made Lindbergh's flight unique was the fact that he was alone. Earlier, two airborne travelers had made the crossing in a plane, thirty-one in a British dirigible, and thirty-three in a German zeppelin.

Ripley's offbeat finds were limited to what he could read in English. In 1923, after playing handball with a banker friend, he confessed that he was running out of source material. The banker mentioned a young Austrian clerk, Norbert Pearlroth, who knew thirteen languages. Asked at an interview if he knew any good believe-it-or-nots, Pearlroth offered a close-to-home startler: A church in Ripley's own hometown of Santa Rosa, California, was built from the wood of a single tree. Soon, Pearlroth was doing all Ripley's research. And, in the late 1940s, it was Pearlroth who noticed that all the presidents elected at twenty-year intervals since 1840 on had died in office. Headlined "Who's Next?" the item left blank the name of the president to be elected in 1960. "Who's next?" turned out to be John F. Kennedy.

At the height of its popularity, "Believe It or Not" appeared in seventeen languages, in more than three hundred newspapers, in 38 countries. It spawned speaking engagements that made Ripley one of the world's highest-paid lecturers; a lengthy series of paperback books; twenty-six Warner Brothers movie shorts; a weekly radio show; a weekly television show; and "odditoriums" in the United States, Canada, and England. At one point Ripley was receiving—believe it or not!—a million letters a year.

BIFOCALS: Bifocal glasses are just one of many inventions credited to America's pre-Revolutionary Renaissance man, Benjamin Franklin (1706-1790). When nearly eighty, he grew tired of toting two pairs of glasses with different lenses and halved the impedimenta by devising lenses divided into two areas with dissimilar focusing powers. On May 23, 1785, Franklin described his accomplishment to a friend, George Whatley, in a letter from Paris. "I have only to move my eyes up and down," he wrote, "as I want to see distinctly far and near." Since even ordinary specs cost the staggering sum of one hundred dollars in those days, there was no huge demand for Franklin's even more expensive version. For a century they were referred to as "Franklin spectacles."

The first bifocal contact lens, announced in May 1985, was developed by an eye doctor, Newton K. Wesley, associated with the Eye Research Foundation and Chicago's Plastic Contact Lens Company. The center of the lens contained the prescription for distant vision; the outer circle provided the focus for reading.

BIG BANDS: Benny Goodman (1909-1986), a Chicago-born clarinetist, equally at ease with jazz and classical scores, is credited with launching America's—and the world's—"big band" era in the 1930s and 1940s. Goodman attracted to his seminal band the world's best jazz instrumentalists. Subsequently, many fronted bands of their own, among them Gene Krupa, Lionel Hampton, and Harry James. In 1962, the Goodman band made the first jazz tour of Russia since the 1920s. On opening night, in the Moscow audience, was the Soviet premier, Nikita Khruschev.

Goodman organized his first band in 1934, with so-so success in New York and on tour; but his "big band" style caught on a year later at Los Angeles's Palomar Ballroom. With arrangements by Fletcher Henderson, the Goodman band introduced a new kind of jazz, featuring dynamic ensemble work and virtuoso solo improvisations; and Goodman was promptly crowned the "King of Swing" (see SWING). In 1937, he returned in triumph to New York and filled the Paramount Theater with jiving jitterbugs.

Other big bands that achieved worldwide recognition, via personal appearances or recordings, included those assembled by brothers Jimmy and Tommy Dorsey, Glenn Miller, Woody Herman, Artie Shaw, Charlie Barnet, Duke Ellington, Count Basie, Jimmie Lunceford, Chick Webb, Stan Kenton, Buddy Rich, Benny Carter, Les Brown, and Glen Gray—the latter's Casa Loma Orchestra pioneering on the college prom circuit. Featured "big band" vocalists included Frank Sinatra, Doris Day, Helen O'Connell, and Bob Eberle. The "big band" boom faded after World War II, but Goodman's personal popularity transcended the downward trend. The Goodman band organized in 1955 reaped plaudits at home and abroad.

BIG BANG: In 1929, using the Mount Wilson Observatory's newly completed one-hundred-inch reflecting telescope, the Marshfield, Missouri-born astronomer Edwin Powell Hubble (1889-1953) established a startling fact of physical science. The universe, he observed, is in a state of nonstop expansion in accordance with the following law: The farther a galaxy is from us, the greater—in direct proportion—is its velocity. If one of two galaxies is twice as far away, it is receding twice as fast.

Such an expansion offered intriguing corollaries. First, every galaxy appears to be the center of the expansion as seen from that particular galaxy. Second, at one time in the far distant past, all the matter in the universe must have constituted a single mass. If the expansion were reversed, because of the differences in velocities, everything in the universe, near and far, would reassemble at the same time. Hubble's findings gave rise to what cosmologists the world over dubbed the "big bang" theory of the creation of the universe.

Hubble and his colleagues then tried, using galaxies' distances and velocities, to estimate how long ago that event occurred. Hubble's guess was 1,800,000,000 years, a figure sharply at variance with the British geologist Arthur Holmes's assertion that the earth's crust was more than three billion years old. In 1949, twenty years after Hubble's distance and velocity gauging, Walter Baade of the Mount Wilson staff, working with Henrietta Swope, used the new two-hundred-inch telescope at Mount Palomar to show that the nearby Great Andromeda galaxy was twice as far away as Hubble estimated. Subsequent findings suggested that Hubble had erred to an even greater degree on galaxies farther away. The time of the big bang is now put at twenty billion years ago. By the mid-1950s astronomers using other measurement techniques ascribed that same age to the oldest stars in our galaxy. Concurrently, scientists in nuclear physics laboratories around the world, trying to establish the vintage of unstable radioactive materials, came up with a matching number of years, give or take a few billion.

BINGO: Under a diversity of names—including lotto, keno, beano and pokeno—bingo has become one of the world's most popular gambling games, a favorite fund-raiser for church, fraternal, and social organizations. It is believed to stem from Italy's national lottery, which dates back to 1530. The game was first manufactured under the name of bingo in 1929 by the toy maker Edwin S. Lowe. While near Atlanta, Georgia, during a disappointing sales trip, he decided to relax one night by visiting a small tent carnival, where he watched for hours, fascinated, while a crowd excitedly played a game called beano. Two weeks later, he printed his own game cards, purchased some inexpensive prizes, and invited friends to help him test the game at his Brooklyn home. One exuberant young woman, completing a winning row of numbers, slapped down the final bean and shouted "B-b-bingo!" Eureka!

Lowe began selling a twenty-four-card bingo kit for two dollars. However, a priest in Wilkes Barre, Pennsylvania, phoned to complain that a fund-raising Bingo Night had done little fund raising because Lowe's limited number of cards had resulted in multiple winners. What was needed, the cleric keened, was more unduplicated number combinations. Lowe decided to respond to the priest's plea by seeking expert help. He commissioned an elderly Columbia University mathematician, Carl Lefler, to create six thousand dissimilar cards. Without a computer to ease his labors, Lefler found the task increasingly difficult, but he persisted, spurred on by Lowe's offer to pay him as much as $100 for each acceptable card. Lefler filled the order but at horrendous cost: His mind snapped. Lowe, who claimed that he almost suffered the same fate while trying to check Lefler's juggling of digits, retained enough business acumen to cash in on the bigger and better bingo. Five years later, he had sixty presses turning out copies all day every day. (Bingo, incidentally, is also the name of the pooch on the Cracker Jack box.)

BIONICS: The much-publicized Jarvik-7 (*see* ARTIFICIAL HEART) is only one of numerous American bionic innovations, though no single individual has incorporated as many man-made parts as the eponymous central characters in two network TV series, ABC's 1974-78 "The Six-Million-Dollar Man" and its ABC-NBC 1976-78 spin-off, "The Bionic Woman." After a moon-landing-craft crash, astronaut Steve Austin, portrayed by Lee Majors, was converted into a part-human, part-machine cyborg, crammed with atomic-powered electro-mechanical devices capable of superhuman performance, one of them an awesome left eye with hypervision and a built-in grid screen. Jaime Sommers, played by Lindsay Wagner, was similarly reconstructed after a skydiving accident and equipped with superspeedy legs, a herculean right arm, and the ability to hear faraway sounds.

Among nonfictional prosthetic devices of American origin is the Seattle foot, one of twelve 1985 winners of the first Presidential Awards for Design Excellence. Created by Dr. Ernest M. Burgess, an orthopedic surgeon, and Don Poggi, a Boeing engineer, the artificial foot (with a polyurethane exterior that includes sole and toes) is not only realistic looking but, fitted with a plastic inner spring and foam pad, so resilient that it even leaves a "footprint." Average costs for spare parts in 1980, according to Federation of American Hospitals Review, ranged from $1,000 for a nose to $28,000 for a heart. Other items enumerated, in ascending order of cost, included: ear, $1,715; wrist, $3,400; heart pacemaker or heart valve, $3,500; finger, $3,600; toe joint, $3,650; interocular lens, $4,000; ankle, elbow, knee, or shoulder, $6,600; hip joint, $9,500; lung, $10,000; and kidney, $13,000. In 1985, Dr. Robert Jarvik, already well launched into the bionic business with his artificial heart, was touting an $11,000 computerized ear that, after $5,000 worth of surgery, would equal "the cost of a new automobile." In 1985, a panel of fourteen experts estimated that an implantable artificial heart would eventually cost about $150,000.

No thought has been given yet to making available for humans what the Cleveland neurosurgeon Robert J. White began offering monkeys in 1974: head transplants.

BIRTH CONTROL PILL: The first successful oral contraceptive, commonly identified as "the Pill," was the result of a 1950 request made by the Planned Parenthood Movement, which was seeking the perfect parenthood preventive, one that would be "harmless, entirely reliable, simple, practical, universally applicable, and aesthetically satisfactory to both husband and wife." The recipient of the request was Dr. Gregory Pincus, of the Worcester Foundation for Experimental Biology in Shrewsbury, Massachusetts. Pincus and a co-worker, Dr. M. C. Chang, spent five years trying to fill the order.

The first clinical tests of their consumable contraceptive, from the chemical compounds progestin and estrogen, were conducted in 1954. Dr. John Rock, a professor of gynecology and obstetrics at Harvard University Medical School and an authority on infertility and birth control, organized the field trials and conducted the research that proved the Pill both effective and safe. In 1956, 1,308 women in San Juan, Puerto Rico, volunteered to participate in a large-scale test. Most (811) were given Conovid, the rest Uvulen. Of 830 women who continued to test the Pill for three years, only 17 became pregnant. Rock's research resulted in the 1960 U.S. Food and Drug Administration approval of the Pill for use by the public. The first commercially produced oral contraceptive, Enovid 10, was put on the market by the G. D. Searle Drug Company of Skokie, Illinois, on August 18, 1960.

If Pincus, Chang, and Rock are the fathers of the fatherhood-foiling Pill, the organic chemist Russell Marker would seem to qualify as its grandfather because his contributions to hormone research made the Pill possible. Marker left his mark by finding a chemical process and a source for the abundant production of the so-called "pregnancy hormone," progesterone, in the late 1930s and early 1940s. He never envisioned contraception as a result of his research until Pincus visited him in Mexico in 1952, seeking a supply of progesterone. One of the gynecological researchers who assisted in the development of the Pill, Dr. Edward T. Tyler, moonlighted by writing comedy material for Groucho Marx's "You Bet Your Life" TV quiz show.

BLENDER: L. H. Hamilton and Chester A. Beach perfected a high-speed, lightweight universal electric motor in 1912. Their original intention was to link it to home sewing machines, but they decided to augment their motor's sales appeal by adding attachments for sharpening knives, polishing silver and brass, and mixing cake batter. In 1923, Stephen J. Poplawski, who doted on milk shakes, patented a device to facilitate their preparation; it consisted of "an agitating element mounted in the bottom of a cup and a driving motor mounted in a base." However, it was Pennsylvania's Fred Waring, a well-known bandleader, who, with his Waring blender, first exploited the commercial possibilities of using a similar device to macerate fruits and vegetables. Blenders and food processors have become increasingly versatile and, for serious—and solvent—cooks, increasingly indispensable.

BLOODY MARY: George Jessel, the entertainer who became the self-styled Toastmaster General of the United States, claimed in an autobiography that he invented the Bloody Mary—that bracing blend of tomato juice, vodka, salt, black pepper, Worcestershire sauce, and lemon, with or without tabasco—to halt a hangover. Instant relief was essential, he noted with name-dropping casualness, because he had to keep a volleyball date with Alfred Gwynne Vanderbilt. However, the man usually credited with first assembling the red rouser was Fernand Petoit, a French bartender, who experimented with vodka and tomato juice mixtures at Harry's New York Bar in Paris. The drink reportedly was given its name by an American entertainer, Roy Barton, who said it reminded him of a Chicago nightclub, the Bucket of Blood. That explanation was rejected by Joseph Scialom, once head bartender at Shepheard's Hotel in Cairo and, later, maitre d' at New York's Four Seasons and Windows on the World. The drink's true name, Scialom insisted, was Bloody Meyer; and its inventor was "someone named Vladimir," who operated a New York bar during Prohibition. According to Scialom, Vladimir made up what he called Vladimir's Special, perhaps to conceal the fact that the tomato juice contained verboten vodka. "Vladimir," Scialom claimed, became first "Bloody Meyer" and then "Bloody Mary."

BLOOMERS: Amelia Jenks Bloomer (1818-1894), of Seneca Falls, New York—the petite and reputedly pretty publisher of the *Lily*, the first women's magazine in America—scandalized her fellow townspeople when she sashayed down Main Street wearing an outlandish costume created by wealthy abolitionist Gerrit Smith, whose daughter, Mrs. Elizabeth Smith Miller, first modeled it. Below a drawn-up, corrugated skirt were baggy trouser legs gathered at the ankles. Amelia Bloomer wore the strange getup to protest the voluminous, inconvenient hoopskirts then in vogue. The *Lily* launched a crusade for dress reform and printed patterns of the new, more maneuverable style that became permanently linked to its editor's name. A London Bloomer Committee sponsored a Grand Bloomer Ball; but in England the fashion seemed to appeal most to disreputable women. American feminists continued to wear bloomers for a few years, but like every other wardrobe enthusiasm, that, too, passed.

BLUES: American blacks produced the blues, a distinctive kind of mournful music, usually lamenting a lost or faithless lover, that has acquired ardent adherents throughout the world. Among its most popular practitioners were Bessie Smith, "queen of the blues," who recorded 160 examples of the genre; Ma Rainey, "mother of the blues"; Mamie Smith, first black singer to record the blues, and such subsequent black entertainers as Ethel Waters, and Louis Armstrong.

A Florence, Alabama-born composer and musician, William Christopher Handy (1873-1958), merits the title of his 1941 autobiography, *Father of the Blues*. W. C. preferred secular music to the clerical career his parents had in mind for him and left home to study music, in general, and the cornet, in particular. Between nonmusical jobs, he organized a quartet in 1893 to perform at the World's Columbian Exhibition in Chicago. Later, he settled in Memphis, Tennessee, to develop "the blues." His written scores combined elements of music he had grown up with: spirituals, work songs, folk ballads, and "jass."

Basically ragtime, the music achieved a melancholy quality through its generous use of "blue notes," largely flatted thirds and sevenths. A twelve-bar song titled "Mr. Crump," which Handy wrote in 1909 for the mayoralty campaign of E. H. (Boss) Crump, was published in slightly modified form two years later as "Memphis Blues." Departing from tradition, Handy's band deviated from the "Mr. Crump" score with the kind of solo variations that later characterized instrumental jazz improvisation. Unable to find a publisher for "Mr. Crump," Handy sold the instrumental version, "Memphis Blues," to a white promoter for $100. A bonanza for the buyer, it was the first song with "blues" in its title. Among more than sixty subsequent Handy-dandy compositions were "St. Louis Blues," which Handy profitably published himself; "Beale Street Blues"; and "Yellow Dog Blues." Although he was blind and in poor health, he continued to direct his own New York publishing house until his death.

Bessie Smith's 1937 demise after being denied admission to a segregated Mississippi hospital inspired several plays. "Ma Rainey's Black Bottom" was an award-winning 1984-85 Broadway entry.

BLURB: Testimonials to books' contents are now emblazoned on dust jackets, fore and aft, around the world; but that kind of bibliopuffery was first practiced by two New York publishers, Harper and Dodd Mead. Three 1899 examples of such tome extolling survive: John Barrett's *Admiral George Dewey* and J. K. Bangs's *The Enchanted Type-writer*, both published by Harper; and P. L. Ford's *Janice Meredith*, published by Dodd Mead. The word to describe the sometimes suspect encomiums was coined by the Massachusetts-born humorist Gelett Burgess, who vowed in a memorable poem that he would rather see, than be, a purple cow. At an American Booksellers Association banquet in 1907, Burgess defined the verb "to blurb," as "to make a sound like a publisher." As for the noun, "blurb," that was "a check drawn on Fame, and it is seldom honored." For the cover of his book, *Are You a Bromide?* he drew a picture of a pretty young woman, whom he identified as Belinda Blurb. (Any blurb accompanying the present volume is, of course, understated.)

BOARDWALK: The world's first boardwalk, a notion subsequently borrowed by seaside resorts around the world, was erected in Atlantic City, New Jersey, in 1870. It was ten feet wide and only one foot above the beach. When the summer season was over, the primitive plankway was disassembled and stored in a barn, at a cost of seventeen dollars.

A railroad conductor named, by curious coincidence, Alexander Boardman and a hotel proprietor, Jacob Keim, are both credited with what was first considered a nutty notion. Boardman was bored by the frequent need to brush sand from Camden and Atlantic Railroad seats; Keim kept keening about the amount of beach that ended up in his lobby. Within twenty years the boardwalk had replaced the ocean as Atlantic City's most potent attraction. Its fifth version is, with minor changes, the one that exists today.

On April 16, 1876, the boardwalk became the site of the first Easter Parade, now an annual tradition. On August 17, 1896, it was officially dubbed the boardwalk and proclaimed a street. When snow falls on the city, the boardwalk is always the first "street" cleared. Electricity arrived in 1882, and by 1908, the boardwalk was bordered by huge electric signs. One, advertising Gillette razors, contained fifteen hundred bulbs. Later boardwalk adornments included the world's largest lightbulb, the world's largest toothpaste-oozing tube, the world's largest tire, and the world's largest functioning typewriter. The latter, 1,728 times larger than a standard Underwood, weighed 14 tons, contained 45-pound type bars, and used a ribbon 5 inches wide and 100 feet long to tap out messages on stationery measuring 9 by 12 feet. Every time its bell rang at the end of a line, the sound could be heard for blocks.

BOTTLE CAP: In 1892, William Painter, a Baltimore, Maryland, Quaker, invented the bottle cap, the machinery to manufacture it, and the method to affix it. To make and merchandise his invention, he created the Crown Cork and Seal Company, which eventually made him a millionaire. His bottle cap was unchallenged until the advent of the twist-off variety in the 1960s. The success of Painter's invention and its inventor's counseling about the profits to be derived from a throwaway everyday necessity inspired a Painter salesman, King Camp Gillette (*see* RAZOR BLADE, DISPOSABLE).

BOURBON: Bourbon, America's contribution to international tippler-tempters, had its nativity not long after the nation's. A Baptist minister, the Rev. Elijah Craig, distilled the first corn whiskey in 1789. He resided in Georgetown, Kentucky, part of Bourbon County, named as a thank-you for aid rendered to the American Revolution by a French king of the Bourbon dynasty, Louis XVI. The "western country," rechristened "Bourbon County," encompassed northeastern Kentucky and part of Virginia. Craig's distillations were considered duds.

The first bourbon to earn profuse praise was manufactured in 1823, by Dr. James C. Crow, a Scottish physician. Crow had something to crow about—he invented the sour mash process, which greatly enhanced bourbon's flavor. According to Civil War legend, when a Congressman complained to President Lincoln that General Ulysses

S. Grant was drunk during the Battle of Shiloh, Lincoln replied, "I wish I knew what brand of whiskey he drinks. I would send a barrel to all my other generals." Historians say that Crow's elixir was Grant's favorite. Spreading the stuff around would not have bankrupted Lincoln; at the time, a barrelful cost only twenty-five cents.

Although bourbon is not quite two hundred years old, a puling infant next to many of the world's more potent potables, bourbon is partial to such hoary brand names as Early Times, Ancient Age, Old Grand-Dad, Old Taylor, Old Forest, Old Red Fox, Old Charter, Old Sunny Brook, and of course, Old Crow. No distiller, so far, has had the chutzpah to escalate these antiquity-claiming antics by marketing an Older or Oldest. Best-seller, with nary a mention of venerability, is Jim Bean. To qualify legally as bourbon, whiskey must be distilled to a proof not exceeding 160 (80 percent alcohol) from a grain mash with a corn content between 51 percent and 80 percent. It must then be stored in charred new-oak buckets, at 125 proof or less. "Kentucky straight whiskey" is bourbon bottled at no less than 80 proof, with nothing but water added. A close cousin to bourbon is "Tennessee sour mash whiskey," which reuses "beer" from an earlier fermentation, adds fresh yeast and fresh corn mash, and is filtered through ground charcoal before aging.

BOX CAMERA: In the late 1870s, Waterville, New York-born George Eastman (1854-1932), working as a bank clerk in Rochester, New York, wanted to take souvenir pictures during a vacation. When he learned that he would have to tote a formidable amount of heavy equipment, he decided to skip the trip and concentrate on the photography. Using his mother's kitchen as a workroom, he developed a dry plate that markedly reduced the amount of impedimenta required by the wet-plate method. In 1880, he rented a loft and started manufacturing dry plates. Four years later, he introduced a revolutionary new product; film in rolls with a roll holder that could be used in most available cameras. In 1888, the Eastman Dry Plate and Film Company began marketing the first box camera, the twenty-five dollar Kodak, with enough film for a hundred photos already inside. When that number of pictures had been snapped, the camera was returned with ten dollars for developing and reloading.

Eastman invented the name Kodak after trying various combinations beginning and ending with K, which he considered a "strong, incisive" letter. The following year, George Eastman wrote to his partner, Henry A. Strong, that he was working with the camera-maker Frank Brownell on a more simple, less costly model. In February 1900, came the result: a boxlike camera made of heavy cardboard, reinforced with wood, and covered with black imitation leather. It was virtually goofproof and, as introductory ads promised, could be operated "by

Any School Boy or Girl." The camera cost $1; a "transparent-film cartridge" for six 2¼ by 2¼-inch exposures, fifteen cents; and a developing and printing outfit, seventy-five cents. It was named the Kodak Brownie, which may have been a salute to Brownell or to the artist Palmer Cox, whose cartoons of tiny "brownie" elves adorned ads for the new camera and its package. For years the Brownie was America's most popular camera. It was the progenitor of such Eastman Kodak products as the 1963 cartridge-loaded Kodak Instamatic (*see* INSTANT PHOTOGRAPHY) and the 1982 automatic Disc 4000.

Kodak's cameras are merely means to a more profitable end: selling and developing film. The Kodak name and the company's distinctive yellow film boxes are familiar everywhere. Almost half of Kodak sales are outside the United States, and in 1979, the company began selling its film in the Republic of China.

An astute businessman, Eastman bought out many rivals, acquired numerous patent rights, and blocked competitors by compelling his wholesale and retail outlets to sign exclusive contracts. These practices triggered several antitrust actions, but Kodak virtually monopolized the field by 1927.

The inventor was also a straitlaced bachelor who lived with his mother in a Rochester mansion, and subscribed to a Victorian code of morality that was continued by his Kodak successors. A brouhaha erupted in 1980 when *Penthouse* magazine sued for the return of some allegedly lewd color photos of Cheryl Rixon, the magazine's Pet of the Year, which had been sent to the Kodak color lab for development. As late as the 1970s, all Kodak executives who needed their secretaries past the 5 P.M. quitting time were required to summon chaperones, and purchase of liquor was not an acceptable expense-account entry. In 1931, when he was seventy-seven, an ailing Eastman asked his doctor to point out precisely where his heart was located; then, he went home and put a bullet through the designated spot. "My work is done," he wrote in a suicide note. "Why wait?"

BRA, MODERN: Many countries claim the invention of the mammary supporter. According to a Chinese legend, the first brassiere was designed as camouflage, to conceal a general's love bite from the eyes of a concubine's patron, the T'ang dynasty emperor Hsuan Tsung. He found the red silk titillating. The French say they dreamt up the often-deceptive device. In 1912, a German immigrant, most appropriately named Otto Titzling (1884-1942), working in his uncle's undergarments factory, devised a chest halter to halt the laments of an overendowed young opera singer, Swanhilda Olafsen.

An American socialite who was a descendant of the steamboat inventor Robert Fulton, Mary Phelps Jacob (known as Caresse Crosby by fellow expatriates in Paris during the 1920s), created her own variation, one evening, to prevent the embroidery of her corset cover from poking between the flowers on her rose-garlanded evening gown. Deciding to dispense with the corset, she sent her maid for a couple of handkerchiefs, pink ribbon, needle and thread; folded and pinned the handkerchiefs on the bias; anchored them by tying the ribbon behind her back; and donned her dress. She approved, she discovered, of both the way she felt and looked. Envious friends asked her to free them, too, from the tyranny of unseen armor forged from whalebone; but it wasn't until she received a request for a "contraption" from a total stranger, with a dollar bill tucked inside, that she realized that her improvisation had moneymaking possibilities. She was awarded a patent for her "backless brassiere" design but, after an unsuccessful attempt to do her own marketing, sold it to the Warner Brothers Corset Company of Bridgeport, Connecticut, for a picayune fifteen thousand. During the next two decades, sales exceeded $20 million.

The Warners, not the same siblings who made Hollywood history, created the A, B, C, D cup-size categories for bras in 1939 and, later, the two-way stretch girdle. Other American and European corsetieres quickly invaded the breast-bracing business. To describe the new product, American manufacturers borrowed a French word, *braciere*, which means "arm protector." The French themselves preferred *soutien-gorge*, "throat supporter"—a choice that hints at anatomical anarchy.

BREAKDANCING: This mind-boggling blend of mime, acrobatics, martial arts, and jazz and jitterbug dance steps could easily result in the breaking of bones, especially when its practitioners are spinning on their backs at an incredible number of revolutions per minute; but that's not where breakdancing gets its name. There are several explanations of the nomenclature. The form is attributed to blacks in the South Bronx ghetto and Hispanics in the Los Angeles barrio, who, sometime in the late 1960s, began waging anything-you-can-do-I-can-do-better dance competitions during breaks or truces between street battles.

Another version attributes breakdancing's label to the percussive instrumental break in soul-music songs. A carefully choreographed conglomeration of styles, breakdancing is performed to an insistent beat provided by music or rhythmic talk. The style was popularized in the 1983 *Flashdance, Breakin'*, and subsequent movies and was quickly copied in Canada, England, France, West Germany, and other countries, spreading from the street to high school gyms, stages, and nightclubs. Dance schools began to offer specialized courses. Hospitals reported an increase in sprained necks and battered backs. In San Bernardino, California, an ordinance banning breakdancers from any public passageway, because of protests from storekeepers at a downtown shopping mall, was quickly rescinded when youth leaders and child psychologists lauded the razzledazzle dance style as a relatively harmless way for young people to let off steam.

Breakdancing has acquired some unlikely recruits. One, as attested by a series of magazine photos, is England's Prince Charles, who, in April 1985, wandered into a disco in the Sussex village of Middleton-on-the-Sea and soon began trying to emulate the commoners' demonstrations of the King Tut, Michael Jackson-style moonwalking and a shaky-legged "collapse" step. Other common steps are tagged the back spin, the head spin, the knee spin, the spider, the windmill, the hand glide, the turtle, the crazy legs, and ominously, the suicide.

BREAKFAST CEREAL: Morning oatmeal was a European tradition long before 1850, when a German immigrant, Ferdinand Schumacher, wondered why Americans fed oats to horses instead of to humans. Deciding it was because they lacked the patience to steam the oats for hours, he created a variety that could be prepared in much less time. That paved the way for the development of numerous quick-serve cereals. After Tom Avidon, a Grand Forks, North Dakota, miller, shipped boxes of ground wheat in homemade containers, New York City brokers ordered more of what they dubbed "cream of wheat."

Henry D. Perky, a Denver lawyer plagued by dyspepsia, met at a Nebraska hotel a fellow sufferer who claimed he gained relief (not spelled R-o-l-a-i-d) by breakfasting daily on boiled whole wheat with milk. That inspired the first ready-to-eat breakfast cereal. Perky's product, airy biscuits made by drawing heat-softened wheat through rollers, sold poorly in 1892 as "Ceres" but, later, became world famous as shredded wheat. At first, it was sold only in Denver and Colorado Springs, but in 1895, Perky founded the Natural Food Company and opened a factory in Worcester, Massachusetts. Samples of shredded wheat reached John Harvey Kellogg, resident doctor for a health institute operated by Seventh-Day Adventists in a farmhouse just outside Battle Creek, Michigan. Kellogg, a vegetarian who kept asking, "How can you eat anything that looks out of eyes?" began similar experiments with grains. John and his brother, Will, devised a system for flaking or flattening wheat. Result: the first flaked cereal, Granose, announced in 1895. Three years later, after the siblings had a tiff, Will, on his own, concocted corn flakes. (*See* KELLOGG'S)

A patient at the Battle Creek Sanitarium, Charles W. Post, decided to start his own breakfast cereal company. Its products included a dry cereal he called Elijah's Manna but, later, renamed Grape-Nuts, and Postum, a coffee substitute made from grain. Post's company evolved into General Foods. Virtually all breakfast cereals are made from some variety of grass, a category that encompasses oats, barley, corn, and wheat.

BROOM: Brooms made from broomcorn, a variety of sorghum, were common in Europe long before the 1790s, when Levi Dickinson, of Massachusetts, raised enough broomcorn to make thirty brooms and launch an American industry. Brooms acquired a new look and greater efficiency when the Shakers—as members of the United Society of Believers in Christ's Second Appearing were commonly called—converted the traditional round sweeper made of twigs or straws into the flat model now used throughout the world.

BUBBLE GUM: The strategic placement of lips, tongue, and breath enables children, assorted athletes, and other skilled gum-chewers throughout the world to produce awesome bubbles. Each is a tribute to a twenty-three-year-old cost accountant, Walter Diemer, who, in August 1928, created the formula for the Frank H. Fleer Corporation, the Philadelphia firm previously responsible for candy-coated Chiclets. Fleer named its product Blibber Blubber, then re-christened it Dubble Bubble.

Early U.S. bubble gum was invariably pink, reportedly because that was the only coloring available to Diemer during his experiments. In Germany, however, because of food laws, it was white. In 1974, a soft bubble gum, Bubble Yum, was introduced by Life Savers. The Warner-Lambert Company's American Chicle Division quickly countered with Bubblicious.

After enjoying a munchers' monopoly for nineteen years, Double Bubble was challenged in 1947 when the Topps Chewing Gum Company began peddling the five-cent Bazooka, so named because of its resemblance to a World War II weapon that, in turn, recalled a peculiar-looking wind instrument devised by the hillbilly comedian Bob Burns. Topps attempted to boost its sales in 1951 with a "Freedom's War" line of Atom Bazooka Gum wrapped in picture cards showing American forces triumphing over Russian, Chinese, and North Korean Communists. When these sparked "brutalizing children" accusations, Topps borrowed an idea used earlier as a bonus for other products and substituted likenesses of major league baseball players. In 1961, Topps signed 446 of the 450 major league players and 6,500 minor league players to exclusive contracts for $5 token fees and $125 per year. Fleer tried to lure some of them away, without success. An antitrust action brought by the government ended after four years, with Topps still tops. Bubble gum became a worldwide favorite, reputedly serving as ransom for a kidnapped British diplomat in Borneo, barter for wives in central Africa, and currency for Eskimos (*See also* CHEWING GUM.)

BURBANK, LUTHER: Luther Burbank (1849-1928) was Mother Nature's energetic aide. After reading Charles Darwin's *Varia-*

tion of Animals and Plants Under Domestication when he was nineteen, this superhorticulturist born in Lancaster, Massachusetts, acquired a small plot of land and began developing new and improved vegetables. One result was the highly successful Burbank potato. After five years he moved to Santa Rosa, California, where his experiments expanded to include fruits and flowers. Hybridizing and grafting, he created 90 varieties of vegetables, including tomatoes, corn, squash, asparagus and peas; 113 new kinds of plums and prunes, and at least 10 new berries, plus assorted nectarines, quinces, cherries, apples, and peaches. His floral breeding included calla lilies, roses, poppies, and, most notably, the Shasta daisy. "I shall be content," he said, "if, because of me, there shall be better fruits and fairer flowers."

BURLESQUE: U.S. burlesque in the early 1800s was utterly unlike the kind presented by the Minsky brothers in New York a century later. Instead of baggy-pants slapstick, unsubtle double entendres, and female flesh, its emphasis was on parody and caricature. The first successful example was John Poole's 1828 hamming-up of *Hamlet.* It was followed by numerous needlings of prominent plays and players. One entry of this type was titled *Much Ado About a Merchant of Venice.* In the same style, decades later, were travesties like the 1874 *Evangeline* and the 1884 *Adonis,* stage vehicles for the comedy teams of Weber and Fields, and Harrigan and Hart, and full-scale gagathons like the 1891 *A Trip to Chinatown* and the 1938 *Hellzapoppin'.* Burlesque also comprised the final third of minstrel shows, lampooning what had preceded it (*see* MINSTREL SHOW).

Burlesque or "burleycue," U.S. style, stemmed from growing male preoccupation with female thigh-hugging tights. Such convention-defying attire made its American stage debut at New York's Thalia Theater on February 7, 1827, via a Mlle. Hutin, and became a national scandal on June 7, 1861, when Adah Isaacs Menken wore tights while strapped to a real horse in a play based on Byron's poem, "Mazeppa." Mazeppas multiplied. A transition to later-day burlesque was represented by Michael P. Leavitt's 1869 accent-on-legs opus, *Mme. Rentz's Female Minstrels,* in which boy-girls wore tights and girl-girls wore teasingly slit skirts. Distaff minstrels disrobed to tights as they swung over the heads of male oglers. Partial nudity became a burlesque staple in the 1920s, first motionless, then accompanied by energetic action. Burlesque gradually evolved into a commercialized sex show, with amply endowed "queens of burlesque" progressively showing more epidermis. The hootchie-kootchie degenerated into bumps and grinds, tights were replaced by the G-string. Gypsy Rose Lee and other strippers (dubbed "ecdysiasts" by H. L. Mencken) became international celebrities, whose techniques were emulated and "improved" in overseas theaters and nightclubs.

C

CABBAGE PATCH KID: Xavier Roberts, the North Georgia country boy who fathered the millions of dolls that have been "adopted" into families all over the world, called them Cabbage Patch Kids because local lore claimed that the cabbage patch, rather than the stork, was where babies came from.

In 1978, he was waiting on customers at the Unicoi State Park gift shop when the thought struck him that there just might be a market for one-of-a-kind soft-sculpture dolls with bloated bodies that were dough faced, chinless, and beady eyed. Grabbing a needle and some cloth, he set to work. Although many prospective customers had the same immediate reaction: "God, they're ugly!" Roberts put a thirty dollar price on his progeny. Moreover, he insisted that they were "babies" to be "adopted" by "parents," not dolls to be sold to customers. The idea appealed to little girls' maternal instinct, and by 1983, the annual cabbage patch crop being harvested by Coleco Industries of West Hartford, Connecticut, had reached the three million mark. During 1985, Coleco expected the dolls—oops! babies—to gross $2 billion worldwide.

Each Kid comes with a personalized "oath of adoption." Each has its own name—based on 1938 Georgia birth records, assigned by computer—and computer-controlled differences in wardrobe, in hair and skin color, type of mouth, location of dimples, and sprinkling of freckles. A supply shortage the first Christmas the Kids went on sale resulted in a mad scramble by the parents of would-be parents. Long lines formed. Fist fights erupted. One Kansas City postman flew to London to buy a Cabbage Patcher for his five-year-old daughter. At his rural Georgia gallery, Roberts dressed his salespeople in doctor and nurse whites and plunked the dolls into bassinets and incubators. Forty-eight of the Kids were kidnapped from a Holland, Michigan, collector and briefly held for ransom. Although Roberts condemns such connubiality—"They're too young!"—two of his Kids were wed in a telecast ceremony in Davenport, Iowa, on February 29, 1984. In March 1985, an Arlington, Texas, orthodontist began adorning Cabbage Patch faces with braces. Later ramifications were horoscopes and personal insurance policies.

CABLE: The first telegraph cable was an insulated copper wire laid in New York Harbor between the Battery and Governors Island by Samuel Finley Breese Morse. One day after its completion on October 18, 1842, it was put out of commission when a vessel raised its anchor and ripped up two hundred feet of the wire. The following year, Samuel Colt linked New York City with Fire Island and Coney Island, using an insulated cable encased in a lead pipe. The first transatlantic cable, ramrodded by Cyrus West Field, was completed on August 5, 1858, after two unsuccessful tries. The day after a splice was made in midocean on July 28, 1858, the cable was dipped into the deep by two American ships, the *Niagara* and the *Georgia*, heading for Trinity Bay, Newfoundland, and two British ships, the *Agamemnon* and the *Valorous*, bound for Valencia, Ireland. The cable was 1,950 statute miles long, and two-thirds of it nestled more than two miles down. Congrats were swapped by President James Buchanan and Queen Victoria on August 16, but they were premature. Because of inadequate power, service was discontinued two weeks later. The first successful transatlantic cable was completed on July 27, 1867. The first transpacific cable, between San Francisco and Honolulu, was completed on December 14, 1902, and the first message was transmitted the same day. On July 3, 1903, the Pacific cable network also encompassed Midway, Guam, and Manila. Round-the-world messages between President Theodore Roosevelt and Clarence Hungerford Mackay, president of the Pacific Commercial Cable Company, who were both at Roosevelt's home in Oyster Bay, New York, required eleven minutes for the westward transmission and nine for the eastward response.

CAMPBELL SOUP: Campbell soups—which have made possible their parent company's expansion into some six hundred products and food manufactories in England, France, Belgium, Australia, Japan, and other countries—are only remotely connected with anyone named Campbell.

Joseph Campbell, a fruit merchant, and Abram Anderson, an icebox maker, joined forces in 1869 to establish a Camden, New Jersey, company to can jellies, mincemeat, fruits, and vegetables; but Anderson withdrew in 1876 and Campbell retired in 1894. Arthur Dorrance took over management of the company. His chemist nephew, Dr. John Thompson Dorrance, added soup to the company's array of canned foods. After inspecting Parisian kitchens and soup tureens, Dr. John felt there had to be a more economical and more appetizing way to distribute canned soup than via the bulky, often waterlogged cans then being utilized by three other soup companies. He invented condensed soup, consisting of all the ingredients of soup except water. At last count, Campbell was packing fifty-four varieties of condensed soup, to which water must be added, plus—since 1970— even more profitable Chunky ready-to-serve soups, which already contain the water Dorrance went to such pains to eliminate.

Tomato soup, the first variety the company produced, has always been the unchallenged champ, with chicken noodle and cream of mushroom in the place and show positions. The gold medal displayed on Campbell soup cans since 1900 was acquired at the Paris Exposition. In 1940, to help reach housewives through their children, Campbell's advertising began to feature the Campbell Kids, "round roly-polies" created by Grace Gebbie Drayton, the artist wife of a Campbell salesman. The Campbell colors, red and white, were borrowed from Cornell's football uniforms. The distinctive soup cans are displayed in galleries, thanks to pop artist Andy Warhol. When Dr. Dorrance died in 1930, he left a $115 million estate. Although soups now represent less than half its business, the company is still called Campbell Soup.

CANCER RESEARCH: The Baltimore-born pathologist Francis Peyton Rous (1879-1970) and the Halifax, Nova Scotia-born surgeon Charles Brenton Huggins (1901-   ), whose work was conducted in Chicago, shared the 1966 Nobel Prize for physiology and medicine for their research on the causes and treatment of cancer. In 1909, Rous was given a Plymouth Rock hen with a cancer he diagnosed as a sarcoma and decided, contrary to prevalent medical opinion, that the barnyard spread of the disease was due to a virus rather than the transfer of cancer cells. In 1912, he published a landmark paper, "Transmission of a Malignant New Growth by Means of a Cell-free Filtrate." Critics indulged in *raus mit Rous* sniping at his laboratory methods, and not until 1923, did independent researchers confirm his findings. Even when he was first proposed for a Nobel Prize in 1926, it was generally assumed that his research was applicable only to barnyard cluckers, but later investigators discovered viral causes for various animal and, perhaps, human cancers. During World War I, Rous developed a method to store blood for transfusions, making blood banks possible and, later, did research on the liver and gall bladder. After 1940, however, he concentrated on cancer and made other important contributions in that field.

Huggins's general field was genitourinary surgery, but he specialized in the treatment of cancer of the prostate and mammary glands.

He discovered that both cancer types were linked to the bloodstream level of certain hormones and, using female hormones and cortisone, developed a set of radical procedures for treating otherwise untreatable cancers. Huggins found that many cancer-causing chemicals possess structures similar to those of certain hormones and utilized large doses of hormones to control cancers afflicting rats, as a preliminary to human therapy.

CANDY BAR: Although even the early Egyptians found candy dandy, candy *bars* are among America's sweetest creations and universally hailed by kids, adults, and income-seeking dentists. The first bar, an inexpensive palate-pampering blend of sugar, cocoa, chocolate, and milk was concocted by the Lancaster, Pennsylvania, confectioner Milton Hershey in 1894. Two years later, Leonard Hirschfeld introduced the first paper-wrapped candy, the chewy Tootsie Roll— its name a salute to his young daughter. Peter Paul Halijian of New Haven, Connecticut, made two notable contributions to the candy-bar buffet: the bittersweet chocolate-and-coconut Mounds in 1921 and the nut-adorned Almond Joy in 1947. In 1921, Otto Schnering mixed fudge, peanuts, caramel, and chocolate and named the result (*see* BABY RUTH) in honor of President Grover Cleveland's daughter. Two years later, by concocting the Butterfinger, Schnering demonstrated that, even like lightning, candy-bar fame and fortune can strike in the same place twice.

Hershey ruled the candy bar roost until the early 1970s, when Mars spurted ahead. The Minnesotan Franklin Mars sired what was to become a delicious dynasty by stirring together sweet milk chocolate, corn syrup, milk, sugar, cocoa, malt, butter, and frothy egg whites to form what he dubbed the Milky Way. Later his son, Forrest Mars, Sr., parlayed the Milky Way recipe into a thriving candy business of his own in England before returning to the United States to rejoin his candy-concocting clan. Subsequent additions to the Mars family of candies included Snickers, in 1930; 3 Musketeers, in 1932; and M&Ms, in 1940.

In 1979, Snickers was the best-selling candy bar, followed in the Top Ten by Hershey's Reese Peanut Butter Cup, peanut M&M, plain M&M, Hershey chocolate bar with almonds, 3 Musketeers, Hershey's Kit Kat, Hershey chocolate bar, Milky Way, and Baby Ruth. The next five were Butterfinger, Nestle Crunch, Almond Joy, Reese Crunchy Peanut Butter Cup, and Mounds.

CARBONATED DRINKS: Centuries-old efforts to duplicate naturally carbonated mineral waters finally succeeded in 1772, thanks to England's Joseph Priestley, and "soda water" was soon being bottled and peddled. Ginger ale, first produced about 1850, became a popular import from Ireland. However, American chemist Townsend Speakman, commissioned by the Philadelphia physician Dr. Philip Syng Physick (how's *that* for a vocation-suiting name!) to provide a supply of carbonated water, made a major contribution. Dr. Physick, who later was saluted as the father of American surgery (in 1831, he extracted one thousand stones from the bladder of U.S. Chief Justice John Marshall), thought the drink would have spalike health qualities. However, it was Speakman's idea to add fruit juices to make it more palatable.

Americans have created many of the world's most popular soft drinks. One, Dr. Pepper, was the indirect result of a temporarily blighted romance. A Dr. Pepper, the owner of a Virginia drugstore in the latter part of the 19th century, fired a young soda fountain attendant who was showing too much interest in a Miss Pepper. The lovelorn lad fled to Waco, Texas, and resumed his soda fountain career at Waco's Old Corner Drug Store. One of his experimental concoctions especially pleased the store's patrons, who dubbed it Dr. Pepper, in honor of the man whose intervention in a romance had brought them their taste treat. According to legend, Dr. Pepper's creator and Dr. Pepper's daughter eventually wed. A Waco beverage chemist, R. S. Lazenby, who had been an Old Corner Drug Store patron, experimented with the formula and put the result, officially dubbed Dr. Pepper, on sale at local soda fountains in 1885.

A year later, John S. Pemberton, an Atlanta pharmacist, created Coca-Cola (*see* COCA-COLA). In 1898, a North Carolina pharmacist, Caleb Bradham, introduced what was to become "Coke's" foremost competitor, Pepsi-Cola. Other bubbly birthdates: Hires Root Beer (*See* ROOT BEER), 1886; Canada Dry Ginger Ale, 1904; 7-Up, 1933; No-Cal, 1952; Diet-Rite, 1962; Tab, 1963; Diet Pepsi, 1965; the "new" Coca-Cola, 1985.

CARE: The acronym identifying the organization founded in 1945 to provide help where needed once represented Cooperative for American Remittances to Europe, but that was later changed to Cooperative for American Relief Everywhere.

The first of its "CARE packages" to World War II-ravaged Europeans—consisting of all-purpose flour, canned meats, margarine, sugar, powdered milk, coffee beans, bacon, dried whole figs and seedless raisins—reached Le Havre, France, on May 11, 1946, and soon were being distributed in twelve countries. Originally a nonprofit, nonpolitical, nonsectarian cooperative effort by twenty-two major American organizations, CARE USA promptly acquired a CARE Canada affiliate and, later, overseas siblings like CARE Europe, CARE Deutschland, and CARE Norge. Care International, established in 1982, also includes France, Italy, and Great Britain.

CARE packages to indviduals were phased out in the 1960s. They have been replaced by health, nutritional, and educational programs that benefit entire communities in thirty of the world's poorest countries, variously situated in Central and South America, Africa, Asia, and the Middle East. In 1984, CARE staff members distributed 854,842,000 pounds of food to twenty-two million children, refugees, pregnant women, and nursing mothers on three continents. Emergency relief was provided to refugees fleeing drought and civil disorders in Chad, Somalia, and Uganda. CARE for the Earth programs of soil conservation, reforestation, and land management encompassed sixteen countries. In Bangladesh, CARE-built irrigation systems enabled farmers to produce and sell three crops a year instead of one. Other programs provided help in building schools, health clinics, and roads and in developing small businesses.

In 1985, CARE estimated that for every dollar contributed, it was able to provide, with the help of host governments, $9.21 in goods and services.

CARPET SWEEPER: Melville Reuben Bissell of Grand Rapids, Michigan, the owner of a china shop, suffered nonstop headaches because he was allergic to the dusty straw in which his merchandise was packed. Looking for a way to keep down the dust, he invented the first practical carpet sweeper, patented on September 19, 1876. Other carpet sweepers had been attempted earlier, but none was equally effective on different kinds of floor coverings. Bissell's innovation was the "broom action" principle. Varying pressure on the handle made a brush roller adjust to various thicknesses. Parts made by women working in their homes were assembled by Bissell and his spouse, who formed the Bissell Carpet Sweeper Company to market their product.

CASH REGISTER: One day in 1879, James J. Ritty, a vacationing Dayton, Ohio, saloonkeeper, was exploring the engine room of a transatlantic steamer when he noticed a piece of maritime equipment that counted the revolutions of the ship's propeller. He decided a similar system could provide a more accurate way than haphazard pencil jottings to keep tabs on saloon sales. It could also, he hoped, dissuade larcenous bartenders from tapping the till. With his brother John, he devised "Ritty's Incorruptible Cashier"—a bulky mechanism that included two rows of keys with amounts printed on them, a large clockface with the little hand indicating dollars and the big hand showing cents, and a bell whose tinkle signaled the completion of a cash transaction. The device lacked a cash drawer control and any way to maintain a permanent record. Several improvements were made before Ritty, because of inadequate funding, sold his business to a local group that renamed it the National Manufacturing Company.

In 1884, the name was changed again, to National Cash Register, after a fellow Ohioan, John Henry Patterson, acquired a controlling interest for sixty-five hundred dollars. Patterson, a skillful merchandiser and a benign employer, gussied up Ritty's crude "thief catcher" with an internal printing mechanism that kept a running record of sales and spewed out sales slips. By 1910, the company monopolized the U.S. cash register market to such a degree (90 percent) that an antitrust suit was filed by the Justice Department. Patterson was sentenced to a five thousand dollar fine and a year in jail, but the sentence was reversed after the Dayton flood of 1913, when Patterson was credited with saving the city by providing company property to feed, house, and hospitalize flood victims and by reorganizing his assembly line to produce one rowboat every seven minutes.

In more recent years, under William Anderson—who in 1974 streamlined its name to NCR—the company has gone electronic, diversifying into computers and automated twenty-four-hour bank tellers (*see* BANKING, AUTOMATED). With forty-five foreign units, it does more than half its business outside the United States.

CELLULOID: Sometimes prize contests produce true prizes. Celluloid, the first in what was to become a profusion of plastics, was invented by siblings John Wesley Hyatt of Albany, New York, and Isaiah Smith Hyatt, of Rockford, Illinois, to win a ten thousand dollar prize offered by Phelan and Collender. The New York company wanted something other than ivory for the manufacture of billiard balls.

The Hyatts produced their versatile compound by dissolving cotton in nitric acid (this combination, in some forms, is the explosive called gunpowder), adding camphor, and then, subjecting the mixture to heat and mold pressure. The result was a material that could be made to look in any color like ivory, amber, bone, horn, mother-of-pearl, or tortoise shell. A patent was granted on June 15, 1869, and manufacture began three years later. The word "celluloid," which became common, was registered as a trademark in 1873. It was derived from cellulose and the suffix "oid," meaning "like."

Celluloid's hundreds of uses included photographic film, lacquers, artificial leather, combs, brush and knife handles, buttons, and of course, billiard balls. Because all materials made with nitric acid are highly flammable, cellulose acetate, substituting acetic acid for nitric acid, has inherited many of celluloid's uses.

CHAIN LETTER: Although they're legally a no-no, chain letters—promising each participant deluges of such goodies as dollars, benevolent prayers, or sex partners—pop up periodically in the United States and elsewhere.

The first chain letter, proclaiming a Depression-time Prosperity

Club, had its origin in Denver in 1935. Theoretically, if you sent a dime to the name and address at the top of a list of five, crossing the first one out and adding your own, and mailed copies of the letter to five other people, your ten-cent investment plus postage could burgeon into $1,562.50. Almost immediately there were rumors of needy persons who had actually achieved such providential payoffs. A few weeks later, three chain letters emanating from Springfield, Missouri, upped the ante from a dime to a dollar. Springfield residents went berserk in their eagerness to share in the bucks bonanza. At least printing shops profited, charging first fifteen cents and, then, twenty-five for form letters. The entry fee rose to five dollars, and mailing was replaced by hand-to-hand list selling. Soon there was a glut of sellers but few buyers, and in a matter of weeks, the get-rich-quick craze abated. Before it vanished, however, a Kansas City, Kansas, cleric used chain letters to enlarge his congregation, and the National Republican Committee borrowed the idea to solicit anti-New Deal dimes.

Other variations included a "send-a-pint" letter, a "good-riddance" letter ("shoot the guy at the top of the list"), and a "kiss chain" for unwed participants only. In 1951, a Dallas-based "pantie club" was quickly quashed by Texas postal authorities. Chain letters became an international phenomenon, with variations surfacing in such seemingly unlikely locales as England, Germany, Japan, China, and Abyssinia.

CHEWING GUM: According to legend, when Antonio López de Santa Anna (the general who commanded the Mexican attack on Texas's Alamo in 1836) was deposed thirty years later as Mexico's dictator and sought refuge on Staten Island, he brought with him a large wad of chicle—a gummy substance made from the sap of the sapodilla tree that had been a favorite tension-easer for uptight Mexicans since ancient Mayan days.

When he returned to Mexico a few months later, he left the chicle chunk behind. Thomas Adams, a Staten Island acquaintance, began experimenting with it. Efforts to vulcanize the sticky stuff into a new kind of rubber failed. So did attempts to convert it into an adhesive for false teeth. Finally, Adams boiled it and rolled it out with a rolling pin. When tested at a New Jersey candy store, this improved version of Santa Anna's jaw exerciser proved so popular that Adams developed, and in 1871 patented, a gum-making machine. Long ribbons of gum were notched so that sellers could break off penny pieces. Adams's first gum, sold as "Adams' New York Gum—Snapping and Stretching," was tasteless. He named a licorice-flavored variety Black Jack. Competitors soon proliferated, offering assorted flavors in brightly colored wrappings. William F. Semple of Mount Vernon, Ohio, was the first to add flavors, using such substances as "orrisroot, myrrh, licorice, sugar, barytes, and charcoal." Adams topped his rivals by putting his product in hundreds of vending machines. Then in 1899, the financial tycoon Charles R. Flint masterminded the merger of Adams's firm and five rival companies into the mammoth American Chicle Company. However, one major manufacturer, William Wrigley, Jr., declined to join the "chewing gum trust." Instead, he kept upping the ad budget for his gum until it became the world's most advertised product. Wrigley first became involved with chewing gum as a premium to boost sales of baking powder, offering two sticks of "chewing candy" with every can. With such flavors as spearmint and juicy fruit, he eventually cornered a giant's share of the world's chewing gum market. That was huge, thanks to the popularization of gum by cud-munching GIs in both theaters of World War II.

CHICKEN: Because of the widespread operations of franchisers, American barnyard fowl are becoming an international staple. Two native breeds, the Plymouth Rock and the New Hampshire, account for about half of all the poultry being raised today. Technological advances have made chicken virtually a "manufactured" product. Once considered a luxury food (President Herbert Hoover, seeking reelection in 1928, dangled before a dubious electorate the prospect of "a chicken in every pot"), it is now cheaper than beef and pork.

The booming agribusiness, deceiving chickens about the hour and the season by substituting lightbulbs for sun and fans for wind, can now produce in less than fifty days chickens ready for eating that weigh slightly over four pounds, with plump bodies and skinny legs. Chicken is also being put to new uses. Robert Baker, chairman of Cornell University's poultry science department, functioning as a sort of Edison of chicken, has helped invent 52 processed-chicken products since 1960, including chicken steak, chicken chili, chickalona (white chicken balony) and, most popular of all, the chicken hot dog, which has captured almost 20 percent of the hot dog market. The first fast-food franchiser to realize that chickens could lay golden eggs was Harland Sanders, of Louisville, who subsequently acquired an honorary colonelship from the governor of Kentucky for "contributions to the state's cuisine." In 1956, when he was sixty-six and on Social Security, Colonel Sanders, of the white hair and goatee with suit to match, created Kentucky Fried Chicken. In less than twenty years it was grossing more than one billion dollars annually from outlets in thirty-nine countries, an amount that later doubled. Hardly chickenfeed!

CHIROPRACTIC: In 1895, the medical practice based on the theory that all disease is caused by discombobulation of nerve functions resulting from displacement of body parts, especially vertebrae, was introduced by Toronto-born Daniel David Palmer (1845-1913). After his wife's death in 1883, he left a small business in What Cheer to practice "magnetic healing" in other Iowa cities. The first patient to be treated with the "spinal adjustments" Palmer devised after becoming interested in osteopathy (*see* OSTEOPATHY) was his janitor, Harvey Lillard, who had been deaf for seventeen years. After manipulation, Palmer claimed, Harvey's hearing was restored. The claim was arguable, but Palmer apparently was quite successful with other patients. One suggested as a name for the new discipline "chiropractic," derived from two Greek words, *cheir* and *praktikos,* which Palmer translated as "done by hand." The Palmer School of Chiropractic in Davenport, Iowa, founded in 1898, prospered under the leadership of one of its earliest graduates, Palmer's son, Bartlett Joshua Palmer. Father and son published *The Science of Chiropractic* in 1906, but four years later the father alone authored *Textbook of the Science, Art and Philosophy of Chiropractic,* which rapped all other practitioners of medicine and chiropractic, including his son.

Since 1977 physicians have been authorized to recommend chiropractic treatment, which encompasses massage, manipulation, exercise, and the application of heat, cold, and light. The treatment is now licensed in every state. Sixteen four-year chiropractic colleges graduate about 17 hundred students annually. By 1985 there were approximately 23,000 chiropractors in the United States alone.

CHOP SUEY: Now a staple in Chinese restaurants near and far, chop suey was unknown in China when the first batch was served in America. However, when and where is subject to dispute. According to some sources, the dish originated in a California mining camp when some unheralded Chinese cook tossed his accumulated leftovers into a pot and called the resultant mishmash "chop suey," a sound-alike for a Mandarin phrase, *tsa sui,* which is freely translatable as "various things." Other authorities say that chop suey was created in New York City on August 29, 1896, by visiting Chinese Ambassador Li Hung-Chang's chef after his boss requested a new dish that would please both Oriental and Occidental palates.

CHORUS LINE, A: American musicals are presented in many countries in many languages, as was attested when Michael Bennett celebrated the 3,389th record-breaking Broadway performance of *A Chorus Line* on September 29, 1983, by assembling 332 top-hatted strutters who had appeared in its various companies.

Bennett brought on the stage of New York's Shubert Theatre all the members available from the troupe then appearing in New York, the original company, the bus-and-truck company, and the regional and international companies. During the gala performance performers took turns playing the same roles or played the same roles simultaneously. At one point Donna McKechnie, portraying Cassie, the solo dancer desperately seeking a chorus job, was joined by eight other Cassies. But what underscored most the impact of American musicals outside their home country was the singing of "What I Did for Love" in a medley of languages, including Japanese, Norwegian, German, Spanish, Portuguese, and Swedish. (It was United Nations time, with participants whose names were as nationally and ethnically diverse as Scott Allen, Sandahl Bergman, Roxann Caballero, Tim Cassidy, Karis Christensen, Rene Clemente, Lillian Colon, Nancy Dafgek, Glen Ferrugiari, Mark Fotopoulos, Deborah Geffner, Ganine Giorgione, Zoe Vonder Haar, Angelique Ilo, Chikae Ishikawa, Baayork Lee, Kenji Nakao, Cilda Shaur, Sacchi Shimizu, Victoria Tabaka, and Cookie Vazquez.)

At the time it was estimated that since the show's Broadway premiere on July 25, 1975, approximately 22.3 million theater patrons had paid $260 million to see it in 184 U.S. cities, Toronto, Mexico City, London, and Berlin, plus cities in Australia, Argentina, Brazil, and Sweden. By late 1985 the worldwide gross exceeded $300 million. Japan is especially fond of *A Chorus Line*. The show has toured the country, had four lengthy engagements in Tokyo—first by a visiting troupe and then by an all-Japanese company—and was presented in the Shiki Production Company repertory, two or three times a month, for five years. A record-shattering Broadway run ended April 28, 1990 after 6,137 performances. A movie version, directed by *Gandhi's* Richard Attenborough, was released in December 1985.

CHRISTIAN SCIENCE: The Church of Christ, Scientist, established by Mary [Morse] Baker Eddy (1821-1910), encompasses principles based on its founder's interpretations of Christ's words and acts. Because Christian Scientists contend that illness and sin exist only in the mind, they refuse medical help.

Born in Bow, New Hampshire, Mary Baker was a sickly child, who received little formal education but read at home. Subject to seizures and nervous collapse, Miss Baker nevertheless became Mrs. George W. Glover in 1843, only to be widowed the following year. Ten years after her first marriage, she was wed to Daniel Patterson, a dentist and homeopath. Because of her poor health, she became interested in spiritual healing and sought help from the prominent practitioner Phineas Parkhurst Quimby. Claiming an instant cure, she became Quimby's ardent disciple. In 1866, a momentous year, Quimby died; she suffered a relapse; she divorced her husband, taking again the name of her earlier spouse; and she turned to the Bible for guidance. She attributed her complete physical recovery to New Testament references to Christ's power of healing. In 1870, she began healing and teaching, gradually replacing Quimby's methods with her own. In 1875, she published the first of many versions of *Science and Health with Key to the Scriptures,* embodying her beliefs. One of her adherents, Asa G. Eddy, became her third husband in 1877, two years before her church was chartered. In 1881, she founded Massachusetts Metaphysical College in Boston. The First Church of Christ, Scientist—of which all Christian Science churches throughout the world are branches—was established in Boston the following year. *The Christian Science Journal,* begun in 1883, was succeeded by the *Christian Science Sentinel* and, then, in 1908, by the prestigious *Christian Science Monitor.*

Despite failing health, Mrs. Eddy remained firmly in control of all aspects of Christian Science until her death. Some of her pronouncements had nothing to do with religion. She once warned against daily bathing: "Cleanliness is next to godliness," she pontificated, "but washing should be only to keep the body clean, and this can be done with less than daily scrubbing the whole surface."

CIGARETTE: The Indians of North America were early tobacco users; but the first smokers of cigarettes were probably their Mexican cousins, who filled hollow reeds nearly a foot long with crushed tobacco. Paper-wrapped cigarettes are said to have been invented during an 1832 battle between Egyptians and Turks, when after a cannonball destroyed their communal clay pipe, Egyptian cannoneers stuffed tobacco into the hollow paper torches used to ignite their guns.

In 1876, the first patent for a cigarette-making machine was granted to Albert H. Hook of New York City. Like a similar machine invented in 1880 by James Albert Bonsack of Virginia, it produced a single attenuated cigarette that was sliced into shorter lengths. They reputedly were used as a medium of exchange for various wartime favors. After World War II, as president of Philip Morris, the Benson & Hedges alumnus Joseph Cullman III launched the first major campaign for overseas buyers. Now Philip Morris International earns $2.5 billion annually.

The most profit-making cigarette manufacturer, however, is R. J. Reynolds, which postdates Philip Morris and Liggett and Meyers. Its founder, Richard Joshua Reynolds, reputedly first visited the twin North Carolina towns of Winston and Salem as a barefoot, illiterate farm boy, accompanying a load of his father's tobacco. After earning a college and business school education, he returned to his father's Virginia farm and began peddling plugs of chewing tobacco, sometimes swapping them for barter items. Then, in 1874, he began his own chewing tobacco business in Winston; and thirteen years later, eighty-six brands of Reynolds tobacco were on sale. Experiments with smoking tobacco, begun shortly after the turn of the century, resulted in particular success with the Prince Albert brand. In 1913, "RJR" introduced four kinds of "blended," rather than "straight" (pure Virginian or pure Turkish), cigarettes. The most successful variety was Camels, in packages of twenty for ten cents—half the going price. In 1954, the Reynolds company introduced filtered Winstons and, later, the filter-tipped menthol Salem.

American cigarettes are prized the world over by puffers who ignore lung cancer warnings.

COCA-COLA: All the Atlanta pharmacist John Styth Pemberton had in mind on May 8, 1886, was "a Brain Tonic and Intellectual Beverage" that would relax tremblers and tipplers. Because its two main ingredients were coca, the dried leaves of a South American shrub, and cola, the extract of the kola nut, Pemberton's bookkeeper, Frank M. Robinson, suggested "Coca-Cola" as the new drink's name. Robinson's fancy script also provided the familiar Coca-Cola trademark. After mixing a batch of the syrup in a backyard kettle, Pemberton took a sample to the pharmacy of Dr. Joseph Jacobs, who agreed to sell it, mixed with plain water, for five cents a glass. One day, Willis E. Venable, who presided over Jacobs' soda fountain, used carbonated water by mistake, and *voila*! After Pemberton's death in 1888, another Atlanta pharmacist, Asa Briggs Candler, acquired complete ownership for $2,300 and created the Coca-Cola Company. By 1895, the drink was on sale in Canada, Hawaii, and Mexico. Candler's son introduced it to England in 1900. By 1906, there were bottling plants in Panama and Cuba. Essentially, Coca-Cola was still a one-product soda fountain business when Robert Winship Woodruff took over the troubled company in 1924. Woodruff put Coca-Cola into its distinctive bottle. Under his stewardship the company introduced the six-pack carton, the king-size bottle, the soft-drink vending machine, and about 250 "Coke"-linked products.

For many years chronic Coca-Cola imbibers in Southern states called the drink "a dope"; and in fact, until 1903, because of early methods used to extract the flavoring from the coca leaves, it did contain cocaine. In those days, however, cocaine, opium, and morphine were available without prescription in popular patent medicines. Fourteen of the beverage's ingredients are known, but the fifteenth, "Merchandise 7X," was a secret that the company refused to divulge to the Indian government in 1977.

In April 1985, Coca-Cola underwent a formula change, including substitution of corn syrup for sugar, that made it taste sweeter and more like its arch-rival, Pepsi-Cola. Protests proliferated. Three months later, the company announced it would bring back "Coca-Cola Classic."

Coca-Cola is bottled and sold in 155 countries and advertised in almost every language.

COCKTAIL: Although its dictionary definition is "an iced drink of distilled liquor mixed with flavoring ingredients," the word has been watered down to apply to mixtures of all kinds, such as the tomato juice cocktail (sans alcohol it's often called a virgin or bloodless Mary) that sometimes begins a meal and the fruit cocktail that sometimes ends it. The dining room, dedicated guzzlers keen, has co-opted the barroom.

The first cocktail, according to elbow-bending lore, involved barnyard tail feathers served by the barmaid Betsy Flanagan at Halls Corners, a small tavern in Elmsford, New York, in 1776. The bar was festooned with feathers the Revolution-endorsing Betsy had saucily plucked from a neighborhood Tory's rooster. When a plastered patron ordered a glass of "those cocktails," Betsy complied, bringing him a mixed drink with a feather inserted as a swizzle stick. An elaboration on this yarn has a soldier applauding "the beverage that offers the palate the same charming sensations as the feathers of the cock's tail offers the eye" and eliciting a Frenchman's toast: "Long live the cocktail!" Could be. Another possibility links the drink with a type of horse, used mainly for hunting and stagecoaches, once called the cocktail because its tail was cut so short that it stuck up rooster style. Such horses were never thoroughbreds, but a mixed-drink-like mixture. Yet another version has early doctors treating certain throat diseases by applying "a pleasant liquid" with the tip of a long feather. Patients referred to the procedure as "the cocktail." Other sources say "cocktail" is a mispronunciation of the names of beauties who served historic drinks, the Aztec Zochitl or the Mexican Coctel.

The Bronx cocktail was named for the New York City borough in 1919. Of earlier vintage is another borough booster, the Manhattan, which actually toasts New York's Manhattan Club, where it was first dispensed in the 1870s at a dinner given in honor of Governor Samuel J. Tilden by Lady Randolph Churchill. The "screwdriver" was named by American oilfield workers, who reputedly used that tool to stir it. The daiquiri derives its name from an iron mine in Daiquiri, Cuba, where American civil engineers used local ingredients to create it. The Harvey Wallbanger is said to have been named about 1970 for a California surfer, Tom Harvey, who would gulp too many "Italian screwdrivers" (orange juice, vodka, and Galliano) and then lurch into walls.

The martini reputedly was the Martinez when the bartender Jerry Thomas created it between 1860 and 1862 at San Francisco's Occidental Hotel. Possibly, but martinis are frequently made with Martini and Rossi vermouth.

According to barroom bards, the gibson, a martini adorned with a pearl onion instead of an olive, was created when an American diplomat, Hugh Gibson (1883-1954), appalled by the amount of liquor he was supposed to imbibe in the line of duty, asked a bartender to substitute water for gin in his martinis. Substitution of the onion enabled him to distinguish mocktail from cocktail on a serving tray. Other guests at the same diplomatic dos marveled that the American lost neither his cheerfulness nor his equilibrium despite nonstop chug-a-lugging and surmised that the onion had some special salutary effect. Eager to get in on a good thing, they, too, began requesting onions in their martinis. That's one story. Another is that the Gibson was named for artist Charles Dana Gibson when a New York Players Club bartender, running out of olives, plunked a pearl onion into Gibson's martini.

Not one, but two American cocktails share the name "suffering bastard." Among regional drinks, one of the most celebrated is the mint julep, which immediately conjures up leisurely warm days on Southern verandas. Ah, there, Scarlett!

COLOR TELEVISION: Primitive color TV was first shown in the United States in 1929. The first demonstrations of increasingly sophisticated color TV systems were made by England's John Logie Baird in 1928, 1938, and early 1941; but all relied on problem-plagued mechanical, rather than electronic, scanning. CBS began TV networking in 1948, later than NBC, DuMont, and ABC because it wanted to offer programming in color from the start. The first scheduled experimental colorcasting from CBS's WCBW, New York, began on June 1, 1941. CBS began regular commercial color transmissions on June 15, 1951, with a 4:35 P.M. variety show that featured Ed Sullivan, Arthur Godfrey, and Faye Emerson. The first color series, Ivan T. Sanderson's "The World Is Yours," bowed the following day. Although CBS's electromechanical system with a spinning disc inside each set had been endorsed by the Federal Communications Commission (FCC), it was not compatible with existing black-and-white sets and was jettisoned by the FCC three years later in favor of RCA's all-electronic system.

Colorcasting with the RCA system began on December 17, 1953. CBS dragged its heels because color meant added costs that could not be passed on to advertisers; but NBC went all out to help its parent company, RCA, sell color sets. NBC-owned WNBQ (now WMAQ-TV) in Chicago became the world's first all-color station. Because of high prices and, at first, inferior color, only about two hundred thousand sets were sold in the United States during the first decade of commercial colorcasting. In 1965, when color TV sets began selling in quantity, CBS announced that virtually all its programming during the upcoming season would be in color, even if it meant reshooting black-and-white pilots. A year later, ABC followed suit. By 1970, there were more than twenty million U.S. color sets; and by 1977, they were providing multihued pictures in more than 75 percent of the nation's TV-equipped homes. (*See also* TELEVISION.)

COMIC BOOK: Comic books evolved from the adventure comic strips that replaced the newspaper "funnies."

Among the first comic books were compilations of "Mutt and Jeff" comic strips in 1911, but the mother of Superman and all the other comic-book superstars with superhuman powers was probably—surprise!—prepubescent Little Orphan Annie. Harold Gray's 1924 strip about Daddy Warbucks's blank-eyed ward introduced the idea of serial melodrama. On the same day, January 7, 1929, two notable "action" strips made their debuts: Harold Foster's "Tarzan" and the Philip Nowlan-scripted, Dick Calkins-drawn "Buck Rogers." In short order their macho heroes were joined by Dick Tracy (*see* "DICK TRACY"), Brick Bradford, Flash Gordon, Mandrake the Magician, Terry and the Pirates, Prince Valiant, and the Phantom. Most of them soon were doubling in derring-do in the thick, three-inch square Big Little Books, which substituted alternate pages of text for dialogue in balloons.

The *Funnies*, a 1929 color comic tabloid that lasted thirteen issues, and many Sunday comic supplements were printed by New York's Eastern Color Printing Company. Two Eastern employees, the sales manager Harry I. Wildenberg and the salesman M. C. Gaines, fostered the idea of using the company's presses for comic books; first, as a giveaway for Gulf Oil, Procter and Gamble, and other companies and, then, as a newsstand entry. Eastern's presses, printing newspaper-size sheets that folded conveniently into sixteen pages measuring about eight inches by eleven inches, dictated the comic book's look. Harry Donenfeld launched "Detective Comics" as a D.C. Comics Publication in March 1937. Even after his firm became National Periodicals, it continued to use a "D.C." ID. Gaines, who had become a newspaper-syndicate agent, brought to Donenfeld's attention as a possible comic book subject a strip submitted by two D.C. employees, the writer Jerry Siegel and the artist Joe Shuster, which had been nixed for newspaper use. Superman, launched in D.C.'s June 1938 Action Comics (*see* SUPERMAN), ushered in the Golden Age of Comic Books, which continued for about seven years. Among golden agers who acquired multitudes of fans at home and abroad were Batman, Wonder Woman, "Shazam!"-uttering Captain Marvel (who was deshazammed in 1953 because of a Superman lawsuit), Plastic Man, Phantom Lady, The Spirit, Blackhawk, and the Justice Society of America.

COMIC STRIP: Richard F. Outcault's black-and-white panel, "Down in Hogan's Alley," the first nonpolitical newspaper cartoon, first appeared in the *New York World* on February 16, 1896. It dealt with New York City slum life and featured a jug-eared, bald-headed boy who wore a nightshirt that reached to his bare feet. Joseph Pulitzer, publisher of the *World,* wanted to test a new yellow ink for his Sunday supplement's rotary press and decided to use the cartoon character's nightshirt. The "Yellow Kid" became so popular that a covetous William Randolph Hearst hired Outcault away for his *New York Journal.* Because the Yellow Kid appeared in newspapers that featured sensational, often inaccurate, stories, that kind of news coverage became known as "yellow journalism."

Hearst, who had been interested years before in the German illustrator Wilhelm Busch's "Max und Moritz" drawings, instructed a staff artist, Rudolph Dirks, to build a running story around the same characters, renamed Hans and Fritz. "The Katzenjammer Kids," the first strip to use dialogue "balloons," made its debut on December 12, 1897. The first successful daily strip, Bud Fisher's "Mr. A. Mutt"—later "Mutt and Jeff"—bowed in in 1907. The name changed after tall, skinny Mutt met a small, chunky sanitarium inmate who imagined that he was the heavyweight champion Jim Jeffries. "Mutt and Jeff" reprints were among the earliest comic books in 1911.

The first comic strip to become an international favorite was George McManus's 1913 "Bringing Up Father," about low-class Maggie and Jiggs, who became wealthy by winning the Irish Sweepstakes. "Funnies" and "jokes" began to share space with Saturday seriallike adventure stories (*see* "DICK TRACY"). By the time Garry Trudeau's topical and satirical strip (*see* "DOONESBURY") won a 1975 Pulitzer Prize, it was estimated that daily comic strips were being read by more than 100 million buffs in America and more than twice that number in forty-two languages in 102 other countries. "Peanuts," the current circulation champ (*see* "PEANUTS"), appears in 2,018 newspapers in fifty-six countries. France's "Barbarella" and England's "Modesty Blaise" introduced comic-strip strippers.

COMMERCIAL, RADIO: In 1922, President-to-be Herbert Hoover, then the secretary of commerce, predicted, "The American people will never stand for advertising on the air." Some prophet! Shortly after, at 5:15 P.M. on August 28, 1922, the first radio commercial, touting the attractions of Hawthorne Court, the Queensboro Corporation's new apartment building in Jackson Heights, was broadcast over the American Telegraph and Telephone Company's Long Island station WEAF. It was 10 minutes long and consisted of a tedious panegyric by a "Mr. Blackwell." The station's fee was $100. The Hawthorne droneathons, which claimed that Nathaniel Hawthorne, the author of *The Scarlet Letter,* would have approved the borrowing of his name for what he had once advocated, "a home removed from the congested part of the city, right at the boundaries of God's great outdoors," made no mention of price. Hawthorne commercials continued until September 21, but in two months, WEAF sold only three hours of time for a total of $550. Linking ads to orchestral programs proved more effective, and by the end of 1922, WEAF had fourteen sponsors. Other stations also began cashing in. "The Eveready Flashlight Hour" introduced "intermittent commercials" during its 1923 broadcasts. By 1928, "sponsors" were investing $10 million a year in radio advertising.

COMMERCIAL, TV: The first television commercial was a twenty-second plug for Bulova watches on WNBT, New York, on July 1, 1941. Consisting of a close-up of a watch accompanied by a voice-over announcement, it cost the sponsor nine dollars. The station's first rate card, issued June 27, offered sponsorship of the hour-long "Truth or Consequences" for $120 plus production costs. The maximum potential audience was a mere forty-seven hundred households, but the paucity of viewers did not deter early advertisers like Bulova, Adams Hats, Ivory Soap, and Botany Worsted. The 1948 "Texaco Star Theater," starring Milton Berle (who was dubbed "Mr. Television" and "Mr. Tuesday Night"), was the first major sponsored TV program.

The programming on commercial TV is designed primarily to lure sizable audiences for advertising. The putatively most popular shows are scheduled during the "sweeps" rating months of November, February, and May because audience size at those times, as proclaimed by the Nielsen and Arbitron rating services, determines where advertising budgets are allocated and how much will be charged for each time slot. The minimum length for a sponsor's network time buy was originally sixty seconds, but in 1970 CBS led the way in reducing it to thirty seconds. In 1986, there was an upsurge of fifteen-second spots. Up to nine minutes of every prime-time hour (8 P.M. to 11 P.M.) is devoted to sales spiels, but just because commercials are there doesn't mean that the audience is compelled to watch them. During the early 1960s, surveys indicated that 15 to 18 percent of the audience was lost during commercial breaks. Later, the defection zoomed to 50 percent; although many claim that the commercials are often better than the main attraction.

Compounding the ad ignoring has been the emergence of the videocassette recorder (VCR), enabling viewers to watch a show whenever they please. VCR owners, after taping programs, often fast-forward through the commercials. Nevertheless, sponsors continue to patronize "the only game in town."

In July 1985, NBC became the first network to sell $1 billion worth of commercial time before the start of a TV season. The estimated 1985-86 income of all three networks was $2 billion.

COMPUTER: The development of the computer can be traced as far back as China's abacus. There also were seminal French, English, and German contributions. But the first large-scale automatic digital computer, the five-ton Mark I, was created during World War II by American engineer Howard H. Aiken.

The world's first general-purpose electronic computer, substituting vacuum tubes for electromechanical switches, was the Electronic Numerical Integrator and Computer (ENIAC), constructed for the army at a cost of four hundred thousand dollars by a University of Pennsylvania task force headed by J. Presper Eckert, Jr., and John W. Mauchly. It was completed in 1946, too late for World War II use. Capable of five thousand calculations per second, it weighed thirty tons and was housed in a space equivalent to eighty average living rooms. Eckert and Mauchly were fired by the university when they refused to relinquish commercial rights. On their own, they created the first commercial computer, a streamlined five-ton unit, but sold their financially strapped company to the Remington Rand Corporation before UNIVAC I's debut on June 14, 1951.

UNIVAC I could add, subtract, multiply, divide, sort, collate, provide square and cube roots, and store data. Fifty were manufactured. The transistor (short for transfer resistance), invented by three Bell Laboratories scientists in 1947, made possible solid-state computers with printed electrical circuits. In 1971, the microchip, with hundreds of thousands of transistors etched on a tiny silicon chip the size of a pea, begat the microprocessor, which in turn begat the personal computer. The first mass-market personal computer was the Apple, conceived in a garage workshop; but primacy in the field eventually went to the industrial giant IBM. American personal computers are being purchased in virtually every industrialized country. In 1985, they were selling at a faster clip in Europe than in the United States. Although they produce their own, American business software dominates in England, France, and West Germany. The most recent American and Japanese development has been superrapid "supercomputers."

COMPUTER MUSIC: Computer-produced sound, first described by the Bell Laboratories researcher Max Mathews in a 1964 article, enables a composer to be his own orchestra. The article explained how musical sounds could be created, stored, reproduced, and manipulated on computers by using digital formulas. Intrigued, John Chowning, a graduate student in music, and four colleagues, using computer time when it was not required by the Stanford Artificial Intelligence Laboratory, experimented with fusions of engineering and the arts, which produced what sounded like music. In 1975, with grants from the National Endowment for the Arts and the National Science Foundation, Stanford University established the Center for Computer Research in Music and Acoustics (its CCRMA acronym appropriately pronounced "karma"), with Chowning as director.

CCRMA became the prototype for similar research centers in other countries, most notably Pierre Boulez's Institute for Research and Coordination of Acoustics and Music (IRCAM), which began operation in subterranean Paris facilities in January 1977. Using computers, composers are able to make their music seem to emanate from various places, just as Giovanni and Andrea Gabrieli did with famous sixteenth century "echo" pieces that sounded as if an orchestra was moving around St. Mark's Basilica in Venice. Moreover, they can simulate existing instruments; increase their capabilities by making them go higher or lower; or create, in effect, entirely new ones (*see* MUSICAL INSTRUMENTS). One objection raised is that computer music offers no variation that reflects a human performer's personal interpretation. However, some computer pieces are programmed for "deviations" from performance to performance, and others are designed as man-and-machine collaborations. In the latter category is Janis Mattox's "Shaman," which received its world premiere on the Stanford campus on September 29, 1984. The hour-plus composition, three years aborning at CCRMA, blended a multitrack tape with live performances by the drummer George Marsh, the bass player Mel Graves, the Grateful Dead vocalist Bob Weir, and the belly dancer Rachel Dutton. (*See also* MOOG SYNTHESIZER.)

CONSTITUTION: The brevity, clarity, and adaptability of the Constitution of the United States, which in 1787 became the world's first written document of its kind, has made it the model for all or part of the constitutions adopted by more than 160 other countries (150 since World War II), beginning in 1791 with Poland on May 3 and France on September 3.

The fact that the Constitution, its Bill of Rights, and its amendments have proved continuously serviceable for the world's oldest functioning republic has not been lost on other nations. Initially, numerous countries in the Western Hemisphere borrowed from the Constitution to legitimize their own revolutions: Venezuela in 1811, Mexico in 1824, the Central American Federation in 1825, Argentina in 1826. In some cases, the U.S. Constitution's influence has been second- and third-hand. France's short-lived 1791 document, based on America's —which introduced what has been termed the most famous

American "invention," the concept of federalism—inspired the Spanish constitution of 1812, which in turn was reflected in the documents adopted by Portugal, Brazil, Naples, Sicily, and Latin America. Norway's 1814 constitution, based on France's, is the world's second oldest. The influence of the United States persists in France's present 1958 constitution. In some instances an American-style document has been a postscript to military action. Examples include the Philippines, Cuba, Panama, Haiti, South Vietnam, and post-World War II Germany and Japan.

Widely borrowed everywhere—only six countries are without constitutions—are such American concepts as separation of powers, judicial review, and specification of individual rights. The United Nations 1948 Declaration of Rights, drafted primarily by Eleanor Roosevelt and her American staff, was based on the U.S. Bill of Rights. The U.S. Constitution was signed on September 17, 1787, and ratified by the requisite nine of the thirteen original states by June 21, 1788.

In 1874, an obscure composer named Greeler set all the words to music. His score, which vanished sometime in the 1880s, received several public performances, each lasting more than six hours. According to contemporary critics, it wasn't bad.

COPPERTONE: The world's best-selling suntan lotion provides Green browning. It was formulated in 1944 by Dr. Ben Green as a protective lotion for World War II U.S. airmen forced to bail out over the Pacific. Previously they relied on amber petrolatum, alias axle grease.

After the war, Coppertone was marketed by its creator with the slogan "Don't Be a Paleface." In 1957, he sold out to Plough, which in 1971 was merged with the Schering antibiotic company (founded in Germany) to form Schering-Plough. Coppertone and other antisunburn Plough products, including Solarcaine, account for more than half the sales in that field.

Memphis-born Abe Plough plowed ahead after turning a profit with his very first business venture. In 1908, while still in his teens, he borrowed $125 from his auctioneer father; whomped up a batch of cottonseed oil, camphor, and carbolic acid; and peddled it to druggists as "antiseptic healing oil—the sure cure for any ill of man or beast." After achieving tycoonship, he became so impressed with radio's potency as a sales-booster for his products that he purchased five AM and five FM stations. One of Coppertone's principal lures, however, is relayed by nose rather than ear. Its aromatic smell is attributed mainly to essence of night-blooming jasmine. Another sunburn-easer, Noxema skin cream, was first known as Dr. Bunting's Sunburn Remedy. "Noxema" is a coinage from "knocks eczema."

CORKSCREW: M. L. Byrn of New York was granted the first American patent for this handy-dandy device on March 27, 1860. "Corkscrew punch" is not a drink containing a foreign object, the result of a pourer's failure to retract the bottle opener; it was a pugilistic favorite during the 1920s, a jab accompanied by a twisting of the fist.

CORTISONE: By 1934, the South Norwalk, Connecticut-born biochemist Edward Calvin Kendall (1886-1972) and Mayo Clinic colleagues succeeded in separating from animal adrenal extract a small amount of crystalline material of uncertain composition and physiological effect. Soon crystals were being precipitated from cortical extracts almost simultaneously in New York, Minnesota, and Switzerland. By 1942, twenty-eight crystalline compounds, steroids derived from cholesterol, were isolated. It wasn't easy. Three thousand pounds of adrenal gland were required to produce about a gram of the crystalline materials. Of at least five that were biologically active, "compound E"—on which Kendall began to concentrate his efforts— had the greatest effect on carbohydrate metabolism.

In 1941, the Pittsburgh, Pennsylvania-born physician Philip Showalter Hench (1896-1965), conducting Mayo Foundation research on rheumatoid arthritis, decided to try colleague Kendall's compound E in the treatment of that malady, but experiments were delayed because of problems posed by the synthesis of compound E and the outbreak of World War II. During the war years, Merck and Company developed a way to increase the yield of compound E, but the price—two hundred dollars per gram—limited its use. In 1948, Merck's compound E, which had been renamed cortisone, was injected into a severely arthritic patient. Within three days the patient showed dramatic improvement. By early 1949, Kendall and Hench were able to show movies of previously bedridden patients who were not only up but running. For their contributions to the discovery of cortisone and other hormones of the adrenal cortex and their functions, Kendall, Hench, and Switzerland's Dr. Tadeus Reichstein shared the 1950 Nobel Prize for physiology and medicine.

Cortisone subsequently proved to be beneficial in the treatment of innumerable ailments, including asthma and other allergic reactions, eye lesions, acute leukemia, and various skin diseases. The compound is now produced synthetically. The term "cortisone" is often used collectively to include other glucocorticoids, natural and synthetic.

COTTON GIN: There's gin, the drink, and gin, the card game; but the gin that has exerted the greatest impact on America and the world is the cotton gin. Although most kinds of cotton in use today originated in India, America has become the world's foremost source. Cotton has been a crop in the American South since the establishment of the Jamestown colony in 1602. Initially, it was produced only in small quantities because separating the seeds from the fibers was so difficult. Deseeding just one pound was a day's work for a man before the invention of the cotton gin, and it would take him many months to clean an average-size bale of cotton. The cotton gin made it possible to produce from three to fifteen bales a day.

In 1793 Westborough, Massachusetts-born Eli Whitney (1765-1825), who first demonstrated his mechanical ability as a maker of violins and eventually became rich as a manufacturer of weapons (*see* INTERCHANGEABLE PARTS), invented what was first called the cotton engine and later called the cotton gin. Basically a variation on the charha, used in India since antiquity, it consisted of a toothed cylinder revolving against a grate that ripped the cotton fiber from the seeds and a revolving brush that freed the fiber and guided it into a receptacle.

A quick consequence was the invention of various cotton-manufacturing machines. One, invented in 1797 by Amos Whittemore (1759-1828), produced in quantity (twelve thousand dozen a year) the leather cards required for the hand carding of both cotton and wool. Samuel Slater, dubbed the father of the American cotton industry, opened a cotton mill in Pawtucket, Rhode Island, in the early 1790s; but the first totally mechanized mill was established by Francis Cabot Lowell in Waltham, Massachusetts, in 1814. It was also the world's first mill to combine all the operations required to convert raw cotton into finished cloth. A revolutionary new process known as "ring spinning," used for most of the world's spindles, was patented in 1828 by John Thorp (1784-1848.) Pattern printing on cotton, in various designs and colors, made financially feasible by the cylinder press, became an important part of cotton manufacture between 1820 and 1830.

COTTONSEED: Two-thirds of the weight of freshly picked cotton is seeds. For many years any that were not needed for planting were discarded or burned, but the seeds have since germinated into hundreds of products. In 1859, when cottonseed was considered garbage and planters were plagued by the problem of how to dispose of it without incurring a fine, one prescient dealer predicted, "Cotton seed and cake (the dried mush after the oil has been extracted) could add 50 percent to the profit of the cotton industry." By 1870, cottonseed had become fertilizer; by 1880, cattle feed; by 1890, table food and much more.

The shells, removed by machine, are sometimes mixed with other ingredients for cattle or horse feed or, more frequently, burned to an ash that provides excellent fertilizer. After shelling, the seeds are pressed to squeeze out the oil. The hard residue is ground into cottonseed meal, an even better animal food and fertilizer than the shells. Pure, high-quality cottonseed oil is used on salads, for cooking, and in the manufacture of such items as lard, margarine, and lipstick. Lower-grade oil is utilized for numerous products, including paint, soap, detergents, candles, putty, artificial leather, oilcloth, and tar. The cottonseed-oil industry became increasingly important to cotton growers as cotton fiber was challenged by cheaper, stronger synthetic fabrics. Even the stems of the cotton plant benefit man. Mashed into a pulp, they become an ingredient in cardboard.

COUGH DROP: The Smith brothers, "Trade" and "Mark," often referred to by those names because the words appear under their bewhiskered visages on packages of Smith Brothers Cough Drops, were actually William and Andrew, sons of James Smith, a carpenter who moved from St. Armand, Quebec, to Poughkeepsie, New York, to open Smith's Dining Saloon. Among Papa's skills was candy making; and when a transient patron volunteered a recipe for a tasty and effective "cough candy," Papa Smith saw the local sales possibilities and whipped up a batch on the kitchen stove. The fame of Smith's cough-inhibiting confection spread up and down the cold, wind-swept Hudson River valley, by word of cough-spared mouth and newspaper ads inviting "all afflicted with hoarseness, coughs or colds" to "test its virtues." His sons were James's enthusiastic collaborators. They helped mix the secret formula and hawked the anti-hawking nostrum in the streets. Poughkeepsieites became familiar with the sight, sound, and product of the Smith brothers. When James died in 1866, the sons took over the thriving business under the "Smith Brothers" name.

Success breeds imitation, and soon look-alike cough drops were being peddled by Schmitt brothers, Smythe sisters, and other Smith spin-offs. *The* Smith brothers, needing a distinctive trademark to distinguish their cough drops from all others, decided to put their own pictures on the large glass jars from which storekeepers dispensed drops by the envelopeful. However, that did not prevent unscrupulous storekeepers from filling Smith Brothers jars with cheaper imitations. In 1872 came *voila!* time. The brothers put their drops into something new—factory-sealed packages. As a result of this innovation, production at two factories soared to five tons a day. The Smiths retained their Trade & Mark trademark and became two of the world's most familiar faces.

COUPON: Because some buyers of his soap rebelled at the idea that they might be paying extra for the paper wrapper, New York's

Benjamin Talbert Babbitt searched for a way to convert a liability into an asset. Then in 1865, he printed the word "coupon" on each wrapper, making the wrapper itself valuable. For ten coupons the customer was offered "a beautiful lithograph picture." As the idea grew more popular, different premiums were added. The first penny-off coupon was offered in 1895 by the C. W. Post Company, which eventually became one of the world's largest conglomerates: General Foods. Variously referred to as "cash-offs" and "cents-offs," coupons have become the single most popular promotional gimmick, printed by the billions annually for use in newspaper and magazine advertising and as bonuses inside containers or on wrappers. The Department of Agriculture estimates that four out of every five U.S. families engage in at least occasional coupon clipping.

Reflecting rising food costs, "couponing" became epidemic in America in the 1970s. At the beginning of the decade, money-off or money-back coupons were offered by about 350 manufacturers. By 1978, more than one thousand companies were printing a total of about seventy billion coupons with a reclamation value of $500 million. Moreover, dedicated collectors of discounts and refunds had access to more than fifty specialized newsletters.

COVERMARK: Lydia O'Leary, born with a large port-wine birthmark covering most of her face, sought employment that shielded her from public scrutiny. In the early 1930s, while at work painting flowers on place cards, she tried to cover a darkened petal on a painted iris. That triggered a provocative thought: If a mistake in a painted flower is camouflagable, why not a facial blemish? Consulting a chemist, she developed a covering cream that hid her birthmark for an entire weekend. She was awarded a patent at a time when products considered cosmetics were denied such protection from copycatting. Her creation—now marketed as part of a Covermark line that includes a foundation in eleven natural skin-tone shades, finishing powder, cream rouge, shading cream, lotion, and a removing cream—is recommended for victims of disfiguring birthmarks, scars, vitiligo, and other skin conditions by plastic surgeons, dermatologists, and hospitals like Baltimore's Johns Hopkins Burn Center. It is also used to conceal lesser problems like varicose veins, dark circles under the eyes, and brown skin blotches. Among those who have benefited from Lydia O'Leary's appearance-improver are Japanese survivors of World War II's atom bombs.

COWBOY: Thanks to dime novels (*see* WILD WEST), pulp magazines, touring Wild West shows, movies, and television shows, the American cowboy has become a romantic figure far beyond the United States. Kids everywhere play cowboys and Indians. Members of

Wild West clubs in many countries periodically don cowboy garb and swagger about like tough hombres. England alone has reported some fifty make-believe ranches, with hitching posts, corrals, and bunkhouses, where would-be buckaroos convene. In Germany the fascination with "der Wild West" was attributed in considerable part to the sagebrush sagas of Karl May (1842-1912), which have been translated into twenty-five languages. May wrote his Wild West yarns about Old Shatterhand and his Tonto, Winnetou, while serving an eight-year prison term for theft and swindling. He did not get to see the United States until after his last cowboy opus had been published, so his descriptions of cowboys' stomping grounds are utterly inaccurate, but he gave eager Europeans what they wanted: stalwart heroes, honorable Indians, and hissable troublemakers. Among his devoted readers were Adolf Hitler and Albert Einstein. May's counterparts in other countries included Mayne Reid in England, Gustave Aimard in France, and numerous lesser hacks elsewhere. Contradictory early European attitudes toward American frontiersmen were replaced by unqualified admiration for the knight of the wide open spaces, the cowboy.

The American range riders who engendered all this romantic adulation numbered perhaps forty thousand from 1865, when the Civil War ended, until the mid-1880s, when meat prices dipped and the accessibility of railroads eliminated long, grueling cattle drives. Until then, the cowboys had been urgently needed by the cattle raisers in Texas, Montana, and other western states. They were mainly in their early twenties and a grubby lot, often dirty, cold, and hungry as they went about their decidedly unromantic chores, sometimes guiding a few hundred head of cattle fifteen hundred miles from Texas to Kansas. After the 1880s, few merited description as cowboys. Almost all were merely ranch hands.

CRACKER JACK: The candied popcorn and peanuts confection, permanently linked to one of America's favorite sports by the 1908 Jack Norworth-Al Von Tilzer baseball anthem, "Take Me Out to the Ball Game" ("Buy me some peanuts and Cracker Jack . . ."), is a favorite munchie in fifty-three other countries. One source of its popularity is the free toy that has been nestled in every package since 1913. For three years before that date, the bonus was a coupon that could be exchanged for a gift. When F. W. Rueckheim, a German immigrant, first concocted the mixture, it was neither Cracker Jack nor Santa Claus-in-a-box. In 1871, after saving two hundred dollars while working on a farm, Rueckheim trekked to nearby Chicago to help clean up the fire-gutted city. He went into business with a friend who owned a small popcorn stand and, soon, bought out his partner and summoned his sibling Louis from the fatherland. Between 1875 and 1884, F. W. Rueckheim and Brother kept growing, moving, and adding confectionary products. The candied popcorn was introduced to the world at the 1893 Columbian Exposition. The taste was great, everyone agreed, but the kernels often formed unappetizing lumps. In 1896, Louis solved that problem. A salesman, testing the improved version, exclaimed "That's crackerjack!" The Rueckheims promptly trademarked the name and the slogan suggested by a customer: "The more you eat, the more you want." A new partner, E. G. Eckstein, developed wax-sealed and moisture-proof packages that kept Cracker Jack crisp.

In 1916, a little sailor boy, Jack, reputedly resembling F. W.'s grandson, Robert (who died of pneumonia when he was eight years old and is buried under a tombstone bearing his Cracker Jack image), and a black-and-white dog, Bingo, began figuring in Cracker Jack ads. Three years later, their pictures were imprinted on every package. The miniature prizes are picked by a committee and are certifiedly harmless toys whose average cost is less than half a cent. However, in 1980, as a promotional stunt, Borden's—which now owns Cracker Jack—inserted fifty-seven thousand coupons redeemable for far more valuable prizes, including toy-filled Mazda GLC station wagons.

CRAPS: Dice, honest and loaded, were used even by prehistoric man. Perhaps the earliest precursor of those little spotted cubes, so beloved of gamblers, were cubicle knucklebones or the anklebones of sheep. (In Arabic the same word denotes dice and knucklebone.) Ancient man also used plum and peach pits, stones, seeds, bones, horn, pottery, pebbles, shells, and beaver teeth. "Hazard," a dice game popular in Europe, supposedly was brought to New Orleans in 1813 by the Frenchman Bernard de Mandeville. According to legend, because Creoles were called Johnny Crapauds, the game became known as Crapaud's game, subsequently abbreviated to craps. Could be, but the 1-1 and 1-2 combinations in hazard were tagged "crabs" as far back as the sixteenth century. American blacks in and near New Orleans are said to have developed craps as the game is played today and to have contributed much of its jazzy jargon, like "snake eyes," "box cars" and "Little Joe from Kokomo!" A New York dicemaker named, almost incredibly, John H. Winn reputedly created open craps, the kind most often played in alleys and pool halls. It was spread abroad by GIs during both World Wars. A variant, bank craps, is played in casinos around the world.

CRAYON: Wax crayons, an American innovation, were developed near the turn of the century by the firm of Binney and Smith, which initially manufactured anything-but-colorful lampblack—used to darken printing inks, rubber boots, stove polish, and later, carbon paper and typewriter ribbons. In 1912, the firm (started in 1864 by Joseph W. Binney of Peekskill, New York, and continued by his son, Edwin, and a cousin from England, C. Harold Smith) hit it rich. Binney's son-in-law, Allan Kitchell (who later became head of the firm) landed a steady buyer for its award-winning carbon black—a tire manufacturer who wanted to darken the visible portion of his product to distinguish it from the usual zinc-white tires of his competitors. The carbon black not only made tires look better, Binney and Smith lab technicians discovered, it also made their treads last four and five times as long. (Tire manufacturers still use carbon black to increase longevity.)

While all this was going on with black carbon, Smith paid a visit to his native heath and returned with the American rights to new red iron oxides. Edwin Binney used them to produce a red paint that was soon being slathered on many a barn and "little red schoolhouse." After Edwin's chance meeting on a train with John Ketchum, who owned a talc mine in North Carolina, Binney and Smith began manufacturing slate pencils. Soon after, the company added the first white "dustless" chalk stick to its list of products. Talking to teachers, salesmen noticed that the wax crayons being used by young students were costly, easily broken, and of inconsistent color. The company's technicians rose to the challenge. The first Crayolas—a name coined by Joseph Binney's wife, Alice Stead Binney, who combined the French word for chalk, *craie*, and "oil"—went on sale in 1903 for a nickel a box. The first boxes contained eight crayons, made by heating liquid paraffin and mixing it with various pigments. By the mid-1960s, the color choice had increased to sixty-four, including eight fluorescent shades and such exotic hues as bronze, peach, and goldenrod. In 1977, Binney and Smith added to its products another small-fry favorite: Silly Putty (*see* SILLY PUTTY).

CREDIT CARD: Credit cards were envisioned as early as 1888 by American novelist Edward Bellamy in his *Looking Backward, 2000-1887*, which predicted a new social order and influenced economic thinking in the United States and Europe. Bellamy foresaw a day when every citizen toted a government-issued "credit card" showing his share of "the annual product of the nation." Almost all purchases, he opined, would be charged against the balance on the card, eliminating the need for currency or monthly bills. New "smart cards," with built-in computers, serve a similar function (*see* LAZER CARD).

The first multipurpose card, Diners Club, came into existence in 1950 after businessman Frank McNamara reached for his wallet in a restaurant and realized it was somewhere else. McNamara and a lawyer friend devised a system to eliminate embarrassment when restaurant tabs exceeded diners' cash. Earlier, "courtesy cards" issued by oil companies had been in existence before World War I, and regular gasoline credit cards arrived in 1924. After World War II, department stores distributed metal or cardboard charge cards, later replaced by plastic. The American Express card—initially purple, to match American Express traveler's checks—made its debut in 1958. In 1985, it was being used in more than 120 countries. The BankAmericard, initially intended for use only at stores near Bank of America's California branches, granted licenses to other banks in 1966. Master Charge was created because other California banks were reluctant to augment their biggest competitor's profits. Visa came along a decade later. International Art Credit Company offered art collectors a card with a $1 million line of credit. In 1984, Buffums, a Southern California department-store chain, inaugurated credit cards for kiddies, entitling charge-accounters under eighteen to spend up to two hundred dollars if an adult cosigned their applications. (The youngest card-seeker was one year old.) In January 1986, Sears, Roebuck and Company introduced its own general-use Discover credit card.

In 1980, Walter Cavanagh (a Santa Clara, California, real estate man) claimed that since 1972, when he and a friend wagered a dinner on who could accumulate more credit cards, he had acquired 1,003—a world record. They weighed thirty-four pounds and entitled him to $1.25 million in credit. His goal, he said, was ten thousand cards.

CROSSWORD PUZZLE: Word games predate crossword puzzles and Scrabble by centuries, going as far back as pre-Christian Hindu and Chinese cultures; but Arthur Wynne devised the world's most popular variant as an emergency half-page filler for the December 13, 1913, "Fun" page of the *New York Sunday World*. Labeled "Word Cross," it consisted of a diamond-shaped puzzle built around a geometric blank. It contained thirty-four numbers for thirty-one words, the clue-word FUN, and no black squares. As a weekly *World* feature, it was rechristened "cross word" in 1924 and, later, "crossword." Margaret Farrar, née Petheridge, the Sunday editor's Smith College alumna secretary, was arbitrarily picked to check the puzzles and, then, in 1921, to supervise their preparation. At the *World* and, then, from 1942 until her retirement in 1969, at *The New York Times*, she established numerous crossword rules, insisting on symmetrical patterns; limiting black blocks to one-sixth of the total space; and banning two-letter words, cliché definitions, and, when possible, cheerfulness-chasing references to death, disease, and taxes.

In 1924, she and two other *World* editors split a seventy-five dollar advance to prepare a collection of crossword puzzles that launched the publishing firm of (Richard L.) Simon and (M. Lincoln) Schuster. A $1.35 mail-order item, complete with Venus pencil and eraser, *The Cross Word Puzzle Book* sold 123,000 copies and, during the next sixty years, begat 132 sequels and numerous auxiliary tomes,. including crossword dictionaries replete with esoteric words like anoa, esne, oud, and zebu. One collection was published by the Broadway composer Stephen Sondheim, a confessed addict. The form's appeal was virtually universal. Other nations redubbed it *les mots croises; las crucigramas; le cruciverbas; kreuzwortratsel; kruiswoord;* and in Russia, *krestoslovitsa.*

Numerous complex variants have been devised, including the ultradifficult double crostic. Most difficult of all, however, is a crossword puzzle with 2,008 downs and 2,007 acrosses created by Robert M. Stilgenbauer of Los Angeles between 1938 and 1945. It has never been entirely solved.

CUTEX: Northam Warren, born in 1879, merits a niche in any Manicurists' Hall of Fame. After graduation from the Detroit College of Pharmacy, he addressed himself to women's peskiest finger-furbishing problem other than the acquisition of engagement rings and wedding bands: cuticle control. The liquid cuticle remover he invented, developed, and began merchandising in 1911 revolutionized the art of digital beautfication. Cuticle Remover, an instant success, pared dramatically the time required to prettify fingernails. No toilet aid ever had speedier or wider acceptance. On a roll, in 1916, Warren added America's first liquid nail polish, naming it Cutex by taking the first syllable of his ultrapopular Cuticle Remover and adding the suffix "ex." The colorless liquid was welcomed by women everywhere as a handy improvement over existing powders and pastes. In 1917 came a tinted version in the rose-colored shade reputedly the favorite of the famed French courtesan Madame Du Barry.

During the Depression years, Warren tried to provide a sense of luxury by introducing bolder shades that were deeper and darker. The Northam Warren Corporation's pioneering as the world's oldest manufacturer of manicure preparations and of Cutex, the world's best-selling brand, invited considerable copycatting in other countries. One brash entrepreneur helped himself to both Cutex's name and packaging on the subsequently court-rejected grounds that "cutex" was synonymous with "nail polish." Since 1960, Cutex nail polish, lipstick and polish remover have been manufactured by Chesebrough-Pond's.

CYBERNETICS: The science of cybernetics, dealing with information control and communication, was created by the Columbia, Missouri-born mathematician Norbert Wiener (1894-1964) after World War II radar and missile-guidance stints for the U.S. government. He coined the word "cybernetics"—which he used as the title of a seminal 1948 book that he revised in 1961—from the Greek word for "steersman." It became the everyday designation for the entire field of automated machine control of information. Wiener, a child prodigy who learned to read and write by the time he was three, was graduated from Tufts College at fifteen and had a Harvard Ph.D. before he was nineteen. His World War II assignments, relying heavily on automatic information processing, cued a deeper study of computers and their similarities to animal nervous systems. Wiener kept expatiating on the possibilities of cybernetics and warning of its dangers, especially the possibility that intellectual laziness could result in humans relinquishing control to their own machines. (*See also* ARTIFICIAL INTELLIGENCE.)

D

DANCE MARATHON: Despite objections by local and federal officials, dance marathons first sprouted in the early 1920s in scattered metropolises like Pittsburgh and Chicago and smaller communities like New Kensington, Pennsylvania.

In 1923, Surgeon General Hugh S. Cumming warned participants that they were flirting with permanent disability or death. But not even the demise that year of Homer Morehouse, twenty-seven, of North Tonawanda, New York—after eighty-seven hours of hopping and gliding—dissuaded dollar-hungry dancers. City after city banned the exhaustion exhibitions, but promoter after promoter scouted new locations.

The fad peaked with a "Dance Derby of the Century" at New York's Madison Square Garden, concocted by the ex-Pittsburgh newspaperman Milton Crandall, who became one of the more imaginative Hollywood press agents. It began on June 10, 1928, with ninety-one couples on the floor, and ended 481 hours later, summarily halted by the local board of health, with nine couples sharing the five thousand dollar first prize. The rules called for hour-long stretches of dancing interrupted for fifteen-minute rests on canvas cots in a tent just off the dance floor. The music was supplied by a saxophone, banjo, trombone, kazoo, and phonograph endlessly repeating the same waltzes and fox-trots. Tickets to watch the ordeal cost $2.20. A headline-hunting humanitarian, Earl Carroll, producer of Broadway's *Vanities,* offered defecting duos one hundred dollar consolation prizes. On the seventeenth day, speakeasy hostess Texas ("Hello, sucker") Guinan, indignant because she felt Crandall was not giving the contestants a fair share of the proceeds, upped the bonus for immediate quitting to one thousand. There were no takers.

The U.S. dance marathon craze inspired an even crazier European variation, the nonstop dance, in Paris, Edinburgh, Marseilles, and

Sunderland, England. The Paris record—twenty-two hours twenty minutes—was quickly topped by a succession of energetic Americans; the crown finally settling on the head of a nineteen-year-old Ohioan, June Curry, who during ninety hours ten minutes of whirling pared off 12 of her 161 pounds. In 1965, a New York discotheque, Our Place, tried to update the venerable fad with a twistathon. Evie Asnes, eighteen, a member of the final couple, offered a succinct assessment of the proceedings: "Pretty stupid!"

DANCES: America has introduced a wide variety of dances that have subsequently become the rage in other countries. If the waltz and tango were European creations, the fox-trot was strictly American. So were other dance-floor steps with barnyard or menagerie monikers like the turkey trot (what could be more indigenous than America's traditional Thanksgiving dinner guest?), the bunny hug, the grizzly bear, and the kangaroo dip.

Perhaps the greatest international impact on the he-she dance style was effected around 1911 by the professional ballroom dance team of Vernon and Irene Castle, who popularized the one-step, the fox-trot, and the Castle walk. The latter, featuring great freedom of motion although the man still led and the woman moved backward, established a new standard of gracefulness. Performed in contemporary clothes, with more flexible undergarments, it stressed lissomeness; and soon, women everywhere were going on diets and enrolling at dancing schools. The new steps encouraged improvisation by the male partner and almost instinctive female response. Descriptions of new steps appeared in magazines, and there was much practicing to screechy phonograph music in parlors.

The Charleston, reputedly born on the South Carolina wharves, emerged about 1924. The dance most closely associated with the Roaring Twenties flappers, it had particular appeal for energetic, exuberant young people, as did such subsequent dances as the black bottom and the varsity drag. Also extremely difficult and almost acrobatic were a crop of world-favorite newcomers in the 1930s and 1940s, including the big apple, the little apple, the boogie-woogie, the jitterbug, and the lindy.

Later American additions to the international dance repertory were the twist, popularized in 1960 by Chubby Checker, a Philadelphian named Ernest Evans, Jr., whose *nom de show biz* saluted an earlier black musician, Fats Domino; the hully-gully, the mashed potato, the watusi, the frug, the bump, the Kung Fu, the boogaloo, the monkey, the hustle, and many more, including whatever bowed in in discos or other dance floors last week. For most humans some dance steps of recent U.S. origin seem downright impossible (*see* BREAK-DANCING).

DATA PROCESSING: An 1880 Washington "date," of the boy-girl variety, developed into data processing. The twenty-year-old male involved was Buffalo, New York-born Herman Hollerith (1860-1929); the nubile female, a daughter of Dr. John Shaw Billings, Hollerith's co-worker at the census office. During the family supper, Papa Billings complained about the tedium of toting up with dip-pen and ink the data provided by a U.S. population already exceeding fifty million. If a machine wasn't invented, Billings grumped, counting wouldn't be completed before the next census started.

Hollerith, a graduate mining engineer who was working as a six-hundred-dollar-a-year statistician, promptly turned his thoughts from lips and hips to numbers and notches. At first, he considered perforated rolls of paper, like the player-piano rolls that were to become popular twenty years later, with a line of holes for each individual, but abandoned the idea because it would require miles and miles of paper. During a railroad trip, he noticed that the conductor made several passenger-identifying punctures on each ticket. That started a new—oops!—train of thought. He eventually devised an electric tabulating machine that registered how many cards fit into each of several categories, determined by the location of nicks. A nick on the right edge of a card, for instance, meant male; on the left edge, female. Each notch allowed a pin to slip through, completing an electric circuit that advanced a numbered dial. Financing was a problem, but in 1887, he was able to test his system by tabulating Baltimore death records. In days his battery-operated machine compiled statistics that would have required weeks of hand tallying.

Another Hollerith invention, a keyboard punch machine, replaced the hand punch before he achieved his goal: a contract for the 1890 U.S. census. Canada, Great Britain, Norway, France, Italy, Germany, Austria, and Russia also leased his machine for population counts. Companies around the world became customers for the Hollerith technology that paved the way to sophisticated digital computers. Hollerith sold his Tabulating Machine Company in 1911. After merging with two other firms it became, in 1924, International Business Machines (IBM). (*See also* COMPUTER.)

DAVIS CUP: Tennis is of British ancestry, but the Davis Cup, the treasured trophy awarded to the nation that wins the world's men's tennis championship, is of U.S. origin. In 1884, Americans first played—unsuccessfully—at England's Wimbledon, which had already been the site of tennis championship matches since 1877. In 1900, after a series of informal Anglo-American encounters on both sides of the Atlantic in the 1880s and 1890s, a Harvard undergraduate, Dwight Davis, instructed a Boston silversmith to melt down almost fourteen pounds of silver and refashion the metal into an International Lawn Tennis Challenge Trophy. An American team won the first Davis Cup tournament that year, amid English complaints about mushy balls and high grass at Boston's Longwood Cricket Club. Though its lengthy official name is engraved on the trophy, it became popularly known as the Davis Cup. In 1903, tennis players in France, Germany, and other countries were invited to participate.

DECLARATION OF INDEPENDENCE: The Declaration of Independence, adopted July 4, 1776, in which representatives of the thirteen American colonies announced their separation from Great Britain, begins: "We hold these truths to be self-evident, that all men are created equal, that they are endowed by their Creator with certain unalienable Rights, that among these are Life, Liberty and the pursuit of Happiness." Another declaration of independence, signed September 2, 1945, begins: "All men are created equal. They are endowed by their Creator with certain unalienable rights; among these are life, liberty and the pursuit of happiness." The latter document signaled the determination of the Vietminh, the Marxist party founded by Ho Chi Minh, to resist any post-World War II attempt by France to reestablish its sovereignty in Indochina. Two decades later, despite their virtually identical statements of governmental dedication to individual welfare, America was locked in battle with North Vietnam.

Another irony: Although the Declaration of Independence was drafted by English-speaking colonials, the first announcement of the historic document's adoption appeared in German. That was not a reflection of the Declaration drafters' disdain for anything English, but because the day after, July 5, was a Friday, and Henry Miller's *Der Wochentliche Philadelphische Staatsbote* was the only Philadelphia newspaper published on that day.

The British press ignored the Declaration. The *London Morning Post* accorded it six lines, under a theatrical notice. Ideas expressed in the Declaration of Independence are echoed in many other countries, as in the French Revolution's rallying cry "Liberty! Equality! Fraternity!" The Declaration of Independence was written by Virginia's Thomas Jefferson, after Boston's John Adams declined, deferring to Jefferson's superior stylistic elegance. Only one man signed the document, in effect a declaration of war, on the day of its adoption: Boston's John Hancock, as president of the Congress. His signature dwarfs all those appended one or more months later by delegates to Congress who were either too busy or too timid to sign earlier.

DELICATESSEN: Although many a similar cornucopia of aromatic ethnic foodstuffs can now be found in cities around the world, the "deli" is uniquely American. The first surfaced in colonial Philadelphia, but New York became the nation's mecca for lox, bagel, corned beef, pastrami, chopped liver, baklava, Brie, feta, and Greek olive mavens, with some fifteen thousand delis within its borders by 1959. Many subsequently emerged in other parts of the United States.

DENTAL DRILL: A drill that loosened decayed dental tissue when the fingers holding it were twisted in alternate directions was described in a 1728 book by the Parisian dentist Pierre Fauchard. More like contemporary dental drills was the one invented in 1790 by John Greenwood of New York, who borrowed from contemporary spinning wheels the idea of using a foot treadle to provide the necessary power. Another of Greenwood's ouch!-earning achievements was making a pair of false teeth from elephant and hippo tusks for dental-problem-plagued George Washington.

The first electric dental drill was patented by George F. Green of Kalamazoo, Michigan, on January 26, 1875. (Greenwood and Green, brothers in groan!) The patent application referred to "electromagnetic dental tools" for sawing, filing, dressing, and polishing teeth. The electromagnetic motors, powered by costly batteries, made the equipment too heavy and too expensive for widespread use. Dental drills that plugged into electrical sockets were not available until 1908. The water-driven turbine, capable of 50,000 revolutions per minute, was created in 1953 by the American Robert J. Nelsen and two colleagues. It was followed four years later by John Victor Borden's "air-driven turbine angle handpiece with ball bearings," with an r.p.m. reading of 250,000. The last fundamental change occurred in 1962 with the advent of the "air-driven turbine angle handpiece with air bearings," with an r.p.m. potential of 800,000 which was reduced to about half that when it made contact with a tooth. The most recent development, with Japanese manufacturers in the forefront, is toward small turbines costing under $100, compared to the previous $700-$1,500 price range. Diamond bits and carbide burs were introduced around 1925. One slightly daft dentist opines "Diamonds are a drill's best friend."

The modern dental chair, with a headrest and repositionable seat and back, was patented by Waldo Hanchett of Syracuse, New York, on August 15, 1848.

DEPARTMENT STORE: In the mid-1800s, dry-goods and clothing stores gradually added other kinds of merchandise in separately located "departments." It has been suggested that the first store to segregate its wares in that manner was Zion's Cooperative Mercantile Institution, affectionately known as ZCMI, which was established in Salt Lake City by the Mormon leader Brigham Young. Perhaps the first institution qualifying as a "department store," because it encompassed a sizable number of specialized sales areas, was Alexander Turney Stewart's Marble Dry-Goods Palace, which opened in New York City in 1848. Stewart, an underpaid schoolteacher in Ireland, emigrated to the United States to start a business. At the time it opened, his Marble Dry-Goods Palace was the largest shop in the world, occupying an entire city block. When Stewart died in 1876, the store was grossing $70 million per year and he had a personal fortune exceeding that amount. Among Stewart's innovations was fixed prices, not subject to alteration by bargaining. Other policies that became standard for department stores included guarantees of customer satisfaction, refunds for faulty merchandise, distinctive wrapping paper and shopping bags, closeout sales, bargain basements, and use of irregular prices ending with "and ninety-nine cents" (*see* BARGAIN PRICE).

DEPO-PROVERA: The World Health Organization is supporting the efforts of America's Upjohn Company to get Food and Drug Administration (FDA) approval of Depo-Provera, an injectable, long-acting contraceptive already being used in eighty-three countries. A fifteen-year battle with consumer-advocate groups prefaced a five-day Washington hearing in January 1984. The following October, an advisory board recommended an FDA ban on general U.S. marketing, citing carcinogenic effects on female laboratory animals. Even without FDA approval, Upjohn has already earned more than $25 million from the drug.

A single injection halts human ovulation for at least three months. It is reportedly as effective as the Pill, but it is less costly and more convenient. Depo-Provera is a synthetic acetate of the hormone progesterone, which FDA experiments in the 1970s linked to breast tumors in two of sixteen beagles and to uterine cancer in two of fifty-two rhesus monkeys. The World Health Organization counters such clinical evidence with reports of successful tests involving eleven thousand women and reports of continuous, unregulated use in countries like Thailand, where eighty-six thousand women have been injected since 1965.

Depo-Provera is already in authorized U.S. use, but the injectees are men. Since 1966, Johns Hopkins Hospital has been giving injections of the cloudy fluid every week to about seventy-five sex offenders—pedophiles, rapists, sadists, exhibitionists, and voyeurs. Reputedly, it diminishes the male sex drive. The usual rate of recidivism for such offenders is nearly 75 percent. After use of Depo-Provera, backsliding slips to 10 percent. In a most ironic twist, a Michigan judge prescribed a one-year jail term and five years of treatment with the Upjohn drug for the heir to the Upjohn pharmaceutical fortune, convicted of raping his fourteen-year-old stepdaughter from the time she was seven. Although there is no certainty that the drug causes cancer in women, other effects reportedly include weight gain, muscle aches, and high blood pressure.

DETECTIVE STORY: Whodunits—which enjoy worldwide popularity via books, magazines, movies and television shows—all stem from Edgar Allan Poe's grisly tale in the April 1841 edition of *Graham's Magazine,* "The Murders in the Rue Morgue," which he followed with the three-installment "The Mystery of Marie Roget," and, finally, in 1845, "The Purloined Letter."

The first important American detective novels were those of Anna Katharine Green, whose most popular opus was *The Leavenworth Case,* published in 1878. Detective novels became popular abroad through the writings of such European authors as Gaboriau, Willkie Collins, and the creator of Sherlock Holmes, Sir Arthur Conan Doyle. Holmes, who was extremely popular in the United States, was pre-dated by several home-grown dime-novel detectives, most notably Nick Carter.

Many American writers have made memorable contributions to the genre, including (Samuel) Dashiell Hammett, who is credited with substituting hard-boiled private eyes for more gently deductive sleuths; Chicago-born, London-raised Raymond Chandler; S. S. Van Dine (Willard Huntington Wright, whose books, written under his real name before he suffered a serious illness, included *What Nietzche Taught, Modern Painting,* and *The Future of Painting*); Erle Stanley Gardner (alias A. A. Fair); Ross Macdonald (Kenneth Millar); John D. McDonald; Ed McBain (Evan Hunter); Rex (Todhunter) Stout; Earl Derr Biggers; Leslie Charteris (Leslie Charles Bower Yin); Ellery Queen (a *nom de gore* for cousins Frederic Dannay and Manfred Lee); Mickey Spillane; and Elmore Leonard. Many "serious" U.S. authors have also written stories about sleuths, including Ernest Hemingway, William Faulkner, John Steinbeck, and Pearl S. Buck. Even presidents have been bitten by the bug. Abraham Lincoln published "The Trailor Murder Mystery" in the Quincy, Illinois, *Whig,* and Franklin D. Roosevelt dreamt up a whodunit plot but asked six professional writers to develop it.

Fictional crime-solvers of U.S. manufacture, known worldwide, include the aforementioned Ellery Queen, Sam Spade, Philip Marlowe, Perry Mason, Nero Wolfe, Mike Hammer, Nick and Nora Charles, Mr. and Mrs. North, Travis McGee, Lew Archer, The Saint (Simon Templar), Philo Vance, and Charlie Chan.

DIAPER, DISPOSABLE: Babies' bottoms were traditionally swathed in cloth that required laundering at home or by pick-up-and-deliver services before the first discardable diapers became available.

The disposables were crude, pulpy pads, neither comfortable for the baby nor especially convenient for those assigned the messy task of making infants socially acceptable; but they soon generated a $10 million business. To develop a more satisfactory product, Procter and Gamble allocated more time and money to research than Henry Ford spent on his first automobile. One of the company's engineers began thinking of possibilities immediately after being drafted for the first time to change his first grandchild's soggy cloth diaper. The first Procter and Gamble solution was elasticized plastic pants that became unbearably steamy. The company introduced Pampers—an amalgam of rayon, plastic and fluff—in 1961 and Luvs—designed by Kenneth Buell, an alumnus of the Gemini space program—in 1975.

Pampers, Luvs, Kimberly-Clark's Huggies, and other snug-fitting disposables now constitute an estimated 75 percent of all diapers in use. There's big money to be made from an infant's need for underwear replacement six to eight times a day, and in 1983, Pampers and Luvs were accounting for 17 percent of Procter and Gamble's worldwide sales but an estimated 22 percent of the company's profits.

"DICK TRACY": In the late 1950s, "Dick Tracy," the first literally dead-serious comic strip, its panels often littered with corpses, was read daily in nearly one thousand worldwide newspapers by an estimated sixty-five million buffs of make-believe mayhem. This revolutionary departure from the traditional pen-and-ink "funnies" was conceived by Pawnee, Oklahoma-born Chester Gould (1900-1985). Son of the editor of a weekly Oklahoma newspaper, he decided early that he was more interested in newspaper pictures than words. At fifteen he spent twenty dollars for a correspondence course in drawing and, while at college, began selling an occasional cartoon. At twenty he headed for Chicago. Fascinated by the shenanigans of Prohibition-era gangsters, he made similar criminals characters in the "Plainclothes Tracy" comic strip that he submitted to the *Chicago Tribune* in 1931.

Letters to the creator of this extremely popular comic strip often protested the names and matching visages of Gould's strange-looking baddies like Mole, Prune Face, Flyface, The Blank, and others of the same ill-making ilk. Gould also had a unique knack for meting out to these villains unusually gruesome deaths. Thus, Flattop, whose head resembled a World War II aircraft carrier, drowned while wedged between underwater pilings, the Brow was impaled on a flagpole, and B. B. Eyes was smothered under a garbage scow's cargo. Adding a note of realism was the fact that square-jawed, snap-brim-fedora-wearing detective Tracy and his sidekick, Sam Catchem, utilized actual police methods both in the strip's story and in an appended "Crimestoppers

Notebook." Ahead of their time were Gould notions like the two-way wrist radio (1946) and the closed-circuit TV lineup (1947).

A poll of teenagers in the late 1940s ranked Tracy as America's second best-known personality, behind Bing Crosby but ahead of President Harry Truman. "Li'l Abner" cartoonist Al Capp lampooned Tracy in "Fearless Fosdick" episodes. (Spencer Tracy's 1937 Oscar for *Captain's Courageous* was accidentally inscribed "Dick Tracy.")

Tracy was portrayed in the 1940s in several B movies and Saturday-matinee serials, usually with Ralph Byrd as the no-nonsense detective, and at the time of Gould's death, a Dick Tracy movie was in preparation with Warren Beatty in the title role.

DIGITAL WATCH: Hailed as "the ultimate time computer," the first digital watch was put on the market in 1972 by the Hamilton Watch Company of Lancaster, Pennsylvania. It was a $21 hundred limited-edition, 18-karat gold Pulsar utilizing a light-emoting diode, or LED, that required the pressing of a button to get a flashing red readout. The LED led to the liquid-crystal display, or LCD, which provided a continuous readout—at least during daylight hours—until another battery and switch were added to light the dial. In 1973 the estimated world sale of digitals totalled 200 thousand; two years later the number exceeded 2.5 million. Digital watches went out of vogue with the advent of a new kind of timepiece, the quartz analog. Now available from Hong Kong for as little as four dollars, digitals have become frequent corporate giveaways. A digital watch bearing a likeness of TV's Gumby, a green cartoon creature, became a popular under-ten-dollars novelty in 1985. Also retaining their appeal for novelty seekers are multi-purpose high-tech digital watches with such extras as wake-up alarms and calculators.

DISCOUNT STORE: Selling at less than full price was a common U.S. practice as early as 1910, but "discount houses," or "mass merchandisers," proliferated after World War II. No-frill "mill outlets," displaying clothing on tables or racks, opened in abandoned factories and warehouses throughout New England. In 1936, Anderson Little, a manufacturer of men's clothing, opened one of the first discount houses because a canceled order caused an oversupply of merchandise. To reduce his inventory in a hurry, he began selling clothes in his Fall River, Massachusetts, factory. Many manufacturers are reluctant to have their retail prices undercut regularly but provide merchandise to discount stores because of the sheer volume of turnover. Increasingly, department stores and other retail outlets have adopted discounters' methods.

DISHWASHER: The first dishwasher patent was granted in 1850 to a man named Houghton, from Ogden, New York, for a wooden contraption that splashed water on dishes. In 1886, a dishwasher built in the home of Mrs. Josephine Cochrane of Shelbyville, Indiana, led to the founding of a company that sold kitchen equipment. She worked on the idea for ten years but could not get her parsimonious husband to provide funding. It was only after his death that, with the financial help of friends, she was able to begin commercial production. Both of the first two dishwashers granted patents required hand cranking as tiring as dish washing by hand. Mrs. Cochrane built various models for both home and hotel use. The larger of the latter were powered by steam engine and, according to a newspaper account, were "capable of washing, scalding, rinsing and drying from 5-20 dozen dishes of all shapes and sizes in two minutes." The first motor-powered dish-washing appliance for home use appeared in 1911. Automatic controls were not added until 1940.

DISNEYLAND: Although Disneyland was not America's first theme park (*see* THEME PARK), it's the first—and only—entertainment center of its kind to acquire an overseas colony, Tokyo Disneyland.

Walt Disney reportedly conceived Disneyland while watching his daughters, Sharon and Diane, on a shabby merry-go-round. According to official legend, he decided then and there that parents and children deserved a clean, attractive, friendly playground where they could all have fun together. He had to mortgage his home to finance the project, but it was an immediate and profitable success when it opened in Anaheim, California, on July 17, 1955. Its lure is not limited to Americans. At Walt Disney World, for instance, where another of Disney's dreams, EPCOT Center (consisting of Future World and the multination World Showcase) was added on October 1, 1982, it is estimated that 9 percent to 10 percent of twenty-two million annual visitors are from other countries, mainly Canada, the United Kingdom, Puerto Rico, Brazil, Mexico, and West Germany. Disneyland has become so irresistible a mecca for foreign tourists that Soviet premier Nikita S. Khrushchev, visiting the United States in 1959, expressed chagrin when security problems prevented Disneyland's inclusion in his itinerary.

Tokyo Disneyland, built at a cost of $600 million, opened on April 15, 1983. It is patterned after the original Disneyland and "Disneyland East," the Magic Kingdom at Walt Disney World near Orlando, Florida, which made its debut on October 1, 1971. The Tokyo Disneyland also has unique features. Visitors enter via a World Bazaar with a weatherproof glass roof rather than through Main Street, U.S.A. Unduplicated attractions include the multi-media Japanese history-stressing Meet the World and the Mickey Mouse Revue. The Disney organization will add a $1 billion outpost near Paris by 1991.

The total number of guests for all three Disneylands has passed the 400 million mark. In 1982 and 1983, annual Disney revenues exceeded $1 billion. In 1985, Walt Disney World announced plans for a $300 million addition, the Disney-MGM Studio Tour.

The first sensationally successful theme amusement park was only one of numerous projects with worldwide reverberations conceived by Chicago-born Walter Elias Disney (1901-1966), sire of a menagerie of internationally beloved anthropomorphic critters, including Mickey Mouse (*see* MICKEY MOUSE), Donald Duck (*see* DONALD DUCK), Pluto, and Goofy. After achieving Hollywood fame and fortune with Mickey Mouse and "Silly Symphony" cartoon shorts, including the 1933 *Three Little Pigs* with a theme song ("Who's Afraid of the Big Bad Wolf?") that became a popular antidote to Depression blues, he produced the first feature-length animated film, the 1937 *Snow White and the Seven Dwarfs. Snow White* was released in ten foreign versions (Russian director Sergei Eisenstein ranked it with his own classic *Alexander Nevsky*). Disney also produced a series of distinguished, if sometimes contrived "true life adventure"wildlife documentaries; a number of live action family films, most notably the 1964 *Mary Poppins,* and several popular TV series.

Notable Disney animated features included *Pinocchio, Dumbo, Bambi, Cinderella, Alice in Wonderland, Peter Pan, Sleeping Beauty,* and the fantastical *Fantasia,* which combined animation with a soundtrack by the Philadelphia Orchestra. In addition to a record thirty-two Academy Awards, Disney received international honors by the hundreds, including the title of *Officer d'Academie,* France's top decoration for artists.

DOG BISCUIT: Dogs the world over—and their halitosisphobic owners—are indebted to the bone-shaped Milk-Bone Dog Biscuit, first made in 1908 by the F. H. Bennett Biscuit Company, a small bakery on New York's Lower East Side. Originally made of cereals, minerals, meat products, and milk, it was one of the company's lesser products; but eventually, after the Bennett operation was taken over in 1931 by the National Biscuit Company, the only one that survived. Nabisco first sold Milk-Bone as "a dog's dessert" and "a nourishing snack for canines," but it became a big seller after pooch fanciers became aware of a fringe benefit: freedom from doggie breath.

DOLLAR: The "almighty dollar" has obviously affected the world's destiny, for good or ill. This American institution has non-American origins. The word derives from the German *t(h)aler,* an abbreviated version of *Joachimstaler,* a silver coin, vintage 1519, initially minted in Joachimstal, Bohemia. *T(h)aler* or *da(h)ler* became widely used for any large German coin and for the basic coins of Denmark and Sweden. By 1581, England was spelling it "dollar."

The first dollars in America were lion-decorated Dutch coins brought to this country around 1620 by the settlers of New Netherland, which was converted by an English takeover into New York and New Jersey. Also available to colonists were pesos, dubbed "Spanish dollars." The dollar became the basis of the "not worth a Continental" paper money issued by the Second Continental Congress in 1775.

American dollars have been issued in assorted sizes, shapes, and materials. In 1776, to bolster its inflated paper currency, the Continental Congress authorized a pewter dollar designed by Benjamin Franklin that was decorated with a thirteen-link chain (representing the United Colonies); a sundial; the Latin word *fugio* ("I fly," an allusion to *tempus fugit,* "time flies"), and the motto "Mind Your Business." The earliest American dollars were paper; later ones, silver (1794) and gold (1849).

After writing a series of articles about finance, Gouverneur Morris, who had been defeated for reelection to Congress, was appointed assistant to the superintendent of finance and submitted a national-currency proposal. His decimal coinage system was improved and simplified by Thomas Jefferson, who had originally proposed using the dollar as the basic monetary unit. Jefferson, who has been dubbed "the father of the American dollar," submitted Morris's amended dollars-and-cents formula to the Continental Congress in 1784. It was adopted by resolution on July 6, 1785.

Even while placing a high valuation on the American dollar, other countries have often sneered at it. "Dollar diplomacy," a phrase dating from 1910, is used pejoratively. However, native Americans have also been disrespectful. "The almighty dollar," Washington Irving termed it, coining the phrase in 1836, "that great object of universal devotion throughout our land."

DONALD DUCK: According to one animated cartoon maven, the gabbling, anarchistic duck was added to the Disney repertory troupe, via the 1934 *The Wise Little Hen* and a bit part in the Mickey Mouse-starring *The Band Concert,* to inject some bite after the Mouse became "respectable, bland, gentle, responsible, moral."

The noisiest member of Walt Disney's stable of anthropomorphic cartoon critters has had international impact. Donald Duck comic books were banned in 1978 by a Helsinki, Finland, youth club committee that charged that he was a reprehensible role model because, after fifty years of courtship, he still gave no sign that he intended to make an honest duck out of Daisy; because his "nephews" (Huey, Dewey, and Louie), were suspected of being his own illegitimate ducklings; and because he persistently ducked donning pants. All was forgiven, however, after a Donald Duck fan club offered comic-book proof that, despite his predilection for high dudgeon, in the romance department Donald was a most discreet duck. The German Society for the Promotion of Noncommercial Donaldism was founded in Hamburg in May 1977 by thirty Donald Duck devotees who announced that they hoped to establish a Donald Duck chair at the local university. In 1964, when a freighter carrying six thousand sheep capsized in the harbor of Kuwait, the local residents were appalled at the prospect of having their drinking water polluted by rotting carcasses. A Danish manufacturer, Karl Kroyer, saved the day—and the drinking water—when he refloated the ship by filling its hull with twenty-seven billion Ping-Pong balls. Kroyer later credited Donald, who had used a similar strategem to conquer a similar problem in a 1949 comic book.

One reason for Donald's cantankerousness may have been the Disney organization's decision to shelve feature-length *Donald Duck Finds Pirate Gold* because of the spectacular success of Disney-style fairy tales. In 1942, what was to have been a movie vehicle became a sixty-four-page comic book, one of several glorifications of the duck assigned to writer-cartoonist Carl Barks. After his 1965 retirement from day-to-day Disney duties, Barks created a series of elaborate oil paintings, parodies of art masterpieces, with Donald as a surrogate centerpiece.

Donald is "Kalle Anka" in Sweden, "Paperino" in Italy, and "Pato Donald" in Latin America.

"DOONESBURY": Newspaper cartoons comprised an initial Pulitzer Prize category; but in 1975, "Doonesbury," created by Garry ("G.B.") Trudeau (1948-   ), became the first comic strip to earn that prestigious award. Its four panels rely on minimal artwork, sometimes a single picture shown four times, to make devastatingly witty comment on contemporary mores, life-styles, and politics. The strip's satire is so pointed that some newspapers have transferred it to the editorial page.

"Doonesbury" has often sparked headlines, notably via sequences lampooning presidents (one of the two dozen compilations of "Doonesbury" cartoons is titled *In Search of Reagan's Brain*); Washington's Watergate scandal; an antiabortion "scare" film; Frank Sinatra (in 1985 strips combining drawing and photographs); and, in 1986, seventeen "sleazy" Reagan Administration appointees.

When it was first submitted to the *Yale Record* in 1968 by undergraduate Trudeau, the chronicle of hapless, date-hungry Oklahoman Michael J. Doonesbury; his football-helmet-wearing roommate B. D. (inspired by the Yale quarterback Brian Dowling); and their cronies was titled "Bull Tales." After the strip's transfer to the *Yale Daily*

News in 1969, it attracted national attention and the interest of the Universal Press Syndicate. Rechristened "Doonesbury" and subjected to excision of the "Y" on B. D.'s helmet, cuss words, and nude female dorm visitors, the strip made its off-campus debut on October 26, 1970. In June 1985, despite a controversial Trudeau-imposed restriction on permissible paring of picture size, "Doonesbury" claimed 835 outlets.

The strip's constantly growing cast includes campus revolutionary-turned-disk jockey Mark Slackmeyer; "perfect tan"-seeker Zonker Harris (Trudeau ended that quest during an anti-skin cancer campaign); middle-aged feminist Joanie Caucus and her daughter J. J.; Washington journalist Rick Redfern; bosomy film actress Bootsie; and the fast-buck-minded Duke and his Chinese Communist aide, Miss Huan, alias "Honey."

For twenty-one months the strip was on sabbatical while Trudeau sought new insights and wrote the book and lyrics for a *Doonesbury* musical that achieved 135 Broadway performances. The strip returned in September 1984.

DOUGHNUT HOLE: The hole in the middle of a doughnut is attributed to Captain Hanson Crockett Gregory, of Rockport, Maine, in 1847. According to one legend, after six of his men fell overboard and were drowned by the weight of the soggy fried cakes in their bellies, the captain mulled ways to make the cakes less lethal, thought logically of life preservers, and using a belaying pin, jabbed a hole into a lump of dough. Another tale has the captain eating a fried cake at the wheel of his clipper when a sudden squall causes him to spike the cake on a spoke.

Both stories were pooh-poohed by one of Gregory's descendants, Fred E. Crockett of Camden, Maine, in October 1941, during the Great Doughnut Debate conducted at New York's Hotel Astor under the auspices of the National Dunking Association. Pointing out that Gregory was only fifteen in 1847, Crockett said his forebear was watching his mother make fried cakes, asked why the centers were so soggy, and when told they never seemed to get cooked, poked out some uncooked centers with a fork. After his mother gave punctured samples to neighbors, a local grocer started selling them, and their fame spread. A plaque commemorating Gregory's 1847 culinary inspiration was affixed to his birthplace 100 years later. In 1921, Adolph Levitt, a Russian immigrant, invented a mass-production doughnut machine. After World War II his Donut Corporation of America made doughnuts as far away as Tokyo. A California entrepreneur, Don Smith, topped Gregory by introducing a doughnut with *two* holes.

The first doughtnut dunker was said to be the silent-screen-star Mae

Murray. Emily Post, former First Lady of Etiquette, condemned the practice and then changed her mind.

DRAMAMINE: The motion-sickness remedy used since 1949 by plane, ship, bus, and train travelers the world over was first considered an antihistamine that might be useful in the treatment of hives. Leslie N. Gay, chief of the Johns Hopkins allergy clinic, was in charge of clinical research on the new drug and prescribed it for a woman who suffered from hives. When she paid her next visit to the clinic, she reported that the new medicine hadn't routed the hives, but that for the first time she wasn't made nauseous by the swaying of a streetcar. Intrigued, Gay and his assistant, P. E. Carliner, substituted a placebo for the medication. Next time the patient returned, she informed the researchers that she was again afflicted with motion sickness. Repetition of the original prescription again eliminated her trolley trauma, and Gay solicited army help for a large-scale test. The drug was given, with beneficial results, to soldiers making a rough transatlantic crossing via troopship. Generically dimenhydrinate, it was produced commercially by G. D. Searle and Company as Dramamine. For five years it was sold by prescription only; but in 1954, the Food and Drug Administration asked Searle to make it available as an over-the-counter motion-sickness remedy.

DRIVE-IN: The phrase "drive-in" was first applied to gasoline filling stations in 1931 but was expanded to encompass movies and restaurants about fifteen years later. Other early appellations for al fresco screening sites were "ozoners" and "passion pits," the latter because many a pubescent patron was more concerned with injection than projection.

The first outdoor film showcase was the Camden, New Jersey, Automobile Movie Theater opened by Richard M. Hollingshead, Jr., on June 6, 1933, after he had tested the feasibility of outdoor exhibition by putting a sixteen-millimeter projector on the roof of his car and using his garage door as a screen. The first feature on the thirty-by-forty-foot screen in the eight-level, forty-car-capacity lot, *Wives Beware*, starring Adolphe Menjou, drew six hundred ticket-buyers at twenty-five cents apiece plus twenty-five cents per vehicle. Initially, three six-foot-square speakers were mounted atop the projection booth, but numbed neighbors nixed the high-decibel results. An early substitute, a speaker about the size of a manhole cover under each car, was eventually replaced by car-side speakers. Hollingshead patented his terraced drive-in design, but in 1938, a federal court ruled that exclusivity could not be granted for something affecting "the formation of the earth." Hollingshead reaped no personal profit as drive-ins proliferated in the United States and also enjoyed transient popularity in other countries, most notably Australia.

Ancillary attractions, originally limited to popcorn, candy, and soft drink concessions, expanded to include Laundromats, baby bottle-warmers, barbeque pits, dog kennels, playgrounds, wading pools, and amusement parks. In a Brattleboro, Vermont, motel every room contained a speaker and faced a 100-foot movie screen—drive-in patrons could watch from their cars for seventy-five cents apiece or from a motel room for sixteen-dollars-and-up per couple.

In 1983, the number of U.S. drive-ins had dropped from a 1958 high of 4,063 to 2,935. Spiraling real estate values, prolonged first-run bookings in hardtop theaters, the competition of commercial and cable TV, and the accessibility via videocassette recorders of X-rated fare (many drive-ins' last-ditch audience lure) have helped ditch the drive-in's appeal.

DUNGEONS AND DRAGONS™: The intricate game played not on a board but in an imaginary cave tenanted by assorted monsters and sorcerers who must be bested by treasure seekers was devised by Gary Gygax, of Lake Geneva, Wisconsin, a fan of simulation war games. In 1973, after failing to interest major game companies in his creation because of its multitudinous rules, he began manufacturing it himself through a company, TRS Hobbies, that he heads. Dungeons and Dragons™ has sold eight million copies, created an international cult, and sparked a popular cartoon show, a Mattel computer game, and similar maze-featuring mind-benders like Milton Bradley's Dark Towers. The game, which holds an almost hypnotic attraction for high-IQ youths, has been denounced as "a form of devil worship" and has been blamed for suicides. In 1983, TSR Hobbies added to its instruction manual a warning against identifying too closely with the game's fantasy characters.

DU PONT: Capital *D* or lower-case *d*? If America's largest chemical company is being referred to, it's *D*. If it's the family that created big *D*, it's little *d*. That's by company lawyers' official *D*-cree in 1961, after 159 years of uppercase, lowercase chaos.

Du Pont, originally America's primary manufacturer of explosives, is now the nation's number one synthesizer, producing an astonishing array of products that benefit people everywhere. The company invented nylon (*see* NYLON), Orlon, and Dacron; developed rayon; created the Teflon resin (*see* TEFLON) used in nonstick cookware, "SilverStone" scratch-resistant cookware finishes; the Freon essential for refrigeration; and Lucite—a clear plastic—used in everything from auto glass to housepaint. Du Pont is still the largest manufacturer of gell explosives made from soft plastic materials. The company also built and operated the world's first plutonium plant in Washington state to fuel the atom bombs dropped on Japan in 1945.

Long a family business centered in the state of Delaware, it now has eighty-seven plants in twenty-seven states, turning out more than seventeen hundred products, mostly for sale to other manufacturers and fabricators. In addition, it has plants at forty-four locations in eighteen foreign countries.

After France's King Louis XVI was beheaded in 1793, Pierre Samuel du Pont—who had been made a nobleman nine years previously because of his part in the negotiations to end the American Revolution—went to prison. In 1797, Pierre and his son, Eleuthère Irénée du Pont de Nemours, who had studied gunpowder making under Antoine Lavoisier, emigrated to the United States. Thomas Jefferson, who knew Pierre from the treaty negotiations, encouraged Irénée to go into the gunpowder business and recommended a site on Delaware's Brandywine River. Financing was arranged in France, and the company, named for its founder, began selling black powder in 1804. Three years after Irénée's death in 1834, his two sons, Alfred and Henry, bought out the French backers. For years the company was strictly a du Pont duchy. Members of the family still own about 35 percent of the stock, worth some $2.3 billion. At last count there were more than seventeen hundred well-heeled descendants of Pierre Samuel du Pont.

DYNAMIC TENSION: Angelo Siciliano, who accompanied his mother from Italy to the United States in 1905, when he was eleven, was a ninety-seven-pound weakling, so frail that he had difficulty climbing the steps to their Brooklyn apartment. He was badly beaten one Halloween by a young tough wielding a sock crammed with ashes. At sixteen, after marveling at the muscles adorning a statue of Hercules, Angelo joined the neighborhood YMCA and began a body-building regimen. At home he improvised a barbell out of two rocks and a broomstick. One day, after watching a tiger stretching, he decided that animals develop their strength by exerting pressure between muscles. Swapping barbells and elastic stretchers for isometric exercises, he was able to double his weight, develop massive muscles—and avenge that Halloween beating. Friends thought his 54¾-inch chest and 17-inch biceps made him look like the statue at a nearby bank and began calling him Atlas. So Angelo Siciliano changed his name to Charles Atlas.

After working as a strongman in Coney Island, tearing telephone books in half and lying on a bed of nails while three adults stood on him, he was hired as a model by several sculptors and posed for the statues of George Washington at New York's Washington Square, Alexander Hamilton in front of Washington's U.S. Treasury Building, and more muscular, if less historic, symbolic figures. Soon after being named "the world's most perfectly developed man" by *Physical Culture* magazine in 1922, he launched a mail-order muscle-building business.

In 1928, Charles Roman took over marketing of the Atlas course and renamed it "dynamic tension." One of Roman's most effective ads was a comic-strip panel in which a ninety-seven-pound weakling, after sprouting muscles, defeated the bully who had once kicked sand in his face and swiped his girl. Atlas's isometric exercises were adopted by armed forces and professional athletes. By the late 1930s, Atlas had branch offices in London and Buenos Aires and six million mail-order students all over the world. Among them were the heavyweight champ-to-be Max Baer, the comedian Fred Allen, the radio announcer Harry Von Zell, the piano manufacturer Theodore Steinway—and a skinny politician in India named Mahatma Gandhi.

E

EARMUFFS: Farmington, Maine-born Chester Greenwood (1858-1937), a grammar school dropout, invented earmuffs, alias earlaps, in December 1873, at the age of fifteen. Testing a new pair of ice skates, a combination birthday and Christmas present, on a frozen pond near his home, he suffered intense ear pain from the biting cold. The next day he skated again with his head wrapped in a thick woolen scarf; though his ears no longer bothered him, the scarf was too bulky and caused unbearable itching. He then made two ear-shaped loops out of short lengths of wire and asked his grandmother to sew fur around them. Neighbors applauded, so in 1877, Greenwood patented an improved model, Greenwood's Champion Ear Protectors, with a tempered steel band holding the earmuffs firmly in place (U.S. Patent No. 188292) and established the Greenwood Ear Protector Factory. (Subsequently, he patented more than one hundred other inventions, including the spring-tooth rake for farmers.) Greenwood became wealthy supplying millions of earmuffs for World War I soldiers.

In 1977, the Maine legislature finally took official note of Greenwood's contribution to cold-weather comfort and December 21 was proclaimed Chester Greenwood Day, "to honor the achievement of one of Maine's most noteworthy sons." Earmuffs enjoyed a resurgence of popularity after NBC's David Brinkley mentioned Maine's belated tribute during a TV newscast. Mail-order houses and department stores still report requests. In Beverly Hills, California, where freezing weather is a newsworthy rarity, exceptionally tender—or chic—ears are sometimes "protected" by puffs of mink or sable.

EDISON, THOMAS ALVA: Probably the world's all-time champion inventor, Thomas Alva Edison (1847-1931), the Wizard of Menlo Park, New Jersey, accumulated more than thirteen hundred U.S. and foreign patents. His contributions have affected life-styles throughout the world. Self-taught, he went to school—in Port Huron, Michigan—for only three months. His first inventions, after he had worked as a railroad telegrapher, were the transmitter and receiver for the automatic telegraph, the quadruplex system allowing for the simultaneous transmission of four messages, and an improved stock ticker system. Then, at one-year intervals, beginning in 1877, came the carbon telephone transmitter, a precursor of the microphone; the first successful phonograph (*see* PHONOGRAPH); and the first practical incandescent light. To power his light bulbs he developed a complete electrical system—including generators, motors, light sockets, junction boxes, safety fuses, and underground conductors. His Pearl Street plant in New York City was the world's first central electric-light power plant. He played a pivotal role in the development of the telephone, the mimeograph, the electric railroad, the storage battery, the movies, and the talkies.

Despite his numerous achievements, he had many peculiar quirks. He once claimed that he was considering a machine to communicate with the dead. He often slept in his clothes because he thought disrobing caused insomnia, yet he rarely slept more than five hours; he almost starved himself because he was convinced that food poisoned the intestines. His habits were so slovenly that his laboratory was overrun by rats. Cables from his company's offices in Europe referred to him as "Dungyard." As a child, he was considered a possible retard. Accident-prone, he burned down his father's barn. At fifteen, experimenting with a battery, he blew up a telegraph station. At sixteen he caused a derailment when he forgot to set a train signal. But at nineteen he signed his first contract for an invention, and by his middle twenties he was already involved in corporative complexities. Scientific curiosity was not his only spur. "Anything that won't sell," he said, "I don't want to invent." (*See also* MICROGROVE RECORD, MOVIES.)

ELECTRIC CHAIR: The world's first electric chair was commissioned in 1889 by New York State penal authorities as a humane substitute for hanging after Thomas Alva Edison, trying to discredit rival inventor Nikola Tesla, charged that Tesla's alternating current, AC, was more dangerous than his own direct current, DC (*see* ALTERNATING CURRENT).

With the equipment Edison placed at his disposal and the assistance of Dr. A. E. Kennelly, Edison's chief electrician, Harold P. Brown, who first conceived of execution by electrocution, experimented on more than fifty stray dogs and cats, a horse, and a cow. Those who did not die promptly in the "hot seat" invented by Dr. Alphonse D. Rockwell were hit on the head with a brick. The entire procedure triggered protests. They were compounded by rumors that

Brown had used Westinghouse generators without authorization in order to put the Westinghouse Electric Company, the principal rival of Edison's General Electric Company, in a bad.light. Because of all the grisly publicity, Westinghouse secured a court order to block use of their generators, but Rockwell's chair was still Westinghouse powered when on August 6, 1890, at New York's Auburn State Penitentiary, William Kemmler, alias John Hart, became the first criminal to die in the electric chair.

Kemmler, who ran off with another man's wife, killed her with an axe when the thrill was gone. Seventeen months after he went on trial, following numerous appeals and stays of execution, he finally played his historic role before an audience of twenty-one invited guests. The execution took place before 7 A.M. as a safeguard against rioting in case of a power failure while the prisoners were in the machine shops. The condemned man, dapper in coat with matching vest and a checked bow tie, bowed after being introduced to the spectators by warden Charles Durston. His death was not instantaneous. The current had to be turned on a second time. According to the official report, Kemmler was dead eight minutes after entering the execution chamber. *The New York Times* termed it "an awful spectacle, far worse than hanging."

ELECTRIC IRON: An electric iron with replaceable heating units was placed on sale in 1896 by Wisconsin's Ward Leonard Electric Company, but it attracted few buyers because of its unwieldy weight and the sporadic availability of electric power, which was usually furnished only after dark. In 1903, to justify daytime operation by increasing demand, Earl H. Richardson (superintendent of an Ontario, California, power plant) devised a small, lightweight iron heated by a glowing wire wrapped around a brass core. The iron became so popular that his company's management agreed to provide power all day on Tuesdays, most housewives' favorite ironing time. To peddle his pressers, Richardson established the Pacific Electric Heating Company but ran into buyer resistance because his product overheated in the center. At his wife's suggestion, he reworked the design so that more heat was directed to the point, facilitating the smoothing of buttonholes and pleats. "The iron with the hot point" was so popular that Richardson renamed his company Hotpoint. Light, practical electric irons enjoyed brisk worldwide sale after World War I. Hotpoint was later acquired by General Electric, which has 127 manufacturing plants in twenty-four foreign countries.

ELECTRIC TOASTER: Primitive electric toasters, with exposed wiring, first appeared at the start of the twentieth century. Before that, in the nineteenth century, simple tin-and-wire toasters were merely placed atop wood and coal stoves. (These yesteryear artifacts are still being manufactured by the Bromwell Wire Goods Company, founded in Michigan City, Indiana, in 1819.) General Electric entered the field in 1905, and Westinghouse introduced its "toasterstove" in 1910.

Electric or not, early toasters still had to be monitored by the eyes and noses of diners chary of charcoal, a nuisance that irked a World War I mechanic, Charles Strite. Exasperated by the burnt toast served in his company's Stillwater, Minnesota, lunchroom, he invented and, in 1919, patented the first successful pop-up toaster. In 1926, his company introduced an improved model, the Toastmaster, with an adjustable timing device for different shades of browning. Strite's firm was purchased by Max McGraw, founder of the McGraw Electric Company, whose merchandising know-how escalated Toastmaster sales. Because of the product's popularity, other pop-ups promptly popped up.

ELEVATOR: Although elevators of various kinds existed in ancient days—the Emperor Nero owned three, and France's Louis XV had a "flying chair" stationed outside his bedroom in the palace at Versailles, for quicker access to his mistress' boudoir—the first "safety elevator" was built in 1853 by Halifax, Vermont-born Elisha Graves Otis (1811-1861).

Otis had previously made his living by building brass beds in Yonkers, and there was little interest in his invention until he arranged for a startling demonstration at New York's 1854 Crystal Palace Exposition. After Otis and a load of freight were hoisted well off the ground, Otis ordered a workman to cut the lift rope. Spectators gasped, but—because a wagon spring at the top snapped out when no longer compressed by the pull of the lift rope, driving metal jaws into cogs in the elevator's guide rails—the elevator platform stayed put.

Even though his invention was hailed, Otis couldn't sell one for the next three years. The first buyer—for three-hundred dollars—was E. V. Haughwout of New York, owner of a five-story china-and-glass emporium. Passengers were lifted by steam-driven belts at the leisurely rate of forty feet per minute. In 1873, to increase the speed in a ten-story building, the elevator was placed at one end of a rope and an iron bucket at the other. When the bucket was filled with water, the elevator went up. When the bucket was emptied, the elevator went down—with only a hand brake to halt the descent. Hydraulic pistons were less scary, but they required deep pits.

The first reliable air cushion for elevators was devised by a Chicago inventor, Colonel Ellithorpe, but its debut at Boston's Parker House in 1880 was a disaster, resulting in minor injuries to eight volunteer passengers and lots of broken glass and twisted steel. The pit wasn't deep enough and an air-escape valve had been omitted. During a later demonstration in Chicago, however, the descent was so gentle that passengers and fresh eggs emerged unscathed and full-to-the-brim water glasses shed nary a drop.

Later developments included soft landings sans deep pits, call signals, and in 1924, automatic signal-control systems. The safety elevator made feasible another American innovation: the skyscraper.

EMBRYO TRANSFER: In October 1983, two doctors at the Harbor-UCLA Medical Center in Torrance, California, John Buster and Maria Bustillo, announced the first successful transfer of embryos from one human to another. In cases in which women were unable to produce ova, their husbands' sperm were used to inseminate donors. When conception occurred, the fertilized ova were removed during the first week of pregnancy and transferred to the wives' wombs. In two of twenty-five cases the procedure worked, and in both cases the women gave birth to normal children early in 1984. The technique was an adaptation of a method frequently used with cattle, except that the embryos were live instead of frozen.

It is seen as a scientistsend, rather than a godsend, for women who want to bear their spouse's children but are afflicted with blocked Fallopian tubes that cannot be surgically rectified. Although they are carried for nine months by the husbands' wives, the babies are not genetically related to the wives, a situation that could cause legal complications. Just such a problem occurred in 1984 when a wealthy couple died in a plane crash while frozen, artificially inseminated ova were awaiting transplantation in Australia. The couple's only potential heirs were frozen embryos. The Australian government established an ethics committee to draw up appropriate regulations for such future bizarre situations.

ENZYMES: Their pioneering research into the chemical basis of life, especially the role played by enzymes, brought a 1972 Nobel Prize in chemistry to three American biochemists, Christian Boehmer Anfinsen (1916-   ), Stanford Moore (1913-1982) and William Howard Stein (1911-1980). All three concentrated on the analysis of protein structure, especially the enzyme ribonuclease—Anfinsen on his own and Moore and Stein as colleagues at the Rockefeller Institute for Medical Research (now Rockefeller University). Monessen, Pennsylvania-born Anfinsen bridged a wide gap in the world's knowledge of the chemistry of living organisms, providing data on how the enzyme was formed in a living cell and making intelligible the relationship between the structure of proteins and their genetic function. Chicago-born Moore was a principal contributor to post-World War II knowledge of cellular protein synthesis and the enzyme's function as the specific catalyst for the chemical processes of metabolism. New York City-born Stein helped explain the chemical processes essential for the existence of a cell and how it synthesizes protein, showing how amino acids become attached to ribonuclease and are then linked together by peptide bonds in a sequence ultimately determined by deoxyribonucleic acid (DNA), the genetic material of the cell. In essence what the Nobel laureates produced was a chemical analysis at the molecular level of cell metabolism and reproduction. Shortly before receiving their international kudos, Moore and Stein published their analysis of the action of a more complex enzyme, deoxyribonuclease.

ERASER: Methods to correct errors have undoubtedly been utilized from the earliest days in which *Homo sapiens* tried to record his exploits. In 1770, Joseph Priestley, the English discoverer of oxygen, proclaimed that rubber was better than bread crumbs for rubbing out mistakes, but it was the discovery of vulcanized rubber in 1839 that made rubber erasers practical.

In 1858, Hyman L. Lipman of Philadelphia earned one hundred thousand dollars and the first patent for a pencil with an eraser by coming up with the notion of inserting lead into one end of a pencil and gluing "a piece of prepared rubber" into the other. Buyers sharpened one end of the pencil to expose the lead and the other to freshen up the eraser. In 1867, another Philadelphian, J. B. Blair, invented a rubber eraser cap into which a pencil could be tightly wedged. Because of the prior existence of pencils with rubber nubbins, Blair's version precipitated an 1874 patent suit before the U.S. Supreme Court.

The advent of the typewriter (*see* TYPEWRITER) in the 1870s was accompanied by a demand for means, other than retyping entire pages, to avoid messy erasures. Correction paper, consisting of thin paper strips coated with a chalklike substance, appeared in the 1960s and finally solved the erasure problem. About the same time, a correction fluid invented in 1951 by Bette Nesmith Graham, an artist, to paint out errors, was put on the market by the Liquid Paper Corporation. Mrs. Graham's multi-million dollar heir was her son, Michael Nesmith, of the Monkees. Typewriters are now being produced with built-in correction devices.

ERSATZ FOOD: American food technologists are busy creating test-tube cuisine that merchandisers consider preferable to the real thing. Consumers may not agree, but wittingly or unwittingly, they're purchasing phony fare. Some of the products developed over a hot lab table by the twenty-one thousand chemists, microbiologists, and nutritionists who comprise the Institute of Food Technologists address such legitimate consumer concerns as the reduction of health-endangering salt, sugar, and cholesterol content. Others are intended primarily—taste be damned!—to cut costs, save time, and prolong shelf life. An example is extruded foods. Extrusion consists of chopping or powdering a basic ingredient, then reassembling it to look like an authentic veal chop, chunk of chicken, or other familiar menu item. Extruded foods widely available include reconstituted onion rings, french fries, and shrimp. About ten years ago, Ralston Purina put on the market the Gourm-egg, developed initially at Cornell University. It is a foot-long rod of hard-cooked egg that saves caterers, institutions, and restaurants the time and trouble required to shell real eggs. The chef merely slices off what he needs.

Culinary counterfeiters are importing from Japan large quantities of surimi (the boned, minced, and frozen base of an ocean fish like pollack), which can be extruded, textured, colored, and flavored to become a look-alike for Alaskan king crab legs, scallops, and shrimp. Surimi shrimp, fried in "microwavable" batter prepared by Griffith Laboratories U.S.A., are dubbed "seafood curls." Fake crab is given many names, including "seafood legs," "seafood sticks," and less deceptively, "artificial crab" or "imitation crab." On restaurant menus it is sometimes listed only as "seafood" or is an unidentified "Neptune salad" ingredient. JAC Creative Foods in Los Angeles labels its surimi crab "King Krab." JAC, which also processes surimi into fishcakes and is planning to add molded lobster tails, is hoping to create surimi salami and bologna, to be tagged "Sea-lami" and "Sea-Loni." A Rutgers University food chemist has concocted Fish Chewies, a chocolate-flavored, fish-based confection like a soft Tootsie Roll.

ESCALATOR: The first patent for an escalator was granted to Nathan Ames of Saugus, Massachusetts, on August 9, 1859. He described his arrangement of steps on an endless inclined chain as an improvement in revolving stairs. The first escalator actually built, however, was the Reno Inclined Elevator, for which Jesse W. Reno of New York City received a patent on March 15, 1892. It consisted of an endless-belt conveyor made up of wooden slats and plush-covered rubber handrails that an electric motor kept hurtling along at approximately 1½ miles per hour. Installed at the Old Iron Pier in Coney Island in 1896, its grooved slats slid under comb-plates at each end like present-day escalators.

The first practical escalator, with flat steps, was patented by Charles A. Wheeler on August 2, 1892, but it had no comb-plate landing device, so those using it had to enter and exit at side entrances. Wheeler's escalator was never actually built, but his patent was purchased in 1898 by Charles D. Seeberger, who wanted the flat-step feature for his own improved version of an escalator. The following year, Seeberger made a deal with the Otis Elevator Company in Yonkers, New York, which was already in the business of propelling people up and down (*see* ELEVATOR). Otis registered the word "Escalator" as a trademark in 1900 and renewed the registration in 1930.

Seeberger's escalator was put into service later in 1900 at the Paris Exposition. After its return to the United States, it was installed in Philadelphia's Gimbel Brothers department store and remained in use until 1939. The first step-type escalator incorporating both flat steps and the comb-plate landing device was the Otis "L," introduced commercially in 1921. There have been no major changes in escalator design since that time. The longest outdoor escalator in the world has been installed by Otis in Hong Kong. Riders get a striking view of Victoria Harbor while ascending thirty stories.

F

FADS: Fads surface everywhere in the world, in every epoch, some remaining local, others finding eager acceptance in other communities and other nations. America has contributed generously to the world's passing fancies. Random examples, including a number in CAPITAL LETTERS that are accorded separate entries as (*see*   ) elsewhere in this tome: ZOOT SUIT, HULA HOOP, coonskin Davy Crockett hats, propeller beanies, mood rings, FRISBEE, DANCE MARATHON, flagpole sitting, telephone booth squashing, automobile stuffing, SKATEBOARD, 3-D movies, pet rocks, live-goldfish gobbling, nude "streaking," pie-in-the-face throwing, piano axing, toothpick-castle erecting, CHAIN LETTER, Nehru jackets, platform shoes, tie-dyed shirts, designer jeans, assorted dolls, goo-goos, YO-YOs, paddle balls, SLINKYs, SILLY PUTTY, MONOPOLY, SCRABBLE, jigsaw puzzles, DANCES, "Jaws"-mania, Ouija boards, coed panty swiping, bed pushing, and diet after diet after diet.

A postscript about the pet rock, which was invented in 1975 by Gary Dahl, a Los Gatos, California, advertising man. It was, in a way, an ancestor of the Cabbage Patch Kid, whose Cabbage adoption papers are akin to the pet rock's care-and-training manual (*see* CABBAGE PATCH KID). Dahl, hearing pet owners keen about broken vases, clawed furniture, cat urine, and doggy do, casually commented that he was spared such inconveniences because he had a pet rock. The quixotic quip then became a national nuttiness when Dahl imported tons of egg-sized rocks from a Mexican beach and sold them, nestled in excelsior inside miniature pet-carrying cases with breathing holes, at $3.98 apiece. His instruction manual advised new owners on how to housetrain their pet ("Place it on some old newspapers; the rock will know what the paper is for and will require no further instruction") and how to teach them to roll over (on hills), come to heel, and—the breed's specialty—play dead. His pet was the world's least troublesome, Dahl contended, because it didn't have to be fed, walked, boarded, or spayed.

FAST FOOD: Fast-food restaurants are not a twentieth-century phenomenon. Street stalls undoubtedly catered to toga-clad customers. One American innovation, the self-service restaurant, first appeared in New York in 1885; but self-service "cafeterias" had been popular in San Francisco since the 1849 gold rush days. However, modern fast-food serving may have started on the day—June 9, 1902—that a weary Philadelphia waiter, Frank Hardart, decided that restaurant patrons should serve themselves. Using mechanisms imported from Germany, Hardart and a partner, Joe Horn, opened the first automat—a new kind of restaurant in which customers dropped nickels into slots to gain access to glass compartments displaying various foods. At its peak Horn and Hardart owned forty-four restaurants and automats in Philadelphia and New York, but by 1985, they had dwindled to a single restaurant in a different part of the chain's home city.

Quick service—but not *that* quick—was provided by the Harvey girls, the personable waitresses at a chain of American restaurants assembled by an Englishman, Fred Harvey, which grew between 1876 and 1912 from a single Topeka, Kansas, eatery to seventy-seven restaurants and sixty railway dining cars. A major contribution to "convenience food" preparation was made by Howard Johnson, who in the late 1920s began selling homemade ice cream in his Wollaston, Massachusetts, patent medicine store and, then, sought customers at Massachusetts beaches and at roadside restaurants. Johnson instituted a "commissary" system (preparation of all foods at a central location) to maintain uniform quality and cut costs. The restaurants with the orange roofs and twenty-eight ice-cream flavors became family favorites throughout the U.S. in the forties, and still attract hungry crowds. The McDonald's hamburger chain, whose golden arches now span the globe, borrowed the central-kitchen policy, as have most of the other successful franchise operations (*see* McDONALDS).

Fast foods are dispensed at varying speeds by such chains of varying size as McDonald's, Burger King, Wendy's, Roy Rogers, Kentucky Fried Chicken (*see* CHICKEN), Hardee's, Pizza Hut, Dairy Queen, Taco Bell, Arby's, Church's, Jack in the Box, Long John Silver's, Domino's, Godfather's, Popeye, Wimpy, Gino's, White Castle, Bojangles, Grandy's, Chick-fil-A, Chili's, G. D. Ritzy's, Fresher Cooker, Nankin Express, D'Lites, Flakey Jake's, and Fuddrucker's.

FERRIS WHEEL: The directors of the 1893 World's Columbian Exposition in Chicago wanted a spectacular attraction to rival the

Eiffel Tower, the 984-foot-high structure that had evoked oohs and ahs from visitors to the Paris exposition four years earlier, so they offered a prize for the best contender. It was won by George Washington Gale Ferris (1859-1896), an engineer from Galesburg, Illinois, who designed and erected a gigantic revolving steel wheel that carried thirty-six 60-passenger cars high into the air. The top of the wheel was 264 feet above the ground. The wheel—825 feet in circumference, 250 feet in diameter, and 30 feet wide—hung by tension rods from a shaft resting on two 140-foot towers. Total weight of the wheels and cars was 2,100 tons; of the levers and machinery, 2,200 tons; and of a full load of passengers, 150 tons.

Smaller versions have become a popular feature of amusement parks and traveling carnivals everywhere. At nineteen, Jim Bakich of San Jose, California, claimed a world's record by revolving in a ferris wheel for 337½ hours. His gondola was equipped with a telephone. Asked if he had received many calls, Bakich replied, "Just from the crackpots."

FIVE-AND-TEN: Only nickel merchandise was initially contemplated by the founder of the dime stores. A self-confessed klutz when he left his parents' farm to work as an unpaid apprentice clerk at a Watertown, New York, store, Frank Winfield Woolworth (1852-1919) helped launch the store's "five-cent counter." He persuaded his employer to lend him $315.41 worth of "Yankee notions" to open The Great Five Cent Store in Utica, New York, on February 22, 1879. It flopped, but Woolworth bought a railroad ticket to Lancaster, Pennsylvania, with his last twenty dollars and tried again. On a single day, he exuberantly wrote his father, he grossed $127.65. To allow for more varied merchandise, he made a modest adjustment of his price structure, putting nickel items on one side of the store and dime items on the other. After aborted attempts to expand to two other Pennsylvania cities (Harrisburg and York), he duplicated his Lancaster success in a third (Scranton).

When Woolworth's variety-store chain went international in 1909, the British outlets were dubbed Three-and-Sixpence stores. Further nomenclatural changes were needed as Woolworth stores moved into Germany, Mexico, Spain, and other countries and re-revision became necessary in 1932 when, for the first time in fifty-three years, the price limit was upped to twenty cents. In 1935, all price ceilings were removed—West German branches even sell costly furs.

Aside from establishing a fixed price limit, Woolworth departed from custom by allowing customers to handle the merchandise and by instructing his sales clerks to keep on the move, asking customers if they needed help. Such offbeat notions caught on and "F. W. Woolworth" stores, their founder's name emblazoned in gold letters on red storefronts like those Woolworth admired on A&P grocery stores, spread across the country and beyond its borders. When New York's 792-foot Woolworth Building opened in 1913, it was the world's tallest until 1930, and Woolworth paid its $13 million cost in cash. Downstairs, at company headquarters, is a sculpture of the founder, counting nickels and dimes.

FLASHLIGHT: The first flashlight grew out of an idea discarded by Joshua Lionel Cowen, who went on to create Lionel miniature trains (*see* LIONEL TRAINS). Cowen, a student at Cooper Union, was told by his instructor that he was wasting his time working on a doorbell. After switching from that project to another—perfecting a tiny electric motor that he installed in a skillfully designed fan that had only one major flaw: it failed to stir up any semblance of a breeze—Cowen also developed a slender battery in a tube with a lightbulb at one end. Stuck into a flower pot, it illuminated the plant. Conrad Hubert, a restaurant owner, thought that lighting up greenery in that manner was a great idea, and he quit the meal-merchandising business to become a traveling salesman for Cowen's gadget. Cowen was not equally enthusiastic, and preferring to tinker with his miniature motor, he transferred all the rights to Hubert, who later came up with a new use for it.

The first flashlight produced by the American Electric and Novelty Manufacturing Company in New York in 1898 consisted of a paper tube with metal fittings; a rough brass stamping used for a reflector, without any lens; and a spring contact switch. Both lamp and battery were handmade. The company later changed its name to the American Eveready Company, which eventually became part of the National Carbon Company.

FLIP-TOP CAN: In 1959, Ermal Cleon Fraze (1913-1989), of Dayton, Ohio, was enjoying a summer picnic with his family-until he discovered that he had left the can opener at home and couldn't find a handy substitute. On that occasion he finally used the bumper guard of his car to supplement the sandwiches with sodas, but the inconvenience started him thinking. A professional mechanical engineer, president of the Dayton Reliable Tool Company, he developed the rivet needed to hold a pull-ring to a metal tab. For several years the notion was shunned because it upped the cost of cans. Then Iron City Beer became Fraze's first client (*see* BEER CAN). In 1988 more than 150 billion cans were opened, world wide, with his pull tab.

FLUORIDATION: In 1908, a Colorado dentist, Frederick Sumter McKay, observed that many of his patients had mottled tooth enamel but few cavities. He decided that the peculiar pairing of good and bad effects was due to some substance in their drinking water; but not until 1931 was it identified as decay-resisting fluoride. In 1938, the United States Public Health Service checked out two Illinois communities—Galesburg, where the water had a high fluoride count; and Quincy, where it was fluoride-free—and confirmed McKay's opinion. Tests elsewhere helped establish a ratio of fluoride to water—one part per million—that kept teeth both healthy and unsullied.

In 1942, David B. Abst, who was the director of the New York State Bureau of Dental Health, plumped for artificial fluoridation of water. Two years later, it was tested in Newburgh, with the fluorideless neighboring community of Kingston as a basis for statistical comparison. After tests demonstrated that the water additive reduced school children's cavities by as much as 60 percent, fluoridation was adopted throughout the United States and in Canada, England, Australia, and other countries.

Although the process has been endorsed by the American Dental Association, the American Medical Association, and other scientific bodies, vehement protests have been lodged in some communities by fluoride flouters who oppose what they term compulsory medication and consider what's being stirred into reservoirs a potentially harmful poison.

FLY SWATTER: Attending a Topeka softball game in 1905, Dr. Samuel J. Crumbine, a member of the Kansas State Board of Health seeking ways to exterminate the state's bumper crop of flies and to combat public indifference to the pesky insects, heard fans screaming, "Swat the ball!" The next issue of the *Fly Bulletin* bore a front-page headline: SWAT THE FLY. A schoolteacher, Frank H. Rose, created a fly-flattening device out of a yardstick and a piece of wire screen. The holes were essential because a fly can sense the air pressure of a hand or any other solid object. Rose dubbed his invention a "fly bat." Crumbine renamed it.

FM RADIO: Even before his graduation from Columbia University in 1913, New York City-born Edwin Howard Armstrong (1890-1954) invented the regenerative or feedback circuit that virtually revolutionized the still fledgling field of radio. However, similar innovations by others caused patent litigation that was not settled until 1934, when the Supreme Court, despite chronology that apparently supported Armstrong's claims to being first, ruled in favor of Lee De Forest. While serving with the U.S. Signal Corps in France during World War I, Armstrong developed the superheterodyne circuit that greatly increased radio receivers' selectivity and sensitivity and became the basic design for amplitude-modulation (AM) radios. In 1920, he played a major role in the development of shortwave and police radios.

Armstrong's greatest achievement, in 1933, was frequency-modulation (FM) radios, which eliminated static and, by using a wider band than AM radios, made possible broadcasts of high fidelity. Although FM has become the preferred medium for radio transmission of music, it was not until 1939 that FM receivers were marketed. An impatient Armstrong built his own FM station on the New Jersey Palisades. He subsequently devised multiplexing (a system for broadcasting more than one FM program on the same frequency)—making possible the broadcasting of background music in stores, restaurants, and factories—and, later, broadcasting of programs in stereophonic sound. Although he earned $15 million from FM, he was constantly involved in litigation with the Federal Communications Commission (FCC) over the licensing of FM stations and with several radio companies over patent rights. The lawsuits depressed him to such a degree that he committed suicide by jumping from a thirteenth-story window. When the suits then in progress were completed, his widow received settlements totaling about $5 million.

FOLDING CHAIR: Some of the nation's founders invented things other than the world's first government with a written constitution. Benjamin Franklin, for one, was an inveterate innovator. The folding chair is attributed to Thomas Jefferson, who wrote the Declaration of Independence and, in 1800, after the House of Representatives resolved in his favor an electoral tie with Aaron Burr, became the third president of the United States. The folding theater chair was patented in 1854 by an Aaron other than Burr, Aaron H. Allen of Boston. A chair that folded all the way back, enabling a sitter to become a recliner, was invented in 1841 by a Philadelphia cabinet maker and upholsterer, Henry Peres Kennedy.

Among Jefferson's other creations were another kind of chair, one that swiveled 360 degrees, a more effective plow, an adjustable music stand that could be converted into a table, a walking stick that doubled as a stool, and a turnstile-style clothes hanger.

FOODS: Foodstuffs native to America have found warm welcomes in other countries. One of the first items exported from the American colonies was the cranberry, which was perhaps the country's only uniquely indigenous fruit. It was used by the Indians as a food, dye, and medicinal poultice.

Corn, the Indians' all-purpose food ("maize," the Indian word for corn, means "our life"), has become similarly indispensable throughout the world. The Indians made versatile use of the crops available to them, many unknown in Europe, including white potatoes, sweet potatoes, Jerusalem artichokes, pumpkin, squash (an abbreviation of the Indian word *askutasquash*), peppers, peanuts, and sunflower seeds. An Indian dish, succotash (green corn cooked with lima or shell beans), may have been served by the Pilgrims at the first Thanksgiving dinner in 1621. The melting-pot nation has provided many cooking-pot cuisines, including Tex-Mex, Creole, and soul foods. It has also produced a long list of "ethnic" dishes like chop suey (*see* CHOP SUEY), chow mein, chili con carne, English muffins, cioppino, and vichysoisse (*see* VICHYSOISSE), which are erroneously thought to be of foreign origin. Among American contributions to gourmets' contentment are lobster Newburgh, née lobster à la (Ben) Wenberg, named initially for a friend of the owner of Delmonico's restaurant in New York; chicken à la king, which was chicken à la Keene, named for the Delmonico diner Foxhall Keene; the Waldorf salad, created by Oscar Tschirky, alias Oscar of the Waldorf; eggs Benedict, requested as a hangover remedy by the socialite Samuel Benedict at New York's Waldorf Astoria in 1894; oysters Rockefeller, so named because a patron at Antoine's in New Orleans dubbed the dish "as rich as Rockefeller"; and baked Alaska, invented by Charles Ranhofer, chef at Delmonico's, to celebrate America's purchase of Alaska in 1867. American-produced hybrids include James Logan's loganberries and Rudolf Boysen's boysenberries. Also all-American are apple butter, apple pan dowdy, barbecued spareribs, cheeseburgers, codfish cakes, clam fritters, gumbo, ham and shrimp jambalaya, ham hocks and greens, hasty pudding, Indian pudding, maple sugar, clam chowder, scrapple, pumpkin pie, and pumpkin soup.

FORMICA: The decorative plastic laminate that makes kitchens and bathrooms everywhere more utilitarian has become so common that in 1978 the Denver regional office of the Federal Trade Commission (FTC) filed a petition to convert the identifying word from a trademark to a generic term. The FTC argued that the name has become so much a part of everyday language that the Formica Corporation, a subsidiary of American Cyanamid—which also operates forty other chemical and medical companies around the world—had an unfair advantage over its competitors. Arguing that its trademark appeared conspicuously on a number of exclusive products and that the FTC wasn't authorized to challenge trademarks that predated the 1946 Lanham Act, Formica succeeded in retaining its capital *F*.

Herbert A. Faber and Daniel J. (D. J.) O'Conor, fellow employees at Westinghouse, discovered a new way to make high-quality insulation materials for electrical products coming into existence just before World War I. They started their own two-man operation in Cincinnati on May 2, 1913. Their first order was for Chalmers Motor Company commutator rings in which their laminate would serve as a substitute for mica. Eureka! A name for their product! To secure financing for their jerry-built factory, they persuaded three local businessmen to join with them in establishing the Formica Insulation Company.

A crisis occurred when the company decided to expand by adding sheet laminates to its line of products. An essential component was resin, which Faber and O'Conor were purchasing from the Bakelite Company. Bakelite's sales manager advised O'Conor that his company would continue to provide resin for Formica's rings and tubes but that it was licensing only Westinghouse to use its resin for flat sheet laminates. Refusing to be forced into abandoning what they saw as a major potential source of business, Faber and O'Conor began searching for an alternative source of resin ·and found it in a small Chicago plant operated by Dr. L. V. Redman. The first sheet of Formica laminate rolled off the press, appropriately enough, on July 4, 1914. The company introduced today's sturdy, decorative laminate in 1938.

FORTUNE COOKIE: Although the cookie part of the fortune cookie hails from China, the fortune part—like such "traditionally" Chinese dishes as chop suey (*see* CHOP SUEY) and chow mein— reputedly is of strictly U.S. origin.

The cookies have sometimes contained patriotic messages ("Enlist; Uncle Sam needs you") or political exhortations ("Vote for so-and-so"). Usually, however, they contain innocuous statements like "There is nothing permanent except change"; puns like "Love is a softening of the hearteries"; ethnic advice like "Eat, eat, you need strength to worry"; or mild gags like "Smile—people will wonder what you are up to." In recent years some cookie communiqués have merited an X rating. George Yep, a Philadelphia fortune-cookie fabricator, prepares to order Valentine cookies that contain engagement rings and king-size cookies that encompass large gifts. Also earning a Yep yep are green cookies for St. Patrick's Day, cookies that contain "lucky" numbers for lottery players, and prospectively, fruit-flavored and chocolate-chip varieties. A 1985 variation by Susie's Kitchen, a New Jersey bakery, contains trivia questions.

Chinese bakeries turn out the cookies and stuff them with often perplexing "Confucius say"-level philosophizings they create themselves or buy ready-made from printers, but no one seems to know for certain when and where the custom started or the identity of its instigator. One New York distributor, the China Bowl Trading Company, which gets its fortune cookies from the Key Key Cake Company, has hazarded a guess. On the China Bowl's boxes of cookies appears this legend: "The history of messages in cakes goes back to the 13th century in China when the people were oppressed by the barbarian rule of the Mongol conquerers. In those days, instructions calling for local uprisings and attacks on guards were transmitted on rice paper in steamed cakes." Another theory is that the cookies are linked to an ancient Chinese parlor game. However, Melvin Chin, of New York's Hing Lung Fortune Cookies, stoutly maintains, "They're as American as apple pie."

FOUNTAIN PEN: Fountain pens were available in Paris and London as long ago as the seventeenth century. The quill pen was still favored, however, even after a British inventor, Joseph Bramah, patented the Compound Fountain Pen in 1809. It consisted of a thin silver tube, filled with ink, that tapered to a quill nib. Gently squeezing the tube generated a flow of ink. A major problem, how to regulate the flow of ink so that it was neither more nor less than required, was solved by Decatur, New York-born Lewis Edson Waterman (1837-1901). According to legend, Waterman, an insurance salesman who carried a dip pen and a vial of ink for signing contracts, ruined a suit and lost an account when the dipper became a dripper. He resolved to prevent a recurrence of the messy accident and in 1884 patented the fissure feed, a hard-rubber insert with tiny channels that allowed ink and air to flow in the pen in opposite directions at the same time. Assembling the pens by hand on a kitchen table at the rear of a small New York tobacco shop, he turned out about two hundred the first year. Later he devised machinery that stepped up production. The first Waterman pen was called "the Regular" and was filled with an eyedropper. In 1903 Waterman's company developed a pen with a retractable point called the safety pen. About the time of World War I, both Waterman and another American company, Shaeffer, introduced lever-fill mechanisms. Although the great majority of the pens sold today are of the ballpoint variety, fountain pens still have their adherents who believe that they make handwriting more distinctive.

FRISBEE: The Frisbee flying saucer, which launched an international fad, is a Plastics-Age variation on the prehistoric practice of pebble propelling. Its name is a trademarked Wham-O Manufacturing Company homage to the Joseph P. Frisbie Pie Company of Bridgeport, Connecticut, whose tin pie plates reputedly kept being swiped many years ago by Yale students for scaling across open fields. In 1955, Princeton undergraduates converted random tossing into a competitive sport that soon became a widespread campus favorite.

Before World War II, Walter Frederick Morrison, a one-time Los Angeles building inspector, dazzled spectators with his masterful manipulation of airborne pie pans and peddled them at beaches, fairs, and carnivals. The inventor of a machine for making popsicles in home freezers and of the Crazy Eight Ball, a saggy water-filled bowling ball, Morrison devised a plastic version of the pie tin, in 1948, and named it the Pluto Platter to distinguish it from other flying saucers. In 1957, Wham-O, a San Gabriel, California, manufacturer of novelty items, bought the rights to Morrison's throwaway disk, added grooves (suggested by Ed Headrick), and tested various names before opting, in 1959, for Frisbee. Players vied in contests involving distance, time aloft, accuracy, and boomeranging. More sophisticated developments included Frisbee tennis and golf, the latter with target poles or baskets instead of holes; guts Frisbee, with the disks thrown as forcefully as possible between teams fifteen feet apart to prevent their being fielded with one hand; and ultimate Frisbee, created in 1968 in the parking lot of Columbia High School in Maplewood, New Jersey, which has seven-member teams vying to work a disk down a football-field-sized area and across a goal line.

The first world Frisbee champ was crowned in 1968. Pasadena's Rose Bowl became the site of an International Frisbee Tournament in 1974. It was sponsored by the International Frisbee Association, which was in turn sponsored by Wham-O. The 1979 tournament drew 139 participants from thirty-five states and eleven countries. The first Canine World Frisbee Catch and Fetch Championship, with 365 cans of dog food as first prize, was added in 1977.

FROZEN FOOD: Brooklyn-born Clarence (Bob) Birdseye (1887-1956), who is credited with the idea of quick-freezing food on a commercial scale, kept reminding people that for centuries the Eskimos had been freezing meat for later use.

Birdseye, whose king-size curiosity resulted in more than 250 inventions, including harpoon guns and heat lamps, lived with his wife in Labrador during World War I while participating in a U.S. Geographic Service fish and wildlife survey. He had suitable credentials. Earlier he had earned money trapping black rats for biology researchers at Columbia University and live frogs for menu preparers at the Bronx Zoo. He decided that fish and caribou meat frozen in midwinter tasted better than the same items frozen at warmer times. What made the difference, he concluded, was the speed of freezing— the faster the process, the less danger that ice crystals would rupture cell walls and release natural juices. He packed cabbages in a barrel, freezing each layer in salt water. When cabbage was on the family menu, he would chop out a layer with a hatchet and let it thaw. After his Arctic stay ended, Birdseye spent seven dollars on brine, ice, and an electric fan to continue his experiments. What worked best, he found, was placing packages of fish between two metal surfaces with a below-zero temperature. He patented his process and, in 1924, began marketing quick-frozen fish through his General Seafoods Corporation in Gloucester, Massachusetts. He tried freezing everything that seemed edible, even an alligator.

In 1928, he ran into financial difficulty because retailers were reluctant to invest in the special refrigeration needed to store frozen food. He received backing from the Postum Cereal Company and, in 1929, sold his thriving company to what was to become the General Foods Corporation. General Foods installed frozen food storage cases at its own expense and invited shoppers to sample its Birds Eye foods. World War II gave frozen foods (until then, primarily "luxury" items) their greatest impetus because Japan's conquest of Southeast Asia deprived America of its major source of tin, and most foods in tin cans were reserved for the military.

G

GAS CHAMBER: Like another American alternative to such traditional forms of capital punishment as hanging and shooting (*see* ELECTRIC CHAIR), the gas chamber was envisioned by its proposer, Major D. A. Turner, of the U.S. Army Medical Corps, as a more humane method. The procedure was tested for the first time on February 8, 1924, when the state of Nevada executed Gee Jon, a Chinese who had been convicted of multiple murders. He died after inhaling hydrocyanic gas for six minutes. Gas chamber executions consist of strapping the condemned prisoner in a chair in an airtight room and producing a lethal gas by dropping cyanide pellets into a bucket of acid. If the prisoner breathes deeply, death is almost instantaneous, but many delay their demise by holding their breaths or taking short, shallow breaths. Under such circumstances, observers claim, death is painful. By the second half of the twentieth century eleven of the fifty states had adopted the method.

The gas chamber was devised to punish the guilty; Hitler's Germany used a variation to murder the innocent, herding minorities condemned by the Nazis into gas chambers disguised as bathhouses. During World War II, victims in concentration camps included an estimated six million Jews.

GASOLINE: During the oil industry's early days, gasoline—alias gas, gasolene, and petrol—a volatile, inflammable liquid derived from petroleum, was distilled off at a lower temperature than kerosene and largely discarded. That changed with the realization that gasoline provided a superior fuel for the internal-combustion engine because of its high-energy hydrocarbons and a volatility that enabled it to be easily inserted into engine cylinders, when mixed with air by a simple, inexpensive carburetor. Its widespread use as automobile fuel became feasible, however, only after William M. Burton of Chicago invented a way to "crack" crude petroleum, greatly increasing gasoline yield. He was awarded a "manufacture of gasoline" patent on January 7, 1913. His method, treating the residue of the paraffin group of petroleum by distillation and condensation of the vapors, was adopted by the Standard Oil Company of Indiana.

After a seven-year search for an antiknock ingredient for gasoline, during which at least thirty-three thousand compounds were tested, Thomas Midgley, Jr., of the General Motors Research Laboratories in Dayton, Ohio, found that tetraethyl lead, made from alcohol and lead, affected gasoline's combustion rate. Ethyl gasoline went on sale in Dayton on February 1, 1923. Years later, because of concern about air pollution, the Environmental Protection Agency, to reduce the amount of lead from automobile exhausts, passed regulations requiring that all new cars be designed to operate on unleaded gas. In 1984, because 13 percent of the owners of no-lead vehicles were illegally using "regular" gas, the EPA announced that by 1986 the amount of lead in leaded gas would be cut by 91 percent and threatened to ban lead entirely as a gasoline additive.

In the 1980s, gasoline was chiefly produced by means of synthetic compounds. A search continues for new sources, with oil shale and tar sands considered promising alternatives. One-hundred-octane aviation gasoline resulted from the catalytic cracking method devised by Eugene Houdry. It was commercially produced for the first time by the Socony-Vacuum Oil Company in Paulsboro, New Jersey, on June 6, 1936.

GAS STATION: The French claim the first service station or garage—an establishment opened in Bordeaux in December 1895 by A. Borol, the local Peugeot agent—to provide overnight parking facilities for motor cars; a workshop for repairs, maintenance and cleaning; and refills of oil and "motor spirit." Visiting "autocarists" were advised of the availability of "storage for car and supply of petrol" in an April 1897 Brighton Cycle and Motor Company ad in an English periodical, *Autocar*. However, the gas pump and the fill-'er-up station are American innovations.

The first gas pump was made by Sylvanus F. Bowser of Fort Wayne, Indiana, who delivered it to a storekeeper, Jake Gumper, on September 5, 1885. The transaction had nothing to do with automobiles. Gumper had been receiving complaints about the taste of what was coming out of the butter cask next to his leaking kerosene barrel. Instead of simply moving one or the other, Gumper asked Bowser for a less messy way to dispense measured quantitites of lamp oil. Bowser's solution was a round tank containing a cylinder and an outlet pipe. When a wooden handle was raised, a system of valves and plungers sent a gallon of kerosene from the tank to the cylinder; when it was lowered, the kerosene flowed out the pipe. Twenty years later, Bowser began manufacturing the first self-measuring gasoline pump. In 1925, his company added a clock that registered quantity, and in 1932, an automatic price indicator.

The first bulk-storage filling station was operated in 1905 by the Automobile Gasoline Company in St. Louis, founded by Harry Grenner and Clem Laessing. A garden hose connected to a gravity-fed tank was used to fill 'er up. The first filling station with a projecting canopy was opened in Seattle two years later by Standard Oil of California. In 1912, a Standard Oil of Louisiana superstation featuring thirteen pumps, a ladies' rest room, and a maid who served ice water to waiting customers lured Memphis motorists. In those days, the gasoline to fuel automobiles was delivered to filling stations by mule. In December 1913, the first drive-in service station was launched in Pittsburgh by the Gulf Refining Company. It was a twenty-four-hours-a-day operation and offered free crankcase service.

In the 1920s, service stations dotted all America. Some were awesomely elaborate, resembling Greek temples, Chinese pagodas, or Spanish missions. Services provided gratis included fuel pumping, oil and water checking, windshield washing, and tire inflating. Now many "service" stations invite their customers to do-it-yourself.

GEODESIC DOME: A gold-tinted version of the multi-purpose geodesic dome designed by Milton, Massachusetts-born (Richard) Buckminster Fuller, Jr. (1895-1983), drew so many Russians when it housed the American National Exhibition in Moscow in 1959 that the U.S. State Department later erected similar exhibition domes in Burma, India, Thailand, Afghanistan, and Japan. The domes, based on a mathematical principle, "energetic synergetic geometry," devised by Fuller in 1917, provided maximum strength with minimal material. They were built of numerous contiguous tetrahedrons made from lightweight alloys with high tensile strength, a design that effectively withstood any external pressure.

The dome, widely used in the 1950s for military and industrial purposes, was only one of "futurologist" Fuller's revolutionary concepts to solve problems of modern living. Others included the 4-D house, a self-contained dustless unit that was transportable by air; the three-wheeled Dymaxion automobile ("Dymaxion" was a Fuller coinage pairing "dynamic" and "maximum"); and the spacious, comfortable Dymaxion house, supported by a single central column. Another Fuller fabrication, the Dymaxion world map, showing the continents without distortion, was the only map ever granted a U.S. patent.

The 1933 Dymaxion automobile could be parked in an area no larger than its length. It traversed difficult terrain with ease, attained a speed of 120 miles per hour, and ran 30 to 40 miles on a gallon of gasoline. An accident during a well-publicized demonstration tour, due to human error and not because of any mechanical flaw, is said to have caused cancellation of marketing plans.

GIDEON BIBLE: The practice of leaving Gideon Bibles in hotel and motel nightstand drawers around the world, to provide solace for "lonely men on the road," stems from an 1898 meeting of the Christian Commercial Men's Association of America in Boscobel, Wisconsin. Initial implementation of the organization's free-testament policy occurred on July 1, 1899, when three traveling salesmen, whose thoughts obviously did not dwell on farmers' daughters, convened at the Superior Hotel in Iron Mountain, Montana, and distributed the first of what eventually became millions of Bibles. Repositories, in addition to hotels, have included schools, prisons, ships, and military camps. In 1985, Gideons International, named for the faithful servant of God chronicled in the Book of Judges, claimed eighty-three thousand members in some thirty countries. Since the late 1960s, the Gideons have printed modern-English Bibles as well as the King James Version. To blend with dissimilar room decors, Gideon Bibles, originally available like early Fords in "every shade of black," are now offered to hotel managers in bindings of assorted colors, including beige, olive, walnut, and "burnt orange."

GOLD RECORD: A single record is certified "gold" by the Recording Industry Association of America (RIAA) when actual sales, not shipments, total one million copies and "platinum" when sales reach two million. For albums, "gold" means five hundred thousand; "platinum," one million. Since 1970, three-million-seller albums have been accorded the titanic "titanium." Similar metallic adjectives have been adopted by record makers in other countries.

The first "gold record" went to Glenn Miller's "Chattanooga Choo Choo," a novelty number originally heard in the 1941 movie *Sun Valley Serenade* and recorded by RCA Victor the same year. When sales zoomed past the million mark in only a few months, RCA had a "master" record sprayed with gold paint and presented it to Miller during a February 10, 1942, radio broadcast. However, "Choo Choo" was not Miller's first seven-digit disk; "Sunrise Serenade," recorded in 1939, sold more than a million copies; as did his orchestra's theme song, "Moonlight Serenade," Miller's best-known composition. No documentation exists for the first record ever to sell a million copies. A likely candidate is Al Jolson's "Ragging the Baby to Sleep," which was waxed by the Victor Talking Machine Company on April 17, 1912. It reputedly sold a million copies within a year or two and was probably the only pre–World War I record to achieve that distinction. The first 33 1/3 RPM long-playing (LP) record to pass the million-

138

sales mark was Decca's 1949 original-cast album of the Rodgers and Hammerstein musical *Oklahoma!* By 1956, before any other LP had reached a million, *Oklahoma!* had soared to 1.75 million.

GOLF BALL: Golf derives its name from the German word for "club" and almost everything else from Scotland. One noteworthy exception is the strictly American ball. Many materials were utilized before a lighter, tightly wound, rubber-threaded ball with a solid rubber core was devised by Coburn Haskell, a Cleveland golfer, and Bertram G. Work, of the B. F. Goodrich Company in Akron, Ohio. In 1951, the United States Golf Association and the Royal and Ancient Golf Club of St. Andrews, Scotland, agreed on a codification of golf rules that received worldwide endorsement the following year. However, British golfers continue to use a slightly smaller ball because of dissimilar wind and terrain.

GOLF TEE: In Scotland, where golf originated, the player would position his ball on a small clump of earth before driving. On December 12, 1899, a wooden tee with a tapering base and a concave shoulder to hold the ball was patented by a black Bostonian, George F. Grant.

GONE WITH THE WIND: Margaret Mitchell's 1936 novel about the Civil War and the Reconstruction was an international smash hit. A million copies were sold within six months. It became the best-selling novel in U.S. publishing history, eventually toting up twenty-four million sales worldwide, including translations into eighteen languages for forty foreign countries. Foreign readers, especially in Germany, flipped over the romance between the tempestuous Scarlett O'Hara and the supermacho Rhett Butler.

Also an international sensation was the multi-Academy-Award-winning 1939 movie version of the book, with English actress Vivien Leigh and Clark Gable as Scarlett and Rhett. The three-hour thirty-nine-minute saga became Metro-Goldwyn-Mayer's all-time top money-earner, seen in theaters by more than 300 million people. Atlanta, Georgia-born Margaret Mitchell (1900-1949) (ironically, she died in an automobile accident on Peachtree Street, an important address in her book) worked as a writer and reporter for the *Atlanta Journals* from 1922 to 1926. When she broke her ankle, she stopped newspapering and spent the next ten years writing the voluminous (1,037 pages) novel. It was initially titled *Tomorrow Is Another Day*, a sentence excerpted from Scarlett's final lines: "I'll think of it all tomorrow at Tara. I can stand it then. Tomorrow, I'll think of some way to get him back. After all, tomorrow is another day." When the publisher opined that too many novels had titles containing the word "tomorrow," Miss Mitchell borrowed a line from Ernest Dowson's poem, "Cyanara": "I have forgot much, Cyanara! Gone with the wind."

Margaret Mitchell sold the motion picture rights for fifty thousand dollars, certain her novel would not make a good movie. Seventeen scriptwriters, beginning with Sidney Howard, labored to prove her wrong. In 1978, CBS paid $35 million for a twenty-year lien on TV rights. One line uttered in the movie by the irked Rhett, "Frankly, my dear, I don't give a damn," triggered a censorship brouhaha, but the producer David O. Selznick refused to permit its deletion. A Frankly, My Dear, We Do Give a Damn Committee organizes commemorative celebrations for *Gone with the Wind* cultists, most recently in Chattanooga, Tennessee, in 1984.

GRAHAM CRACKER: Sylvester Graham (1794-1851), a West Suffield, Connecticut-born lay minister who evangelized for better eating habits, toured the East Coast to tout the benefits of food that wasn't "compounded and complicated by culinary process"—fresh fruits and vegetables, cereals containing roughage, pure water and unsifted whole-wheat flour (which became known as "graham flour"). The white flour used by many bakers, he contended, was unhealthy and was sometimes adulterated with chalk, clay, and plaster of paris; meat caused constipation and excessive desire for fornication; and condiments like mustard, vinegar, salt, and pepper overstimulated the system, producing depression and insanity.

A controversial figure because of his emphatic opinions, he had both sneering detractors and dedicated devotees. The former included bakers, butchers, and distillers. The latter joined Grahamite societies, stayed at Graham hotels, and patronized stores selling Graham-endorsed foods. Among his most ardent admirers were the inventor Thomas Alva Edison, the editor Horace Greeley, the breakfast cereal pioneer J. H. Kellogg, and the Mormon prophet Joseph Smith.

As a lecturer for the Pennsylvania Temperance Society, Graham began inserting comments on temperance in diet as well as drink. Most of his proposals are now considered commonsensical. He advocated avoidance of alcohol and other stimulants, taking cold showers, sleeping with open windows and on hard mattresses, exercising regularly, and moving the bowels daily. Because of the latter advice, newspapers pronounced him "the Peristaltic Persuader." He also wrote and lectured about other aspects of health, anatomy, and childbearing, often in terms so outspoken that more sensitive readers and listeners were shocked. Among his many crusades was one intended to alert the nation to the evils of masturbation, which he denounced as a cause of lethargy, lunacy, and death.

The still-popular Graham cracker uses whole-wheat flour as its principal ingredient but departs from its creator's intent by adding preservatives.

140

H

HAMBURGER: The Big Mac is now as universal as Coca-Cola, but America's own fondness for hamburger on a roll began long before McDonald's erected its first golden arch. Most sources credit St. Louis' 1904 Louisiana Purchase Exposition, which also introduced two other U.S. food favorites—the ice-cream cone and iced tea, but there are conflicting claims to the initial blending of hamburger and bun.

Although steak tartare, Salisbury steak, and hamburger steak were already staples in other countries, the concessionaire Frank Menches of Akron, Ohio, allegedly was the first to use ground beef in a sandwich, when he ran out of sausage at the 1892 Summit County, Ohio, Fair. Also credited is Louis Lassen, proprietor of a three-seat restaurant in New Haven, Connecticut, who, in 1895, began serving sliced steak sandwiches and, later, added a ground steak by-products platter. In 1900, a customer in a hurry asked him to put the ground beef between slices of toast. Louis's Lunch was given landmark status by the New Haven Preservation Trust in 1967, but eight years later, the entire building was moved two blocks, to make way for a medical complex. During World War I, hamburger retained its popularity but, because of anti-German sentiment, was often dubbed "liberty steak."

The first drive-in hamburger chain, White Castle, was launched in Chicago by Walter Anderson and Edgar Waldo Ingram in the early 1920s. The first store in the McDonald's chain—outgrowth of a single San Bernardino, California, hamburger stand operated by Maurice and Richard McDonald—opened in Des Plaines, Illinois, on April 15, 1955 (*see* McDONALD'S). It begat Burger King, Roy Rogers, Wendy's, Wimpy (which disclaims any connection with the hamburger-gobbling Wimpy in E. C. Segar's Popeye-starring "Thimble Theater" comic strip), and other franchise chains.

According to a study conducted in 1980 by the Brooklyn psychiatrist Dr. Leo Wollman, hamburger munchers are more introverted than hot dog buffs.

HAWAIIAN SHIRT: Ellery J. Chun, who reputedly named those flamboyant short-sleeved Hawaiian garments "aloha shirts," began manufacturing the eyeball-blasting prints in 1936. In those days Hawaiian shirts retailed for about a buck. In 1985, high-fashion designers in Italy, France, and Japan seized upon the gaudy garb as a challenge to untrammeled imagination, which could be peddled for hundreds of dollars. Just as Clark Gable's torso baring in the 1934 *It Happened One Night*—revealing that he didn't bother to wear an undershirt—affected the dress habits of many a non-movie star male, so the widespread alohaing of Hawaiian shirts is being linked to their constant display in CBS's "Magnum, P.I.," draped on the formidable frame of another bemustached sex object, Tom Selleck. An earlier, less beefcakey model who helped sell those shirts was President Harry Truman, who appeared on a 1951 *Life* magazine cover in a resplendent example of the genre. Soon after, however, Hawaiian shirts became an object of ridicule, supposedly worn only by gauche vacationers from the mainland. In the 1970s, rock stars were responsible for a revival of the style as a symbol of counterculture nose thumbing at conventional taste.

H-BOMB: The hydrogen bomb (H-bomb), with many times the explosive force of the atom bomb used by the United States with devastating effects in Japan during World War II (*see* ATOM BOMB), uses fusion (the joining together of lighter elements into heavier elements), instead of fission (the splitting of uranium or plutonium into lighter elements). In both cases, the end product weighs less than its components, the rest being converted into explosive energy. Because fusion requires extremely high temperatures, the hydrogen bomb is also known as a thermonuclear bomb. It is a comparatively "clean" bomb, with less radioactive fallout.

H-bomb development was spurred by the physicist Edward Teller (1908-   ), a refugee from Nazi Germany who became a naturalized U.S. citizen in 1941. That same year, he joined Enrico Fermi at Columbia University to conduct atomic-fission research and became a member of the Manhattan Project that eventually sired the atom bomb. During the five years that Teller was associated with the project, he formulated the H-bomb's theoretical basis and was one of its strongest supporters. His advocacy of nonstop improvement and testing of nuclear weapons was in sharp contrast to most scientists' calls for a moratorium on such testing. In 1954, he testified at security hearings involving J. Robert Oppenheimer (1904-1967), who helped staff and then directed the U.S. government's atomic-energy laboratory at Los Alamos, New Mexico, and was considered by laymen the father of the atom bomb. Oppenheimer's failure to provide "moral support," Teller claimed, delayed H-bomb development. After Ronald Reagan's accession to the presidency, Teller emerged as a leading proponent of H-bomb-nullifying technology.

The first thermonuclear bomb was exploded by the United States at Eniwetok in 1952; the second, a year later, by the USSR. Subsequently, Great Britain, France, China, and India have also unleashed "Biggest Yet Booms." In 1961, the Russians exploded a fifty-eight-megaton bomb with an impact equal to that of fifty million short tons of TNT. Electronic radiation belts circling the earth, the result of such detonations, are expected to persist in measurable form for many years.

HEARING AID: A year after his November 15, 1901, patenting of the Acousticon (the first electric hearing aid), Miller Reese Hutchinson of New York received a medal of appreciation from the consort of Great Britain's King Edward VII. Alexandra, partially deaf since infancy, was a fan of Hutchinson's hearing-enhancer. Manufactured by the Hutchinson Acoustic Company, it housed batteries in a case about the size of a portable radio. A telephone-type receiver attached to the case was held to the ear.

A prolific inventor, Hutchinson held some ninety patents, including one for the high-decibel Klaxon. A Hutchinson crony, Mark Twain, accused him of double-dipping duplicity: "You invented the Klaxon horn to make people deaf, so they'd have to use your acoustic device in order to make them hear again!"

The first transistorized hearing aid was put on the market by the Sonotone Corporation of Elmsford, New York, on December 29, 1952.

HEIMLICH MANEUVER: During the Middle Ages drowning victims were rolled over a barrel to get them to disgorge swallowed water. That primitive method had a basic resemblance to the effective first-aid technique for resuscitating choking and drowning victims introduced in June 1974 by Dr. Henry J. Heimlich of Xavier University in Cincinnati, Ohio. He demonstrated that pressing upward into the abdomen dislodges breathing-impeding food and water.

Initially, the Heimlich maneuver was recommended when other methods had failed; but in 1985, Dr. Heimlich opined that a reshuffling of priorities might be in order—especially in the case of drowning—with precedence given to the maneuver (which expels water from the victim's lungs) over mouth-to-mouth respiration. He also plumped for use of the maneuver, rather than chest thumping, in cases of cardiopulmonary resuscitations (CPR) because, when hearts stop, pressing the chest literally squeezes blood out of the heart and into the head. Doctors at Purdue University and the South Alabama Medical Center have been experimenting with a new technique that combines CPR and the Heimlich maneuver, but Heimlich feels that it is the maneuver that most improves blood flow and that CPR techniques can cause crushed chests and injuries to hearts and lungs. In 1985, the American Red Cross and the American Heart Association concurred.

The maneuver can be performed on both horizontal and vertical subjects, but the preferable method is to have the victim on his back, the rescuer astride his thighs. The rescuer places his hands, one atop the other, just above the victim's navel and presses the victim's abdomen with quick upward thrusts. In the case of choking, the victim's face should be straight up, to enable whatever solid object is the cause of distress to pop out. In the case of drowning, the victim's head should be turned to the side so that water can run out.

HIPPIE: The birthplace of the hippie counterculture was San Francisco's Haight-Ashbury section, where it flourished during the sixties through the early seventies. The hippie movement evolved from the earlier Beat generation. Hippies, who frequently referred to themselves as "freaks," were characterized by ultracasual wardrobes and alienation from conventional ("straight") values. In general they "dug" rootlessness, hirsuteness, sandals, jeans, rock music, jug wine, drugs, communes, and random sex. They also dug love and peace and were active in anti-war demonstrations. Their attitudes and colorful, tie-dyed clothes earned approbation, envy, and imitation from restless teenagers and reluctantly aging adults everywhere. Hippies sometimes scraped up enough cash, usually from tolerant relatives, to go abroad, where they often found others affecting a similar life-style. Some of the ragtag tourists stayed, and that distressed the local authorities because the hippies often represented little money and much trouble.

The word "hippie" evolved from numerous jazz terms. "Hep," for "knowledgeable," was being used as early as 1903. It led to "get hep," "hep to the jive," and "hepcat." The bandleader Cab Calloway called frenetic dancers "hepsters." By 1931, "hep" was being replaced by "hip," as in "hip chicks" and "hipsters." The latter word became a descriptive for any unemotional, or "cool," youth. The *San Francisco Chronicle* columnist Herb Caen coined "beatnik" (*see* BEATNIK) after author Jack Kerouac invented "beat" for "beatific," but "hippie" became the more common synonym.

The East Coast counterpart of Haight-Ashbury (or Hashbury, connoting hashish) was New York's East Village. The hit Broadway play *Hair!* (later, a movie), with its music and satirically witty anti-war lyrics, helped popularize the hippie movement in America and internationally.

Hippies took themselves seriously but were often derided. Sample hippie jokes: "One hippie, imbibing pot and acid, tells another, 'Hey, man, turn on the radio.' So the other hippie walks across the room and says, 'Hey, radio, you're sexy!'" "A hippie, high on drugs, is stopped by a policeman for driving in the wrong direction on a one-way street. 'Didn't you see the arrows?' the policeman asks. 'Hell, man,' the hippie replies, 'I didn't even see the Indians!'" "A cannibal restaurant charges twice as much for a hippie dinner as for a missionary dinner. Asked why, the owner says, 'Have *you* ever tried to clean a hippie?'"

HOLLYWOOD: To brainwashed TV watchers, Rolaids spells relief; but to movie buffs the world over, Hollywood spells glamour, excitement, and escape. That was especially true in the days when the major studios boasted lengthy rosters of superstars, instantly recognizable in the farthest corners of the earth. But even today, when more and more film shooting is being done "on location" (far from Hollywood) and when America's filmmaking eminence is constantly under challenge, the word "Hollywood" retains its efficacy as an evoker of pleasurable images.

The movie industry's switch from New York, where it was centered during its pioneer years, to a quiet, rural suburb of Los Angeles was dictated only in part by the area's persistently sunny weather—a cost-saver for independent filmmakers operating on a shoestring and doing most of their shooting out-of-doors. Another major lure was Hollywood's proximity to the Mexican border. Threatened with injunctions by the Motion Picture Patents Company (an association of Thomas Alva Edison and other leaders in the fledgling industry, who owned virtually all the patents required for movie making), many independents opted to relocate where they could make a quick exit from the United States to avoid punitive legal action. Some went to Cuba, where there was danger of disease, and others to Florida, which was judged too hot. Hollywood seemed the ideal solution. After 1913, it became the national—and, then, international—movie capital.

The word "movies" was first applied by the earliest Hollywood residents to filmmakers (not their product) because actors, directors, and cameramen were always bustling about, disrupting the even tenor of everyday life. Sabotage and violence were frequent during the movie industry's formative years. In 1913, while filming his first movie, *The Squaw Man,* Cecil B. deMille toted a loaded six-gun—and it was not intended for goof-offs like the aide in a legendary gag who, after hundreds of actors and animals have gone through their elab-

orate paces amid toppling buildings, shouts "Ready when you are,
C. B.!"

HOPE: Project HOPE, an acronym for Health Opportunity for
People Everywhere, was founded in 1958 by New York-born Dr.
William B. Walsh with $150 in seed money. During the next two
years, $3,500,000 was raised to refit the 15,000-ton Navy hospital ship
U.S.S. *Consolation,* originally an ugly, gray vessel tagged the *Marine
Walrus.* Painted a gleaming white and rechristened the S.S. *Hope,* it
became the world's first peacetime hospital ship.

American doctors, nurses, and technologists were invited to come
aboard for voyages to developing nations, where they could use their
expertise to heal the sick and train native medical specialists. More
than a thousand doctors and nurses volunteered for the 250 medical
berths. The first sailing was from San Francisco on September 22,
1960. Destinations: Indonesia and Vietnam. Some of the patients had
never seen a white face.

The S.S. *Hope*'s final voyage, in 1974, was to Maceio, Brazil. The
ship was retired because it became too costly to operate and its visits
had been limited to countries with adequate harbor and docking
facilities, but land-based HOPE programs continue. Fifty nations
have received HOPE's help, the most recent Swaziland.

HOT DOG: The frankfurter is an import from Frankfurt, Germany, where members of the butchers' guild created and named it in
1852. Its shape reputedly was inspired by one butcher's pet, a dachshund. In America "dachshund sausages" were avidly gobbled up.
They were renamed "hot dogs," according to one story, because a New
York newspaper cartoonist couldn't spell "dachshund."

Baseball, another American innovation, and hot dogs are inextri-
cably interlinked. According to the legend mentioned above, their
christening occurred at the New York Polo Grounds in April 1900.
Because it was a cold day, concessionaire Harry Stevens told his
vendors to shout, "Get your dachshund sausages while they're red
hot." Hearst cartoonist Tad Dorgan, in the press box, heard the yells
and began sketching dachshund sandwiches barking at each other. A
notoriously bad speller, he scribbled an easier phrase on his drawing:
"hot dog." The hefty home-run hitter Babe Ruth was so fond of the
heated canines that he once ate a dozen of them during a game and had
to be rushed to a stomach pump.

Not all of the early vendors approved of the "hot dog" nomenclature. Some felt it suggested that one ingredient was dog meat. In 1913,
the Coney Island Chamber of Commerce briefly banned the phrase,
announcing that thereafter a hot dog would be called a "Coney."
Hot-dog buffs barked back.

Technically, a hot dog merits that terminology, at home or abroad, only when it is ensconced in a roll. That marriage was first consummated in 1883 by a St. Louis sausage peddler, from Bavaria, named Antoine Feuchtwanger. Because customers at his small stand found his sausages too hot to handle, Feuchtwanger first lent them gloves but, then, decided that nonreturnable rolls were more practical. A rival claimant to the title of "Father of the Hot Dog" is Charles Feltman, a pushcart peddler who sold frankfurters in toasted rolls on the Coney Island boardwalk in the 1890s. Nathan's, the world's most famous hot doggery, was started in Coney Island in 1916 by Nathan Handwerker, who reputedly halved the going price of ten cents on the advice of a couple of aspiring entertainers, Eddie Cantor and Jimmy Durante.

HULA HOOP: This category requires a bit of fudging to make it fit our overall theme, as does the yo-yo. Three-foot bamboo rings, previously used only in Australian gym classes, were becoming popular with other Aussies in 1957, when Richard P. Knerr and Arthur K. (Spud) Melin, the owners of the Wham-O Manufacturing Company—the San Gabriel, California, novelty firm that also popularized the Frisbee (see FRISBEE)—first heard about the new fun phenomenon. After testing hoops made of scrap wood on their own and other kids plus cocktail-party guests, they ordered full speed ahead on the production of brightly colored polyethelene plastic Hula Hoops, which sold for $1.98 apiece and cost about fifty cents to make. In 1958, this colorful American version of the Australian gimcrack whetted an international hunger that the hula hoop and its copycat U.S. cousins, Spin-a-Hoop, Hoop Zing, and Hooper Dooper, couldn't sate. It was hoop, hoop, hooray—and away, around the world. Not only children gyrated. Japan's Prime Minister Kishi received a "hura hoopu" as a sixty-second birthday gift. Jordan's queen mother, Zaine, took one home with her. A Belgian expedition, about to leave for Antarctica, ordered twenty. Industrialists in several countries complained that too much plastic tubing was being diverted from important uses. Jacques de-Saint-Phalle, a Paris manufacturer of plastic tubes for hospitals and laboratories, drafted novelist Francoise Sagan to pose for a photo, proving that not even intellectuals were immune; but the euphoria induced by mounting profits was lessened by the fear that the pelvic movements of shapely customers would draw clerical censure. A Polish publication deplored that country's poor record in "Hula-Hoop progress." In Germany, the former world heavyweight champion Max Schmeling and other celebrities twirled what the Germans called *Swing Reifen, Sport Reifen, Hula Reifen,* or *Hulahupp.* A store in Hanover boosted sales by delivering hoops after dark—in brown paper wrappers?—to childless couples reluctant to be seen carrying them home. In sold-out Tokyo department stores, queues formed for "rainchecks." In Geneva, a new word emerged to express surprise: "Hula-la!" Almost everywhere an old word was evoked by slipped disks and aching backs: "Ouch!"

HYBRID CORN: American geneticist George Harrison Shull (1874-1954) made possible vast expansion of the world's food supply by his experiments with hybrid corn. Today, virtually all corn grown in the developed countries, 20 percent of China's rice, and superior varieties of tomatoes, spinach, cucumbers, and other vegetables come from seed derived by crossbreeding unrelated strains.

Shull's first plantings of corn in 1904 reflected no particular interest in that grain. He merely wanted to develop an interesting way to illustrate Mendel's laws of inheritance for visitors to the Station for Experimental Evolution at Cold Spring Harbor, New York.

I

ICE-CREAM CONE: Although ice cream's origins go back several thousand years, America can claim the ice-cream cone as one of its more mouthwatering, and practical, innovations. There are conflicting claims to its invention. A special mold for cones was patented by the Italian immigrant Italo Marcioni of New Jersey on December 13, 1903; but there is general agreement that the baked cone, that convenient and tasty conveyance for ice cream, did not achieve popularity until the Louisiana Purchase Exposition in St. Louis the following year. Ernest A. Hamwi, an immigrant from Damascus, obtained a permit to sell zalabia (wafer-thin Persian waffles topped with sugar or jam) to exposition visitors. A few steps away another concessionaire sold ice cream in small dishes. According to one story, on a warm day when Hamwi found little demand for his hot waffles, his neighbor ran out of dishes. In a moment of inspiration, Hamwi rolled a zalabia into a cornucopia and his fellow vendor added a scoopful of ice cream.

Another version is that customers themselves decided that there was a natural affinity between the adjacent waffles and ice cream and started buying the one and requesting that it be topped with the other. Hamwi noticed that the result was sometimes on the messy side, with ice cream dripping off the flat waffle, and began shaping his cornucopias. Either way, the idea caught on, and soon, numerous stands were offering the "world's fair cornucopia." Hamwi, who later established first the Cornucopia Waffle Company and, then, the Missouri Cone Company, gets the nod as the cone's creator from the International Association of Ice Cream Manufacturers, the National Geographic Society, and assorted historians.

A more romantic tale credits an anonymous inamorata of Charles E. Menches. Menches, who sold ice-cream sandwiches at the fair, supposedly gave the young woman two tokens of his affection: an ice-cream sandwich and a bouquet. Since she had nothing in which to hold the flowers, Menches's miss lifted the sandwich's top layer and rolled it into a makeshift vase. What was left of the sandwich, according to this legend, was reshaped into the world's first ice-cream cone. In 1912, Frederick A. Bruckman of Portland, Oregon, invented an automatic cone maker that was purchased by cone companies all over the country.

ICE-CREAM SODA: Claims to the invention of the ice-cream soda have come from numerous directions, all of them American. Chambers of Commerce have touted local talent in Texas, Massachusetts, Nebraska, Michigan, and Colorado; but documents unearthed by Carl J. Palmer, then executive secretary of the Soda Fountain Manufacturers Association, for a definitive 1947 history of the soda fountain industry, name Robert M. Green as the man, Philadelphia as the place, and October 1874 as the time. Green, a concessionaire at the semicentennial celebration of Philadelphia's Franklin Institute, offered a single soda-fountain drink from a three-foot-square dispenser. He did a brisk business with a blend of sweet cream, syrup, and carbonated water. Too brisk, because one day he ran out of cream. His spur-of-the-moment inspiration was to substitute ice cream. The first customers for the new concoction were so congratulatory that Green retained the dollop of ice cream. His receipts zoomed from six dollars a day to more than six hundred dollars. When he died in 1920, after making a fortune manufacturing soda fountains, his will specified that the inscription over his grave should read "originator of the ice cream soda." Two years after Green's first ice-cream soda, James W. Tufts paid fifty thousand dollars for the exclusive right to peddle ice-cream sodas at the Philadelphia Centennial in 1876 marking the 100th anniversary of the signing of the Declaration of Independence.

In 1893, an American magazine characterized the ice-cream soda as "the national beverage." By then it had crossed the Atlantic, as attested by a chapter in a book published that year, *Soda Fountain Beverages,* by a British analytical chemist, G. H. Dubelle, American clerics viewed with alarm the emergence of yet another temptation-causing taste treat. As late as 1890, a minister in Newport, Vermont, inveighed against "sucking soda" and eating ice cream on the Sabbath. Some midwestern towns banned the sale of sodas on Sundays, paving the way for . . . the next category.

ICE-CREAM SUNDAE: Evanston, Illinois; Two Rivers, Wisconsin; Ithaca, New York; Philadelphia, Pennsylvania; and an unnamed town in Connecticut are among the communities credited with first blending ice cream and syrup in the late 1890s; but it's generally agreed that the cooling confection was initially sold only on Sundays.

According to one version, when Evanston passed a law banning the sale of ice-cream sodas on Sundays because ministers complained that too many parishioners were "sucking sodas" at the neighborhood ice-cream parlor instead of going to church, soda fountain proprietors circumvented the law by offering "ice-cream Sundays"—ice-cream sodas without the soda. When such use of the Sabbath was denounced as irreverent, "Sunday" became "sundae."

According to another version, a Two Rivers youth, George Hallauer, asked the shopkeeper Ed Berner to enhance his dish of ice cream with a dribble of the chocolate syrup used in sodas. Berner began selling "ice cream with syrup" for the same nickel he charged for ice cream alone. George Giffy, who owned an ice-cream parlor in nearby Manitowoc, was persuaded by his customers to follow suit but decided that he could afford to offer the new dish only as a Sunday loss leader. When he found the dish was profitable, after all, he began advertising "ice-cream sundaes," changing the spelling so that prospective customers wouldn't think the delicacy was available only one day a week.

Still another version credits a small Ithaca pharmacy that did little soda fountain business on weekdays because it was across the street from a busy hotel bar. On Sundays, however, when the bar was closed, devout drinkers ordered ice-cream sodas to cool their alcohol-roughened throats. One patron, complaining that the fizzing of the carbonated water aggravated his hangover, urged the pharmacist to eliminate the soda. Result: "The Sunday Special." By 1900, midwestern salesmen were peddling tulip-shaped dishes especially designed for sundaes.

IDENTIKIT: The Identikit, consisting of five hundred photographs of assorted facial features, which, when assembled at the suggestion of victims and viewers, help identify the perpetrators of crimes, was conceived by a Los Angeles detective, Hugh C. McDonald, shortly after World War II. McDonald, assigned to the L. A. Identification Bureau, cut up approximately fifty thousand photos before picking the basic elements: 37 noses, 40 lips, 52 chins, 102 pairs of eyes, 130 hairlines, and various eyebrows, beards, mustaches, wrinkles, eyeglasses, and headgear. It was successfully used for the first time in February 1959, by Sheriff Peter Pitchess of the Los Angeles County Police, after the robbing of a liquor store. When an Identikit likeness, assembled with the storekeeper's help, was posted in the neighborhood, a suspect was quickly named, arrested, and convicted.

England's famed Scotland Yard and other foreign police forces subsequently adopted the U.S. system of finger-pointing face making. In March 1961, the first British use of the Identikit enabled a junior police constable stationed in Soho to recognize and arrest the murderer Edwin Albert Bush.

IN-FLIGHT MOVIE: The first airline to introduce in-flight movies on a regular basis was TWA. The initial film, shown in the first-class section during a flight from New York to Los Angeles on July 19, 1961, was the 1961 film *By Love Possessed*, with Lana Turner, Efrem Zimbalist, Jr., Jason Robards, George Hamilton, and Thomas Mitchell.

INNERSPRING MATTRESS: Leaning on a wagon one day in the 1850s, waiting to go home to the pesky chore of tightening the ropes of his lattice bed, James Liddy of Watertown, New York, fell against the spring seat of his buggy. Inspired, he hurried home and designed the American coiled bedspring. By the 1930s, beds everywhere used machine-made innerspring mattresses.

INSTANT PHOTOGRAPHY: The Polaroid Land camera, despite its name, is equally effective at sea and in the air. This revolutionary instant camera came into being during Edwin H. Land's 1943 vacation in Santa Fe, New Mexico, when Jennifer, Land's three-year-old daughter, after posing for a snapshot, asked her father how long she'd have to wait to see it and why couldn't she see it right away. That started Land thinking about the possibility of developing and printing a photograph inside a camera, and in 1947, he startled optical scientists with the first demonstration of instant photography. His Polaroid Model 95 was introduced the following year. It weighed slightly over four pounds, produced sepia-toned prints of varying quality in sixty seconds, and cost ninety dollars. After a picture was taken, the negative inside the camera was brought into contact with a positive print sheet; then both were drawn between rollers, breaking a tiny pod of jellylike chemicals.

The Polaroid 95 was an instant success. When New York's R. H. Macy and Company wangled one-month's department store exclusivity, Gimbels stealthily made out-of-town purchases and devoted a window display to the new camera—until Macy's sent "shoppers" to buy most of Gimbels' supply. Later, picture quality and speed improved, color was added, and the SX-70, introduced in 1972, became the best-selling camera ever.

Land had originally approached Kodak with his invention. When they didn't show any interest, he proceeded on his own. Later, Kodak decided to enter the fast-photo field after all, and to avoid patent infringement, sought to develop a totally dissimilar system. Land didn't agree that it was all that different and sued. In 1986, while still appealing an adverse verdict, Kodak quit the field.

Back in 1928, as an eighteen-year-old Harvard undergraduate, Land had experimented with light waves and discovered a way to polarize light and reduce glare. Nine years after dropping out of school, he founded Polaroid and submitted his process to automakers for use in sun visors and headlights. They turned it down because the polarized sheets deteriorated in heat. Polaroid manufactured sunglasses and filters with great success during World War II, but income sagged afterward. In 1947, the company lost $2 million. It needed a new product, and Land, with his new invention, had it. Like Gillette, which makes razors to sell blades, Polaroid makes cameras to sell film.

INTERCHANGEABLE PARTS: Although Westborough, Massachusetts-born Eli Whitney (1765-1825) is renowned as the inventor of the cotton gin (*see* COTTON GIN), which in 1793 enabled a single operator to separate fifty pounds of short-staple upland cotton daily from its seeds, another major Whitney contribution had nothing to do with cotton. In 1798, foreseeing costly litigation involving infringements on his cotton-gin patent (his claim was not validated until 1807), Whitney obtained a government contract to supply ten thousand muskets, using a system he had devised for manufacturing interchangeable parts. His technology was so superior that when Samuel Colt (*see* REVOLVER) received a rush army order for one thousand of his six-guns for use in the Mexican War, he subcontracted a substantial part of the order to the factory Whitney established in an area near New Haven now known as Whitneyville. Whitney built nearly all the factory's tools and equipment, including what is considered the first successful milling machine. His system, enabling workers with little skill to assemble a complex product, effected a revolutionary change in international industrialization. Though the cotton gin brought Whitney fame, the musket factory brought him financial gain. Whitney's principle of interchangeable parts was refined by Henry M. Leland, who used close machining to make the parts fit with absolute precision. In 1913, Henry Ford linked interchangeable-parts and Ransom E. Olds's assembly-line techniques (*see* MASS PRODUCTION, AUTOMOBILE).

IRON LUNG: An 1892 version of the iron lung was Alexander Graham Bell's snug-fitting metal "vacuum jacket," conceived as an aid for premature babies and drowning victims. A bellows pumped air in and out, alternately squeezing and releasing the wearer's chest. However, the first experimental model of a body-encasing respirator, designed to aid infantile paralysis victims, was assembled in 1927 by Harvard University's Professor Philip Drinker from bits and pieces of cast-off machinery, including two household vacuum cleaners for alternating positive and negative pressure. Manufactured by Boston's

Warren E. Collins, it was first used at Boston Children's Hospital on October 12, 1928, for a small girl suffering from respiratory failure.

The Drinker Respirator scored its first overseas success in England in September 1932 after a night nurse at the Wingfield Morris Orthopedic Hospital near Oxford noticed that a seventeen-year-old polio patient wasn't breathing properly. An American member of the hospital staff, Dr. T. C. Thompson, remembered reading that a Drinker Respirator had been sent to London for experimental purposes. After numerous telephone calls, it was located and rushed to Oxford by truck. The patient was kept alive by artificial respiration until the iron lung's arrival. After several weeks inside the lung, he was able to end total dependence on its breathing mechanism. As the result of a letter the grateful teenager wrote to the *London Times,* Lord Nuffield offered an iron lung to every hospital in the British Empire.

The first person compelled to spend an entire postpolio lifetime, from 1936 until 1954, in a respirator was Frederick B. Smite, Jr., the son of a wealthy American railroad executive. After contracting polio in Peking, he was brought back to the United States in a respirator and, still encased, was transported in a private train, accompanied by a special medical staff. Smite, who subsequently spent a considerable portion of his wealth making respirator treatment available for polio victims unable to afford it, came to be known as "The Man in the Iron Lung." The first artificial heart-lung machine, for use during surgery, was invented in 1953 by the surgeon John Heysham Gibbons.

IVORY SOAP: The world's first buoyant bar of soap was the result of a serendipitous 1878 accident. The Ohio operator of a Procter and Gamble soap-stirring machine went to lunch without pushing the "off" switch. When he returned, the soap mixture had been beaten to a froth so light that chunks containing air bubbles were floating about. Instead of reboiling the "spoiled" batch, someone suggested shaping and shipping it. Customers later requested "the floating soap," so the original formula was altered to make the mishap standard operating procedure.

When originally marketed, the product was identified as White Soap, but Harley Procter, a son of William Procter, cofounder of Procter and Gamble, rechristened it in 1879 after hearing his minister intone, during a reading of the 456th Psalm, "All thy garments smell of myrrh, and aloes, and cassia, out of the ivory palaces, whereby they have made thee glad." Harley also had the novel notion of carving a groove in the middle of each laundry-size bar so that housewives could break it into convenient toilet-size halves. He ordered the soap chemically analyzed, to ascertain the percentages of useless impurities; and after getting the report—uncombined alkali, 0.11; carbonates, 0.38;

mineral matter, 0.17—coined the potent slogan, "99 44/100 percent pure."

An adept advertiser, Procter promoted the idea of purchasing a dozen bars of Ivory at a time and keeping one handy in every room. To dramatize his product's mildness, he sent shopkeepers life-size posters of "the Ivory baby." He submitted preprinted full-color ads for insertion into magazines that had previously employed color on only their covers. He offered reproductions, suitable for framing, of paintings of babies that well-known artists created for Ivory Soap ads. He awarded prizes for verses extolling the product. By the time Harley Procter resigned, one year earlier than the age (forty-five years) deadline he had set for himself as a young man, and left Cincinnati to live in his wife's home state of Massachusetts, the Ivory Soap bar had become the cornerstone for one of the world's richest and most pervasive industrial empires.

J

JACKPOT: The slot machine dubbed "the one-armed bandit," one of the more lucrative lures in gambling casinos around the world, dates back to the 1880s, when a number of coin-operated devices paid off in money or in tokens that could be cashed in for drinks or merchandise. To make these Lady Luck-challenging devices seem more wholesome, manufacturers adopted patriotic and similarly ingratiating motifs. After Charles Frey built the "Liberty Bell" in San Francisco in 1889, the slots in general were referred to as "bells." To avoid difficulty with communities' antigambling laws, the gambling devices ostensibly vended gum or candy, a pretense reflected in the slots' use of fruit and gum symbols as well as "Liberty bells." The machines' popularity soared in the mid-1920s with the invention of the jackpot, which produced a deluge of coins for the player who achieved a particularly fortuitous alignment of symbols. Chicago, the nation's coin-operated machine-manufacturing mecca, began installing jackpots in bars, restaurants, drugstores, and even small-town filling stations throughout the country. The early machines were rigged to pay off as little as 60 percent of the money deposited, but that was subsequently upped to 80 percent.

During Prohibition, gangsters began supplying speakeasies with slot machines as well as illegal liquor, and nickel-and-dime gambling became a source of huge profits and political corruption. Reform groups, startled by the revelations resulting from federal investigations, demanded new laws, and the Chicago-based coin-machine industry, already judged guilty by association, seconded the motion, striving to prevent its pinball machines and jukeboxes from being linked with the unsavory jackpots. The Johnson Act of 1951 prohibited interstate shipment of gambling equipment to states where gambling was illegal. Ten years later, the Illinois legislature banned the out-of-state sale of all Illinois-manufactured gambling equipment. After two years, this prohibition was revoked and all-out production resumed in Chicago. Long Island's Kenilworth Systems Corporation has developed a device that enables slot-machine addicts to insert a special credit card instead of coins.

JACUZZI: The whirlpool sitz bath bearing the name of its inventor evokes images of jet-set opulence; of sybarites steeping in warm, muscle-soothing water. Actually, it was created in the early 1950s by a concerned father who wanted to ease the discomfort of his rheumatoid arthritis-plagued young son. The father was Candido Jacuzzi (1903-1986), one of seven brothers from Italy who jointly operated Jacuzzi Brothers, a Berkeley, California, firm then manufacturing industrial pumps, filters, and water systems and nonindustrial swimming pool equipment.

While son Kenny was receiving hydrotherapy, Candido noticed that the water jet principle involved was not unlike that used by the siblings' pumps. He had the company's engineers whomp up a portable whirlpool that could be used in a bathtub, enabling Kenny to end his hospital commuting. Several years later, when this pioneer Jacuzzi was made available to nonrelatives, it was touted as an invention that "grew out of a father's love."

Initially, it was sold only at medical supply stores to victims of rheumatism, bursitis, and other muscular maladies, but as word spread about the pump's salubrious effects, athletes and mere relaxation-seekers also became buyers. To glamorize what had previously been considered only a medical aid, Jacuzzi publicized paid testimonials by Jayne Mansfield and Randolph Scott. A Jacuzzi also figured prominently in a 1966 movie starring Jack Lemmon and Walter Matthau, *The Fortune Cookie.*

In 1968, a Jacuzzi grandson, Roy Jacuzzi, designed the first self-contained, aesthetically pleasing whirlpool tub. It became a hot item in the mid-1970s. Richard Nixon and Gerald Ford added a Jacuzzi to the list of presidential perquisites. A torrid tome, *The Sensuous Woman,* endorsed it as a source of sexual pleasure. Kenny Jacuzzi, whose aches and pains inspired it, helped sell Papa's pain-easer as head of the company's Italy-based European division. Because of intrafamily dissension, however, the company was sold in 1979 to Kidde Inc., for $70 million.

JAZZ: Ferdinand Joseph (Jelly Roll) Morton (*see* JAZZ BAND) claimed that he coined the word in New Orleans in 1902, to give his new kind of music an identity separate from that of its black predecessor, ragtime. Historians challenged the claim, asserting that the new sound lacked a label until it was christened in Chicago about 1916. Bandleader George Morrison challenged the challengers, insisting that he was playing "jazz" in Colorado as early as 1911 and had signs on his car's running boards advertising his jazz orchestra. The word "jass" first appeared in print in the *Chicago Herald* of May 1, 1916, referring to a performance by Johnny Stein's "New Orleans Jass Band," the forerunner of the Original Dixieland Jazz Band. "Jass" was the common spelling until *The New York Times* ran a January 1917 ad for "The Jasz Band." The following month *The Times* spelled it "Jazz Band."

In a 1919 Swiss periodical, it was predicted, after audiences were enthralled during London concerts by the artistry of Will Marion Cook's Southern Syncopated Orchestra and especially by the clarinet tootling of young Sidney Bechet, that Bechet's approach to authentically American music represented "the mainstream along which the whole world will be swept tomorrow." The comment was prophetic because the following decade became identified as the Jazz Age. Another ten years and names like Louis Armstrong, Duke Ellington, and Benny Goodman were household words around the globe. Fifty years later, jazz, under many labels—Dixieland, New Orleans, swing, bebop, cool, avant-garde (and later, progressive)—had been universally accepted as music far more important than something merely to dance to. Other categorizations that have been assigned to the Afro-American styles that have emerged from the rural South and the urban North include ragtime, blues, rhythm and blues, gospel, country (née hillbilly), and rock 'n' roll (a blend of numerous earlier ingredients).

Jazz developed in the latter part of the nineteenth century from black work songs, field shouts, sorrow songs, hymns, and spirituals (with predominantly African harmonic, rhythmic, and melodic elements) and spread from New Orleans to Chicago, Kansas City, New York City, and the West Coast. Ragtime and the blues were seminal elements. Jazz, in general, was characterized by exuberant improvisation. The classically trained Scott Joplin was the first to commit ragtime to score sheets and to insist that his compositions be performed as written.

For many years the U.S. State Department sponsored international tours by jazz virtuosi and the "Voice of America" beamed it to non-American buffs. In Tokyo's jazz coffeehouses, java-drinkers request selections from well-stocked jazz libraries, and it is generally conceded that U.S. jazz composers and players are accorded greater respect in other countries. For instance, French admirers of Bechet pay homage via a monument in Juan-les-Pins and a street in Nancy. Louis Armstrong is similarly saluted by a statue in Nice.

JAZZ BAND: Usually credited as the original jass, jasz, or jazz band (*see* JAZZ) is the New Orleans combo formed by black trumpeter Buddy Bolden about 1900. It included cornet, clarinet, trombone, violin, guitar, string bass, and drums. A recorded demonstration of the Bolden style made by Bunk Johnson in the 1930s indicates that it had the distinctive characteristics of pure jazz as well as marching and ragtime elements. According to one of Bolden's contemporaries, his style, at variance with previous black music making, was inspired by a church visit. Bolden's band continued to play New Orleans gigs until 1907, when its leader went mad and had to be institutionalized.

The first jazz orchestration was by Ferdinand Joseph (Jelly Roll) Morton, who claimed that he was the "inventor" of jazz and that his first jazz orchestration, "New Orleans Blues," was composed in 1902. His "Jelly Roll Blues," composed in 1905, was the first jazz orchestration ever printed. It was published in Chicago in 1915. In June 1916, members of Johnny Stein's Dixie Jass Band quit after a dispute with their leader and organized the Original Dixieland Jazz Band. That band, led by the cornetist Nick LaRocca and including the trombonist Emile Christian, the clarinetist Larry Shields, the pianist Russel Robinson, and the drummer Tony Sbarbaro, made the world's first jazz recording in 1917. Seeking new worlds to conquer, the Original Dixieland Jazz Band made its European debut at the London Hippodrome on April 7, 1919, in a musical revue, "Joy Bells." The band was fired after a single performance at the insistence of the show's star, George Robey, who feared playing second fiddle to the invading instrumentalists. They were quickly rehired for a post-"Joy Bells" Palladium stint, and Lord Donegall, a jazz buff, arranged for a command performance before King George V. The band was also honored by being invited to perform at London's Victory Ball.

When it left England in July 1920, the Original Dixieland Jazz Band left behind the beginnings of a British jazz movement and, at the dock, a shotgun-toting Lord Harrington, who furiously asseverated that leader LaRocca had despoiled his debutante daughter.

JEEP: The small motor vehicle that became familiar the world over during World War II derived its name from the initials G. P., an abbreviation for "general purpose," its official designation. It had a 45-horsepower four-cylinder motor, 80-inch wheelbase, ¼-ton capacity, and 4-wheel drive. The latter characteristic enabled it to surmount such battlefield obstacles as ice or mud. Designed in July 1940 at U.S. Army request by Karl K. Fabst, consulting engineer for the Bantam Car Company in Butler, Pennsylvania, the prototype was completed two months later and tested at Camp Holabird in Maryland. The oldest surviving jeep, the seventh of seventy preproduction models subsequently ordered, is enshrined at the Smithsonian Institution in Washington. After both Ford and Willys-Overland submitted prototype jeeps for the acceptance trials, the Willys version was approved; but then, both companies manufactured it. The versatile vehicle was affectionately dubbed "the jeep" by GIs. However, the word "jeep" had been used in the late 1930s by other manufacturers of general purpose vehicles because of the popularity of a comic-strip character, Eugene the Jeep, who "could do almost everything."

The English military found the jeep especially useful for airborne assaults because it fit conveniently into a glider transport. Nearly 649,000 jeeps were produced during World War II. The Willys-Overland plant in Toledo spewed out one every eighty seconds. Redesigned for civilian use, Willys' "Universal Jeep" went into production in September 1945. In 1985, sans fanfare, the Pentagon announced that the military version of the jeep was getting a twenty-five thousand dollar replacement, the "High Mobility Multipurpose Wheeled Vehicle (H.M.M.W.V.)." Army brass hopes it will be called the "Hum-Vee," rather than "hummer," which rhymes with "bummer." In January 1986, American Motors replaced the CJ (for civilian Jeep) with a fancier, smoother-riding YJ (for Yuppie Jeep?). In Manila, minibuses are called "jeepneys," an amalgam of "jeep" and "jitney."

JEHOVAH'S WITNESSES: The sect founded at the end of the nineteenth century by Pittsburgh, Pennsylvania-born Charles Taze Russell (1852-1916), a haberdasher who quit the Congregational church because he rejected its doctrine of eternal punishment, claims approximately two million members, all considered ministers of the gospel and about 75 percent of them living outside America. Witnesses are active in virtually every country. Until 1931, when the cult was renamed by Russell's successor, Joseph Franklin Rutherford, Jehovah's Witnesses were called Russellites. An alternate name is the Watch Tower Bible and Tract Society. Abroad, the movement is usually known as the International Bible Students' Association.

Russell's views were expounded in an 1872 booklet, "The Object and Manner of Our Lord's Return," that announced that Christ's Second Coming would occur, without public awareness, in the fall of 1874 and that it would be followed by a forty-year "millennial age," culminating in 1914 (the year in which World War I began) when Jesus would cast out Satan, thus precipitating cataclysmic events. Witnesses believe that the Battle of Armageddon between Christ and Satan is imminent and that after its happy resolution, with good triumphing over evil, exactly 144,000 humans will proceed to heaven, while repentant sinners, granted a second chance for salvation, enjoy paradise on earth. Witnesses believe that theirs is the only true faith and the only reliable path to salvation. They have no churches but convene in meeting places invariably dubbed Kingdom Hall. The organization's headquarters were moved to Brooklyn in 1909.

Convinced that governments are tools of Satan, the Witnesses refuse to salute any nation's flag, bear arms in war, participate in governmental affairs, or permit blood transfusions. Their snooting of saluting was upheld by a 1943 U.S. Supreme Court decision. Their views are expounded in the *Watchtower*, *Awake!*, and other publications and by the nonstop door-to-door proselytizing of the "ministers."

Commonly addressed as "Pastor Russell," though he was never ordained in any church, Russell traveled and preached all over the world and died in Pampa, Texas, during one of his tract treks.

JELL-O: A gelatin dessert was patented in 1845 by Peter Cooper, inventor of the "Tom Thumb" locomotive, but he did nothing to promote it. In 1895, Pearl B. Wait, a carpenter in Le Roy, New York, who augmented his income by making patent medicines, decided to augment it even more by cashing in on the popular trend toward packaged foods. He created a tastier version of Cooper's concoction, for which his wife, May Doris Wait, suggested a snappy name: Jell-O. The Waits waited and waited for customers, but few appeared. In 1899, they sold out for $450 to an enterprising entrepreneur, Orator Frank Woodward, a school dropout at twelve who by twenty had started a business of his own, selling balls for use as shooting targets and cement nest eggs chemically treated to kill lice on laying hens. Woodward also merchandised several patent medicines; Raccoon Corn Plasters; and a roasted cereal coffee substitute, Grain-O. Grain-O and Jell-O may have seemed predestined stablemates. At first, sales were so slow that Woodward offered to sell the rights to Jell-O to his plant superintendent for thirty-five dollars. The offer was declined, to Woodward's subsequent relief, for suddenly, spurred on by intensive advertising, Jell-O jelled.

By 1902, sales had soared to $250,000; by 1906, nearly $1,000,000. To drum up trade, Woodward dispatched nattily dressed salesmen, first, in elegant horse-drawn rigs and, later, in vans emblazoned with the Jell-O name to scout out picnics, church socials, and other gatherings where they could demonstrate preparation of the dessert and dole out samples. One great impetus to sales was the distribution of as many as fifteen million copies a year of a Jell-O recipe book containing the favorites of celebrities like the actress Ethel Barrymore and the diva Ernestine Schumann-Heink. The booklets, illustrated by artists like Maxfield Parrish, Norman Rockwell, and Kewpie-creator Rose O'Neill (*see* KEWPIE), were printed in virtually every language, including Yiddish. In 1923, Woodward's Genesee Pure Food Company was renamed Jell-O Company. Its merger two years later with the Postum Cereal Company was a factor in the creation of the General Foods Corporation.

JUKEBOX: Manufacturers prefer to call the jukebox a "coin-operated phonograph," perhaps, because "juke" has unsavory overtones. The Gullahs, southeastern blacks, coined "jook house" for "roadhouse." Elsewhere in coastal communities "juke" was a slang term for disorderly. Authorities trace the song-for-a-nickel (or -dime or -quarter) dispenser back to the time Thomas Alva Edison attached a coin mechanism to his eighteen dollar "talking machine."

The first commercial jukebox, an electrically operated Edison phonograph with four listening tubes activated by separate nickel-in-the-slot devices, was installed in San Francisco's Palais Royal Saloon by phonograph manufacturer Louis Glass in 1889. The preselective juke first surfaced in Grand Rapids, Michigan, in 1905. The first disk-playing juke was manufactured in Chicago a year later. Interest dipped in 1910 but re-zoomed when electrostatic speakers were introduced in 1927. Chicago's Wurlitzer Company entered the field in 1933 as Prohibition ended and taverns became numerous. The first light-up model was offered by Wurlitzer in 1937, and other manufacturers promptly dittoed.

After World War II, some two million jukes—mainly Wurlitzer, Seeburg, Rock-Ola, and Rowe—were in operation in the United States alone. Collectors hail as the all-time classic the Art Deco Wurlitzer Model 1015 Commercial Phonograph, still shown four decades later in TV commercials and NBC's "Cheers" series. The jukebox's popularity peaked in the 1950s when it could be found in almost every tavern, soda fountain, pizza parlor, diner, and truck stop. Its subsequent decline was blamed on the proliferation of fast-food outlets, eager to speed patrons on their way; the competition of pinball and electronic games; portable radios; cassette recorders; discos; piped-in FM music; and more recently, music videos, plus urban renewal, which hastened the demise of many neighborhood taverns.

In 1974 Wurlitzer stopped production, but a year later, Seeburg introduced a 160-selection model. In recent years, half of a dwindling supply of new jukes has been sold abroad. Collectors everywhere (jukebox junkies) still vie for old models.

K

KAZOO: Should the kazoo, which produces a buzzing sound when the kazooist's humming causes vibration in a membrane (a bit of plastic, waxpaper or tissue paper), be classified as a nonmusical instrument or as a musical noninstrument?

Reputedly invented in Macon, Georgia, in 1850, it is still a favorite of would-be music-makers in all age groups, from small-fry to senior citizen. At last report, the world's only manufacturer of metal kazoos—an Eden, New York, firm appropriately named the Kazoo Company—was selling about a million kazoos annually worldwide at prices ranging from ninety cents to four dollars. Plastic kazoos are produced in quantity by a harmonica company, Hohner, Inc.

Kazoos come in various configurations, but they all work on the same principle. The tones produced by a saxophone-shaped kazoo and a trombone-shaped kazoo are identical. Some models, like those in the shape of whiskey bottles that were used to celebrate the demise of Prohibition, are no longer available. The Kazoo Company claims that it is "the one and only original" manufacturer of the cigar-shaped "King" kazoo, first produced in 1915 at the same location on the same twenty-seven cast-iron metal presses. The company's president, Maurice Spectoroff, an engineer who once hosted an opera show on Buffalo radio, donates kazoos to schools where deaf students are taught to speak by feeling vibrations.

A Kaminsky International Kazoo Quartet, consisting of five members, has performed in concert at New York's Town Hall and Alice Tully Hall and as a warm-up for musical programs featuring the "classical" compositions of "P.D.Q. Bach," (Peter Schickele). A 54,500-person kazoo chorus greeted 1986 in Rochester, New York.

KELLOGG'S: An earlier entry under BREAKFAST CEREAL merits separate consideration because of its unusual paternity. Maternity, really. Kellogg's, with plants in twenty-one countries, is a consequence of the crusade for purity of mind and body conducted by Sister Eileen Harmon White. Sister White, a dedicated Seventh-Day Adventist, decided that she had a special mission in life after a futile nightlong vigil on a Maine hilltop with coreligionists who were waiting to be yanked into heaven in laundry baskets. Her postponed ascension, Sister White was convinced, meant she still had holy work to do. Subsequent revelations led her to Battle Creek, Michigan, where, in 1866, she opened a sanitarium, the Western Health Forum Institute. There, to cultivate spiritual thoughts and stifle sexual surges, she recommended a diet of bread and water, augmented by fruits and vegetables. The bread, to be eaten sparingly, was the kind devised by health-food pioneer Sylvester Graham (see GRAHAM CRACKER).

In 1876, Sister White chose as her spa's director Dr. John Harvey Kellogg, who had edited the institute's magazine, *Good Health*, before enrolling at New York's Bellevue Medical College. Kellogg changed the institute's name to Battle Creek Sanitarium and hired his younger brother, William Keith (W.K.), as business manager. The first patients included Warren Gamaliel Harding, later to become the twenty-ninth president of the United States, and the business tycoons Henry Ford, John D. Rockefeller, and Harvey Firestone. Culinary experiments to make the spa's vegetarian menus more palatable accidentally produced wheat flakes, which patients enjoyed with milk and sugar. After going home, many began requesting supplies of the tasty flakes, so Kellogg created the Sanitas Food Company to produce wheat, rice, and corn varieties. W.K. improved the corn flakes by discarding the tough kernel, using only the heart, and adding malt. In 1906, he started his own firm, W. K. Kellogg's Toasted Corn Flake Company. To differentiate it from forty-two other Battle Creek-based cereal companies, he had his own signature printed on each package.

KEWPIE: The Kewpie doll, which has been produced and sold in virtually every country, is a three-dimensional representation of a pen-and-ink creation by Wilkes Barre, Pennsylvania-born Rose Cecil O'Neill (1874-1944). It first appeared with an O'Neill poem in the December 1909 *Ladies Home Journal*. The initial drawing was accompanied by a footnote that explained, "The reason why these funny, roly-poly creatures are called Kewpies is because they look like Cupids. You can tell by their little wings. Kewpie means a small Cupid, just as puppy means a small dog." Besides wings, all members of the Kewpie clan had starfish hands, angelic smiles, and a distinctive topknot. More than five thousand illustrated Kewpie stories appeared in women's magazines.

Because children kept writing for a Kewpie doll, Miss O'Neill advertised for a sculptor. Joseph Kallus, a Pratt Art Institute student, fashioned the bisque and celluloid dolls; and in 1913, O'Neill arranged to have them manufactured in nine sizes by Germany's George Borgfeldt Company. As Kewpiemania spread across the globe, Kewpies were reproduced in comic strips, cutouts, and calendars and adorned hundreds of objects, including chinaware, glassware, lamps, scarves, pillows, jewelry, and even radiator caps. The royalties made the Kewpies' mama wealthy. After her death, Kallus, who had founded the Cameo Doll Company in 1925, inherited full merchandising rights. Since 1982, vinyl Kewpies have been manufactured by the Jesco Company in California. Collectors pay considerably more for vintage examples of earlier versions, distinguished from carnival prizes and other inferior imitations by the fact that they are made of smooth, pinkish-tan bisque and not of a rough, plasterlike material.

Branson, Missouri, which became Miss O'Neill's home, is the site of a Kewpie museum at the Shepherd of the Hills Farm and is the headquarters of the International Rose O'Neill Club, founded in 1967. Foreign chapters once existed in Norway and Germany, but only Japan's remains active. Club members subscribe to Miss O'Neill's philosophy: "Do good deeds in a funny way. The world needs to laugh, or at least to smile more than it does."

KILROY: Many non-Americans became aware of an invisible American during World War II. Graffiti that appeared in every part of the world visited by GIs proclaimed, "Kilroy was here." Often the phrase was accompanied by a drawing of a cartoon character, visible from his big and pendulous nose up, peeping from behind a wall.

"Kilroy was here" was not only an export; it was also lettered on the Statue of Liberty's torch, on high girders of New York's George Washington Bridge, and in similarly "inaccessible" places from Maine to California. It appeared almost magically in various battle zones. The ubiquitous message-writer seemed to reach fought-over objectives before anybody else. When the Fourth Infantry Division stormed Utah Beach at Normandy, Kilroy's name was emblazoned on a German pillbox. Concurrently, at Omaha Beach, more than ten miles away, the First Infantry Division found his name on another troublesome pillbox. Kilroy's terse claim surfaced throughout the Pacific—in Australia, New Guinea, the Philippines, and hundreds of remote islands. American troops sifting through the rubble of Hiroshima, the first A-bomb target, found a variation on the theme: "Kilroy doesn't want to be here!" When Truman, Churchill, and Stalin had to respond to calls of nature in a top-security restroom, during the 1943 Potsdam Conference, they discovered that Kilroy had been called sooner.

The army claimed Kilroy, saying he was a GI who first began

leaving his trademark in Africa. The air force counterclaimed that one of its sergeants was responsible for the greetings that repeatedly awaited infantrymen. So many people wrote to the U.S. Army's adjutant general in Washington, asking, "Who's Kilroy?" that he had a search made through the files, only to announce in 1946, "As far as we're concerned, Kilroy doesn't exist." Many ex-GIs demurred, insisting that they knew the man—in fact, many men—responsible for the legend.

The *real* Kilroy may have been James I. Kilroy of Boston, a wartime shipyard inspector. To indicate that tanks, planes, ships, and assorted crates had been properly checked off, he made it a practice to chalk his name on each item. GIs constantly exposed to the name may have perpetuated it.

KING KONG: King-sized Kong, the forty-foot title star of a highly successful 1933 Hollywood film, fathered a succession of gigantic movie monsters at home and abroad, including Mighty Joe Young, Mothra, and, especially notable, Japan's repeatedly resuscitated saurian, Godzilla.

What distinguishes the gargantuan gorilla from other towering menaces (what a basketball team they'd make!) is the fact that he's a lovelorn loser. *King Kong*, good old Beauty and the Beast, became an international kitsch classic. Several scenes are indelibly etched in movie buffs' memories: Kong holding a sexy squirming sacrifice, Kong scaling the Empire State Building, Kong slapping at hostile planes like so many buzzing hornets. *King Kong* was conceived by Merian C. Cooper, a pioneer aviator and moviemaker, who correctly judged the erotic—and box-office—impact of pairing a nubile heroine and a horrendously huge and hirsute hero. *King Kong* spawned sequels, both American *(Son of Kong)* and Japanese *(King Kong Escapes)*, but not as many as Japan's 1956 *Godzilla, King of the Monsters.* (The title terrors shared billing in Japan's 1963 *King Kong vs. Godzilla*—in the United States, Kong conquered; in Japan, Godzilla was the victor.)

The 1976 remake of *King Kong* by Dino de Laurentiis was a conspicuous flop. Its most notable aspect was, perhaps, the fact that a changed movie morality permitted showing more of Jessica Lange than of Fay Wray. Both versions employed special effects plus a man in a gorilla suit. The original camouflaged Kong was Carmen Nigro, a five-foot-six-inch stuntman who used a show-biz alias, Ken Roady. Roady, who had twice accompanied the "Bring 'Em Back Alive" animal collector Frank Buck to the Malayan jungle and claimed he had studied gorillas in their natural habitat, portrayed numerous gorillas, including the title star of the 1949 variation on *King Kong,*

Mighty Joe Young. In the second U.S. coming of Kong, the man in the costume was its fabricator, the six-foot makeup man Rick Baker.

KITTY LITTER: This housebreaking, deodorizing product, a boon to cats—and their owners—everywhere, was invented in 1947 by Ed Lowe of Cassopolis, Michigan, after a neighbor lamented that she had run out of sand for her cat box. Lowe offered her some of the sawdust his father sold to factories for sopping up grease spills. It worked, but the sawdust scattered. Lowe then substituted some of his father's new line, dried pulverized clay, which absorbed even better and stayed put in the cat box. Later, deodorants were added to the kiln-dried clay granules. Lowe dreamed up the name, Kitty Litter, which—like Kleenex—identifies a single manufacturer's product but is often incorrectly used as a generic term. Before Kitty Litter, Lowe once observed, "most cats were not kept inside unless you had a hell of a constitution." Felinephobes may therefore consider the product a mixed blessing.

KLEENEX: In 1925 Kleenex and Kotex were the first Kimberly-Clark Corporation products to go on sale abroad. Today the company has manufacturing operations in 21 countries and sells its products in about 160. Both the K-C K trade names have become virtually generic words, synonyms for disposable handkerchiefs and females' sanitary napkins, but Kleenex was conceived as a cold cream-remover and Kotex as a World War I substitute for surgical cotton. The switchover to their more usual uses reflects the venerable adage that the customer is always right. Both Kleenex and Kotex stemmed from a search for ways to utilize a kind of cotton wadding.

The tissues, initially dubbed Celluwipes and then Kleenex Kerchiefs, were considered a disposable substitute for facial towels. Ads linking the product to Hollywood makeup departments, sometimes including endorsements by movie stars, claimed that Kleenex represented a "scientific way to remove cold cream." That was the thrust of most Kleenex advertising until 1930, when the manufacturer became intrigued by the number of customers who wrote saying that they used Kleenex mainly as an expendable handkerchief. To test customer preference, ads of similar size and layout, stressing dissimilar purposes, were run in January and February 1930 editions of Peoria, Illinois, newspapers, and those who wrote in response to either ad received a free box of Kleenex. When the results indicated that 60 percent of the respondents used Kleenex primarily for blowing their noses, advertising emphasis was changed. Sales promptly doubled.

In 1944, Little Lulu, a cartoon character Margaret Buell drew for the *Saturday Evening Post,* was enlisted for Kleenex sales pitches. Curtis Publishing gave its permission for Lulu's use in ads, as long as they appeared only in newspapers. A few years later, Curtis changed its mind and told Mrs. Buell she'd have to choose between the *Saturday Evening Post* and the everyday product. She opted for Kleenex, and the relationship continued for sixteen years. In the early 1950s, a not-so-little Lulu, thirty-five feet tall, stood next to a huge Kleenex box above New York's Times Square.

KODACHROME: "God" and "Man" collaborated to produce the first color-film process. Those were the nicknames of Leopold Godowsky, Jr., and Leopold Mannes, who met in 1916 as fifteen-year-old students at New York City's Riverdale Country School. Both from musical families, God and Man, respectively aspiring violinist and pianist, found they also shared an interest in photography. When together they went to what was advertised as a color movie, they decided that they could produce a more satisfactory process. The 1922 result, while God was at the University of California and Man was at Harvard, was a film that required filters and complex projection. A better solution, they decided, was to build color directly into the film emulsion itself. Eastman Kodak offered technical support and, in 1930, invited them to join the company's staff. Three years later, they produced a two-color slide film for home use, which Kodak was eager to introduce pronto, but the inventors persuaded the company to hold off until they could develop a film containing all three primary colors. That goal was finally achieved and Eastman Kodak introduced Kodachrome on April 15, 1935. Faster versions were added in 1961 and 1962.

Kodachrome is the only color film that is black and white when exposed. The color is produced when dyes are added, layer by layer.

L

LASER: The "maser," an acronym for "microwave amplification by stimulated emission of radiation," begat the "laser," alias "light amplification by stimulated emission of radiation."

In the 1950s, Charles Hard Townes, a Greenville, South Carolina-born physicist, developed the maser, which became the basis for the atomic clock, the world's most accurate timing device. For his pioneering microwave research and its subsequent developments, Townes shared a 1964 Nobel Prize with two Soviet physicists, A. M. Prokhorov and N. G. Basov. On May 16, 1960, Theodore Harold Maiman, working alone with a minimal budget at Hughes Research Laboratories in Malibu, California, used a ruby crystal and won the race by American and European researchers to build the first laser.

The uses, present and prospective, for the laser's narrow, intense beam of coherent light are numerous and varied. Made up of waves of identical length and phase, sharply focused laser beams are used for communications, repairing torn retinas, excising tumors, cauterizing surgical incisions, erasing birthmarks, expanding computer capabilities, drilling, welding, cutting, reading grocery prices at checkout counters, creating holographs, aiming artillery . . . the list goes on and on. Lasers are widely used to transmit information to telephones, video disks, and computers through fiber-optical strands, replacing acres of copper. It was laser that first bounced a light signal off the moon.

Of the greatest eventual consequence to mankind, however, are experiments utilizing the world's most powerful laser, Nova, housed in quarters the size of a football field at the Lawrence Livermore Laboratory near San Francisco. Officially opened in April 1985, this $176 million assemblage of ten bright blue tubes, each a conduit for an intense laser beam, was designed to weld the nuclei of hydrogen atoms, releasing bursts of energy at temperatures higher than those at

169

the sun's core. If Livermore efforts to harness nuclear fusion succeed, they could lead to a limitless supply of cheap, clean power. Access to fuel would cease to be a reason for war. Nova, however, is also being used to improve thermonuclear bombs by simulating their explosion under controlled laboratory conditions.

LASER CARD: The medical memory card, containing the bearer's entire medical history, from allergies to X rays, on a wallet-sized piece of plastic, was devised by nineteen-year-old Douglas Becker of Baltimore, after reading about laser cards in computer magazines. Slated for wide use by insurance companies in the United States and abroad, the laser-encoded "LifeCard" is capable of encompassing eight hundred pages of medical data, a digitalized personal photograph, a facsimile of the bearer's signature, and an explanation of the insuree's policy. It is expected to speed up emergency medical treatment by making vital information about everything from vaccinations to electrocardiograms instantly available.

Like the videodisc and the compact audio disc (CD), the laser card, which was developed by Jerome Drexler's Drexler Technology Corporation of Mountain View, California, depends on laser optic technology. A low-power laser beam is used to inscribe digital information and to "read" it by subsequent scanning. Target cost for the inscribing-scanning mechanism, in hospitals and doctors' offices, is one thousand dollars. The cards themselves cost about $1.50. Drexler envisions use of laser cards for cashless purchases, like gift certificates. The buyer would pay a predetermined amount, say fifty dollars, and would use the card to make purchases at vending machines until the last dollar of the card's face value had been spent. Laser cards are also being used by existing credit card companies, including Visa and Master Card. (*See also* CREDIT CARD.)

LAUNDROMAT: Establishments providing, for a fee, washers, dryers, and the requisite soap powders are a boon for apartment dwellers everywhere. The world's first Laundromat was the Washateria, equipped with four washing machines rentable by the hour, opened in Fort Worth, Texas, by J. F. Cantrell on April 18, 1934.

Outlets offering facilities for clothes washing as well as assorted ways to mark time while awaiting the end of the wash, rinse, and spin cycles proliferated under various names. Barwash, the first combination Laundromat and deli, was opened in 1984 by Robb Walsh of Austin, Texas. Unlike most Laundromats, which tend to look bleak, Barwash is awash in glass, wicker and white-and-blue tile. It boasts a bar that dispenses ten kinds of wine, sixteen varieties of beer, and five brands of detergent. It is the first Laundromat ever rented out as the site of a wedding reception. To comply with health rules, clothes cleansing takes place on one side of a glass wall, elbow bending on the other.

LEVI'S: One of the most famous logos in the world includes a galloping horse and rider, a woodsman swinging an axe, and a miner panning gold. It appears conspicuously on the back of blue denim work trousers manufactured by the San Francisco firm of Levi Strauss and Co. Initially intended for West Coast miners, Levi's acquired style-conscious, as well as hard-working, customers in the late 1930s and early 1940s, after the *New York Herald Tribune* recommended them for prospective dude ranchers. They zoomed in popularity in the 1960s, during the hippie era, and even more after the release of a 1980 John Travolta film, *Urban Cowboy*. In the peak year of 1981, an estimated 600 million pairs of jeans were sold in the United States alone. Levi's "classic" model, the "501 Double X blue denim waist overall"—with five pockets and button fly, extra strong, snug, low-hipped, and tapering at the legs—first came on the market in the 1870s. Levi Strauss boldly announced that its garments were guaranteed to "shrink, wrinkle and fade."

After working as an itinerant peddler of clothing and housewares in and near New York City, Levi Strauss (1829-1902), a Bavarian immigrant, headed for San Francisco in gold rush days with rolls of brown canvas intended for tents and wagon covers. When he discovered that the miners needed sturdy workpants, Strauss, barely twenty-one, had a tailor make "waist-high overalls" from his stock of canvas. Later he switched to a cotton fabric loomed in France, *serge de Nimes* (or, in shortened form, "denim"). He dyed some of the trousers indigo blue and, borrowing the idea from a Nevada tailor, Jacob Davis, added copper rivets at "stress" points. To assure a snug fit, he had his customers sit in a watering trough while the material shrank. Levi's quickly became standard garb for miners, loggers, farmers, railroad workers, oil drillers, and cowboys everywhere. During World War II, Levi's were declared an essential commodity and sold only to bona fide defense workers. Levi's were originally sold for twenty-two cents. In Russia, on the black market, the post-World War II price zoomed to $140. Fancified versions by other manufacturers, almost skintight at the thighs and buttocks, became high style as "designer jeans."

LIEDERKRANZ: Despite its German-sounding name, Liederkranz is one of only two cheeses considered all-American. It was the result of a serendipitous accident in 1892, when the German-American cheesemaker Emil Frey of Monroe, New York, was trying to reproduce the Old Country favorite, Bismarck Schlosskase, Frey sent a sample of his mishap mutation to Adolph Tode, a delicatessen owner who belonged to a Liederkranz ("wreath of song") Choral

Society. When slices distributed to Tode's co-carolers were enthusiastically approved, Frey began marketing his new product under the cheese-cheerers' name. The other native cheese, little known outside the Midwest, is Brick, created in Wisconsin in 1877 by John Jossi.

LIFE SAVERS: When sales of his homemade chocolates lagged during the summer of 1912, Clarence A. Crane of Cleveland decided that he needed a warm-weather replacement. A nonmeltable mint seemed a wise choice, but many European brands were already available. Most resembled miniature pillows, so Crane opted for something that would look different—a round mint with a hole in the center. An unofficial version is that the hole was caused by a glitch in the machinery of the pill manufacturer Crane hired to stamp out round mints. Life Saver was the obvious name. Crane promptly registered it and began marketing the confection in paperboard tubes bearing the slogan "for that stormy breath."

Edward John Noble, who sold advertising space in New York streetcars, immediately realized Life Savers' potential and tried to persuade Crane to advertise the product. Crane replied that his principal interest was chocolate making, and if Noble was all that excited about Life Savers, he could buy the rights for five thousand dollars. When Noble and a friend, Roy Arlen, couldn't raise that much financing, Crane lowered the price to thirty-eight hundred dollars. To retain the spicy peppermint taste that was quickly absorbed by paperboard, Noble devised the industry's first tinfoil wrapper. Retailers were offered fresh Life Savers for the stale ones, with the suggestion that they could boost sales by putting a few packages next to the cash register and including nickels in a customer's change. One flavor, wint-o-green, differed from all the others because it sometimes produced chemical fireworks. Because of triboluminescence, the result of the rapid breakdown of sugar crystals and its effect on the flavoring, it generated visible sparks when chewed in a dark room.

Huge metal Life Saver rolls, used to advertise the product, were borrowed by Columbia University students as a downhill vehicle. The radio humorist Henry Morgan caused a stir at Life Savers headquarters when he ignored the prepared advertising copy and ad libbed that the Life Savers company was making huge profits by shortchanging the public—substituting holes for candy.

LIGHT BULB: Although the first lighting of Thomas Alva Edison's carbon filament lamp, on October 19, 1879, is considered the dawn of the Electric Age (this was the first commercially practical incandescent electric light), efforts to create artificial illumination go back to 1706, when England's Francis Hauksbee was able to produce a dim glow inside a vacuumized glass globe. There were other later

172

efforts, including one in 1850 when Sir Joseph Wilson Swan first utilized a carbon filament for an incandescent lamp. Paris used blazing carbon lights at the Paris Opera for theatrical effect even before the 1870 Battle of Paris, when they helped to detect enemy troop movements. Illuminated by the arc of an electric current between two carbon rods, they consumed a great deal of electricity from wet cells or primitive dynamos, produced a harsh light, burned out quickly and emitted smelly gases. Flickering gas jets and kerosene lamps were, respectively, the urban and rural preferences until 1878, when Edison vowed that he would perfect a *practical* electric light within six weeks.

Edison proceeded to test some twelve hundred filaments, including hair from an assistant's beard, before discovering—after fourteen months of searching—that cotton sewing thread, heated until it was charred black and, then, placed in an evacuated glass sphere and used as a conduit for electricity, glowed continuously for forty hours. A major help was the improved vacuum pump devised by Hermann Sprengel that enabled Edison to produce a lamp with a better vacuum. Almost immediately after patenting his enlightening creation in 1880, Edison began working on improvements. A Shelby Electric Company bulb, installed in 1901 in a Livermore, California, firehouse has been burning continuously ever since!

Because of their cheapness, "warm" color, and convenience, however, they waste much of their power in heat and are far less efficient than other kinds of lighting. Filaments today are made of tungsten, a metal that resists melting below 6,170 degrees Fahrenheit. After Edison's world-changing light bulb (*see* EDISON) came such sources of illumination as the fluorescent lamp, which uses less electricity, and the even more efficient mercury-vapor and sodium-vapor lamps.

LINK TRAINER: Pilot-training methods were revolutionized by the Link Trainer, the "blue box" flight simulator that made possible the rapid training of more than five hundred thousand U.S. and Allied forces fliers during World War II.

A contemporary of Orville Wright and other aviation pioneers, Edwin Albert Link learned to fly in the 1920s and barnstormed with alumni of World War I's Lafayette Escadrille. At twenty-two, deploring the high cost of pilot training and its slow pace while long lines of fledgling aviators impatiently waited to become airborne, he built his first flight simulator in the cramped basement of his father's Binghamton, New York, factory. It consisted of a cockpit with an instrument panel that enabled novices to learn flight procedures without leaving the ground. His invention found few buyers until 1934, when the U.S. Army Air Force unexpectedly found itself saddled with airmail delivery. Trained to fly by watching the ground, ten air force pilots cracked up before the army turned to Link for counsel.

In 1959, Link's interest turned from up in the air to down in the sea. Returned, actually, because he had drawn the schematic for an utterly impractical submarine before his twelfth birthday. After designing and building an oceanographic research vessel, *Sea Diver*, which was used on archeological research cruises, he proceeded from atop the ocean to its inner depths. He created submersible craft with 360-degree vision that helped revolutionize oceanography, including—after the June 1973 underwater death of his thirty-one-year-old son, Edwin Clayton Link, and another minisub crew member—the Cabled Observation and Rescue Device (CORD), equipped with TV cameras and hydraulically powered claws and cutters to rescue trapped divers. At Link Port, an oceanographic complex near Fort Pierce on Florida's Atlantic coast, the former flier headed a staff of 150 scientists, engineers, and support personnel who had at their disposal scientific and engineering laboratories, a computer center, electron microscope, library and reference museum, acquaculture-mariculture facility, dry dock, and more than a dozen research vessels.

Link Trainers are now produced for pilots, maritime vessel operators, and astronauts.

LINOTYPE: After emigrating from Germany in 1872, Ottmar Mergenthaler (1854-1899) went to work in Washington, D.C., for the scientific-equipment-manufacturing firm owned by the son of the German watchmaker to whom he had been apprenticed. The company was commissioned to prepare the patent model of a typewriting device that used papier-mâché molds for typesetting. It didn't work, but Mergenthaler found its intent intriguing. He experimented with various methods of mechanical typesetting before opting for individual copper molds, or matrices, for each letter. By tapping a keyboard, an array of letters lined up at preset widths and were then cast as a single "slug" in a molten, fast-cooling alloy.

Mergenthaler patented his "matrix-making machine" on August 26, 1884. The *New York Tribune* was the first buyer, installing the equipment on July 1, 1886, and using it to set type for the edition that appeared two days later. Examining a slug, Whitelaw Reid, the *Tribune's* owner, exclaimed, "It's a line of type!" Mergenthaler liked the description and adopted it. At the time of his death, more than three thousand Linotypes were in use, and others were being produced at factories in the United States, England, and Germany. Although the Linotype was credited for an unprecedented boom in global publishing activity, numerous metal-scrapping technological advances have made the cumbersome machines obsolescent. The first typesetting machine patent was granted to Adrien Delcambre and James Hadden Young of Lisle, France, in 1841, but the first pre-

Mergenthaler model that actually operated was invented by Timothy Alden of New York City in 1857.

A post-Mergenthaler typesetter devised by James W. Paige so impressed the Linotype executives that they offered a share-for-share stock swap to protect investors in both companies if one machine put the other out of business. The deal didn't go through because a major Paige backer balked. He was the celebrated author Mark Twain, who lost his entire investment because Paige, an oddball perfectionist, kept dismantling his machine whenever it seemed ready for marketing.

LIONEL TRAINS: Joshua Lionel Cowen, who invented and discarded the miniature battery in a tube that became a lucrative product, the flashlight (*see* FLASHLIGHT), prospered with another novel notion, miniature electric trains. Although as a youngster he enjoyed carving toy locomotives, in 1902 he constructed his first battery-powered flatcars not as toys but to transport the merchandise in a New York display window. He was surprised when customers coveted the conveyances. The first models, with a thirty-foot circle of brass track, sold for six dollars.

In 1903, after his toy trains had produced a considerable stir, he issued what was then a merchandising rarity, a hyperbole-crammed catalog. The three-rail track system he later patented was adopted as a standard by other manufacturers of miniature trains. The sequence switch was a post-World War I Lionel innovation that enabled model railroaders to reverse their trains by remote control. Among the most popular Lionel models have been a handcar bearing Mickey and Minnie Mouse, which was the nation's most popular toy in 1934; the company's first diesel locomotive, the Santa Fe F-3, which was its best-selling model engine, and a $10.95 automated milk car with silver milk cans, which had 180,000 purchasers between 1950 and 1953. The Lionel Corporation eventually became the world's largest toy company, and before Cowen's death in 1965, Lionel trains had acquired fanatic fans of all ages in many countries.

In 1985, the Toy Train Collectors of America, with headquarters in Strasburg, Pennsylvania, estimated that seventeen thousand collectors regularly participated in train meets and the buying and selling of train sets, which have advanced in value to more than a thousand dollars apiece. Celebrity buffs have included Frank Sinatra, Roy Rogers, Gene Autry, Tommy Dorsey, Paul Whiteman, and Gypsy Rose Lee. (*See also* MICKEY MOUSE WATCH.)

LISTERINE: The world's best-selling mouthwash for more than a hundred years, Listerine was invented in a small St. Louis laboratory by Dr. Joseph Lawrence, whose choice of a name was intended as a homage to a distinguished predecessor with, coincidentally, the same initials, Sir Joseph Lister, developer of the first antiseptic. It was originally manufactured by the Lambert Pharmacal Company in St. Louis.

During the 1940s and 1950s Listerine ads boosted sales with scare tactics, using soap-operatic situations to pound home the idea that gargling with Listerine could save unwary individuals with bad breath from becoming social outcasts. When Lambert merged in the late 1950s with the New York-based William R. Warner Company, owned by Gustavus A. Pfeiffer and Company, to become the Warner-Lambert conglomerate, Elmer Holmes Bobst, the top Warner executive, proposed an advertising campaign that would imply that Listerine was effective against real ailments as well as those concocted by ad agencies. Amid rumblings that an Asian flu epidemic was imminent, he wanted to prescribe in full-page *Life* magazine ads three ways to elude the malevolent malady: "See your doctor for flu shots, avoid crowds and gargle twice a day with Listerine." The ad agency handling the Warner-Lambert account couldn't believe Bobst was serious but complied with his instructions and Listerine sales promptly zoomed. However, the Federal Trade Commission was not as pleased as Warner-Lambert accountants. In 1978, after a lengthy legal battle, the Supreme Court upheld the commission's ruling that Warner-Lambert had to include in $10 million worth of Listerine advertising the admission that the product "will not prevent colds or sore throats or lessen their severity."

LITTLE LEAGUE: Carl Stotz of Williamsport, Pennsylvania, wanted to provide baseball fun for his nephews, aged six and eight, and other neighborhood boys when he launched the Little League in 1938. With thirty-seven dollars in contributions, he bought three dozen playsuits (as uniforms for three teams) at the local five-and-ten. The first season, 1939, consisted of merely supervised sandlot play. By 1947, there were so many leagues that Stotz organized a World Series between all-star teams from Pennsylvania, New Jersey, and New York. In 1949, he solicited financial assistance from the U.S. Rubber Company, later Uniroyal, which was developing a line of rubber-spiked shoes for Little League players. Peter McGovern, one of the firm's executives, began devoting all his time to bantam baseball and, in a 1955 power struggle, ousted Stotz, who complained of the Little League's increasing commercialization.

The Little League is a federally chartered tax-exempt corporation that promotes the United States, through baseball, in thirty-one countries; franchises teams; and licenses use of its trademark. According to recent reports, more than 2.5 million preteen youngsters belong to some eleven thousand leagues worldwide. A World Series is played each August in a ten thousand-seat Williamsport stadium. A Cana-

◄ ALFRED E. NEUMAN
The idol of nonconformists everywhere, Alfred E. Neuman, alias Melvin Cowznofski, was *Mad* magazine's write-in candidate for President. (Mad *magazine)*

ATOM BOMB Naval observers eye the spectacular cloud produced by an atomic bomb during its testing on Bikini atoll on July 1, 1946. *(NASA/ Temple University Libraries Photojournalism Collection)*

◄ **ACADEMY AWARD** Janet Gaynor, first recipient of a Best Actress Oscar, receives her 1929 trophy from Douglas Fairbanks, first Motion Picture Academy President. *(© Academy of Motion Picture Arts and Sciences)*

ADVICE Twin dispensers of ► worldwide wisdom, Ann Landers (right) and Abigail Van Buren, born Esther Pauline and Pauline Esther Friedman, attend a 1976 high school reunion. *(AP/ Wide World Photos)*

▲ **AIRLINE STEWARDESS** The world's first stewardess corps was assembled for United Airlines by Ellen Church (upper left), who became the first airborne aide on May 15, 1930. *(United Airlines photo)*

▲ **AIRPLANE** Orville Wright demonstrates one of the Wright Brothers' early planes in France for the king of Spain, who wanted to go aloft but was dissuaded by his wife. *(Smithsonian Institution Photo No. A42962A)*

▲ **AUTOMOBILE** In 1914, at Henry Ford's
Highland Park Plant, a Model T body slid
down a ramp to be affixed to a chassis and
driven off. Total assembly required one hour.
*(From the Collections of Henry Ford Museum
and Greenfield Village.)*

▲ **BATHING BEAUTY CONTEST** Finalists in the world's
first bathing beauty competition display 1921 beachwear.
The first "Miss America" is third from left. *(Temple
University Libraries Photojournalism Collection)*

▲ **BREAKDANCING** Created by American blacks and Hispanics, breakdancing has been eagerly adopted by agile members of other races and nationalities. *(Courtesy of the Courier-Pst, a Gannett newspaper, Cherry Hill, N.J.)*

CABBAGE PATCH KIDS Xavier Roberts, ▶
creator of the Cabbage Patch Kids, dandles on his knee one of the multitude of "babies" that have been "adopted" worldwide. *(AP/Wide World Photos)*

▲ CHORUS LINE, A *A Chorus Line,* especially popular in Japan, is accorded frequent revivals by the Shiki Theatrical Company. *(Shiki Theatrical Company)*

◄ DONALD DUCK Donald Duck the most cantankerous of Walt Disney's cartoon creations, has been given hell in Helsinki and kudos in Kuwait. (© *Walt Disney Productions*)

▲ DISNEYLAND Walt Disney, creator of Mickey Mouse, Donald Duck, and other pen-and-ink super-stars, earlier had in his menagerie of animated animals Oswald the Lucky Rabbit. (© *Walt Disney Productions*)

► MICKEY MOUSE Mickey Mouse, briefly dubbed Mortimer Mouse, is affec-tionately known by dozens of other names throughout the world. One example: Mai Kay Shiu Shu. (© *Walt Disney Productions*)

▲ THEME PARK The world's most successful theme park, California's Disneyland, with its Fantasyland castle, has sired similar Disney-designed outposts in Florida and Japan. (© *Walt Disney Productions*)

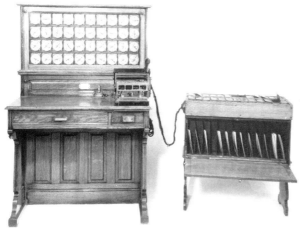

◄ DATA PROCESSING
Herman Hollerith's electric
tabulating machine, fore-
runner of modern data
processing, was first used
for the 1890 U.S. census.
*(Smithsonian Institution
Photo No. 64563)*

HOPE The S.S. ►
Hope, the world's
first peacetime hos-
pital ship, glides
under the Golden
Gate Bridge at the
start of its maiden
voyage. *(HOPE)*

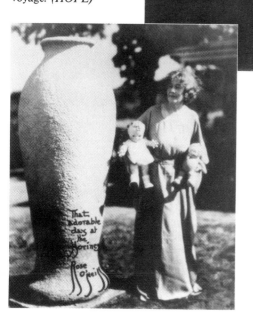

◄ KEWPIE Rose O'Neill holds
dolls representing the kewpie
characters that were originally
illustrations for her poems and
stories in women's magazines.
*(International Rose O'Neill
Club)*

MACHINE GUN Dr. ►
Richard J. Gatling was
convinced that his 250
shots-per-minute machine
gun, invented in 1862,
would diminish the
number of wartime
casualties. *(Smithsonian
Institution Photo No.
44412)*

◄ **MISS AMERICA**
Margaret Gorman, Miss
America 1921, was the
first, the youngest (15),
and the least buxom (30″
bust) to bear the title.
(Miss America Pageant)

▲ **MOON LANDING** Apollo 11 astronauts Neil
Armstrong (left) and Edwin Aldrin, first men
on the moon, conduct the July 20, 1969, flag-
planting ceremony. *(NASA/Temple University
Libraries Photojournalism Collection)*

PEANUTS

By Schulz

▲ "**PEANUTS**" Charlie Brown and his "Peanuts" troupe, the world's most widely syndicated comic-strip characters, changed considerably between their debut in 1950 (top) and 1968. (© *United Feature Syndicate, Inc.*)

◄ **SNOOPY** Snoopy, the top star of the "Peanuts" comic strip, has surpassed the Teddy Bear and Mickey Mouse as the world's most beloved nonhuman. *(© United Feature Syndicate, Inc.)*

© 1950, 1952, 1958, 1960, 1965, 1966 United Feature Syndicate

MONOPOLY ► Charles B. Darrow went from unemployment to affluence after inventing Monopoly, challenged only by Scrabble® as the world's bestselling game. *(Parker Brothers)*

◄ **PEACE CORPS** A Peace Corps volunteer supervises as a Sierra Leone work crew constructs a small dam to control the water in a swamp at Koriboido. *(Peace Corps)*

▲

◄ **PHONOGRAPH** Both Thomas Alva Edison and his wax cylinder phonograph changed in appearance between April 18, 1878 (left) and June 16, 1888 (right). *(U.S. Department of the Interior, National Park Service, Edison National Historic Site)*

Shave Yourself

No Stropping—No Honing

EVERY man's shaving troubles were my troubles—before I invented the Gillette Safety Razor.

I was not satisfied with a device that would merely shave the beard without cutting the face—my idea was to shave comfortably without irritation—quickly without lost motion—smoothly without leaving stray hairs or rough patches of beard in the corners and places hard to get at.

All these things are accomplished in the Gillette Safety Razor and in no other razor in the world. Its keen flexible blade takes a hollow form when fixed in the guard and drawn down by turning the handle. This micrometer adjustment is original with me—no other razor can be adjusted for a fine or coarse beard or for a light or close shave.

My razor will do for you what it does for me and for the three million other users the world over. It costs $5 and it lasts a lifetime. Standard Set, in velvet-lined, full leather case, $5. Combination Sets, specially adapted for gift purposes, $6.00 to $50.

TRADE ◆Gillette◆ MARK

GILLETTE SALES CO.
48 West Second St., Boston

New York, Times Bldg.
Chicago,
Stock Exchange Bldg.
London Office,
E Holborn Viaduct
Factories, Boston, Montreal, London, Berlin, Paris

Canadian Office,
63 St. Alexander St.
Montreal
Eastern Office,
Shanghai, China

◄ **RAZOR BLADE, DISPOSABLE** About 1908, assorted approaches were used in the United States and abroad to proclaim the virtues of the disposable razor blades invented by King Camp Gillette. *(The Gillette Company)*

ROCKET, LIQUID- ►
FUELED Dr. Robert H. Goddard stands beside the first liquid-propelled rocket, launched at Auburn, Massachusetts, on March 16, 1926. *(Smithsonian Institution Photo No. 45914D)*

◄ **TELEPHONE** Initially a teacher of the deaf, Alexander Graham Bell, inventor of the telephone, communicates in 1901 with blind, deaf international phenomenon Helen Keller, 21. *(Reproduced with permission of AT&T Corporate Archive)*

▲ **TELEPHONE OPERATOR** Telephone operators, male and female, plug in calls at the Tremont, Boston, switchboard in 1883. The first Boston operator, five years earlier, was Emma Nutt. *(Reproduced with permission of AT&T Corporate Archive)*

▲ **UNICORN** The world's first man-made mythical creature, a certified unicorn, was introduced in 1985 by the Ringling Brothers and Barnum & Bailey Circus. *(Ringling Brothers and Barnum & Bailey)*

RADIO   SCREEN   STAGE

VARIETY

PRICE 15¢

Published Weekly at 154 West 46th St., New York, N. Y., by Variety, Inc. Annual subscription, $6. Single copies, 15 cents.
Entered as second-class matter December 22, 1905, at the Post Office at New York, N. Y., under the act of March 3, 1879.

COPYRIGHT, 1935, BY VARIETY, INC. ALL RIGHTS RESERVED

Vol. 119   No. 5   NEW YORK, WEDNESDAY, JULY 17, 1935   72 PAGES

STICKS NIX HICK PIX

INTERESTED FARM DRAMA   Stars Favor Own Picture Firm For Tax Conservation Purposes

▲ **VARIETY** This frequently quoted headline in *Variety,* the show-biz weekly, typifies lingo universally adopted by entertainers and impressarios. *(Variety)*

◄ **ZOOT SUIT** Clyde Duncan, a Gainesville, Georgia, busboy, models the world's first zoot suit, tailored to his specifications in 1941 for $33.50. *(AP/Wide World Photos)*

WILD WEST ►
"Je viens" ("I am coming"), on posters for Buffalo Bill's Wild West Show, triggered stampedes to French box offices in 1889. *(Buffalo Bill Historical Center, Cody, Wyoming)*

dian team participated in 1952, and in subsequent years, there was increasing representation from other countries. The first foreign Series winner was Mexico, in 1957. Oriental teams began a three-year reign ten years later. Foreign participation was ended in 1972 when a riot followed the 6-0 victory of Taipei, Taiwan, over Hammond, Indiana. Police said afterward that only Taiwanese, for and against Taiwan's government, were involved. The ban was lifted in 1975, with the proviso that teams were to represent areas with specified population limits, not an entire country; were not to engage in all-year practice; and were to stress fun, not victory *uber alles.*

Girls were first permitted to play in Little League games in 1974. In August 1984, Victoria Roche, aged twelve, a Korean orphan adopted by British parents and playing with a Brussels team (composed of Belgian, American, British, French, and Japanese members) became the first girl to play in a Little League World Series.

M

MACHINE GUN: An "improved automatic cannon"—patented by Charles E. Barnes of Lowell, Massachusetts, on July 8, 1856—was operated by a hand crank. The quicker the crank was turned, the greater the speed with which ammunition was propelled. The first really practical rapid-firing machine gun, however, came along six years later—the brainchild of a nonpracticing doctor who insisted that his motives were strictly humanitarian. Dr. Richard Jordan Gatling (1818-1903) opined that most Civil War casualties were caused by sickness and exposure, rather than wounds. A rapid-fire weapon, enabling one soldier to replace a hundred, he figured, would lessen the need for large armies, thus minimizing the number of men exposed to battle and disease. His first model was a six-barrel weapon that could fire 250 shots per minute at a time when rifles were still being muzzle loaded. President Lincoln nixed adoption of the weapon by the Union army because Gatling, a native North Carolinian, was suspected of Confederate sympathies. Later, the number of barrels was increased to ten, firing 350 rounds per minute. In 1866, the Gatling gun became part of the U.S. Army's arsenal.

The fully automatic Maxim, capable of 660 rounds per minute, was perfected in England in 1884 by Maine-born Sir Hiram Stevens Maxim (1840-1916). A prolific inventor, Maxim accumulated numerous U.S. patents before he became an expatriate and a Sir. While working for an engineer uncle in Fitchburg, Massachusetts, he invented a gas lighting machine. Subsequent Maximizings included an improved curling iron, a widely adopted locomotive headlight, an automatic sprinkler-type fire extinguisher, and regulators for gaslight and electrical pressure. Because of the latter device, exhibited at the Paris Exhibition of 1881, he was awarded the French Legion of Honor. While in Vienna he told a fellow American tourist about his triumph in Paris. The wry rejoinder, "If you want to make a pile of money, invent something that will enable these Europeans to cut each other's throats with greater facility," prompted him to proceed to London—and his lethal machine gun. It was quickly adopted by every major power, including the United States. It helped Western imperialism conquer Africa, but whites were reluctant to use it against whites. However, concepts of warfare changed during World War I when British soldiers, conditioned to rely on bayonets and cavalry charges, were mowed down by German machine guns. Almost 80 percent of World War I's casualties were attributed to that weapon alone.

After World War I, the Thompson submachine gun, alias the "Tommy gun," invented by U.S. Col. J. T. Thompson, became the weapon of choice among Chicago gangsters. Gatling's "humane," unprecedently lethal creation was commonly referred to as a "gat" long before that abbreviation became a synonym for any kind of gun in the lexicon of real and fictional gangsters and private eyes.

MAD: As comic book, eight-times-a-year magazine, and sporadic paperback book series, madcap *Mad*, which made its debut in 1952, has influenced generations of jesters at home and abroad. It is published in a dozen countries, with foreign language editions in Mexico, Brazil, Sweden, Holland, Denmark, Norway, Finland, and West Germany. An entire school of highly regarded French cartoonists credits *Mad* for its wacko style. *Mad* was also an acknowledged influence in the creation of England's sardonic TV program "TW3," unabbreviatedly "That Was the Week That Was." Terry Gilliam and John Cleese, cofounders of England's "Monty Python," first met in the office of *Help!*, a *Mad* clone. British zany Marty Feldman likened *Mad*'s anything-goes needling of society and its values to the satire of Voltaire, Swift, and Rabelais.

When *Mad* first appeared in color comic-book form, identified on the cover as "Tales Calculated to Drive You MAD: Humor in a Jugular Vein," it was published by Bill Gaines and edited by Harvey Kurtzman. Kurtzman, who lived in the Bronx, was producing two realistic war comic books for Entertaining Comics (E. C.) when he developed jaundice. While recuperating, he decided to create a comic book that would not require painstaking research. The idea of *Mad* was worked out with E. C.'s three top artists: Will Elder, Wally Wood, and Jack Davis. Kurtzman—who later gave birth to *Playboy* magazine's comic-strip sexpot, Little Annie Fannie—exited in 1955, shortly after *Mad* became a magazine, and was replaced by Al Feldstein, who had previously edited Gaines's horror comics. It was Kurtzman who first made big-eared, silly-grinned Alfred E. Neuman—also known as Melvin Cowznofski (*see* ALFRED E. NEUMAN)—*Mad*'s mascot in 1954; but it was Feldstein who cast Alfred as *Mad*'s very own cover kid.

Mad has always stressed weird and wild parodies, peculiar phonetic sounds like KAPOKA KAPOKA KAFONK, and—a favorite— Yeccch! In 1965, *Mad*'s influence with collegians was so great that its introduction of a game with utterly incomprehensible rules, 43-Man Squamish, resulted in the formation of teams on various campuses.

MAIL ORDER: The first exclusively mail-order business, not an adjunct to a store, was established in 1872 by Aaron Montgomery Ward in a single Chicago room. The initial Montgomery Ward price list consisted of one 8-by-12-inch sheet of paper. The first catalog, issued in 1874 and tagged *The Great Wish Book*, was a twenty-four-page pocket-sized booklet. By 1893, it had grown to 544 pages. In 1904, Montgomery Ward mailed three million catalogs weighing four pounds apiece. One customer, a Minnesota woman, certain that her husband's death was imminent, ordered embalming fluid and asked, "Must I pour it down his throat just before he dies, or must I rub it on after he is dead?" Despite its fifteen-year head start over Sears, Montgomery Ward by 1908 was millions of dollars behind in annual sales. In 1974, the company was purchased by Mobil. Montgomery Ward's final catalog was issued in December 1985.

MALTED MILK: James and William Horlick of Racine, Wisconsin, manufactured an extract of wheat and malted barley, to which milk had to be added, as an easily digested food for infants and invalids. In 1886, William decided to include the milk in the initial mix before reducing the combined ingredients, by evaporation, to a dry product, which was easily stored and transported and required only water.

First dubbed diastoid, it was described in the 1887 patent application as a nutritious drink intended for "infants, Invalids, the Aged, and Travelers." Horlick coined the phrase "malted milk" to identify his product. Walgreen, the oldest and largest U.S. retail drug chain, is credited with making the malted milk a soda-fountain favorite by augmenting Horlick's mix with chocolate syrup and ice cream. Sans malt, the "malted milk" becomes the "milk shake." In the 1930s, knowledgeable "soda jerks" were advised to provide a nutmeg shaker with every malted or shake. Nutmeg, soda-fountain sages opined, was to a proper malted "what salt is to soup."

MARINER'S QUADRANT: The reflecting quadrant, actually an octant, representing a major navigational advance—it made possible the determination of latitude, despite ship motion, via the altitude of the sun, without the need to fry an eyeball by looking at that fiery orb—was invented in 1730 by the Philadelphia mathematician Thomas Godfrey (1704-1749). Largely self-taught, he made up for his lack of formal education by constant perusal of Governor James Logan's extensive library. The blending of his two major interests, mathematics and astronomy, resulted in the quadrant.

In 1731, when Godfrey was already testing the instrument, John Hadley, who may have heard of Godfrey's discovery from a relative, announced a similar device in England. Although, at Logan's urging, Godfrey was eventually saluted by the Royal Society of London, his navigational aid, precursor of the modern sextant, retained the misnomer "Hadley's quadrant." Godfrey had a second claim to fame. A glazier's apprentice in his youth, he was commissioned in 1732 to install the windows of the Philadelphia building that was later renamed Independence Hall.

MARITIME CHARTS: A vehicular accident on land had far-reaching results on international travel at sea. Lamed at thirty-three when he fell off the top of an overbooked, overturned stagecoach, Fredericksburg, Virginia-born navy lieutenant Matthew Fontaine Maury (1806-1873) was assigned to the navy's depot of charts and instruments. In effect, it was the equivalent of banishment to Siberia, perhaps less because of his physical handicap than in retaliation for his maverick challenging of navy teachings and traditions. A brilliant scientist and mathematician, Maury converted insult into inspiration.

In the depot's archives, gathering dust, he found thousands of logbooks, routinely forwarded at the end of every navy voyage and then never consulted. Maury and his staff collated the more than fifty years of observations by countless navigators on all the oceans at all seasons. These, augmented by newer data assembled at Maury's urging, were encapsuled in 1847 in the navy's first wind and current charts, using simple symbols to note seasonal wind, weather, and current changes in the North Atlantic. The charts disproved the dangers attributed to particular routes and dramatically reduced the sailing time needed to reach specific destinations. By offering free charts to merchant skippers who forwarded their logs, Maury was able, by the end of 1851, to issue information on all the world's major seas.

Reports on the migrations of whales convinced Maury that a Northwest Passage between the Atlantic and Pacific oceans, sought by explorers for more than two centuries, did indeed exist; an assumption confirmed a few years later by the British explorer Sir Robert John Le Mesurier McClure. Prodded by Maury, the U.S. Navy sponsored the world's first International Maritime Meteorological Conference in Brussels in August 1853. Representatives of ten nations voted unanimously to establish an international system of exchange, sharing their logs for inclusion in Maury's charts. During the next fifty years 5.5 million American, 3.5 million Dutch, 7 million British, and 10.5 million German logs contributed toward the substitution of scientific navigational methods for skippers' hunches.

MARSHALL PLAN: In 1947, the year he was named secretary of state by President Harry S. Truman, Uniontown, Pennsylvania-born George Catlett Marshall (1880-1959), who had served as the army chief of staff and a five-star general during World War II, proposed the European Recovery Program, to provide economic aid to nations devastated by that war. Steps to implement the program, which became universally known as the Marshall Plan, were begun a month later at the Paris Economic Conference. The following year, Truman signed into law the Economic Cooperation Administration (ECA), to promote European production, bolster European currency, and facilitate international trade. The beneficiaries of more than $12 billion in aid, between 1948 and 1951, were Austria, Belgium, Denmark, France, West Germany, Great Britain, Greece, Iceland, Italy, Luxembourg, the Netherlands, Norway, Sweden, Switzerland, and Turkey.

Designed in part to counter growing Soviet influence through national Communist parties—especially in France, Italy and Czechoslovakia—the Marshall Plan was denounced by the Soviet Union and opposed by other Eastern European countries. Nevertheless, it played a major role in Europe's economic recovery. In 1953, primarily for this peacetime project to reverse the effects of war, career soldier Marshall was awarded the Nobel Peace Prize.

MASON JAR: The mason jar, with removable threaded zinc top and rubber gasket to prevent contamination of its contents by air, invented in 1858 by John L. Mason, a Brooklyn tinsmith, is still popular. After Mason's patent expired in 1879, in a conspicuous example of Ball gall, two Buffalo, New York, brothers bearing that surname started manufacturing both Mason-like jars, redubbed "Buffalo" jars, and glass-lined zinc caps for the jars, the combined operation producing a tighter fit. In 1886, their first manufacturing year, the on-the-ball Ball brothers sold 12,500 of the containers, commonly called fruit jars, challenging a monopoly shared by the Hero Fruit Jar Company and the Consolidated Fruit Jar Company, which held patents on an improved Mason jar. The two companies notified the trade that the Ball jar infringed on their patents, but the Balls bounced back with confirmation that the Mason-jar patents were up for grabs. In 1902, Alexander Kerr made the lid and gasket a single unit. The Ball variation on the Mason jar became the most popular in the world and provided the funds that enabled the Ball Corporation—headquartered in Muncie, Indiana, after several plant-wrecking fires—to include glass, rubber, and zinc production in its post-World War II operations. In the late 1950s, the Ball Corporation also became involved in the aerospace industry by providing orbiting solar observatories (to study radiation from the sun) for the National Aeronautics and Space Administration (NASA).

MASS PRODUCTION, AUTOMOBILE: The first automobile to be produced in greater quantity than ten per week was the curved-dash Olds, introduced in April 1901. By the end of the year, Ransom E. Olds's Detroit factory had turned out 433, a number that increased to 2,500 in 1902 and zoomed to an unprecedented 5,508 two years later. Because of its extreme simplicity, the Olds was one of the least costly automobiles on the market, selling for a bargain $650. Though its best speed was just over twenty miles per hour, its minimal weight, eight hundred pounds, made it especially effective on hills.

MATCHBOOK: The notion of putting matches in small folding books was patented by Joshua Pusey, of Lima, Pennsylvania, in 1892. Pusey's prototype measured two by three inches, held fifty paper or wooden matches, and was designed to fit in a vest pocket. An igniting surface was on the cover. The matches, in patent application lingo, were "attached to and enclosed by a suitable cover, folded and adapted to be opened and closed as the covers of a book." The Diamond Match Company purchased the patent rights and began producing matchbooks at its Barberton, Ohio, plant in 1896. The first customer to place a sales spiel on a matchbook cover was an opera company. The success of Pusey's invention was assured when a brewery ordered ten million matchbooks as an advertising device, a usage that has been internationally popular ever since.

McDONALD'S: The secret behind the worldwide proliferation of the golden arches that identify McDonald's fast-food emporiums (in 1984, they numbered 8,300 in thirty-four countries and grossed $10 billion) is a Kroc—Ray Albert Kroc, a high school dropout. In 1954, after peddling Florida real estate, paper cups, and milk-shake-making machines, Kroc persuaded two brothers, Richard and Maurice McDonald, proprietors of a thriving hamburger stand in San Bernardino, California, to allow him to franchise their ultraefficient, ultralucrative techniques. The McDonalds reluctantly agreed but insisted that every aspect of their operation, including the golden arches, had to be retained. What had impressed Kroc, then fifty-two and the exclusive sales agent for the Prince Castle Multi-Mixer, was the fact that the McDonalds had ordered forty-eight mixers.

On April 15, 1955, Kroc opened his first McDonald's in Des Plaines, Illinois, near Chicago. Everything was standardized, including the size of the hamburger bun (3 ½ inches wide) and the preparation time for hamburger, shake, and french fries (fifty seconds). In 1961, Kroc bought out the McDonalds, and within twenty years, the McDonald's empire included thousands of drive-ins and restaurants in twenty countries; a headquarters near Chicago, unofficially dubbed "Hamburger Central"; a training academy—Hamburger University—for franchisees, managers, and field inspectors; and numerous McDonaldland playgrounds for children. It even had an "ambassador," the red-headed clown Ronald McDonald. Not all Kroc innovations were as successful as the Big Mac (with a secret sauce), Egg McMuffin, and Filet-o'-Fish. A conspicuous flop was the Hulaburger—grilled pineapple and cheese in a bun.

When Kroc died at eighty-one in January 1984, he was one of the five wealthiest Americans, with a fortune exceeding $500 million. Two months after his death, the Des Plaines restaurant, which lacked a drive-in window, indoor seating, and bathrooms, was replaced, across the street, by a McDonald's three times larger. Its progenitor was reopened on May 21, 1985, thirty years and more than fifty-two billion hamburgers after its debut, as a repository for vintage McDonald's-linked memorabilia—the world's first McMuseum.

MICKEY MOUSE: Mickey Mouse, based on a friendly rodent that once kibitzed while he drew, was conceived by Walt Disney (*see* DISNEYLAND) on a New York-to-Hollywood train just after he had been deprived of his previous source of animated-cartoon livelihood, Oswald the Lucky Rabbit, because the bunny's name belonged to a film distributor. Disney first named his new character Mortimer Mouse, but his wife, Lilly, thought that name "too sissy." He accepted her countersuggestion.

Mickey's looks were the result of a collaboration between Disney and an animator friend, Ub Iwerks. Although Mickey's official birthdate is November 18, 1928, when he made his debut as the star of the first sound cartoon, *Steamboat Willie,* Disney used him in two earlier silent cartoons.

An almost instant international success, Mickey quickly acquired a long string of a.k.a (also known as) identities. He became Mickey Maus in Germany, Miky Maous in Greece, Miki Kuchi or Mickey Mausu in Japan, Michel Souris or Mickey Sans Culottes in France, Mikki Hiiri in Finland, Mikke Mus in Norway, Mikki Maus in Russia, Camondongo Mickey in Brazil, El Raton Mickey in Argentina, El Raton Miguelito in Central America, Miguel Ratoncito in Spain, Musse Pigg in Sweden, Topolino in Italy, Mi Lao Shu in Mandarin, and Mai Kay Shiu Shu in Cantonese.

Mickey was awarded a League of Nations scroll as "an international symbol of goodwill" in 1935. In Japan it was said that only

Emperor Hirohito, who wore a Mickey Mouse (oops! a Miki Kuchi) watch, was more popular. England's King George V refused to go to a movie unless it was prefaced by a Mickey Mouse short, and Queen Mary was late for a tea because she refused to miss the ending of a charity showing of *Mickey's Nightmare.* Among Mickey's fervent fans were other heads of state: America's Franklin D. Roosevelt, Canada's Mackenzie King, France's Charles de Gaulle, South Africa's Jan Christian Smuts, the Nizam of Hyderabad, and Italy's Mussolini.

Il Duce's Nazi crony, Adolf Hitler, banned Mickey because of a short in which villainous cats wore German military helmets, and in 1954, East Germany condemned Mickey as out of step with Marxist principles. In the 1970s, the egregiously clean-living mouse was depicted in underground comic books as a dirty rat who used profanity, took drugs, and engaged in sexual hanky-panky with Minnie Mouse. Disney executives sued to protect Mickey's good name. They also went to court when Mickey Mouse Club costumes and songs were used in a porno film.

MICKEY MOUSE WATCH: Mickey Mouse has inspired hundreds of merchandise items, but none more popular than the Mickey Mouse watch. Just as Yankee Stadium was "the house that Babe Ruth built," the Disney studio was "the house the Mouse built"; but Disney wasn't the only beholden businessman. The Mouse, Disney's affectionate way of referring to the M. M. who long preceded Marilyn Monroe, saved at least two American companies from bankruptcy— the Ingersoll-Waterbury Clock Company in Waterbury, Connecticut, in 1933, and the Lionel Corporation of New York the following year.

Lionel was in receivership when a model-train handcar showing Mickey Mouse and Minnie Mouse moving up and down became a phenomenal success. Ingersoll was *in extremis* when it put Mickey on World War I army surplus watches and introduced its new novelty at the Chicago World's Fair. Eight weeks later, the company's work force had to be increased tenfold to fill the deluge of orders. Over the next two years about 2.5 million Mickey Mouse watches were produced. Wristwatch models sold for $2.98, pocket watches for $1.50. Ingersoll's 1935-36 lapel model is considered the most handsome of all the Mickey Mouse timepieces.

Despite the huge number originally manufactured, Mickey Mouse watches have become a collector's item that commands substantial prices. More than a decade ago, comedienne Carol Burnett bought a 1930s model for six hundred dollars. Cuba's Fidel Castro and Japan's Emperor Hirohito wore Mickey Mouse watches.

The largest Mickey Mouse watch was constructed in 1976 by Paul Persoff, a New York City clock-maker. He estimated that the job would require about three weeks. Instead, it kept him busy for a year and a half. Weighing 140 pounds, with an overall diameter of five feet, it contained a modified tower-clock movement and produced a booming *tick tock* via a tape recording inside the clock housing. The nickel-plated look of an Ingersoll pocket watch was simulated by spraying the watch's wood with silver nitrate. The elephantine frame for a tiny mouse was commissioned by a California toy manufacturer who paid ten thousand dollars. Production costs, Persoff claimed, made the project a labor of love.

MICROCHIP: The microchip, an essential ingredient in such twentieth-century miracles as industrial robots, home computers, pocket calculators, copying machines, videocassette recorders, jazzed-up automobiles, supersophisticated cameras, and many an et cetera, was conceived independently by two U.S. researchers, six months apart. Jack Kilby, an electrical engineer at Texas Instruments, is credited with getting there first—on July 24, 1958—when he jotted this entry in his lab notebook: "The following circuit elements could be made on a single slice (of silicon): resistors, capacitor, distributed capacitor, transistor." The same concept, referred to in engineering circles as "the monolithic idea," was worked out early the following year by the physicist Robert Noyce, who in 1957 had cofounded the Fairchild Semiconductor Corporation.

The monolithic idea solved a problem created by another ultraconsequential American invention (*see* TRANSISTOR), which in 1948 replaced the vacuum tube. The transistor, a chunk of silicon or germanium, could cause a flow of electrons to switch on and off millions of times per second. Packing tens of thousands of transistors and other components into a single circuit made dramatic reductions in the size of electronic equipment possible. An apartment-sized computer, for instance, could be cut to refrigerator size—except for one thing: the intricacy of the wiring. Kilby and Noyce realized that all the electronic components could be made, side by side, of silicon, and the various interconnections could be stamped on the silicon wafer (or microchip) as a gold or copper inlay.

Texas Instruments and Fairchild battled over patents, the microchip market, and the microprocessor (a programmable microchip). In 1969, Noyce and two other scientists started the Intel Corporation, which has acquired a lead in the superchip war being fought among U.S. companies and against Japan because it is part-owned by and supplies IBM, the leading manufacturer of home computers. Also heavy guns in this battle for international primacy are Motorola (linked to Apple) and recently partnered National Semiconductor and Texas Instruments.

MICROGROOVE RECORD: The first long-playing microgroove records, issued by the Edison Company in 1926, were ten inches, twelve minutes per side and sold for $1.75; and twelve inches, twenty minutes per side, for $2.50. The phenolic discs contained 450 grooves to the inch and revolved at an 80-r.p.m. speed. The first releases were twenty-four minutes of selections from *Carmen* and *Aida* performed by the American Concert Orchestra and forty minutes of "Dinner Music," consisting of eight pop numbers by Bernhard Levitow and the Hotel Commodore Ensemble. These pioneer LPs were not successful because they merely repeated what was already available on records released earlier and because the walls of the tightly packed grooves collapsed after repeated use. A diamond stylus made the ¼-inch thick records, which weighed 1 and 1½ pounds, playable on existing phonographs.

The 33 1/3-r.p.m. LP record (*see* PHONOGRAPH RECORD) was introduced by RCA-Victor at New York's Plaza Hotel on September 17, 1931. Two months later, the first release—the first complete symphony to be encompassed in a single, standard-sized disc—was Beethoven's Fifth Symphony, performed by the Philadelphia Orchestra, batonned by Leopold Stokowski. The RCA LPs generated relatively few sales, in part, because of the high cost of the required record players, ranging from $247.50 to $995. The LP that routed the standard 78-r.p.m. discs was Columbia's version, first shown at a Columbia sales convention in Atlantic City on June 21, 1948. Made of lightweight vinylite, with 224 to 300 grooves to the inch, they provided twenty-three minutes of playing time on each side. Among the earliest releases, at an average cost of $4.85, were Mendelssohn's Violin Concerto; Tchaikovsky's Fourth Symphony; and a Broadway musical, Rodgers and Hammerstein's *South Pacific*. An important element in the CBS system's success was that record players were inexpensive. An adapter for standard players cost as little as $29.95.

The most recent microgroove LP development is the compact disc, or CD, a laser-activated 4¾-inch-wide record that has a silvery metal base with plastic coating and is impervious to wear and holds seventy-two minutes of music.

MICROWAVE OVEN: The microwave oven was invented in 1946 when a microwave researcher, Percy L. Spencer, noticed that a candy bar had been melted by a radar vacuum tube. That's one version. Raytheon's official line is that the microwave oven came into being in 1954 after a company engineer sent out for a bag of unpopped popcorn because of his curiosity about the effect of microwave energy on food. The corn popped and with it the inspiration that led to the development of the microwave oven.

When microwave ovens were first introduced, acceptance was slow because housewives feared that the energy waves cooking the food could be the source of dangerous radiation, but such qualms have abated. In 1984, microwave ovens became America's fastest-selling appliances. The boom was attributed to the introduction of smaller ovens, lower average cost, the increasingly hectic life-style of singles and of working couples, and the greater availability of microwave-oven accessories and products. Accessories, which have become a separate major industry, range from bacon racks and coffee percolators to popcorn poppers and steamers. Best-sellers among microwave food products include popcorn, pizza, french fries, frozen soups, pancakes, and Armour and Campbell frozen dinners (*see* TV DINNER).

Various features are offered by three Raytheon companies: Amana, Caloric, and Modern Maid. One countertop model automatically weighs food, to establish optimum cooking time. Another combines microwave-oven speed with convection-oven browning. Varied combinations include a microwave pairing of electric and gas ranges. However, the major producers of microwave ovens are Japan's Sanyo Manufacturing Corporation, which makes Kenmore ovens for Sears, Roebuck and Company, and Litton Industries, a conglomerate with more than a hundred subsidiaries, which turns out 1.5 million microwave ovens a year.

MILK, CONDENSED: Norwich, New York-born Gail Borden (1801-1874) had been a farmer, a cattle rancher, a newspaper publisher, a teacher, a surveyor, and an inventor before he perfected his condensed-milk process in 1853. One of his earlier tries at concentrating foods—a "meat biscuit" that compressed an extract of eleven pounds of meat mixed with flour into a two-pound loaf—won a gold medal at the 1851 London Exhibition but few customers. Returning by ship from the London fair, Borden learned that children aboard who did not look well weren't being fed milk because cows in the hold were too seasick. Borden first tried to rectify that situation by conducting unsuccessful experiments with boiling. Then, while in New Lebanon, New York, visiting friends at a Shakers' religious community, he observed that they used vacuum pans to condense fruit juices and maple sugar. He borrowed one and, after a period of trial and error, discovered the effective procedure. Only after three years, however, did the U.S. Patent Office agree, in 1856, that he had accomplished anything original. The following year, in Wassaic, New York, he established the New York Condensed Milk Company, which in 1899 became the Borden Company.

Consumers did not rush to buy the condensed product and Borden's first plant failed. A second seemed in jeopardy until he happened to take a train seat next to Jeremiah Milbank, a financier and wholesale grocer, who agreed to provide financial help. A big boost in sales came during the Civil War from the Union army's need for light, nourishing rations. Soldiers' testimonials spurred postwar sales. In 1861, Borden returned to Texas, where he had spent his youthful years, and used a town named in his honor as his home base until his death. In March 1836, as copublisher, with his brother, of the *Telegraph and Texas Land Register*, he also demonstrated phraseological flair. His headline over the declaration of independence for the State of Texas became a famous rallying cry: "Remember the Alamo!" Borden's epitaph in New York's Woodlawn Cemetery reads: "I tried and failed; I tried again and again, and succeeded."

MILK BOTTLE: A single glass milk bottle of unknown origin exists that is rather tall and bears a picture of a cow and the date 1866. An Alexander Campbell is said to have made the first delivery of milk in bottles to Brooklyn customers in 1878. "Warren Glass Works Glass Air Tight Milk Jars" were manufactured by Louis Porter Whiteman, proprietor of the Warren Glass Works in Cumberland, Maryland, in 1879. They were first used by New York City's Echo Farms Dairy Company. Whiteman's milk jar, sometimes embossed "Whiteman, Maker," was patented in 1884. That same year, Dr. Harvey D. Thatcher, a druggist in Potsdam, New York, created a milk jar with a glass lid anchored by a metal clamp that fit into two holes near the top of the jar. It was made of clear glass embossed with a picture of a cow being milked by a man on a milking stool. Above the picture were the words "Absolutely Pure Milk" and below it "The Milk Protector." An Italian firm, the Crownford China Company, made reproductions of the Thatcher milk bottle in both clear and colored glass. Unlike the originals, they had porcelain stoppers. In 1889 R. G. Smalley patented a milk bottle with a metal handle on the side, facilitating pouring, that was produced in various sizes, from half a pint to a gallon. (Some old bottles contained one-third of a quart.) In 1892, F. K. Ward produced what he called "a milk preserving jar," with a glass closure embossed with a cow's head and the words "This jar has been stolen if offered for sale."

By 1900, tin or glass closures wired at the top of the bottle were replaced by paper caps, first used in 1889. When the paper cap was pressed onto the top of the jar, it was held by a groove. There were also paper-lined tin caps that were crimped over the bottle opening and paper covers that went over paper caps.

The earliest milk bottles were round. The squared-off shapes, more convenient for refrigerators, did not appear until the 1940s. In the 1930s, cream-top bottles featured a bulbous neck for the cream that rose to the top. Some of the necks were face shaped, depicting a baby or

Cop the Cream, a policeman. Homogenization made cream-top bottles obsolete.

MILK CARTON: The paper milk carton was invented by Victor Wallace Farris, who was born in Buffalo, New York, but spent most of his life in New Jersey. Eventually a multimillionaire with more than 250 patents for inventions involving products like valves and tubing that he produced through seventeen companies with factories in the United States, Canada, England, France, and Australia, he decided while still a youth that glass milk bottles were too heavy to handle. The waxed paper milk carton, sealed at the bottom, made its debut in 1936. After Farris's death in 1985, his widow said that he invented the paper milk carton as "kind of a joke." It proved a highly lucrative jest. In 1943 Farris founded the Farris Engineering Corporation to produce safety valves required by the wartime navy. Later, as a navy consultant, he helped design submarines and destroyers until his retirement. All that and milk cartons, too!

MINIATURE GOLF: The person who first concocted the idea of compressing a multiacre golf course into a small chunk of urban or suburban real estate and of substituting stationary and mobile Rube Goldbergish hazards for trees, lakes, and sand mounds is not a matter of record, but historians of non-earthshaking events seem to agree that the first commercial version was the Tom Thumb Miniature Golf Course that opened in Chattanooga, Tennessee, in 1926. Drives measured in feet and putts in inches (although the traditional shout of "Fore!" was not concurrently deflated to "Two!") quickly became a craze that spread to northern Georgia and points south and, then, rebounded along the eastern seaboard.

Small-scale golf diminished to the point of near invisibility for about twenty post-Wall Street Crash depression years, but regained its popularity after World War II. In 1954, warned by his doctor to find a less blood-pressure-affecting line of work, a Fayetteville, North Carolina, insurance policy peddler, Don Clayton, launched the eighteen-hole Shady Vale Miniature Golf Course, stressing putting skill, rather than gargoylish gimmicks. The next year, he began franchising his Lilliputian layout. Within a year sixty-three look-alike Putt-Putt Golf courses were challenging caddyless golfers coast-to-coast. By 1985, that number had grown to a far-from-mini one thousand-plus in thirty-two states and five foreign nations. In Japan—where the game, with its undersized clubs and colored balls, is known as "baby golf"—the success of the first Putt-Putt, after its 1973 debut in a suburb of Hiroshima, resulted in the opening of twenty more. Since 1959, the Fayetteville-based Professional Putters Association has sponsored an annual Miniature Golf National Open, with eight regional finalists vying for a $150,000 first prize. The National Golf Foundation estimates that between five thousand and seven thousand miniature golf courses now exist in the United States alone.

MINSTREL SHOW: The first uniquely American entertainment form, the minstrel show, began when white song-and-dance men from the North donned black makeup and pretended to be blacks. By the 1840s, the minstrel show, reputedly inspired by slaves' jamborees to please their masters or for their own enjoyment, had become the nation's most popular kind of entertainment—a status it maintained for most of the century. Touring troupes drew enthusiastic audiences in other countries as well.

The minstrel show ridiculed blacks, establishing two stereotypes—the happy, shuffling plantation "darkie" and the inept urban buffoon—that for many years colored the perception of white audiences far from the South as to what blacks and slavery were really like. After Abraham Lincoln's Emancipation Proclamation in 1863, black entertainers discovered that they would have to apply burnt cork, too, and "act the nigger." Early black minstrels, who attracted black fans, learned to please both white and black audiences. They softened the caricatures, added touches of black culture, and injected a mocking humor. White minstrel shows began to hire black performers. One leading company, Primrose and West, augmented its fifty make-believe blacks with twenty-five real ones. There were also all-black shows. In 1898, college-educated Bob Cole wrote, produced, and staged *A Trip to Coontown,* the first black musical comedy sans minstrel show elements. The same year, classically trained composer Will Marion Cook wrote and directed the first black show to open on Broadway, *Clorindy, the Origin of the Cakewalk,* featuring ragtime rhythm and high-kicking strut steps. By 1908, some sixteen hundred black entertainers were employed in minstrel shows, vaudeville, circuses, and other live-entertainment forms. At least three hundred of them were accorded billing. The most celebrated black minstrel was Bert Williams, who became a "Ziegfeld Follies" star.

Vaudeville replaced minstrelsy, just as later the movies ousted vaudeville. Among white performers who donned blackface while achieving international renown were Al Jolson, Eddie Cantor, Red Skelton, George Jessel, and Rosetta Duncan, who played Topsy in vaudeville to her sister Vivian's Eva.

MISS AMERICA: The Miss America Pageant—as hallowed an American tradition as the Fourth of July parade, the Thanksgiving dinner, the World Series, and the Superbowl—has had international impact via newspaper accounts, newsreels, radio, and—since 1954—television.

Devised in 1921 as a way for Atlantic City to delay for an additional week the vacationers' Labor Day exodus and to vie with the annual baby parade at another New Jersey summer spa, Asbury Park, it secured contestants the first year by asking newspapers in nearby cities to invite their subscribers to submit photographs. Herb Test, an *Atlantic City Press* reporter, is credited with suggesting that the winner be dubbed "Miss America." Eight cities participated in the first pageant, and the winner was the *Washington Herald*'s entry, Margaret Gorman. When she first learned that she would represent her city, Miss Gorman, fifteen, was shooting marbles at a nearby park. A slender (30-25-32) blue-eyed blonde, she was the flattest titlist in the pageant's history. The first judging was conducted on the beach—as was the second—with city commissioners, policemen, firemen, and band members, like the contestants, in bathing suits. By 1923, the pageant had attracted seventy-five contestants, representing cities and regions encompassing thirty-six states. The 1922 winner, Mary Campbell of Columbus, Ohio, was recrowned in 1923. She tried for a hat trick in 1924 but was defeated. Pageant officials then ruled that no Miss America could make a second bid. In 1941, after Rosemary La Planche, who had lost as Miss California the preceding year, became Miss America, the rules were again changed to ban second tries by any contestant.

A 1926 loser was Rosebud Blondell, later the movie star Joan Blondell. Vanessa Williams, Miss America 1984, was the first black Miss America and the first forced to relinquish her crown—just weeks before the end of her reign, when *Penthouse* published suggestive nude photographs for which she had posed before becoming a contestant. There has been increasing stress on "talent." One contestant unleashed a covey of trained (?) pigeons that treated the convention hall audience like a collection of park statues.

MISS PIGGY: The prima porka of the company of synchronized lip-movement personalities Jim Henson began creating in the 1950s (*see* MUPPETS) is the ostentatiously elegant, relentlessly self-centered, Kermit the Frog-adoring, "C'est moi"-uttering Miss Piggy. She can be excused her excesses, because she was not taught at the trough how to cope with virtually overnight world fame as star of TV, movies, and Muppet merchandising. Like the heroine of *42nd Street*, she was a chorine who capitalized on her first big break. In the 1976 pilot for a globally successful TV series, "The Muppet Show," Miss Piggy was part of a barnyard chorale comprised of cows, chickens, and pigs, when it was decided to have one of the latter step out for a brief solo. Miss Piggy was the selected sow. Instead of directing her song to the home audience, however, she began an onscreen flirtation with Kermit, the show's host and nominal star, with such risible results that she was promptly upped to co-stardom.

If Kermit owes his personality to Henson, Miss Piggy is indebted for her voice and distinctive characteristics to a Henson Associates associate, vice president, director, and puppeteer Frank Oz.

MONOPOLY: Charles B. Darrow, a Philadelphia engineer out of work during the Great Depression, tried to keep his family fed by fixing electrical appliances; patching concrete; walking dogs; and tinkering with inventions, including puzzles, beach toys, and a bridge score pad. If one of his notions clicked, he hoped it would make him sufficiently solvent to resume fondly remembered vacations in Atlantic City. Such musings suggested a game; and one night in 1931, he sat down at the kitchen table, spread a sheet of oilcloth, and sketched in the names of Atlantic City streets. He shaped miniature hotels and housings from wooden molding. He typed out title deeds, added dice, and, with buttons for play money, invited his family to play the new game he had devised. They loved it. So did friends, who requested sets of their own. Darrow obliged, turning out six a day and charging only $2.50 apiece. Word got around and soon local stores began submitting orders.

Darrow offered the game to Parker Brothers, a major game manufacturer in Salem, Massachusetts. After playing a trial game, George and Charles Parker nixed it on the grounds that it took too long to play, was too complicated, and contained at least fifty-two other drawbacks. Darrow had five thousand sets printed at his own expense and distributed them himself. In 1935, after learning that Darrow had landed a sizable order from the John Wanamaker department store, the Parker brothers changed their minds and offered Darrow a contract. They were soon producing twenty thousand sets a week and had Christmas orders stacked up in huge laundry bags, but George Parker felt that the game's appeal would be short-lived; and on December 19, 1936, reluctant to be stuck with a huge inventory if sales sagged, he declared a moratorium on Monopoly manufacturing. He soon had to rescind the order.

Monopoly buffs continue to multiply. By his forty-sixth birthday, Darrow was a millionaire. Published in twenty-eight countries in nineteen languages, Monopoly is challenged only by Scrabble as the world's best-selling trademarked game. In fifty years, its total sales exceed 100 million. There may be Russian fans, too. All six Monopoly sets put on display in Moscow in 1959 were swiped.

MOOG SYNTHESIZER: Although electronic music dates back decades before to pioneers like Edward Varese, Otto Luening, and Vladimir Ussachevsky, the synthesizer in its modern form was created in the 1960s by experimenters like engineer Robert A. Moog of Trumansburg, New York, who put electronic tone generators under computer control, enabling a single keyboard performer to become, in effect, an entire orchestra. (*See also* COMPUTER MUSIC.) Souped-up synthesizer sounds are now frequent in rock concerts, movie sound tracks (a notable example is Vangelis's score for *Chariots of Fire*), and television commercials.

One exponent of "computer music," Suzanne Ciani, who was a Wellesley music student when she first encountered synthesizers during a visit to the Massachusetts Institute of Technology, prepared for a career as a concert and recording artist by doing graduate work in both music and computer science. Ciani's music, on such platters as the Finidar-pressed "Seven Waves," falls in an uncategorizable zone between classic and popular but is on the lighter side. In 1968, the composer Walter (later, Wendy) Carlos adapted ten Bach pieces for the Moog synthesizer. The result, *Switched-On Bach*, was the hottest classical album of the decade. However, engineer Moog's business, R. A. Moog, faltered shortly afterward because he lacked business knowhow and because his invention was pirated by other technicians. When sales of the $5,000-$10,000 instrument—which he personally assembled with an aide—soared in 1969, Moog tried to organize his operation, but by then, debts had mounted and it was too late. He reluctantly sold the rights to his trademark to a Buffalo, New York, entrepreneur who created a new company, Moog Musonics, with Moog as president.

Opting soon after to make Moog Musonics Moogless, he moved to the tiny, remote town of Leicester, North Carolina. There, at the end of a three-mile dirt road, atop a 1,500-foot mountain driveway, he constructed a large prefab house. Behind it, a large tin outbuilding houses Big Briar, a three-man operation that turns out custom-built electronic music systems. "Moog" synthesizers no longer bring him royalties.

MOON LANDING: First-hand information about the moon, by humans who had been there in person, was first provided by the Apollo 11 astronaut crew consisting of Neil A. Armstrong, Jr., Edwin E. (Buzz) Aldrin, Jr., and Michael Collins.

The lunar landing was preceded by about fifty unmanned space probes of the moon by the Soviet Union—which launched the first artificial satellite, the Sputnik I, on October 4, 1957—and the United States—which made its first bid in the space race with Explorer I on January 31, 1958. The first probes were intended as flyby projects (passing near the moon) or hard-landing missions (designed to crash into it). Later probes were in the soft-landing category, with instruments remaining intact. The final probes aimed at stable lunar orbits.

Soviet Luna launches were the first to achieve each of these four objectives; the first two in 1959, the other two seven years later. After repeated failures with Pioneer and Ranger launches, the American probe program scored successes with Rangers, Surveyors, and Orbiters between July 1964 and November 1968. Although later than the Lunas, they provided more detailed scientific data. The Surveyor series, for instance, established the fact that the moon's surface was solid enough to support a manned spacecraft. A Luna mission that may have aimed at a soft landing and the gathering of rock samples was launched thirty-three days before Apollo 11, but it failed.

In 1961, President John F. Kennedy vowed that by the end of the decade U.S. astronauts would land on the moon and return safely. That pledge was fulfilled with less than six months to spare. Armstrong and Aldrin descended from the command module in the lunar landing module (LEM) and stepped out on the moon on July 20, 1969, at precisely 10:56 P.M., eastern daylight saving time, while Collins, in the command ship, remained in orbit. Said Armstrong, as he stepped from a ladder and made contact with the moon, "That's one small step for a man, one giant leap for mankind." After Apollo 11 the Russians apparently abandoned their own manned lunar program. In all, there were six lunar landings by twelve astronauts.

MORMONISM: For many years the Church of Jesus Christ of Latter-day Saints (LDS), popularly known as the Mormon Church, was limited to a few American states; but after extensive proselytizing and missionary activity, it now claims a worldwide membership of nearly six million. Its beliefs are based on the Bible, the Book of Mormon, and subsequent revelations. The Book of Mormon is a translation from inscriptions on tablets of gold that appeared in a vision to Joseph Smith and on which he based the sect he founded in Fayette, New York, in 1830. Ascribed to the prophet Mormon, the book recounts the early history of residents of the American continent from about 600 years before Christ's birth to about 420 years after.

Mormon beliefs include emphasis on revelation, interdependence of temporal and spiritual life, tithing, concern about community welfare, and "celestial marriage" for all eternity. Because Mormons believe that God can make salvation possible for non-Mormon forebears if their descendants can identify them and pray for them, the church maintains the most extensive genealogical data bank in the world, containing more than a million rolls of electronically indexed microfilm bearing sixty million family histories, equivalent in wordage to 4.5 million books. The Mormons' ultimate goal is to record the pedigrees of everyone who ever lived. Also being stored are two hundred thousand historical works about America and all other countries.

Smith led his followers to Ohio, then Missouri, and finally Illinois, where violence broke out between church factions. On June 24, 1844, Smith was jailed for treason; three days later he was murdered by a mob. A new Mormon leader, Brigham Young, resumed the westward trek; and in July 1847, the first settlers arrived in what is now Salt Lake City. In 1852, Young proclaimed the doctrine of plural marriage, which had been quietly introduced in 1841 by Smith, who was convinced that it was a divine requirement. Polygamy exacerbated friction with non-Mormons, and Congress declared the practice illegal. In 1890, thirteen years after Young's death, the Mormon president Wilford Woodruff ended church sanction of polygamy. As a result, Utah Territory was admitted to the union in 1896 as the forty-fifth state.

MORON: Both the word and the concept (neither applicable to a similarly spelled, differently pronounced sector of Buenos Aires) are of American manufacture. Those with intelligence quotients below the "borderline" range of 70 to 80 were initially classified as "morons" (50 to 70), "imbeciles" (25-50), and "idiots" (below 25). "Moron," from the Greek *moros* (meaning foolish) was the name assigned to a fool in a Molière play. Proposed by the psychologist Henry H. Goddard, who believed that mental retardation was hereditary and that its elimination could be accomplished only by sterilization of the feebleminded, the word was *voted* into existence in 1919 by the American Association for the Study of the Feeble-Minded. The entire IQ concept was conceived by the Johnson County, Indiana-born psychologist Lewis Madison Terman (1877-1956), who, in 1916, published the first widely used test for measuring intelligence, the Stanford revision of the Binet-Simon intelligence scale, subsequently known as the Stanford-Binet test. The test was devised so that the IQ of an average child of any age, computed as a ratio of intellectual age to chronological age, would be 100. Terman found, contrary to popular belief, that children in the "genius" category, with IQ's over 140, tended to be healthier and more stable emotionally than those lower on the intelligence scale. His other gradings were "very superior" (120-140), "superior" (110-120), "average" (90-110), and "dull" (80-90). During World War I, Terman also devised the first group intelligence tests, the Army Alpha and Army Beta tests.

MOTEL: Early on, the "hotel for automobile tourists," also known as "the motor hotel," offered several lures for traveling salesmen, vacationing families, concupiscent couples, and other motor-borne visitors. It was informal, inexpensive, and convenient. No parking problems. No tipping of bellboys. No long walks down corridors. No long waits for elevators.

The first hostelry to identify itself as a motel was the Motel Inn in San Luis Obispo, California, which offered chalets equipped with bathroom, telephone, and garage that could accommodate a total of 160 guests. It was opened by Hamilton Hotels under the management of Harry Elliott on December 12, 1925. Its designer, Arthur Heinman, coined the word "motel" in 1924, but it was not used in any dictionary until 1950. "Tourist courts," consisting of little cabins, proliferated during the 1950s. Many were mom-and-pop operations. By the middle of the decade, motels numbered about twenty-two thousand, approximately twice as many as hotels, and the ratio later rose to about four-to-one. Big chains entered the scene, and amenities and costs increased. One-story motels were succeeded by high-rise motor hotels.

Holiday Inns was launched by Memphis realtor Kemmons Wilson after an arduous and expensive 1951 trip to Washington, D.C., with his wife and five children. He opened his own motel in Memphis and offered "free" extras: ice, swimming pool, room telephone, even kennel service. The Holiday Inn chain, the world's largest, encompasses 1,741 properties in fifty-four countries. Other major chains are Ramada, Best Western, Marriott, and Howard Johnson. Early motels were bunched along major highways, on the outskirts of cities. Now they loom downtown, border airports, or constitute self-contained resorts. As prices escalated, there was a move toward frill-free but comfortable accommodations at lower cost—the "economy" chains.

Research techniques enable motel operators to make educated guesses about occupancy periods, check-in times, and other variables. The motels know, for instance, that washcloths are the most frequently swiped items and that mattresses have a 20 percent shorter life expectancy if they're on the first floor of a multilevel building.

MOTHER'S DAY: Medieval England had a Mothering Sunday, the fourth Sunday in Lent, when apprenticed children headed home, bringing Mum almond-paste fruitcake as a gift. Mother's Day, the second Sunday in May, can be traced back to Mary T. Sasseen, a Kentucky teacher who suggested at a teachers' confab that all mamas should be saluted every April 20, her own mother's natal day. Similar recommendations from several other sources nominated other dates, but none of the proposals caught on until Anna M. Jarvis of Philadelphia, a lifelong spinster, bereft after her mother died, conceived the idea of an international observance. After arranging for simultaneous services, mainly to honor her own mother, on May 10, 1908, in churches in her home city and Grafton, West Virginia, where her family had lived previously, she began writing thousands of letters, seeking to enlist the support of influential individuals for the annual honoring of mothers living or dead. Her crusade gradually won adherents.

In 1910, Mother's Day became an official holiday in West Virginia, Oklahoma, and Washington. Within a year every other state had joined the maternal parent-praising parade. In December 1912, Miss Jarvis established the Mother's Day International Association. Both houses of Congress passed resolutions endorsing it as a national holiday, and in May 1914, President Woodrow Wilson concurred, urging annual display of the American flag "as a public expression of our love and reverence for the mothers of our country." The holiday was quickly adopted by Canada, Mexico, Japan, and parts of South America. The wearing of a carnation on Mother's Day (red for a live parent, white for a deceased one) was another Jarvis suggestion. It was her mother's favorite flower.

An early Mother's Day supporter was John Wanamaker, one of several department store owners who quickly began to cash in on the holiday's gift-peddling possibilities. Greeting-card manufacturers greeted the opportunity to convert love into loot, as did confectioners and florists. Appalled, Miss Jarvis denounced the commercialism and withdrew from public life. She was blind and penniless when she died in a West Chester, Pennsylvania, sanitarium.

MOVIES: Noteworthy early experiments in photographing motion were still pictures of racehorses, made in California in 1877 by Eadweard James Muybridge, who set up a row of twenty-four cameras with electrically triggered shutters. (Eadweard was sometimes Eadweird—he changed his name from Edward James Muggeridge.) The first motion pictures using a single camera, inspired by Muybridge's studies of animal locomotion, were produced by a French physician, E. J. Marey, in the 1880s.

In 1889, Thomas Alva Edison and an assistant, William Dickson, developed the kinetograph, a camera using rolls of coated celluloid, and a peep show device, the kinetoscope, for viewing kinetograph pictures. It became a popular penny arcade attraction. Edison's lab was also responsible for the notion of using a perforated filmstrip to assure smooth movement past the lens. In France, in 1895, the Lumière brothers created the Cinematgraphe. In 1896, projection machines developed in the United States, most notably the pantopticon and the vitascope, replaced one-viewer-at-a-time devices. Initially, screenings were part of vaudeville bills, but in June 1896, a four-hundred-seat movie theater (*see* MOVIE THEATER) was established in New Orleans. Among its attractions was *May Irwin's Kiss*, filmed three months earlier by Raff and Gammon. In a short scene from a Broadway comedy, *The Widow Jones*, May Irwin and John Rice performed the world's first onscreen osculation. The first movie hit was Edwin S. Porter's 1903 *The Great Train Robbery*, an eleven-minute epic that ended with a Western bandit's firing of his gun directly at the audience.

"Movie factories" were initially clustered in and near New York City, with Westerns filmed in the wilds of New Jersey. To escape legal action by the Motion Picture Patents Company, an association of leaders in the fledgling industry, many independents moved their operations to Los Angeles so that they could skeedaddle across the Mexican border to avoid injunctions. After 1913, Hollywood (*see* HOLLYWOOD) became the American movie capital. Until 1910, performers were anonymous, to avoid the creation of stars who would demand higher salaries. That policy was discontinued, however, when producers realized that favorite personalities increased box-office receipts. Early stars included Douglas Fairbanks in adventure films, Mary Pickford in sentimental sagas, Theda Bara in sex dramas, William S. Hart in Westerns, and Charlie Chaplin in comedies.

MOVIE THEATER: The first movie theater to remain in operation for a sustained period of time was the four-hundred-seat Vitascope Hall in New Orleans, opened by William T. Rock on June 26, 1896. The admission charge was a dime plus another dime for any patron who wished to visit the projection room and examine Thomas Alva Edison's vitascope projector. For yet another dime, the movie buff could buy a single souvenir frame of discarded film. Most of the films, screened daily from 10 A.M. to 3 P.M. and from 6 P.M. to 10 P.M., were brief scenic items; but there was also the "sexy" *May Irwin's Kiss* (*see* MOVIES). A few months after the theater's opening, the program included *The Pickaninnies Dance, The Carnival Scene, The Irish Way of Discussing Politics, Cissy Fitzgerald,* and *The Lynching Scene.* The vitascope vogue was relatively brief. As superior projection methods were developed, the 1902 conversion of a Los Angeles store into a "movie house" triggered a proliferation of such change-overs.

The first actual movie theater, with piano accompaniments and other trimmings, opened in Pittsburgh in 1905. Reflecting its five-cent admission charge, it was called the nickelodeon. The first giant movie theater was the five-thousand-seat Gaumont-Palace, opened in Paris in 1910. It was one of the first to use two projectors for uninter-rupted showing of multireel films. Its capacity was not exceeded until the advent, in 1927, of the largest movie theater ever built; New York's $8 million 6,250-seat Roxy. The first movie theater to charge more for sitting in the back, where the viewing was better, than upfront, as in theaters with live actors, was the Picture Palace at St. Albans in Hertfordshire, England, opened in 1908.

MUPPETS: "The Muppet Show," which premiered in 1976 and made an instant international celebrity of a brazen barnyard blonde named Miss Piggy (*see* MISS PIGGY), was a favorite of some 250 million viewers in more than one hundred countries.

"Muppet," which suggests a blending of "marionette" and "puppet," was coined by the Muppets' creator, Jim Henson, who first began playing with dolls when he joined a Washington, D.C., high school's puppet club as an aspiring scenery designer. A longtime TV buff, he successfully applied for a puppeteer vacancy on a local station's "Morning Show" after fashioning a puppet from his mother's old green coat. He acquired a five-minute show of his own, "Sam and His Friends," while a fine-arts student at the University of Maryland. A widemouth lizardlike whatzit? that sprouted long legs and became Kermit the Frog (Henson's alter ego) made his national TV debut in 1957 on Steve Allen's "Tonight" show, wearing a long, blond wig and singing "I've Grown Accustomed to Your Face" to a purple monster. Henson furnished Kermit's voice and motions; the monster was manipulated by a University of Maryland classmate, Jane Nebel—later his partner, his wife, and the mother of his five children. Rowlf the Dog became the first Muppet TV star via the 1963-66 "Jimmy Dean Show," but he was eclipsed by Kermit, Bert and Ernie, and Big Bird on the 1969 "Sesame Street." Over the years the Muppet menagerie has encompassed more than four hundred creations, including Gonzo, the Cookie Monster and the Snuffleupagus.

A current Muppet series, "Fraggle Rock," a Home Box Office cable-TV entry in the United States, is being telecast with minor variations in more than ninety countries. Doc, an eccentric inventor in the home version, becomes a lighthouse keeper in England and a retired chef in France. A Muppet chef in the small-fry "Sesame Street" series spouts doubletalk everywhere except in nonsense-nixing West Germany. Three feature films, *The Muppet Movie*, *The Great Muppet Caper*, and *The Muppets Take Manhattan*, have had worldwide distribution. *Big Bird Goes to China*, starring yet another Muppet, won an Emmy award. Muppet merchandise abounds everywhere. *Maclean's*, the Canadian newsmagazine, dubs the fanciful troupe "undoubtedly the world's most original and entertaining puppets."

MURINE: Stinging eyes the world over are soothed because of the shake of a horse's tail. In 1890, while Oris F. Hall, a Spokane, Washington, banker, was chatting with a friend in front of the bank, he noticed that the friend's horse had a broken shoe. When he bent over for a closer look, the horse swished its tail and cut the cornea of Hall's right eye. A painful ulcer resulted; and soon, Hall and his son, who had a minor eye irritation, headed for Chicago to see two renowned opthalmologists, the brothers Drs. James B. and George W. McFatrich. Father and son were both healed by brother and brother. Contributing to the cures was an eye lotion the McFatriches compounded themselves. Hall urged them to make their preparation available for more victims of eye problems than just their own patients, but it took seven years to convince them. The three men formed a company that became the first mass manufacturer of eye drops. The product's name was coined by its creators from the first and last syllables of its chemical formula, muriate of berberine. Murine was being marketed in more than sixty countries even before it was absorbed by Chicago-based Abbott Laboratories, which has seventy-seven foreign subsidiaries and manufacturing facilities in twenty-eight countries.

MUSICAL COMEDY: Opera and operetta are its forebears, but musical comedy is a uniquely American form of stage entertainment that has been enthusiastically embraced by the rest of the world. Many of the more successful examples of the genre continue to get frequent encores in other countries. *Fiddler on the Roof,* translated into numerous languages, is a signal example. *Annie Get Your Gun* and *Hair* had longer runs in London than in New York. (For a more recent U.S. song-and-dance phenomenon, *see CHORUS LINE.*) Although the 1866 *The Black Crook* is generally cited as the first musical comedy, it fits more comfortably into an earlier category, the extravaganza. Moreover, it was preceded by borrowed-from-England ballad operas like the 1735 *Flora,* with tailored lyrics of popular songs inserted in otherwise spoken plays; two home-grown diversions— early1800s "burlesque" (*see* BURLESQUE), which stressed parody, and pre-Civil War minstrel shows (*see* MINSTREL SHOW); plus another import: the song, dance, and comedy pantomime. *The Black Crook,* an unprecedented hit, presaged American fun fare like Flo Ziegfeld's "Follies" by featuring skimpily clad chorines, stunning stage effects, and elaborate song-and-dance numbers.

The first tentative effort to integrate plot, comedy, music, and dance was made in Nate Salsbury's 1879 burlesque extravaganza, *The Brook,* about events at a picnic. In describing his opus, the producer first used the phrase "musical comedy." The success in America of Gilbert and Sullivan's *Pinafore,* concurrently performed by ninety troupes, encouraged American librettists and composers to put more emphasis on story, ushering in a golden age of American operetta. Most were patterned after European models; but in the early 1900s, George M. Cohan changed that by injecting all-American characters, locales, talk, and zest into breezy musicals like *Little Johnny Jones.* In due, perhaps overdue, course, such relatively primitive works were followed by American musical comedies about America that became international classics, like *Show Boat, Pal Joey, Annie Get Your Gun, Guys and Dolls, Oklahoma!, South Pacific,* and with an assist by William Shakespeare, *West Side Story.*

MUSICAL INSTRUMENTS: For centuries the only "native American" musical instrument to travel beyond its home borders was the banjo, developed by blacks in the South in the 1790s, to accompany plantation songs. The ukulele (in Hawaiian, "jumping flea") became "American" when Hawaii was added to the United States. The first attempt to produce music electronically was made in 1895 by Thaddeus Cahill of Massachusetts, who created what he called the Telharmonium from rotary generators and telephone receivers.

Revolutionary new orchestral sounds were made possible by the invention of an electronic device, the synthesizer. The first, introduced in 1955, was created by RCA research scientists Harry Olson and Herbert Belar. In the early 1960s, it was joined by the Moog Synthesizer (*see* MOOG SYNTHESIZER). Synthesizers were used for specially written compositions, fresh versions of classical opuses and rock 'n' roll. Native Californian Harvey Partch, who escalated the musical scale from twelve tones to forty-three, created numerous instruments to encompass it, including the seventy-two-stringed citharalike whang gun, the marimbalike boo, glass bells he termed cloud chamber bowls, and, his favorite, the bloboys. Among Partch compositions were "And on the Seventh Day Petals Fell on Petaluma" and "Visions Fill the Eyes of a Defeated Basketball Team in the Shower Room." "U.S. Highway," also on the Columbia label, featured the chatter of hoboes riding the rods.

Some American instruments have never had concert hall aspirations. One, fabricated by American comedian Bob Burns, was the bazooka, which resembled a toilet plunger. During World War II, the name of this zany creation was applied to a dead serious weapon: a lightweight firing tube, balanced on the shoulder, that launched armor-piercing rockets. A basic weapon in the rock 'n' roll arsenal, the guitar-shaped electric bass, which has almost replaced the upright bass viol in pop music, was invented by Leo Fender of Fullerton, California, who also provided the Fender Stratocaster electric guitars used by such rock superstars as Buddy Holly, Jimi Hendrix, Elvis Costello, and Prince. Ironically, Fender never learned to play his own instruments.

MUZAK: Despite frequent put-downs by musicians and by captive audiences in elevators, in dentists' chairs, and at the other end of a telephone, when Muzak's "background music" celebrated its fiftieth anniversary in 1984, it claimed subscribers in seventeen countries.

Fifteen years before that, it had even been heard on the moon—Neil Armstrong listened to a Muzak tape just before his lunar stroll.

After experimentally feeding commercial-free music into Cleveland, Ohio, homes via telephone lines, George Squire, an army officer, decided in 1934 that Wired Radio lacked zip. Because Kodak seemed an especially effective brand name, he melded "music" and "Kodak" into "Muzak." Initially, Muzak music consisted of recordings available to the general public. In 1941, a new owner, former Connecticut senator William Benton, revitalized his flagging business by suggesting that workers' efficiency could be improved by music that was "scientifically" programmed. He jettisoned as distractions all lyrics and certain instruments and accelerated tempos at times, especially midmorning and midafternoon, when productivity usually sagged. Muzak is also used to spur supermarket buying, to make waiting less exasperating, and when augmented by subliminal "thou shalt not steal" messages, to decrease shoplifting. The service was acquired in 1981 by Westinghouse Broadcasting and Cable. A daily program of 486 constantly augmented and reshuffled songs, specially recorded by orchestras in various countries, is now transmitted by satellite from Stamford, Connecticut, to local FM stations that serve as relays.

The no-words policy has been breached only twice—in 1981, when the American hostages in Iran were released; and in 1985, when Muzak joined thousands of radio stations in playing "We Are the World," an all-star recording made to raise money for famine relief. In 1963, when President John F. Kennedy was assassinated, martial music replaced the scheduled songs. According to a Muzak official, a German bordello once applied for the service, cuing conjecture as to what the proprietor was after—harder-working employees or less irascible customers?

N

NECKTIE: The modern necktie, consisting of four separate pieces of cloth cut on the bias to prevent twisting, was devised and patented in 1920 by an American, Jesse Langsdorf. A "necktie party" in Wild West days was not an occasion for jolly cravat-swapping. It meant a lynching.

NEEDLE: The first machine-made sewing needles of uniform size and shape, not only better, but cheaper than their crude predecessors, were manufactured by the Excelsior Needle Company of Wolcottville, Connecticut, launched on March 2, 1866, with a capitalization of $20,000. Needle-manufacturing consists of sharpening a bit of steel wire at one end and punching the other to produce a non-black "eye."

NEWSPAPER CARTOON: The first newspaper illustration, designed by Benjamin Franklin, was a cartoon of a segmented snake, its eight parts adjacent to the initials for New England, New York, New Jersey, Pennsylvania, Maryland, Virginia, North Carolina, and South Carolina, over the printed slogan "JOIN, or DIE." About three inches wide, it appeared in the first column of the second page in the May 9, 1754, edition of Franklin's *Pennsylvania Gazette,* and was intended to rally the colonies to united action in the prospective war with the French and the Indians. New York and Boston newspapers promptly copied the idea. It was widely reproduced eleven years later as part of the resistance to the Stamp Act, even though that act was intended to repay England for the costs it incurred aiding the colonists during the French and Indian War.

    The first "editorial cartoon" was drawn in 1814 by the portrait painter John Wesley Jarvis for the Washington, D.C., *Federal Republican.* Commenting on President James Madison's repeal of the

Embargo Act, commonly referred to as a "terrapin policy," it depicted a terrapin floating on its back and grasping the body of Madison, who had cut off its head with a knife. The severed head clung to Madison's ear. Editorial cartoons virtually vanished during the Civil War, but they returned in the 1870s as a regular feature of two New York newspapers, the *Evening Telegram* and the *Daily Graphic*. In *Harper's Weekly*, Thomas Nast—whose cartoons had helped rout the notorious Tweed Ring—created a political menagerie, including the Republican elephant, the Democratic donkey and the Tammany tiger. (Other Nast drawings became the "traditional" Uncle Sam and Santa Claus.) Today, cartoons accentuate editorial opinions virtually everywhere. (*See also* DOONSBURY.)

NEWSPAPER PHOTOGRAPH: Henry J. Newton's photograph of New York's Shantytown, converted into a halftone illustration by Stephen H. Horgan, was the progenitor of all those pictures being shot for daily publication by staff photographers, serendipitous amateurs, and pesky paparazzi the world over. It appeared in the *New York Daily Graphic* on March 14, 1880. The *Graphic,* which made its debut on March 4, 1873, and sold for a nickel, was America's first illustrated daily newspaper. Before and after that historic photograph, its illustrations consisted of zinc plate etchings.

James Gordon Bennett is credited with using the first real news illustration, a picture of the fire-ravaged Merchants' Exchange, in an 1835 edition of his *New York Herald.* Newspaper reproductions were so murky that it was sometimes impossible to figure out what a picture represented without consulting the caption. In 1845, when the *Herald* published what purported to be a drawing of General Jackson's funeral, rival newspapers jeered that the same engraving had already been fobbed off on the public as Queen Victoria's coronation, the funeral of General William Henry Harrison, and the Croton Water Celebration. More impressive news illustration was provided by Nathaniel Currier, who in 1840 hawked vivid prints of a disastrous fire aboard the steamboat *Lexington* three days after the tragedy occurred. He sold so many copies that he hired a staff of quick-sketch artists and made spot news coverage his lithographing establishment's prime function. When James Merritt Ives became his partner, Currier and Ives began three decades of exceptional printmaking. Their pictures were sold by direct mail, by designated representatives, and by peddlers for prices ranging from six cents for a small black-and-white print to four dollars for a large full-color print. A similar sales technique was employed by Matthew B. Brady for his graphic Civil War photos. By the end of the 1880s, action photos were an established newspaper ingredient.

NYLON: The first thread of the first totally man-made fiber was created in the laboratories of the E. I. du Pont de Nemours' chemical company (*see* DU PONT) in 1934 when Dr. Wallace Humes Carothers squeezed a chemical solution through a hypodermic needle.

Although "nylon," especially to males fixated on legs, conjures up sheer hose clinging to shapely limbs, the first commercial use for this artificial fabric, a wholly synthetic fiber originally known as Polymer 66, was Exton toothbrush bristles, manufactured at Du Pont's Arlington, New Jersey, plant on February 24, 1938. The bristles made their public debut via Dr. West's Miracle Tuft Toothbrush, which went on sale the following September. Nylon, patented on February 16, 1937, soon proved extremely versatile. Nylon yarn for stockings was first produced at Du Pont's Seaford, Delaware, factory on December 15, 1939. After a marketing test at a Wilmington, Delaware, department store in October 1939, when four thousand pairs were sold in minutes, all the manufacturers of nylon hosiery, by mutual agreement, introduced their products on the same day. Four million pairs went on sale throughout the United States on May 15, 1940, triggering a mass coast-to-coast invasion of department stores and specialty shops.

A silk substitute, nylon became especially prized during World War II when the Allied countries were deprived of Japanese silk. In 1942, nylon was withdrawn from the general market when the War Production Board decreed that the entire supply was needed for parachutes and other World War II military uses. Other uses of nylon include boat sails, rope, clothing fabric, and many an et cetera. The invention of nylon paved the way to the discovery of Orlon, Dacron, and Lycra. Ironically, Carothers never saw the far-reaching results of his laboratory magic. Depressed over his sister's death and convinced, despite his election to the National Academy of Sciences, that he was a failure, he committed suicide in 1937.

O

OIL WELL: Oil was considered a nuisance during America's pioneer years, though Indians in northwestern Pennsylvania skimmed it off streams and drank it in the belief that anything that smelled and tasted so bad had to be a potent medicine. Revolutionary soldiers shared that opinion. Farmers and lumbermen in Pennsylvania disagreed and cursed the pesky stuff as a contaminant, making water undrinkable and ruining fields. In 1818, when an eastern Kentucky salt well inexplicably filled with oil, becoming the first well in America to produce crude oil, its owner was moved to tears, not cheers. Similar salt wells found in the 1830s also evoked cussing. Some oil-afflicted landowners tried to sell it as a liniment for horses and humans. The attitude toward oil changed, however, after the realization that it was an excellent source of light and a cheaper substitute for hard-to-get whale oil.

In the mid-1850s, George Henry Bissell, James M. Townsend, Benjamin Silliman, and others associated with the Pennsylvania Rock Oil Company concluded that oil, like water, could be produced by digging, but the idea was dismissed as nonsense. A Pennyslvania Rock Oil stockholder, former railroad conductor "Colonel" Edwin Drake, contracted to do the digging at Titusville, in the heart of Pennsylvania's oil country. He hired an experienced salt borer, but the man decided that Drake was out of his mind and never showed up. Drake then hired William A. ("Uncle Billy") Smith, a blacksmith who also did salt boring. Drilling began in June 1859. By August 27, the hole was only 69½ feet deep. The next day was Sunday, so Smith didn't return to resume digging until Monday morning. What he found was the unctuous proof that he had produced the world's first man-made oil well. The subsequent oil rush converted tiny Titusville into a boomtown that was tagged "Sodden Gomorrah." By 1900, there were about thirty-seven thousand oil wells in the United States alone.

As development of the internal-combustion engine, which required gasoline, dramatically increased the demand for oil, wells sprouted in Texas, Canada, Russia, Southeast Asia, Latin America, and the Middle East.

OK: Probably the American phraseology most frequently used by non-Americans, "OK" is uttered by Spaniards more often than *"salud"* and is heard more often in England than "right-o." Even Liberians who speak the Djabo dialect say "O-ke." "OK's" origin is uncertain. It has been attributed to dozens of sources, including an invitation to romance extended to American girls by visiting French sailors during the American Revolution—*aux quais* ("at the wharf"); a Choctaw word, *okeh*, meaning "it is so"; a Finnish word, *oikea*, meaning "correct"; the OK Civil War crackers boxed by the Orrins-Kendall Company; a Danish and Norwegian sailors' phrase, pronounced "hah gay," meaning "shipshape"; an abbreviation for *Oberst Kommandant* used on official documents by a Prussian general who served in the American Revolution; an abbreviation for *omnis korrecta* on examination papers; the initials of a freight agent, Obediah Kelly, signed to bills of lading; a Jamaican phrase, "oh-ki", a Surinam expression, "okee"; and, in the 1830s, an intentional misspelling by pixyish Boston newspapermen of "oll korrect."

President Woodrow Wilson reputedly accepted the Indian etymology and used only the "okeh" spelling. One legend credits—or discredits—an earlier president, Andrew Jackson, claiming it was Jackson's abbreviation for an unintentional misspelling of "oll kurrect" that he kept scribbling on legal documents while he was a law clerk in Tennessee. Since 1941, however, almost all authorities have linked OK to yet another president, Martin Van Buren, born in Kinderhook, New York, and affectionately referred to as "Old Kinderhook." Van Buren reputedly used the initials of his nickname to check off documents when he finished reading them. A New York organization dedicated to Van Buren's reelection in 1840 named itself the Democratic OK Club. When the club held its first meeting, the initials caught on and spread rapidly as a synonym for "all right." "OK" reputedly made its first appearance in print in the *New York New Era* on March 23, 1840. However, came the election, OK was KO'd by William Henry Harrison.

OREO: By 1912 Nabisco, the National Biscuit Company, was already selling popular snacks like Fig Newtons, Animal Crackers, and Uneeda Biscuits, but one of three additions to its line that year, the Oreo Biscuit, became the world's all-time favorite cookie. Its fellow newcomers, the Mother Goose biscuit, imprinted with scenes from Mother Goose legends, and the Veronese biscuit, "of beautiful design." were the ones the company considered potential hits, but customers opted for what was described in a company memo to its managers as "two beautifully embossed, chocolate-flavored wafers with a rich cream filling."

Why "Oreo?" No one's certain. One possibility is that the company's first chairman, Adolphus W. Green, a Chicago lawyer who doted on the classics, picked the name because it is the Greek word for "mountain," which aptly described one of the cookie's earlier configurations. Another possibility is that it derives from *or*, the French word for "gold," because the original label identified the product in gold letters.

The Oreo has undergone changes in size, filigree, and nomenclature. It has been both larger and smaller than it is now. The arrangement of twelve small flowers, dots, and lines was designed by William A. Turnier, a Nabisco employee from 1923 to 1973. The Oreo Biscuit became, in turn, the Oreo Sandwich, the Oreo Creme Sandwich and finally, in 1974, the Oreo Chocolate Sandwich Cookie.

Oreos are being used on and in ice cream, inside chocolate popsicles, and as a chocolate-dipped candy. A Sarasota, Florida, bar features an Oreo cocktail with vodka, creme de cacao and ice cream as its other ingredients. "Oreo" has also become a pejorative term among American blacks to describe someone black externally, but white internally.

OSCAR: The trophy presented to winners of Hollywood's annual Academy Awards (*see* ACADEMY AWARD), a male figure, muscular arms pressed close to its sides, hands clasping the hilt of an upright sword, heels planted on a roll of movie film, is internationally recognized by its nickname.

When first presented on May 16, 1929, it was known as "the Statuette," but in 1931 it became "the Oscar," reportedly after Mrs. Margaret Herrick, later the executive secretary of the Academy of Motion Picture Arts and Sciences, commented, "He reminds me of my Uncle Oscar." (The namesake was identified later as a second cousin, Oscar Pierce.) A newspaperman then wrote that Academy employees had "affectionately" renamed the statuette. Bette Davis, who was said to have detected a similar similarity to her first husband, Harmon Oscar Nelson, later denied it. Hollywood columnist Sidney Skolsky, reputedly tired of seeking synonyms for "statuette," a word he couldn't spell, claimed that he picked the name vaudevillians applied to anonymous small-town orchestra leaders. Etymologist H. L. Mencken relayed this version: Donald Gledhill, secretary of the Academy, was in his office awaiting a relative when a jeweler arrived with the sample statuette. At first glance, Gledhill mistook the jeweler for the relative and said to his wife, "Here's Oscar now." Within hearing was a newspaperman who, the next day, wrote that "Academy officials" referred to the trophies as Oscars.

Sculpted by George Stanley from a design by movie art director Cedric Gibbons, Oscar is 13½ inches tall, base included, and weighs four ounces less than seven pounds. Its bronze interior, 92 percent tin and 8 percent copper, is coated with fourteen-karat gold. Actor Conrad Nagel, one of three prime movers in establishing the Academy, opined at an early dinner meeting that any Academy Award should symbolize "continuing progress . . . militant, dynamic." In a few minutes Gibbons drew a suitable sketch on his tablecloth.

To keep Oscars out of pawnshops and other unseemly places, recipients are required to let the Academy repurchase them. Although Oscar winners place inestimable value on their trophies, the Academy's standing cash offer is ten dollars.

OSTEOPATHY: Although practitioners of both therapies engage in the laying on of hands, osteopathic doctors are not chiropractors, and vice versa. Osteopaths possess medical degrees. Their holistic therapy, which subordinates medication to manipulation of bones and muscles, was created in 1874 by the Jonesboro, Virginia, native Andrew Taylor Still (1828-1917). The son of a Methodist minister, he grew up in Tennessee and Missouri. In 1853, a few years after he married, Still moved to the Wakarusa Mission, near Kansas City, Kansas, where he treated live Indians and studied anatomy by dissecting dead ones. He also studied medicine at the Kansas City School of Physicians and Surgeons. After Civil War service, he concentrated on finding treatments in areas where orthodox physicians had failed. The deaths in 1864 of three of his children, due to spinal meningitis, led him to expound the theory that the normal body provides its own defenses against disease and that most ailments are due to dislocations—he called them "subluxations"—of the vertebrae, correctable by massage.

Osteopathy is directed at the removal of "lesions" created by strain that affect bone alignment, muscles, and cartilage. For more than twenty-five years, Still toured the country, teaching and practicing and often encountering hostility from orthodox physicians. The American School of Osteopathy was founded in 1892 at Kirksville, Missouri, Still's home base until his death. Other U.S. colleges are also accredited by the American Osteopathic Association for the four-year training course, including conventional medicine, required for the degree of D.O., Doctor of Osteopathy. Osteopaths are licensed in all fifty states to perform surgery, deliver babies, prescribe drugs, and offer all other medical services. It is estimated that osteopathic physicians, who comprise about 5 percent of the nation's doctors, treat about 10 percent of U.S. patients. Osteopathic and allopathic (M.D.)

physicians once maintained separate hospitals but now work side by side in most institutions. Osteopathy has become a popular therapy in many other countries. (*See also* CHIROPRACTIC.)

OUTBOARD MOTOR: When Ole Evinrude, picknicking with friends on an island near Milwaukee, so the story goes, was advised by his wife-to-be that she yearned for ice cream, he promptly began rowing to the not-so-nearby shore. By the time he had completed the round-trip in the hot August sun, he was left with a containerful of glop and a compelling notion: a portable motor that could be hooked up, when needed, to a small boat. Motorboats were already common, built by the manufacturers of the Steinway piano and other companies, and even detachable motors had been proposed under such names as "boat-propelling device" and "outboard porto motor." However, Evinrude's version, patented in 1909, was the first to succeed commercially. The prototype "outboard motor" was a single-cylinder, two-port, two-cycle battery-ignited engine, weighing forty-six pounds, that developed 1½ horsepower at about 1,000 r.p.m. In 1921, Evinrude introduced a twin-cylinder motor, the Elto, a pound heavier, that upped the outputt-putt to 2½ horsepower at 1,400 r.p.m.

OVERALLS: Outdoor workers, urban and rural, often don a blue work outfit, consisting of loose denim trousers with a high-rise bib secured by shoulder suspenders. Overalls, often pronounced "over-hauls," could easily be hauled over all other clothing—warm pants and underwear in the winter or *le minimum* in hot weather. The most popular version of the ultrautilitarian garment was devised by a former Singer sewing machine salesman in the 1870s. Seeking a more varied selection of sizes for work clothes, he ordered six sewing-machine employees to turn out a standard bib overall in a different material, hard-wearing blue denim, the same material used for Levi's jeans. The sturdy garment was put on sale for seventy-five cents, promptly making overalls popular all over. (*See also* LEVI's.)

OZ: Long before the 1939 Metro-Goldwyn-Mayer movie, *The Wizard of Oz*—which made a superstar of Judy Garland and generated annual TV encores and all-black stage and screen carbons dubbed *The Wiz*—small fry in many lands had been trasported to the magical kingdom of Oz, a name L. (for Lyman) Frank Baum borrowed from the O-Z label on the bottom drawer of his filing cabinet. The story of Dorothy, a Kansas girl whisked by a cyclone into an Alice-like wonderland, *The Wonderful Wizard of Oz* was an immediate success in 1900 and was translated into a dozen languages. As a musical extravaganza it made instant stars of the song-and-dance team of Dave Montgomery and Fred Stone. Baum wrote thirteen more

Oz books, with titles like *Ozma of Oz* (a granddaughter was named Ozma) and *The Tik-Tok Man of Oz*. After Baum's death in 1919, twenty-six Oz books were written by six other authors.

The first movie version, a 1910 series of one-reelers, was followed by a five-reel adaptation in 1915 and a full-length silent version in 1925. A Disney feature, *Return to Oz*, was released in 1985. The M-G-M classic used black and white for the Kansas segments and color for Dorothy's fantasies. Judy's cast colleagues included Ray Bolger as the Scarecrow, Bert Lahr as the Cowardly Lion, Jack Haley as the Tin Woodman, Billie Burke and Margaret Hamilton as good and bad witches, assorted midgets as the Munchkins, and dithering Frank Morgan as the Wizard.

The most enduring song in the Harold Arlen-E.Y. (Yip) Harburg score, "Over the Rainbow," was almost eliminated. Virtually everyone in the M-G-M front office was unenthusiastic about the song that later won an Academy Award. Earlier, there had been qualms about casting Judy Garland, nearing her seventeenth birthday and considered too doddering for Dorothy, but it was decided that she could pass for a preteener because of her small stature, especially if surrounded by tall performers and strapped into a special corset with yards of tape flattening her bosom. To camouflage her topography even more, the M-G-M wardrobe department put her in a loose-fitting gingham gown. Her stipend for undergoing all this hanky-panky was $350 per week.

P

PANAMA CANAL: Building a waterway linking the Atlantic and Pacific oceans across the Isthmus of Panama, after the French had failed there, zoomed America's international prestige. It was the most formidable and most costly ($336,650,000) peacetime enterprise any nation had ever undertaken.

After the Spanish-American War of 1899 gave the United States territory in the Caribbean and the Pacific, President Theodore Roosevelt decided that a canal providing easier maritime access to the West Coast and beyond would be just "bully." There were two feasible sites: Panama and Nicaragua. Philippe Bunau-Varilla, an alumnus of the 1882-1889 French effort, who was associated with the French owners of the Panama rights, helped tilt the scale toward Panama on the eve of a crucial congressional vote by circulating a Nicaraguan postage stamp showing an erupting volcano. Congress then approved purchase of the French rights.

"Bully" acquired an unintended meaning in some quarters when Roosevelt sent a U.S. warship to support a Panamanian revolt against Colombia, which owned the isthmus and had rejected the U.S. installment-plan offer of $10,000,000 down and $250,000 a year. Work on the canal, under Colonel G. W. Goethals, began in 1904. The first three years were spent developing construction facilities, conducting surveys, and seeking means to control the malaria and yellow fever that had stymied Ferdinand de Lesseps, a hero to the French after his Suez Canal opened in 1869. A successful and far-reaching antidisease campaign was led by Colonel William Gorgas.

Between its Caribbean terminus, Limon Bay at Colon, and its Pacific terminus, the Bay of Panama at Balboa, the canal measures forty miles from shore to shore and fifty-one miles between channel entrances. Ships using the facility must be raised above sea level and, later, lowered by a series of locks. The Gaillard Cut was widened in

1969 to permit two-way traffic. When the canal was informally opened August 15, 1914, it rated little newspaper attention because of World War I. Formal dedication took place on July 12, 1920. The lowest canal toll ever paid was by the adventurer Richard Halliburton, who swam the canal in the 1920s. Weighing 140 pounds, he was charged thirty-six cents.

PANTY HOSE: The introduction of panty hose in 1968 was not accompanied by an Emancipation Proclamation, even though the waist-high undergarment freed women from the paraphernalia required by thigh-high stockings: garters and garterbelts. If women cheered the less cumbersome commodity, many men didn't, especially those with fond memories of how garters and garterbelts had made female thighs more seductive. When some manufacturers added knitted opaque fabric to the panty part of panty hose, that improvement eliminated yet another kind of out-of-sight feminine apparel: panties. But there, too, a boon to female comfort and convenience was a blow to male libido. Between 1968 and 1970, the panty hose's share of all ladies' hosiery production zoomed from 14 percent to 70 percent. A major contributory factor was the popularity of an import from England: the miniskirt. A temporary setback occurred in 1971 with the advent of pantsuits and boots, which enabled women to wear stockings with runs without guilt feelings. The world capital of panty hose is North Carolina, site of L'eggs, Hanes, Kayser-Roth, and Burlington mills.

PAPER BAG: Authorities differ on who invented the paper bag. According to one source, Margaret Knight, a grade school dropout, devised a machine in 1850—or perhaps it was 1869, when she was a twelve-year-old Maine miss, or maybe considerably older—that could produce a paper bag with a flat bottom. "Mattie," who was hailed as a "Lady Edison" at her death in 1914, also is credited with dozens of other inventions, including a dress-and-skirt shield, a clasp to hold robes, shoemaking machinery, and a sleeve valve automobile engine. Nevertheless, when she died at seventy-six her estate totalled exactly $275.05.

Another authority reports that the patent for the first paper-bag-manufacturing machine was awarded to William Goodale of Clinton, Massachusetts, on July 12, 1859, and that a patent for "improved" machinery for making square-bottomed paper bags, with two longitudinal inward folds, went to Luther Childs Crowell, of Boston, on February 20, 1872. But wait, here's yet another nominee. Union Camp, which reputedly makes more paper bags than any other company in the world, traces its origin back to 1852, when Francis Wolle, a Pennsylvania schoolteacher, allegedly invented the first machine to make paper bags. However, the American Paper Institute, the trade association of paper manufacturers, gives the nod to Charles B. Stillwell of Watertown, New York, in 1883.

In 1985, seeking corroborative data from "Stillwell's descendants and anyone else with information or documents certifying his activities," the institute offered a 102d anniversary reward of one thousand dollars or 102 paper bags crammed with groceries. Stillwell's great-grandson, Rob Stillwell, provided photos and biographical details, including the fact that his forebear had gone from bag to Bard, trying to prove before his death in 1919 that William Shakespeare's works were actually written by Sir Francis Bacon.

On June 12, 1883, Stillwell was granted patent number 279,505 for a machine to manufacture the "self-opening sack," the brown paper bag with flat bottom and pleated sides that stacks flat, opens wide, holds groceries galore, doesn't topple over—and is used by grocery and fruit stores throughout the world. The rights were assigned to Philadelphia's Union Paper Bag Company, which became the aforementioned Union Camp.

Before manufactured bags became available, grocers made temporary bags by rolling a sheet of paper into a funnel and twisting the bottom so that the contents wouldn't fall through. The brown paper bag didn't achieve its present state of efficiency until 1910, when tear-resistant *kraft* (German for strength) paper became available. It has many auxiliary uses. For instance, it can clean an iron without scratching the bottom—all that's necessary is to put a paper bag on the ironing board, sprinkle salt on it, turn the iron on high, and iron away. Paper bags sop up grease, can be cut up for book covers and wrapping paper, and can be made into Halloween masks. Breathing into one can halt hyperventilation. And brown paper bags are biodegradable, which can't be said of the plastic bags that have become a supermarket competitor.

In 1985, the American Paper Institute estimated that Americans use 25 million paper grocery bags annually.

PARACHUTE JUMP: Parachutes were used in Europe for descents from balloons as early as 1797, but the first parachute descent from an airplane was made on March 1, 1912, by stunt jumper Albert Berry from a Benoist biplane flying fifty miles an hour at fifteen hundred feet over Jefferson Barracks, Missouri. Berry fell about four hundred feet before his canopy opened. He made a safe landing on the parade ground. Then, pretending to be an army captain, he reported to the office of the barracks commandant and delivered what purported to be a military despatch. To aviators, the most important aspect of Berry's jump was that it proved an aircraft could remain stable after dropping a passenger. The first woman to jump from a plane was also a professional stunter, Mrs. Georgia Thompson of Henderson, North Carolina, a member of the Charles Broadwick stunt parachute team, who was publicized as "Tiny Broadwick." Georgia/Tiny, a fifteen-year-old wife and mother when she joined the Broadwick bunch in 1908, made her first jump on June 21, 1913, over Griffith Park, Los Angeles, from Glenn Martin's home-built biplane. In San Diego on July 4, 1914, she made the first descent from a plane entailing a manually operated chute with a rip cord. The preceding year, another American parachutist, H. Leo Stevens, reportedly introduced a rip cord that, in an emergency, could provide a secondary safeguard, but there is no record that it was used before Tiny's try.

A "free parachute" developed by the U.S. Army Air Corps, requiring the operator to jump before pulling his rip cord, was tested for the first time by Leslie Le Roy Irving at McCook Field in Dayton, Ohio, on April 28, 1919. The first free-fall descent was made in 1924 by U.S. Army staff sergeant Randall Bose, who jumped from a height of forty-five hundred feet over Mitchell Field, Long Island. To win a bet that he could open his parachute after dropping one thousand feet, he delayed pulling his rip cord until he had fallen fifteen hundred feet. The first free-fall parachutist to use the spread-eagle technique was another American, Spud Manning, who jumped from fifteen thousand feet in 1931. The following year he performed acrobatics while falling.

PARKING METER: Before the advent of this bane of drivers everywhere (a lucrative source of city and town income), limits on streetside parking were enforced by policemen who put chalk marks on tires. If a car with a marked tire was still in the same spot when the man in blue made a chalk check, an overtime parking ticket was tucked under the windshield wiper. There was a formidable flaw in this modus operandi, since any smart-aleck car owner or any self-appointed public benefactor could erase the chalk. In 1933, to eliminate such hanky-panky, the city fathers of Oklahoma City, Oklahoma, appointed a businessmen's traffic committee and named Carlton C. Magee, editor of the *Oklahoma City News*, to head it. After his research revealed that four of every five cars remained in the same downtown parking spots all day, Magee decided that some sort of timing device was needed. The actual mechanism was provided by mechanical-engineering professor Gerald Hale. For some obscure reason it was dubbed "Black Maria," a phrase previously reserved for paddy wagons or hearses. Magee established the Dual Parking Meter Company, so named because its coin-operated timers were intended to serve a twofold purpose: regulation and revenue. An unintended third R, rioting, was added after the first of one-hundred fifty nickel-an-hour parking meters went into operation in Oklahoma City on July

16, 1935. The National Guard was summoned to restore order. When similar devices were installed the same year in Mobile, Alabama, ax-toting Mobileans mobilized and mercilessly mangled the monstrous meters.

PATCHWORK QUILT: Quilts are an old Chinese and European custom, but the patchwork quilt, composed of multicolored, multipatterned scraps of material, is uniquely American. Although they often qualify as art objects, and some have been sold to collectors for as much as ten thousand dollars, patchwork quilts were inspired by economics, rather than a creative urge. Use of new yard goods for bed coverings was often impossible because of their unavailability and cost. Patching provided an inexpensive way to recycle bits of worn-out fabric. A favorite pattern, called "crazy quilt" or "hit or miss," was actually patternless. However, quilters gradually developed distinctive patterns that have been frequently repeated. Especially beautiful or venerable quilts often are displayed on museum walls.

PATTERNS: Dresses were cut out and stitched from scratch by the women of a family or by hired seamstresses until an American invention of the 1850s, standardized paper patterns in graduated sizes, made an arduous task much easier. Although Ebenezer Butterick is usually credited with paper patterns' paternity, "Mme." Ellen Demorest apparently preceded him. By 1873, sales of her dress patterns made of tissue paper—promoted in the periodical *Mme. Demorest's Mirror of Fashions* and in mail-order catalogues and peddled by numerous representatives—exceeded two million per year.

At about the same time Mme. Demorest had her money-making inspiration, the same idea occurred to Ellen Butterick, the wife of a Sterling, Massachusetts, tailor, while she was laboring over a gingham dress for her young daughter. Why not patterns for people in her circumstances, she wondered, like those that existed for the high-fashion garments of the well-to-do? Her notion of patterns for everyday clothes intrigued hubby Ebenezer, who proceeded to experiment by designing paper patterns for a man's shirt, a baby's dress, and a little boy's suit. After lengthy trial and error, the first ingenious, inexpensive Butterick patterns, cut from stiff paper and hand folded by large and small Buttericks, were shown to neighbors on June 16, 1863. Neighbors quickly became customers. An especially popular Butterick design was the Garibaldi suit for children, copied from the uniform worn by a contemporary Italian hero, Giuseppe Garibaldi. When Ebenezer began getting requests from women eager to augment their own wardrobes, he had to move his cottage industry to a vacant school and, then, with two dexterous partners, to a factory on New

York's Broadway. To keep prospective customers apprised of the latest modes, E. Butterick and Company began publishing a fashion magazine, the *Delineator*, which continued as a bible for sew-it-yourselfers into the 1930s. By 1871, Butterick patterns were being sold at the rate of six million a year; and by 1876, there were Butterick branches in London, Paris, Berlin, and Vienna.

PEACE CORPS: In establishing the Peace Corps in 1961, President John F. Kennedy, in effect, amended his inaugural injunction, "Ask not what your country can do for you: Ask what you can do for your country," to read: "Ask what you can do for other countries." The Peace Corps, a permanent agency of the U.S. Government, was designed to assist, in nonmilitary fashion, underdeveloped countries that lacked trained personpower. In his first State of the Union message, Kennedy called for a Food for Peace Program and a Peace Corps. "The hopes of all mankind," he said, "rest upon us."

Peace Corps volunteers serve for two years, providing more than three hundred skills in such areas as agriculture, vocational training, natural resource development, business and public administration, and the teaching of languages, mathematics, and science. In November 1963, Ethiopia's emperor, Haile Selassie, opined at the White House, after attending memorial services for the assassinated Kennedy, that his country needed no new Kennedy monument because the president's memory was enshrined forever in the work of the Peace Corps.

The idea of Peace Corps volunteers, an expansion and internationalization of Franklin D. Roosevelt's 1935 Civilian Conservation Corps, was first advanced in the late 1950s by Hubert Humphrey and Richard Neuberger in the Senate and by Henry Reuss in the House. Humphrey occasionally used the phrase "Youth Peace Corps." In June 1960, he introduced a Peace Corps bill. During his campaign for the presidency, Kennedy, at the suggestion of an adviser, became an advocate, mentioning the project for the first time at a 2 A.M. get-together with University of Michigan students. The response was unexpectedly enthusiastic. A few days later, a Michigan delegation was waiting for Kennedy in Toledo with a petition signed by several hundred would-be volunteers. Kennedy then broadened Humphrey's concept by including women and older people. The number of volunteers zoomed. In 1986, nearly six thousand, eighteen and over, were in sixty-two countries. In 1981, President Ronald Reagan signed legislation making the Peace Corps an independent agency.

PEANUT: Peanuts, presumably cultivated by South American Indians at least two thousand years ago, are also said to have been introduced to the American South by slaves from Africa. Known as "goober peas," they were considered suitable chomping only for slaves and poor folk. Despite their availability from as far back as the early eighteenth century, for many years peanuts were little known outside Virginia, their principal source. When the Civil War brought Union and Confederate forces to that state, thousands of soldiers tasted peanuts for the first time.

Showman P. T. Barnum helped popularize peanuts by selling nickel packets during performances of his popular circus. A principal beneficiary of the peanut boom was the Planters Nut and Chocolate Company, whose origin dated back to 1896 when Amedo Obici, a nineteen-year-old immigrant from Italy, opened a fruit stand in Wilkes Barre, Pennsylvania. Its major feature was a roaster that cost Obici $4.50 and that required constant turning by hand to prevent the peanuts from burning. Obici, who had had little schooling, spent a year rigging up pulleys that would eliminate the need for manual manipulation. He added salt to his unscorched peanuts and was soon drawing customers from miles around. In 1906, with a fellow immigrant, Mario Peruzzi, he formed Planters. In less than a year, the business had expanded from a twenty-five-dollar-per-month two-story loft to a four-story building. Soon, Planters had to move to Suffolk, Virginia, where its processing plant for raw peanuts eventually covered seventy-six acres.

Meanwhile, in Alabama, George Washington Carver, the black scientist born a slave, was urging non-Planters planters to make peanuts their major crop. Carver created hundreds of peanut by-products—including milk and coffee substitutes, cheese, flour, ink, dyes, soap, bleach, shaving cream, linoleum, synthetic rubber, insulating board, and plastics—which have been utilized around the globe. One of the peanut's more popular derivatives (see PEANUT BUTTER) was created by a St. Louis doctor who conceived the idea of grinding peanuts into a smooth paste that could be easily ingested by invalids.

PEANUT BUTTER: A suspiciously anonymous St. Louis physician is said to have invented peanut butter in 1890 when, seeking a nutritious, easy-to-digest food for elderly patients, he ran some peanuts through his meat grinder and added a pinch of salt. However, there seem to be South American, Asian, African, and even American antecedents. For centuries South American natives have been grinding out a thick, pasty peanut butter and mixing it with cocoa and honey. A note in an 1883 Savannah newspaper suggests that peanut butter was already a Georgia favorite. However, the U.S. peanut butter boom did begin about the time of that St. Louis "discovery." By 1900, grocers in both the North and South were selling peanut butter by the pound from big tubs, stirring the oil that rose to the top before they did any ladling. In the 1920s, peanut butter with sweeteners and hydrogenated fats (to prevent oil separation) forged to the fore. To meet 1971 Food and Drug Administration standards, peanut butter must contain 90 percent peanuts and no artificial flavoring or sweetener, chemical preservative, color additive, or added vitamin.

There is no record of the unsung genius who first established the natural affinity between peanut butter and jelly. Peanut-butter-and-jelly sandwiches have been termed "more quintessentially American than apple pie." A Wisconsin firm turns out one hundred per minute, already wrapped and ready to be frozen.

Peanut butter has become an international phenomenon, although only Canada and Holland have a per capita consumption anywhere near America's. Asians and Africans use peanut butter in un-American ways. In Guana a traditional soup eaten after church on Sundays consists of peanut butter, fish, meat, and vegetables. Indonesian culinary specialties include *peyek*, peanut butter fritters; *gado gado*, a peanut butter salad dressing; a peanut butter sauce for shish kebab; and candy made of peanut butter and brown sugar. Not everyone is a peanut butter buff. Some contend the stuff is for the birds—and birds agree. The less sticky hydrogenated kind, mixed with bird feed, is a favorite snack of wild North American birds.

"PEANUTS": In 1984, the comic strip bearing that title, drawn by Charles M. Schulz, forged ahead of "Blondie" as world champion in the number of newspaper outlets. Distributed by United Feature Syndicate to 2,200 newspapers in 68 countries, it has an estimated daily circulation of 78.5 million. The "Peanuts" cast consists solely of children and nontalking, but thought-conveying, dogs and birds. No grown-up is ever depicted. Also, no cats, although there was once a feline troupe member named Faron, because Schulz feels he can't draw them. And no "little red-headed girl," a small-fry paragon Schulz prefers to leave to readers' imagination.

Although feckless Charlie Brown, a surrogate for the artist, but named for an old Minneapolis friend, is the nominal central character, he is often upstaged (down-paged?) by his pet dog, Snoopy (*see* SNOOPY). Other major characters include crabby Lucy van Pelt; her security-blanket-clutching brother Linus; the Beethoven buff Schroeder; tomboyish Peppermint Patty; her constant companion, Marcie; and Snoopy's feathered pal, Woodstock.

The first "Peanuts" strip—given that title by New York's United Feature Syndicate, over Schulz's objections (he thought it lacked dignity)—appeared October 2, 1950, in only nine newspapers. Schultz earned ninety dollars the first month, five hundred dollars the second month, and one thousand dollars the third—after which his income *really* zoomed. The comic strip has generated four movies, thirty TV specials, two stage musicals, ice shows, books, greeting cards, and a long list of merchandising items. The strip is translated into twenty-six languages that often require a change of title. In Denmark, for instance, "Peanuts" is "Little Radishes."

Charles Monroe Schulz (1922-   ) is known to intimates as "Sparky," a nickname bestowed on him by an uncle when he was two days old, after the comic-strip character Spark Plug, Barney Google's horse. A so-so student during St. Paul school days (he once flunked every high-school course after skipping a year), he prided himself on his drawing, but the sketches he submitted to his high school yearbook were all rejected. To improve his skill, he took a correspondence-school art course.

In 1946, after World War II service in Europe, he landed a freelance job lettering a comic magazine. Two years later, after selling a cartoon of a smug little boy to the *Saturday Evening Post*, he was hired to do a weekly "Li'l Folks" panel for the *St. Paul Pioneer Press*. When his subsequent requests for more money or daily exposure were turned down, he quit and began submitting "Li'l Folks" samples to newspaper syndicates. Eventually, he found one willing to take a chance on a roundheaded perennial loser and his chums.

PENIS, ARTIFICIAL: Codpieces and jockstraps, as well as bras, have been stuffed for many a year by underendowed individuals eager to deceive members of the opposite, or even the same, sex about Mother Nature's niggardliness. Often, of course, the intent is far from frivolous. Manufactured breasts have helped ease the traumatic effects of mastectomies; and nongenuine genitalia, other than recreational dildos, have been put to good, as well as naughty, use by impotent and man-made males. The first artificial penis capable of erection was produced by Dr. F. Brantley Scott, a urologist at Houston's Baylor College of Medicine, in 1973. Utilizing technological advances in plastic surgery and microengineering, Dr. Scott created a functional organ that simulated tumescence when a built-in hydraulic system pumped fluid from a reservoir in the abdomen. The device was installed for the first time by the urologist Dr. Joseph Montie and the plastic surgeon Dr. Charles Puckett during the first female-to-male transsexual operation in April 1977. The beneficiary was described only as a University of Missouri bacteriology student who had neither regrets nor complaints. Dimensions of the pioneer penis were not revealed.

PHONOGRAPH: Sound waves were recorded in 1857 by Leon Scott, using what he called a phonautograph; France's Charles Cros submitted to the Academie des Sciences on April 30, 1877, a method for recording sound on a lampblacked glass disc; but Thomas Alva

Edison, almost concurrently, constructed the first machine that reproduced recorded sound.

Edison wanted to increase telegraphic transmissions by enabling an operator to speed up the playback of Morse code dots and dashes embossed on a piece of tinfoil wrapped around a rotating cylinder. While whirling a recorded cylinder, he discovered that the stepped-up sounds resembled human speech, suggesting the possibility of a "talking machine." Edison made a crude pencil sketch and handed it to John Kruesi, an assistant, with a scribbled notation: "Make this." On December 6, 1877, Edison tested the device by reciting "Mary Had a Little Lamb." When the machine reproduced Edison's voice, both Kruesi and Edison were flabbergasted. Edison named his new find the phonograph, Greek for "sound writer," and established the Edison Speaking Phonograph Company. Recording and playback required hand cranking; and the sound was aimed at a horn that transmitted the vibrations, via a diaphragm, directly to the stylus that cut the groove. In 1885, Alexander Graham Bell patented an improved version that he named the graphophone. In the 1890s, after Louis Glass installed a nickel-a-play cylinder phonograph in a San Francisco saloon, "phonograph parlors" became popular.

Cylinders were replaced by discs (see PHONOGRAPH RECORD), played, after 1896, on a turntable operated by a spring-driven motor that required hand winding. In 1901, Eldridge R. Johnson, who invented the motor, and Emile Berliner, who invented the flat record, established the Victor Talking Machine Company, reputedly adopting "Victor" after winning several patent fights. Its machines were dubbed Victrolas. Electric motors later eliminated the cranking. Subsequent improvements included automatic record changers, high-fidelity ("hi-fi") amplification, and stereophonic sound. The phonograph acquired a formidable competitor when cassette tape recorders became popular in the early 1950s.

PHONOGRAPH RECORD: Thomas A. Edison first considered discs for recording but decided against it. After he tried wrapping paper—glossed with wax—around his cylinders, he substituted tinny-sounding tinfoil, which wore out after five plays. Edison's phonograph (see PHONOGRAPH) utilized a method later known as "hill-and-dale" recording. The groove, cut into the cylinder and traversed by a vertically moving needle, was of unvarying direction but of varying depth.

Cylinders were superseded by discs, which moved a needle horizontally through a groove of unvarying depth but of varying lateral direction. It was invented by Emile Berliner, a German immigrant, who also invented the metal matrix record, from which unlimited copies of the long-lived, easily stored flat discs could be pressed like waffles from a waffle iron. To play his discs, Berliner, in 1887, patented the Gramophone, which still persists as a generic name in England. By 1894, for 50 cents, he was selling seven-inch "plates" made of hard rubber, which revolved approximately seven times a minute and played for two minutes. Later he gave them a durable shellac coating. The English issued shellac discs as carefully polished as Sheffield plates. After patent infringement suits between Edison/ Columbia and Berliner National Gramophone Company, patents were pooled in 1902. Meanwhile, Berliner had joined with Eldridge Johnson in creating Victor Records. They purchased, from Europe's Gramophone Company, the American rights to Francis Barraud's painting of a fox terrier listening to a brass-horned Berliner gramophone. The dog, Nipper, is still the RCA-Victor trademark. In 1901, Columbia Records broke away from the antidisc Edison Company, though it continued to produce cylinders until 1912. Victor steadily expanded, even opening a branch in Russia.

European recording companies began issuing complete symphonies, often requiring a formidable number of weighty 78 r.p.m. records. The 33 1/3 LP record, introduced in 1948 (*see* **MICROGROOVE RECORD**), held up to twenty-three minutes of music per side and made possible an entire symphony on a single disc. Subsequent advances included stereo (1959) and, most recently, the compact disc, or CD, a laser-activated 4¾-inch-wide plastic disc, impervious to wear, that holds seventy-two minutes of music.

PINBALL: The American pinball machine—with its thumper bumpers, flashing lights, and buzzers—has flippered its way into every country but China. Parlor bagatelles date back to the 1870s, but the first commercially successful spring-powered version was produced by Chicago's D. Gottlieb and Company in 1930. The early machines were strictly games of chance. The player provided the initial propulsion and then watched as a small ball followed a tortuous course through the strategically located pins that gave pinball its name. Because no skill was required and because there was an early linkage to Chicago gangsters, pinball machines for many years were widely banned as gambling devices. Harry Williams, who in 1929 founded Williams Electronics, is credited with such early improvements as the "tilt" mechanism, the kickout hole, and bell and gong sound effects. However, what most lifted the onus of gambling from the game was the post-World War II development of the manually operated flipper. The machines were electromechanical until 1976, when Chicago's Bally Manufacturing Corporation inaugurated machines with solid-state electronic components. The games became increasingly elaborate and complicated—with ingeniously diabolical ramps, tunnels, hideaways, and other hazards plus computerized music selections—and gradually achieved upward mobility, as the machines moved from neighborhood stores, seedy luncheonettes, and tacky penny arcades into carpeted pinball parlors and into suburban homes.

In 1939, William Saroyan put a pinball machine on stage in the Pulitzer Prize-winning *The Time of Your Life,* which was converted into a 1948 movie. Then, in 1975, The Who's Roger Daltry, as the title character in another film, *Tommy,* based on The Who's best-selling rock-opera recording, played a blind and deaf youth who competes against pinball whiz Elton John. Tommy becomes the pinball wizard by using his supersensitive fingertips to tune in to the electrical fields and vibrations. In 1977, Bruce Condella, eighteen, established a world record in Atlantic City for marathon pinball playing—one hundred hours. Condella denied that he was "weird." "I just like pinball," he said.

PLASTIC: Plastic is put to so many uses that this has been dubbed The Plastic Age. The multipurpose substance, derived from numerous sources—including cellulose, coal, plant oils and petroleum—becomes "plastic" or "pliable" like putty between 300 and 480 degrees Fahrenheit. Placed in a mold, it can be shaped as desired. Molding material is an old American practice. In colonial days ground animal horns and hooves were mixed with other ingredients and then placed in a mold. The plastics industry dates back to experiments successfully concluded in 1869 by John Wesley Hyatt and Isaiah Smith Hyatt (*see* CELLULOID). Other chemists, at home and abroad, followed the Hyatts' lead. The Quaker Oats Company developed plastics from oat hulls. Other experiments mixed skim milk and other substances to make plastic buttons out of casein. Polyethylene, which has become the most widely used plastic, was developed during World War II to insulate radar cables. (*See also* BAKELITE.)

PLAYBOY: Within two spring 1985 weeks Americans discovered that even hallowed traditions are subject to change. First, after ninety-nine years Coca-Cola announced that it was altering its sacrosanct secret formula. Then Christie Hefner (*Playboy*'s head honcha in continuance of the dynasty established by her founding father, Hugh Hefner) proclaimed that beginning in October 1985, the magazine's celebrated centerfold, a stapled belly-button fixture since its December 1953 Volume 1, Number 1 issue, would be destapled and perhaps repositioned.

Playboy's first issue, published on a ten-thousand-dollar budget, was mainly memorable for its color photo of a nude Marilyn Monroe, originally intended for use on calendars, which Hefner purchased for five hundred dollars. Thanks to that photo, *Playboy* became an overnight sensation. By 1980, it was selling 5,500,000 copies each month in the United States; 680,000 copies in Japan; 450,000 in Germany; 300,000 in Brazil; 180,000 in France; and 175,000 in Australia. (U.S. circulation dipped in 1984 to 4,250,324.) For foreign editions special editing is sometimes required: Japan bans pubic hair, Mexico permits only one bare breast per page. The magazine's success resulted in a proliferation of Playboy clubs and casinos peopled by minimally clad Playboy "bunnies" in the United States, the Caribbean, and Europe.

Hugh Marston Hefner (1926-   ), whose strict Methodist parents banned smoking, drinking, and Sunday moviegoing, became the nation's most conspicuous advocate of hedonism, spending much of his time in pajamas, surrounded on a water bed by compliant "Playmates," and verbosely expounding what he termed "the Playboy philosophy." A three-year graduate of the University of Illinois, he studied psychology for a year at Northwestern University. After working as a subscriptions writer for *Esquire*, he established the men's magazine that put *Esquire* into temporary eclipse. Initially, he wanted to name it *Stag Party*, but a friend, Eldon Sellers, suggested *Playboy*. Its early bare-breasted pin-ups were relatively modest, but competition with *Penthouse, Hustler*, and other "adult" periodicals kept raising the nudity ante to pubic hair and more.

PLAY-DOH: Play-Doh, which has converted youngsters around the world into instant sculptors, was invented by Joseph McVicker in 1955, while he was working for Rainbow Crafts, the Cincinnati soap and cleaning-compounds company owned by his father. When his sister-in-law, a New Jersey nursery school teacher, complained about the problems when small fry used ordinary modeling clay, McVicker concocted a less messy alternative: a compound, made mostly of flour, that could be kept soft and pliant if stored in an airtight container or moistened with water. Although Play-Doh squeezes easily, it does not cling to the hands; if dropped, it leaves no permanent residue; and if munched by knee-high Rodins, there are no harmful effects. Play-Doh can be rolled, stretched, squashed, and molded into innumerable shapes. When initially tested at kindergartens and nursery schools, the compound was greeted with an enthusiasm that has never waned. Manufactured by Kenner Products of Cincinnati, Play-Doh during the thirty years since its invention has sold more than 800 million cans in the United States and twenty other countries.

Although most Play-Doh is sold in four-tin sets for children, Kenner also markets three-pound containers for use by adults in physical therapy programs. In 1976, using 25 hundred bricks of Play-Doh, a Virginia man constructed a strictly grown-up replica of Thomas Jefferson's Monticello.

POGO STICK: The pogo stick, invented in 1909 by the American George B. Hansburg, has had its ups and downs. Hansburg named his toy, a stick containing a spring with footrests near the bottom and a handle at the top, after the heroine of a Burmese legend. Enabling users to hop from place to place by jumping up and down on the footrests while holding the handle, pogo sticks, in the early 1960s, became an international fad, as hot as hula hoops had been a few years earlier; but the furor subsided. However, thanks to improved technology, they bounced back in the mid-1980s.

State-of-the-art models made of high-grade molded plastic and heavy-duty frames sold for as much as one hundred dollars. To keep things hopping, Trileen, manufacturer of the sturdy sticks, sent five all-star pogo performers on a tour of California shopping malls and parking lots to bedazzle onlookers, who presumably switched from the horizontal head motions required by tennis to a vertical equivalent. Among their specialties were straddle jumps and midair whirls. Rob Banis, captain of the team, broke the Guinness world record in 1984 by bounding 125,102 times in seventeen hours and twenty-six minutes.

POKER: Nguyen Cao Ky, South Vietnam's premier, bound from Saigon to Honolulu in 1966 for a critical meeting with President Lyndon B. Johnson and State Department officials, whiled away the thirteen-hour flying time by inducing the six U.S. news correspondents aboard to join him in a marathon game of poker. He lost eight dollars. Many non-Americans love the American pastime. Italian film star Sophia Loren rhapsodized, "It is a very beautiful game—exciting, unpredictable, and courageous."

Poker is said to reflect American individualism because it pits each player against everyone else. Its antecedents include the ancient Persian game of As Nas and an early British game called Brag. Edmund Hoyle, the English authority on card games, described three-card Brag in 1751. Long after Hoyle died in 1769, a five-card version of Brag emerged with closer resemblance to poker.

Almost as a courtesy, Hoyle's name is still attached to poker rulebooks, although the game originated in New Orleans about 1800. The Union general Robert Cumming Schenk published the first treatise on poker in 1872, while he was the U.S. ambassador to the Court of St. James's during Queen Victoria's reign. Initially strictly stud and played with a twenty-card deck, poker became popular on the Mississippi steamboats and in the mushrooming communities of the West. It achieved national popularity during the 1840s when substitution of the fifty-two-card deck permitted an increase from four to eight in the number of players and made possible the introduction of draw poker. Like Ky many years later, soldiers on both sides during the Civil War found poker a favorite relaxant and became ardent peacetime proselytizers.

Numerous variations of the game have emerged, the most popular being seven-card stud. Serious poker players are appalled, however, by the idea of "wild" cards. The joker reputedly was first introduced in 1875 in a version called mistigris. Four-of-a-kind was considered the top hand until it was found that the odds against drawing a straight flush were even greater. The annual four-day Las Vegas World Series of Poker, with a ten thousand dollar entry fee and, in 1985, a seven hundred thousand dollar top prize, attracts international attention.

POLIO VACCINE: In the late 1940s and early 1950s poliomyelitis (also known as infantile paralysis), an acute infectious virus disease characterized by fever, paralysis, and atrophy of skeletal muscles, which often resulted in permanent disability and deformity, was a scourge in America and throughout the world. At worst, its victims were sentenced to spending their lives on crutches or in iron lungs. A series of American medical discoveries virtually eradicated the disease at home (only six cases were reported in 1981, the last year for which full data is available) and helped reduce it markedly abroad, although it continues to be a major public health problem in the world's less-developed countries.

In 1949, New York City-born immunologist Jonas Edward Salk (1914-   ) switched from influenza virus research to pursuit of a serum that could combat polio. He became the director of a three-year project sponsored by the National Foundation for Infantile Paralysis. The task force's assignment was complicated by the fact that three separate strains of viruses are capable of causing the disease. Utilizing earlier findings by John F. Enders and others, which made it possible to cultivate the polio virus in the kidney tissue of monkeys, Salk announced a killed-virus vaccine in 1953, one year after a U.S. polio epidemic had struck fifty thousand and killed thirty-three hundred. Mass innoculations of schoolchildren began in 1954. Two years later, an oral vaccine made from attenuated or inactivated live viruses of the three polio strains capped decades of research by the Russia-born American immunologist Dr. Albert Sabin (1906-   ). The World Health Organization began using the Sabin vaccine on a worldwide basis in 1957, although controversy over the comparative effectiveness of the killed-virus and live-virus vaccines delayed until 1961 its licensing for U.S. use. Sabin's supporters claimed that the oral vaccine was not only easier to administer, cheaper to manufacture, and more prolongedly storeable, but provided as much as lifetime immunity. By 1962, Sabin's vaccine had been administered to some ninety million residents of the Soviet Union.

POLLING: The "Q. and A." technique to ascertain public opinion on assorted subjects has been traced back to 1824, when two newspapers, the *Harrisburg Pennsylvanian* and the *Raleigh, North Carolina, Star,* solicited "show votes" to determine voters' presidential preferences. To accelerate its 1883 election reports, the *Boston Globe* dispatched reporters to various precincts. By the turn of the century many newspapers were conducting local or regional political-preference polls. Then magazines got into the act, notably the *Farm Journal* in 1912 and the *Literary Digest* in 1916. During World War I, a poll was conducted to gauge opinion on U.S. participation.

Early polls did not claim to be scientifically sound. Respondents were random, volunteering oral opinions to canvassers or written ones by mailing in periodicals' "straw ballots." More scientific "sampling," using small selected groups in ratios representative of the general population, was developed in the 1930s. The superiority of this system was dramatically established in the 1936 election when pollster George Gallup, Sr., correctly predicted Franklin D. Roosevelt's victory over Alfred Landon, while the *Literary Digest* was disastrously off base. By the 1940s, the U.S. polls also encompassed social and economic questions. The pollsters suffered a setback in the 1948 presidential election when Harry S. Truman surprised them by defeating Thomas E. Dewey. The TV networks' premature announcements of election results based on limited early polling has been attacked as a subversion of the democratic process because a lopsided early vote may persuade some voters to jump on a bandwagon or dissuade others from bothering to vote at all. Broadcast ratings by Nielsen and the American Research Bureau's Arbitron have also been assailed on the basis of arguable sample size and because of their effect on the quality of programming.

Among respected opinion-soliciting organizations are the Gallup Poll, launched in 1935; the Harris Survey, begun in 1956, and several nonprofit groups. Many other countries have polling organizations. International set-ups like the European Society for Public Opinion and Market Research facilitate data swapping.

POP ART: A reaction in the late 1950s to the solemnity of another American art movement (*see* ABSTRACT EXPRESSIONISM), pop art was a giddy blend of traditional, commercial, and sign-painting techniques, utilizing such all-American kitsch elements as cartoon characters, movie stars, dollar bills, telephones, typewriters, Campbell Soup cans, and Coca-Cola bottles.

Principal practitioners like Roy Lichtenstein, Robert Rauschenberg, Claes Oldenburg, and the ex-window decorator and advertising illustrator Andy Warhol sought to make art more accessible to the general public by erasing the boundaries between popular and high culture. In 1958, Rauschenberg produced what is considered the first pop art painting—a semiabstraction with a hole into which he inserted four Coca-Cola bottles. Warhol, generally considered pop art's Papa, stressed monotony and repetition in multiimage, mass-produced silk-screen paintings sometimes, as in the case of repeated rows of Marilyn Monroes and Jacqueline Kennedys, reproducing newspaper photographs.

An Oldenburg specialty was giant-sized soft sculptures of a ten-foot ice-cream cone, a six-foot tube of toothpaste, and a folded shirt the size of a double bed from materials such as cloth, plastic, and foam rubber. A soft bathroom and a soft car he termed monuments of ordinary useful artifacts. A gigantic lipstick was erected on the Yale campus and a king-size clothespin near Philadelphia's City Hall. Lichtenstein's international reputation was affirmed by his presence in the 1966 Venice Biennale and by a one-man show of eighty works at London's Tate Gallery. In 1985, Rauschenberg, who in 1964 won first prize at the Venice Biennale—a feat previously accomplished by only two other Americans, James McNeill Whistler and Mark Tobey—began a five-year tour of twenty-two countries with a traveling exhibit of his work that will keep growing as he adds pieces inspired along the way. The purpose of the trek, to culminate in a 1988-89 showing of the global additions at Washington's National Gallery, is to "promote world peace and understanding through art."

POPCORN: Popcorn is an American innovation and an American addiction, with more than a million pounds chomped *daily* in living rooms, in movie theaters, and at sports sites. Popping corn predates the kind eaten off the cob. Its kernels are hard even when fresh, and American Indians are believed to have discovered its poppability while experimenting with ways to make it edible.

Why does it pop? The Indian explanation was that a tiny demon inhabited each kernel. A less fantastical answer is that each popcorn kernel consists of a moist, pulpy heart encased in a hard starchy shell. When heated, the heart's 14-percent water content turns to steam, which expands until the outer shell bursts with a resounding *pop*! Archaeologists found estimated fifty-six-hundred-year-old popcorn in New Mexico's Bat Cave. A one thousand-year-old popped kernel, fired by Pueblo Indian ancestors, was found in a dry cave in southwest Utah. In 1612, Iriquois Indians around the Great Lakes reportedly were popping corn in clay urns over hot sands as a soup ingredient. After Indians brought popcorn to the first Thanksgiving dinner, Pilgrim wives served it with cream for breakfast. According to the Popcorn Institute, approximately 10 percent of America's annual popcorn crop is exported.

The idea of selling popcorn in movie theaters, a practice now emulated in other countries, is attributed to Jacob Beresin of Philadelphia. In 1911, when he was twenty and working as an office assistant at Philadelphia's Metropolitan Opera House, he asked for a raise to enable him to get married. His boss, impresario Oscar Hammerstein, said no. Beresin then requested permission to augment his twelve-dollar-a-week salary by selling peanuts, candy, and popcorn at the Met. He was soon selling munchies in all nine of the city's theaters. His firm, a partnership with Edward Loeb, grew steadily larger with the advent of, first, silent movies and, then, talkies. A 1934 merger resulted in the creation of the ABC Vending Company, which placed food-vending machines in all Warner, RKO, and Loews theaters and in all Philadelphia, New York, and Boston subway stations.

POP MUSIC: American pop music has been embraced throughout the world. Recordings of American songs by American performers have huge sales abroad. American melodies are frequently incorporated into the sound tracks of foreign-made films with foreign locales to establish times and moods obviously shared with American contemporaries. Songs by favorite American tunesmiths like Irving Berlin and Richard Rodgers are sung or hummed virtually everywhere. Jazz (*see* JAZZ) has more ardent aficionados in Europe than in the country of its birth. Rock (*see* ROCK 'N' ROLL) started in the United States and swept the world. Individual performers like Louis Armstrong, Frank Sinatra, and Elvis Presley have been idolized. In September 1984, Soviet authorities took steps to crack down on a booming black market in illicit American albums, with young Russians paying as much as one hundred rubles ($130) for a Michael Jackson tape. Authorities in Volgograd closed down a music shop that was earning 250,000 rubles a year by selling tapes by Kiss and others indicted by the youth newspaper *Komsomolskaya Pravda* as "lowly groups." (*See also* BIG BANDS, SWING.)

POP MUSIC CHART: The first listing of records according to sales volume appeared in the New York City-based show-biz weekly *Billboard* on January 4, 1936. Instead of a single Top Ten, encompassing all entries, there were separate Top Ten listings for each of the three major recording companies. For the preceding week, the number-one hits were three big band entries, Tommy Dorsey's "The Music Goes Round" on RCA-Victor; Joe Venuti's "Stop, Look, and Listen" on Columbia; and Ozzie Nelson's "Quicker Than You Can Say" on Brunswick. England's first Top Ten chart appeared in the *New Musical Express* in November 1952.

POPSICLE: Flavored ice on a stick resulted from a happy happenstance. In 1905, on a *brrr!*able San Francisco night, eleven-year-old

Frank W. Epperson left a glass of soda-water powder and water on the back porch. The next morning he found the drink frozen solid around the spoon he'd been stirring with. Seventeen years later, after he had established himself in the real estate business, he introduced his inadvertent invention at a firemen's ball. The crowd loved it; so in 1924, he patented his "handled, frozen confection or ice lollipop." Initially, the concoction was dubbed the Epsicle, but Epperson and his partners made a royalty arrangement with a small company that changed the name to Popsicle. No longer as lucky during the Depression as he had been twenty-four years earlier, the Popsicle's Papa sold his patent to the Popsicle Corporation in 1929. Popsicle Industries became a multimillion-dollar business and is now an Englewood, New Jersey-based division of Consolidated Foods Corporation, which also manufactures the chocolate-flavored Fudgsicle. The Twin Popsicle, with side-by-side sticks, was created during the Depression, so that two kids could share at one price. Over the years the favorite Popsicle flavor has been orange. In 1977, Popsicle Industries introduced a superpop, the Ten Plus, made from whole eggs, egg whites, milk powder, and orange juice. The company claimed that the eighty-seven-calorie confection provided 10 percent of the protein recommended daily for eight-to-ten-year-olds, plus calcium, vitamin C, and other nutrients; but the superpop was a superpoop.

POSTAGE STAMP BOOK: The first postage stamp books were issued by the U.S. Post Office on April 16, 1900. Two-cent stamps could be purchased in books of 12, 24, or 48 for one cent more than the stamps' cost. Great Britain's General Post Office issued books of twenty-four penny stamps in panels of six at a cost 2 shillings ½ pence on March 16, 1904.

POSTCARD: The first postcard was copyrighted by Philadelphia's John P. Charlton in 1861. The rights were acquired by a Philadelphia stationer, Hyman L. Lipman, who issued the cards with a decorative border and the words "Lipman's Postal Card, Patent Applied For." In October 1869, the Austrian Post Office issued the first prepaid postcards, charging only the cost of the stamp. The U.S. Post Office followed suit four years later.

POTATO CHIP: Appropriately, a native American culinary item, the potato chip, was created in 1853 by a *truly* native American, the Adirondack Indian chief George Crum. Crum, a rather whimsical fellow who claimed that he changed his name from Speck because "a Crum is larger," was doubling as chief and chef at the Moon Lake House Hotel, a resort in Saratoga Springs, New York. When a guest, Commodore Cornelius Vanderbilt, kept rejecting his french-fried potatoes as "too thick," an exasperated Crum sliced a potato almost paper thin and plunged the pieces into boiling fat, then had his waitress wife tote a triple-salted plateful to the hard-to-please diner. Vanderbilt judiciously sampled the world's first potato chips and delivered his verdict: Thin enough and more than good enough. The next day the resort's menu featured Chief George Crum's "Saratoga Chips." That's one story. Another is that the pioneer chip chopper was black, not red; an anonymous chef who made his monumental discovery about 1865.

Commercial production began as a cottage industry, with families cooking, packaging, and peddling from their homes what became popularly known after the turn of the century as "potato chips." (The British call them "potato crisps.") In 1925 A. A. Walter and Company built the first plant intended solely for the manufacture of potato chips in Albany, New York. Years later, Procter and Gamble initiated research designed to produce a better potato chip—or at least, one that wouldn't break so easily—and in 1969, the company introduced "Pringle's Newfangled Potato Chips," made from dried potato granules that were moistened, rolled into sheets, cut into uniform bits, and fried. Because they were all of identical size and shape, they could be stacked in hard cylinders like tennis balls. The Potato Chip Institute International complained, so the Food and Drug Administration ruled, in 1975, that the restructured potato product had to be identified as "potato chips made from dried potatoes."

European buffs like chicken-, beef-, or paprika-flavored chips. The Japanese are partial to a seaweed-flavored variety. Favorite snacks, potato chips chomp up 11 percent of America's potato crop.

POTATO SKIN: In 1978 Frederic D. Starret, Jr., who had founded a thriving locker plant in Belfast, Maine, thirty years earlier, figured out a way to utilize a waste byproduct of his Penobscot Frozen Food Company's line of baked stuffed potatoes. Frozen potato skins quickly became a culinary favorite. Starrett was saluted for his ingenuity at a 1984 "National Small Business Man of the Year" White House ceremony.

PUBLIC RELATIONS: Press agentry became upwardly mobile via the 1903 creation of the title of "public relations consultant" by Cedartown, Georgia-born Ivy Ledbetter Lee (1877-1934), who parlayed Princeton and Columbia degrees and reportorial stints for four New York newspapers into publicity posts for a mayoralty candidate and then for the Democratic National Committee. The new, more dignified nomenclature was accompanied by new, more dignified objectives. Press agents were paid to gain publicity, by whatever means, for individuals or products; "P.R. representatives" were often called upon to earn their keep by molding and safeguarding clients' "images." Early Lee clients included politicians, bankers, and a circus; but in 1906, he demonstrated his value to big business when he was hired by leaders of the anthracite coal industry to counteract public hostility during a strike because of their seeming intransigence. While the miners' leader was charming the press and the public with his candor and reasonableness, the operators' spokesman alienated reporters by refusing to answer questions and by rejecting a presidential offer to arbitrate. Lee's first act was to issue a press release in which his clients promised to be more responsive. After the strike, Lee was hired by the Pennsylvania Railroad to handle a press-relations crisis caused by a serious accident. Instead of trying to suppress damaging data, the railroad's previous practice, he provided transportation to the scene of the accident and facilitated reporters' news gathering, and gained unexpectedly sympathetic press coverage. Among Lee's more dramatic accomplishments was the altering of multimillionaire John D. Rockefeller, Sr.'s flinty skinflint image by such strategems as having him dole out dimes to street urchins. Today, Lee's P.R. progeny are omnipresent.

PULITZER PRIZE: The closest all-American equivalent to the internationally prestigious Nobel Prizes, which have had many American recipients, are the annual Pulitzer Prizes established under the will of the Hungary-born newspaper publisher Joseph Pulitzer (1847-1911). Pulitzer, who merged two newspapers to create the *St. Louis Post-Dispatch* in 1878 and acquired the *New York World* five years later, left a five-hundred thousand dollar endowment for gold medals and cash prizes (five hundred dollars and one thousand dollars) to reward outstanding achievements by journalists and creative artists in his adopted country. Initially, in 1917, there were eight journalism categories plus fiction, drama, history, biography, and poetry. A music award was added in 1943 and two more newspaper awards, for "specialized" and "explanatory" journalism, in 1985.

Since 1947, the Pulitzers have been doled out each May, not necessarily in every category, by the trustees of Columbia University. Administered by the university's graduate School of Journalism, the awards are made on the recommendation of a fourteen-member advisory board stipulated in the Pulitzer will. Although these recommendations are supposedly based on the judgments of university-appointed juries, the juries' choices are sometimes ignored. In 1937, for example, William Faulkner's *Absalom, Absalom* was bypassed in favor of Margaret Mitchell's far more popular, if less distinguished novel, *Gone with the Wind*. After Edith Wharton's *The Age of Innocence* was picked over Sinclair Lewis's *Main Street* in 1920, the displeased winner referred to her blemished laurel in a novel as "the

Pulsifier Prize." Not only winners have been subject to change. Category specifications have been reworded. The fiction prize was originally intended for "the American novel . . . which shall best present the whole atmosphere of American life, and the highest standards of American manners and manhood." Nicholas Murray Butler, president of Columbia University, preferred "wholesome" to "whole." Eventually, the word "whole" plus the references to "manhood" and "manners" were dumped. In 1947, to make James A. Michener's *Tales of the South Pacific* eligible, "novel" was replaced by "distinguished fiction in book form."

Q

QUAKER OATS: In 1915, the Religious Society of Friends attempted to remove "Quaker" from Quaker Oats. Its members tried to persuade Congress to ban use of any religious denomination's name for any commercial product. When that failed, the Quakers instituted state-by-state campaigns for such a prohibition but succeeded only in Indiana. The company was formed at the end of the nineteen century by oatmeal millers who decided that collaboration was preferable to competition. The seven-member "oatmeal trust," organized in 1891, was originally named the American Cereal Company. In 1901, it borrowed the name of one of its predecessors and became the Quaker Oats Company. Henry Parsons Crowell, who had headed the Quaker mill in Ohio, succeeded U.S. oatmeal pioneer Ferdinand Schumacher in 1898 as president of the combine and proceeded to display razzle-dazzle marketing know-how. Using newspaper, magazine, billboard, and in-store advertising, Crowell lured purchasers through sales pitches promising better sex, looks, health, happiness, and job advancement. An 1898 ad in several magazines attracted attention by perching a bare-breasted beauty on a Quaker Oats box. To explain her eye-popping presence, she was identified as Ceres, "fair goddess of the harvest fields." Crowell was the first to put recipes on packages and to tuck inside them coupons for premiums like dishes and for discounts on subsequent purchases.

The Quaker Oats company, with subsidiaries in fourteen other countries, still uses the Quaker name and a flat-hatted Quaker, registered on September 4, 1877, for oatmeal, shredded wheat, puffed wheat, and puffed rice. Although it has diversified and now sells toys and needlecraft items, as well as many other foods, its most popular product continues to be the one it started with more than a hundred years ago, hot oatmeal. The company earns even more, however, from the oat hulls it once discarded as worthless. Quaker researchers have developed numerous commercial uses for furfural, a chemical made from the hulls, principally as a solvent in oil refining.

QUIZ SHOW, RADIO: Quiz shows, the broadcast equivalent of venerable parlor games, led to panel and game shows. The three forms, drawing sizable audiences at minimal cost, became popular staples first in radio and then on television, daytime and evening, at home and abroad. Such shows made their debuts as local programming. The first Q. and A. program to achieve network status, on CBS radio in 1936, was "Professor Quiz." The quizmaster Craig Earl dispensed silver dollars for correct answers to his questions. The very first poser was: "What is the difference between a 'lama' with one 'l' and a 'llama' with two 'ls'?"* "Dr. I.Q., The Mental Banker," which made its debut on NBC on June 10, 1939, was similar in format, also doling out silver dollars. "Dr. I.Q." went on tour, visiting cities a month at a time. When a roving assistant, toting one of the show's nine microphones, shouted, "I have a gentleman in the balcony, doctor," Lew Valentine (later Jimmy McClain and, briefly, Stanley Vainrib) would respond, "Six silver dollars if he can answer this . . ." A small-fry variation, "Dr. I.Q. Jr.," substituted silver dimes.

Before "Dr. I.Q." came "Information Please," which bowed in on NBC's Blue Network on May 17, 1938. Its creator, Dan Golenspaul, reversed the standard quiz format by rewarding those who submitted the questions—two dollars for any question used, five dollars for each one that stumped a panel of experts. A younger panel, braintrusters aged six to sixteen, appeared on "Quiz Kids," a program hosted from its inception in June 28, 1940, by Joe Kelly, a singer who had dropped out of school after completing third grade. Also of 1940 vintage was "Truth or Consequences," devised and hosted by Ralph Edwards, which deposed "Information Please" as radio's most popular quiz show. The 1940 "Take It or Leave It," with a sixty-four dollar top prize, led to the high-stakes "$64,000 Question." The post-World War II "Break the Bank," however, was the first radio quiz to offer four-figure cash prizes.

QUIZ SHOW, TV: Many other countries have imitated the American TV quiz-show format, but none has ever doled out comparable cash. The earliest prime-time network TV quiz show was Dumont's "Cash and Carry," hosted by Dennis James, which bowed in on June 20, 1946. The first real national impact, however, was made by "Break the Bank," which moved from radio to TV on October 22, 1948, and was soon offering as much as ten thousand dollars to winners. In 1956, as quiz-show prizes escalated, it became

---

*The first is a monk; the second, an animal.

"Break the $250,000 Bank," but no one ever collected the title total. In 1949, "Stop the Music," another recruit from radio, began offering home viewers twenty-thousand-dollar jackpots, mink coats, and trips to Paris. The show that triggered the big-bucks boom, however, was CBS's "The $64,000 Question," with Hal March as its host and the "isolation booth" as its arena. In its first (1955-56) season it zoomed to top spot in the ratings, ousting CBS's "I Love Lucy." Its dramatis personae became national heroes—a policeman who an expert on Shakespeare, a shoemaker who fielded tough questions about opera, a jockey who knew all about art. It unleashed a deluge of dollar-doling imitators: "The Big Surprise," "Twenty-One," "The $64,000 Challenge." The latter showcased "$64,000 Question" alumni. Tony Nadler, a seventy-dollar-per-week St. Louis civil service clerk with an encyclopedic memory, became the wealthiest quiz-show beneficiary, amassing $252,000.

Trouble began in August 1958 with the abrupt cancellation of "Dotto," when a contestant, waiting in the wings, picked up a woman's notebook and found it contained correct answers. After he told the woman's just-defeated adversary, they confronted "Dotto's" producer, who paid both for their silence. However, when the notebook-finder discovered he'd received less hush money, he blew the whistle. The subsequent scandal rocked the TV industry, ousted the quiz shows, and triggered a congressional investigation. Charles Van Doren, who had become Public Hero Number One on "Twenty-One," became Public Scapegoat Number One. A 1976-78 attempt to revive ultralucrative quizzes, "The $128,000 Question," had only so-so success because it was pretaped, aired at varying times, and lacked the impact of immediacy.

R

RACQUETBALL: The antecedents of this world-popular American game played indoors or out; on courts with one, three, or four walls; by two, three, or four racquet-equipped players include France's court tennis, Spain's jai alai, England's rackets and squash, and Ireland's handball. In the 1920s, after watching tennis players getting off-season practice on a handball court, Earl Riskey of the University of Michigan substituted a solid wood paddle and originated what was called paddle tennis and paddleball. In the early 1950s, Joe Sobek—a squash and tennis pro from the Greenwich, Connecticut, YMCA—decided that a strung racket would give the game's shots more zip. Sobek designed what was in effect a short tennis racket and began to promote the "new" sport of "paddle rackets."

During the ensuing years the rules remained unchanged, but racquet frames switched from wood to aluminum and fiberglass. After the game's first national tournament in Milwaukee in 1968, paddle racket buffs asked the maverick seventy-two-year-old president of the U.S. Handball Association, Robert Wilhelm Gustav Kendler, a multimillionaire Chicago builder and home remodeler, to help them make it an organized sport. Kendler, a handball buff who shared the National Doubles Championship five times, consented. One of his first moves was to change the game's name to racketball and then to substitute a classier "cq" for the mundane "k." The International Racquetball Association (IRA) was formed in 1969 under Kendler's guidance; but two years later, when a schism developed, he established two rival organizations: the U.S. Racquetball Association (to sponsor amateur competition), and the National Racquetball Club (to supervise pro tours). Although he organized, standardized, and promoted racquetball, Kendler never played it himself, claiming it was too mild for a veteran handballer.

Bud Meuhleheisen, a San Diego dentist, became the first national IRA champion in 1969. The following year, Fran Cohen of St. Louis became the first IRA woman champ. National championships for both sexes are now conducted annually in the United States and Canada. Japan, Israel, and Saudi Arabia were early converts.

RADIO: Although Canadian Reginald Fessenden (a former associate of Thomas Alva Edison) and American Lee De Forest were both working on the development of a wireless telephone, both were also interested in voice radio. Italy's Guglielmo Marconi, utilizing theories developed by a German physicist, had perfected the wireless telegraph, but it was De Forest's invention of the audion, a triode vacuum tube that received and amplified signals, that made possible the reassembling of electromagnetic wave impulses into clearly audible speech or music. The first radio broadcast, however, was made by Fessenden, from his laboratory on the Massachusetts coast, on Christmas Eve, 1906. Telegraph operators on ships off the coast of New England suddenly heard words, rather than click-click-clicks, in their earphones. Fessenden read the Christmas story from the Gospel of St. Luke, played some appropriate music, and then wished everyone a merry Christmas.

For years radio received attention primarily from hobbyists using the crystal sets devised in 1910 by Americans Henry Harrison, Chass Dunwiddy, and Greenleaf Whittier Pickard. The possibilities of a "radio music box," suggested as early as 1915 by David Sarnoff, then assistant traffic manager of the Marconi Wireless Telegraph Company, were ignored. Then Westinghouse decided to promote the sale of radio receivers by providing provocative programming. With Westinghouse funding, the ham operator Frank Conrad went to a KDKA, Pittsburgh, microphone on November 2, 1920, to report the results of the Harding-Cox presidential election. Commercial radio became an overnight success. Aside from its popularity with the public, in 1922, radio began to earn money from advertising.

Radio networking was pioneered in 1923 by American Telephone and Telegraph, which left the field three years later. In 1926, nineteen stations formed the National Broadcasting Company, which was followed a year later by the sixteen-station Columbia Broadcasting System. By 1950, the advent of television threatened to steal away most of radio's audience, as well as most of its performers and formats, but the medium survived. FM (frequency-modulation) stations, capable of better musical quality, have outstripped older AM (amplitude-modulation) stations.

RAGGEDY ANN (ANDY): To amuse his ten-year-old daughter, Marcella, who suffered from a heart infection, author-illustrator

Johnny Gruelle painted a new face, with button eyes and an infectious grin, on a faceless rag doll that had once belonged to his mother. Gruelle told Marcella stories about "Raggedy Ann," a name he borrowed from two James Whitcomb Riley poems, "The Raggedy Man" and "Little Orphant Annie." Two years after Marcella's death at fourteen, Gruelle found that his daily stints as an illustrator for the *Indianapolis Star* were completed by noon, but his co-workers resented his early departures. To keep himself occupied while marking time, he began writing and illustrating verses. Raggedy Ann became one of the subjects. A Chicago publisher suggested a switch to prose, and the first Raggedy Ann book appeared on September 10, 1918.

Gruelle subsequently penned seventeen more books about Ann and her brother, Andy, who made his debut in 1920. "The stories write themselves," Gruelle said. "I've written as many as seventeen in one morning." The redheaded miss was an instant success. After Gruelle's death in 1938, other writers and illustrators resuscitated the Raggedys. Ann and Andy have inspired numerous kinds of merchandise, a Jerome Kern song, a 1978 feature-length animated movie, and CBS television specials. Gruelle ended the first Raggedy Ann book by having a "stranger friend" initiate mass production of Raggedy Ann patterns, "shoe button eyes, cheery smile and all."

The first of millions of Raggedy Ann dolls reportedly appeared as part of a Christmas 1920 Marshall Field department store window display. A special division of ITT Publishing was established in 1978 to handle worldwide licensing. Knickerbocker Toys, now a subsidiary of Warner Communications, has been manufacturing the dolls since 1964. A Raggedy Ann doll was on display at Paris' Louvre Museum for about eight months in 1978. Ann was the recipient of the first successful heart implant. After falling into a paint bucket, she was cleaned up and restuffed with a candy heart bearing the words "I love you."

RAILROAD DINING CAR: The first railroad dining cars, stand-up buffets, were introduced on the Philadelphia, Wilmington, and Baltimore Railroad in 1863. The food was precooked and kept hot in steam boxes. Half of each car, separated by a divider, was a "smoker," with seats for those who preferred to sit while eating. Much more elaborate was the dining car aboard the President, designed in 1867 by George M. Pullman (*see* RAILROAD SLEEPING CAR), for Canada's Great Western Railroad. The first dining car to serve full-course meals prepared by a chef, it was equipped with removable tables that were attached to the side of the car. Menus included six hot dishes, four cold meats, eggs prepared seven ways, seasonal vegetables and fruits, and five kinds of bread. One immensely impressed 1869 passenger burbled, "To breakfast, dine, and sup in this style while the train is speeding at the rate of nearly thirty miles an hour is a sensation of which the novelty is not greater than the comfort."

RAILROAD SLEEPING CAR: The first railroad sleeping car, the Chambersburg, introduced in 1836 on the Cumberland Valley Railroad's run between two Pennsylvania cities (Harrisburg and Chambersburg), was a carriage divided into four sections containing a total of twelve bunks. No bedding was provided. The travelers wrapped themselves in shawls and slept with their boots on. Brocton, New York-born George Mortimer Pullman (1831-1897) accumulated enough capital as a construction contractor in Chicago to finance one of his earlier notions, railroad cars with sleeping facilities; and in 1858, he remodeled two Chicago and Alton Railroad day coaches into sleeping cars by hinging upper berths to the sides. Another feature of "Old Number 9," which went into service on September 1, 1859, was a lavatory at each end. Passengers were pleased with Pullman's innovations, but because of their cost, railroads were reluctant to adopt them. Pullman moved to Colorado and stayed there four years, running a store and ruminating on how to make his sleeper slicker. In 1863, he returned to Chicago and patented his folding upper berth. Two years later, he patented his concept of a lower berth converted from a pair of facing seats. Both principles are retained in modern sleeping cars.

The first Pullman car, the Pioneer, was introduced in 1865, and this time, several railroad companies shared the public's enthusiasm, even though the oversized cars were not only costly but also required changes in bridges and station platforms. In 1867, Pullman founded the Pullman Palace Car Company, which became the world's primary manufacturer of railroad cars. The same year marked the advent of the first sleeping car with restaurant, which was followed by such Pullman projects as the first dining car (*see* RAILROAD DINING CAR), the first chair car, and the first vestibule car. He opened his first manufacturing plant in Palmyra, New York, and expanded to several other localities, including Pullman, Illinois, a company town that became a postreferendum part of Chicago in 1889. Long after his death Pullman was still being commemorated by the eventually condemned custom of addressing Pullman porters as "George."

RAT REPELLENT BOX: America's Pied Piper devised a more technological method for routing rodents than his predecessor in Hamelin, but both techniques involved musical instruments. The legendary exterminator who took kids when denied cash used some sort of flute. Bob Brown, of Hipass, California, a polio victim confined to a wheelchair, hit upon his surefire shooer in 1971 while assembling an electric guitar in his garage. Brown inadvertently crossed the wrong wires and produced a shrill sound, pitched at a million cycles per second, far beyond the range of human hearing. It started a mass mouse exodus. Watching their frenzied departure, Brown, who was living on Social Security, realized he had discovered a substitute for the better mousetrap, a rat ridder. In short order he was the millionaire owner of the Amigo Ecology Corporation, the world's only manufacturer of rat repellent boxes. In six years he sold about eighteen thousand units to farmers in the San Joaquin Valley and to the governments of South American nations. Spain ordered a thousand units for its granaries. Not only rodents are devastated by Brown's mechanism; cockroaches lose all sense of balance and flop on their backs. The Venezuelan government purchased three hundred of the boxes for use in Caracas food stores as cockroach confusers. Brown claims that his mechanism is also anti-ant.

RAZOR, ELECTRIC: While participating in a 1911-14 U.S. Army mining expedition to below-freezing British Columbia, Jacob Schick was irked by the time-consuming need to heat water for his daily shave, so he designed a manual razor that required neither soap nor water. When he tried to interest manufacturers in his "dry shaver," he found no takers. After World War I duty and retirement with the rank of colonel, Schick resumed his efforts to create a dry razor that would eliminate the need for soap, water, and—by using electrically powered blades—even the styptic pencil. A decade and one ten-thousand-dollar mortgage later, he patented the first electric shaver, described as a "shaving implement," on November 6, 1928. Three years later it was placed on the market by the Stamford, Connecticut, firm of Schick, Inc. Sales were slow when the shavers were initially priced at twenty-five dollars but picked up when the cost was cut to fifteen dollars. By 1937, when its inventor died, more than 1.8 million Schick razors were in worldwide use. Schick razors for both men and women are now products of the Warner-Lambert conglomerate, which also sells health-care items, cough drops, chewing gum, sunglasses—and nonelectric razor blades.

RAZOR BLADE, DISPOSABLE: Prototypes of the safety razor failed to solve a major problem: how to keep the blade sharp. Fond du Lac, Wisconsin-born King Camp Gillette (1855-1932) came up with the answer. It also enabled him to follow the advice given to him years earlier by an employer, William Painter (*see* BOTTLE CAP). The surefire way to get rich, Painter had counseled, was to devise something that required constant replacement.

One summer morning in 1895, while he was shaving at his home in Brookline, Massachusetts, both Gillette's mind and epidermis were irritated by the razor's dull edge. Getting it sharpened was a recurrent nuisance. Suddenly Gillette envisioned how a razor could hold disposable blades: a thin piece of steel with an edge on both sides and a clamp to center the blade over the handle. For five frustrating years he tried to implement the image, but expert toolmakers and Massachusetts Institute of Technology scientists insisted the idea was impractical. Finally, an MIT instructor, William E. Nickerson, agreed to give it a try. While Gillette went in search of investors, Nickerson assembled the necessary machinery in a friend's shop over a Boston fish market.

In 1903, the first year the Gillete safety razor was offered for sale, only fifty-one were purchased at five dollars apiece—plus fourteen dozen blades. The following year, Gillette was awarded a patent for the original three-piece safety razor. As word spread about its safety and convenience, sales boomed. By 1906, Gillette and Nickerson were producing three hundred thousand razor sets and nearly five hundred thousand packets of blades bearing Gillette's portrait and signature. Between 1911 and 1914, Nickerson invented automatic sharpening machines that vastly increased the company's production capacity. During World War I, the American army adopted the French army's practice of issuing Gillete razors and blades as a sanitary measure. Gillette's creations now have more than a billion buyers throughout the world.

READER'S DIGEST: Originally a clip-and-paste operation conducted by DeWitt Wallace and his wife, the former Lila Bell Anderson, in a basement room under a speakeasy in New York's Greenwich Village, *Reader's Digest* in 1984 had a monthly circulation of 18,299,091 with thirty-six international editions. The first issue, published in February 1922, consisted of sixty-two pages of print sans illustrations or ads. It went to about five thousand subscribers at twenty-five cents a copy.

Six years earlier, while in Montana editing an agricultural digest for farmers, Wallace had wondered why he couldn't similarly pare magazine articles of general, rather than specialized, interest. Recuperating from World War I shrapnel wounds in a French hospital, with plenty of time to pore over American magazines and assess their content, he decided that most were long on wordage and short on pertinence. Later, daily for six months, he selected a Minneapolis Public Library magazine and spent all day cutting a single article, while trying to retain its sense and style. Picking thirty-one of the condensations that he felt had the widest appeal, one a day for a month's reading, he had them printed in pocket-size format, dubbed the assemblage *Reader's Digest,* and sent it off to magazine publishers. Only William Randolph Hearst reacted favorably, but Hearst doubted that circulation could exceed what he considered an inadequate three hundred thousand. After meeting Lila Bell, who shared his enthusiasm, Wallace began mailing pitches directly to prospective subscribers.

The opening article in Volume 1, Number 1, was "How to Keep Young Mentally." Enough copies were sold the first year to enable the one-man-one-woman operation to move to the pony shed adjacent to a modest Pleasantville, New York, apartment. In 1929, Wallace put the *Digest* on newsstands, made exclusive reprint deals with major magazines, and began assigning original articles. A British edition was launched in 1938; a Spanish-language edition in 1940. Today the magazine is published in fourteen languages: English, Spanish, French, Portuguese, Swedish, Finnish, Danish, Norwegian, German, Italian, Dutch, Japanese, Chinese, and Arabic. For the blind there are Braille and recorded editions in five languages.

READING MACHINE: An almost miraculous boon to the world's blind is a machine created in 1976 by Raymond Kurzwell of Cambridge, Massachusetts. The Kurzwell Reading Machine reads aloud from the printed page. Its inventor initially had in mind only something that would make accessible all printed material, not just items in Braille or on tape, for those with little or no sight. However, numerous additional uses have evolved. For instance, a change of software enables the machine to become a talking calculator, reading numbers aloud and recording them. Since it reads phonetically, this conversational computer is not limited to English. In fact, it is more likely to make pronunciation errors in English because of the language's rule-shunning vowels. Although Kurzwell managed, beginning in 1965, to teach the machine, letter by letter, to recognize the alphabet, it is unable to differentiate the "ou" in "rough" from the "ou" in "through," or the "oi" in "noise" from the "oi" in "porpoise." Oi, indeed!

A mute version, the Kurzwell 4000, which can read various type styles in type sizes ranging from six to twenty-four points, is used by the University of Pennsylvania's language department to copy documents in several languages for study of common phrases. Another spin-off, the Kurzwell Voice Writer, which in 1985 was under development by Kurzwell Applied Intelligence, will reverse the read-and-speak procedure. A voice-activated typewriter, it will convert human speech into printed letters, in effect taking dictation. The read-aloud machine manufactured by Kurzwell Computer Products, which was purchased in 1981 by the Xerox Corporation, is about three feet high and two feet square and resembles a small photocopier. It is attached to a smaller component, a keyboard with two numbered, telephone-like keypads. When a book or document is inserted upside down, there is a flash of light and the sound of a camera scanning the text. A robotic male voice reads it aloud. During the 1985 demonstrations of a $28,900 model, the voice proclaimed, "I can read X-rated books, but I don't get excited by them."

READY-MADE MIX: It was well past the dining car's usual dinner hour when Carl Smith, a young General Mills executive making a 1930 train trek, ordered biscuits. Nevertheless, to his pleased surprise, the rolls brought promptly were piping hot and fresh. The secret of this seeming miracle, the chef told him, was that premixed dough had been stored in the dining car's icebox. Smith hastened to bring a premixed biscuit dough's commercial possibilities to the attention of the General Mills lab. There were some problems to be overcome, lab chemists discovered. It was necessary to keep the shortening fresh and the leavening agent potent for prolonged periods of time. Moreover, the resultant biscuit had to be tasty enough to trigger reorders.

Many of the techniques developed by General Mills to meet these requirements also proved useful later in producing the first cake mixes. Bisquick was introduced in 1930, with ads hailing it as "science's most thrilling food invention." Simply adding water, the printed panegyrics promised, would make anyone at all "a perfect biscuit maker." Even "the most inexperienced bride" could now prepare, in ninety seconds or less, "biscuits your husband will say are better than the ones his mother used to make!" Despite this potential roiling of mother-in-law relationships, Bisquick was a quick hit. Within a year ninety-five other biscuit mixes were on the market, but only a half dozen survived. In 1933, with the help of nonfictional General Mills nutritionists, the fictional Betty Crocker authored a booklet offering 101 Bisquick recipes. The versatile mix makes pancakes, waffles, dumplings, meat pies, and assorted pastries, just for a start, and the list keeps growing.

REAPER: A grain-harvesting method more rapid than the scythe and the cradle became imperative when the vast prairies of America's Midwest were divvied up into farms that dwarfed those back East. The first patent for agricultural machinery was granted in 1803; but the first reapers to prove practical were competing horse-drawn versions invented thirty years later by Obed Hussey (1792-1860) and Cyrus Hall McCormick (1809-1884).

Hussey, whose previous creations included a corn grinder, a sugar-cane crusher, and a machine for making hooks and eyes, was awarded a patent on December 31, 1833. Six months later, on June 21, 1834, McCormick was awarded a patent for a similar invention that he had displayed publicly in 1831. In 1848, when the original patents expired, both were denied extensions. What had previously been a two-way competition became a free-for-all. Hussey, no businessman, sold out in 1858 and concentrated on developing a steam plow; but two years later, after stepping off a train at a way station to get a child a drink of water, he slipped while trying to reboard and was killed under the train's wheels.

Robert McCormick, an inveterate inventor, failed to cash in on patents for a hemp rake, a blacksmith's bellows, a gristmill, and other agricultural implements but thought he had a prospective bonanza when he attached a number of sickles to a wooden bar. It worked fairly well on grain standing tall but was useless after a rain, so he abandoned the project. Robert's son, Cyrus, then twenty-two, was not so easily discouraged. Applying new concepts, he created an efficient piece of equipment. A skillful businessman, he established a Chicago factory in 1847, the year the first railroad reached that city, and soon was servicing customers both East and West. He traveled all over the world, demonstrating his product. At London's 1851 Crystal Palace exhibition it was derided by the *Times* as "a cross between . . . a chariot, a wheelbarrow, and a flying machine"; but it won first prize. McCormick was among the first to advertise guarantees, offer discounts for cash, and extend credit. In 1902, the McCormick Harvesting Machine Company merged with the Deering Harvester Company to form International Harvester, which in 1980 had foreign sales totaling $2.3 billion. In 1986, the company was renamed Navistar International Corporation.

REFRIGERATOR: In 1834. Jacob Perkins, an American living in England, was awarded the first patent for a refrigeration machine. According to legend, some of Perkins's assistants were so excited when his mechanism produced ice one summer evening that they wrapped in a blanket the melting proof that the machine worked, hailed a cab, and rushed across London to display it at the inventor's home. The machine embodied the same principles still used for household refrigeration. A volatile fluid (in this pioneer case, ether) was compressed, allowed to evaporate to produce the cooling effect, condensed, and returned to the compressor. Using a hand-turned compressor, Perkins worked up a sweat producing a few chunks of ice. Spectators were impressed but not to the point of buying.

Americans were more receptive to the idea of refrigeration because deliveries of northern ice to southern ports were often delayed by storms at sea and arguments over price. That problem of unreliable ice delivery led Dr. John Gorrie to invent his own ice machine for the comfort of patients in his Florida hospital. Gorrie's refrigerator, using compressant air as a coolant, was awarded the first U.S. refrigeration patent in 1851. Household refrigerators, to replace leaking, ill-smelling iceboxes, were introduced before World War I. The first, the Domelre, consisting of a wooden cabinet with an electrically powered compression-type refrigerating unit on top, was manufactured in Chicago in 1913. In early refrigerator models, the compressor was usually powered by a noisy motor situated in the basement or an adjoining room. The first self-contained model was introduced by the Frigidaire division of General Motors in 1915, and "the fridge" became a common descriptive for all refrigerators. By 1920, more than two hundred brands were on the market. One drawback was the danger of inhaling toxic fumes from the refrigerating agents, a risk that was eliminated in 1931 when Frigidaire introduced safe, odorless Freon, quickly adopted by virtually all refrigerator manufacturers. The 1941 Frigidaire, designed by Raymond Loewy, was manufactured for twenty years and became the world's best-selling refrigerator.

REVOLVER: The concept of a repeating firearm utilizing an automatically revolving set of chambers that became aligned with a single barrel came to Hartford, Connecticut-born Samuel Colt (1814-1862) while he was on a voyage to India. After working at his father's textile factory in Ware, Massachusetts, and attending school, Colt had run away to sea at sixteen. He whittled a wooden model of what he had in mind and, soon after his return from India, completed two functioning prototypes. One exploded. To finance development of his six-shooter, he went on tour as "Dr. Coult," inviting contributions after demonstrating the giggleability of nitrous oxide, "laughing gas."

Colt patented his revolver in England and France in 1835 and in the United States the following year. In March 1836, he established in Paterson, New Jersey, the mass-production Patent Arms Manufacturing Company, which also turned out a breech-loading revolver rifle. Although the Colt revolver was popular with individuals—including Andrew Jackson—the army vetoed it, causing Patent Arms's demise. Colt turned to other interests, including an underwater mine system for harbor defense, telegraphy, and submarine cable. With the outbreak of the Mexican War, Texans and other westerners partial to Colts refused to use anything else. After receiving this ultimatum, the army ordered one thousand revolvers. Colt subcontracted production to Eli Whitney's plant (*see* INTERCHANGEABLE PARTS) in Whitneyville, Connecticut, until he could launch Colt's Patent Fire-Arms Manufacturing Company in hometown Hartford in 1848.

The revolver, the nineteenth century's major small-arms innovation, played an important role in universally popular folklore about the Wild West and in the gradual establishment of a relatively "Mild West."

REVOLVING DOOR: A rose, as Gertrude Stein once proclaimed, is a rose is a rose, but that's not necessarily true of doors. When is a door not a door? When—ahoy, puerile punsters!—it's ajar. That's no laughing matter, of course, especially when winter frost or summer rain zeroes in on the aperture. To eliminate such nuisances and a few others, like indignant or careless slamming, Philadelphian Theophilus Van Kannel, on August 7, 1868, patented a "storm door structure," consisting of circular, or revolving, doors that rotated when a pedestrian passed through them. He envisioned his invention as "an entrance for all seasons." What he didn't foresee was (1) that people could get stuck in them, and (2) that he was providing a prop for numerous slapstick movies.

RH FACTOR: A major cause of infant fatality at birth or shortly after was a disease of indeterminate cause that doctors dubbed erythroblastosis fetalis. Blood transfusions were common years before it was discovered that human blood was of different, incompatible types. In 1940, in the course of blood-typing research, Karl Landsteiner (1868-1943)—who in 1901, before immigrating to America, had classified human blood as A, B, and O—and Alexander S. Wiener injected monkey blood into rabbits and discovered that the rabbits' blood developed a resistance to the alien blood via antibodies. The previously unsuspected blood component responsible for the resistance was named "the Rh factor." Subsequent research revealed that it often occurred in human blood and that humans could be categorized as Rh-positive or Rh-negative. Further studies traced erythroblastosis fetalis to the mating of Rh-positive males and Rh-negative females, with increased maternal antibody building in every birth after the first. With the cause known, preventive measures followed. Why "Rh"?—because Rhesus monkeys were the laboratory guinea pigs.

RICHTER SCALE: The scale for measuring the severity of earthquakes, used by seismologists everywhere, was created by Dr. Charles Francis Richter (1900-1985) in the 1930s. He retired in 1970 as professor emeritus of seismology at the California Institute of Technology in Pasadena. A Richter magnitude of 2.5 is assigned to an earthquake that generally is not felt, although it is instrumentally recorded. An earthquake of 4.5 magnitude causes local damage. A 6.0 on the Richter scale can be destructive in populous regions. A 7.0 is registered about ten times a year by major earthquakes that cause serious damage. An earthquake of 8.0 or more, occurring about once every five to ten years, levels nearby communities. Recent U.S. earthquakes have included one registering 6.5 on the Richter scale in Coalinga, California, on May 2, 1983 (which inflicted heavy damage on the town and may have caused a .2-inch movement of the San

Andreas Fault) and one registering 6.9 in central Idaho on October 28, 1983 (which was felt in eight adjacent states, caused the deaths of two children under a toppling building, left a cliff fifteen-feet high and twenty-five-miles long, and resulted in many hydrological changes).

Richter's interest in earthquakes was so great that he had a seismograph installed in his living room and avidly perused reports on Mexico City tremblers while hospitalized with fatal coronary-artery disease.

RICKSHAW: As ridiculous as it seems, that old-fashioned Oriental conveyance, the two-wheeled rickshaw, was invented by an American. On second thought, why ridiculous, when such "Chinese" specialties as chop suey and the fortune cookie are also of American manufacture? Jonathan Scobie, a Baptist minister stationed in Yokohama, Japan, in the 1860s, concocted the contraption so that his physically handicapped wife could occasionally leave the house. Scobie, rather than a coolie, provided the necessary pull power. His parishioners watched, applauded, and borrowed the idea.

ROBOT: The word "robot," for an automaton, first appeared in Czech playwright Karel Capek's 1921 sci-fi drama, *R.U.R.* The initials represented Rossum's Universal Robots. Robots, mechanical devices serving as surrogates for human operatives—one definition is "a computerized, reprogrammable manipulator"—now perform numerous functions in manufacturing, office procedures, mail delivery, ship and plane steering, medical diagnosis (*see* ARTIFICIAL INTELLIGENCE), even surgery. In 1962, General Motors employed America's first industrial robot in its Wilmington, Delaware, plant. Large-scale delegation to machines of chores considered too dangerous or too repetitive for humans is usually linked to less fantastical phraseology: computerism, automation, mass production. However, the popular concept of a robot is a mechanical humanoid, capable of controlled or independent movement, like HAL, the computer that took control of the spaceship in the 1968 Stanley Kubrick film *2001: A Space Odyssey* (Arthur C. Clarke, who wrote the novel on which the movie was based, denies that he deliberately selected the three initials that precede those that comprise the acronym of the world's leading computer company, IBM), or more recently R2D2 and C3P0 in *Star Wars* and its sequels. Such humanoids are being produced, too. They open doors, greet visitors, serve cocktails and hors d'oeuvres, and perform household chores. Some are being "taught" to read, speak, and distinguish between odors. However, cost of home robots is not expected to come within common reach until the start of the twenty-first century. In 1940, Californian Cecil Nixon parented Isis, a zither-playing robot who reclined on her side and provided any of three thousand tunes if the request was voiced within twelve feet. Her innards included 1,187 wheels and 370 electromagnets. A mechanical-arm robot, Howard, participated in a 1985 California ballet based on Italo Calvino's *Invisible Cities*. At the Third International Joint Conference on Artificial Intelligence at Stanford University in 1973, scientists predicted robot psychiatrists by 1990 and robot chauffeurs by 1992. By 2000, according to another prediction, blue-collar workers will be in the ratio of one nuts-and-bolts to every five hundred flesh-and-blood workers.

ROCKET, LIQUID-FUELED: Worcester, Massachusetts-born Robert Hutchings Goddard (1882-1945) was fascinated by rockets at an early age and started experimenting while still a college student. In 1914, he devised a two-step rocket, the first to use the concept of propulsion by stages. On a grant from the Smithsonian Institution he wrote the rocketry classic "A Method of Reaching Extreme Altitudes," which the Smithsonian published in 1919. In that paper Goddard predicted that rockets would break free from earth's gravity and would travel to the moon and beyond. He was ridiculed as "moon mad." Even his demonstration that rockets could operate in a vacuum was not taken seriously. During the early 1920s, he experimented with various liquid rocket fuels, finally picking as optimum a blend of gasoline and liquid oxygen.

The first liquid-fueled rocket was fired in March 1926. In 1929, with the help of pioneer solo transatlantic pilot Charles A. Lindbergh, he secured a Guggenheim Foundation grant and established a large testing range near Roswell, New Mexico, where he launched the first rocket to transport instruments: barometer, thermometer, and camera. He also began to experiment with gyroscopic guidance. Although he was granted more than two hundred patents, his rocketry expertise was largely ignored in the United States. Many of his findings, however, were duplicated years later by the German scientists who developed the World War II V-2 guided missile. In 1960, the U.S. government paid the Guggenheim Foundation $1 million for infringements on Goddard patents. Two years later, NASA's research facility at Greenbelt, Maryland, was named the Goddard Space Flight Center.

On July 17, 1969, when the Apollo 11 astronauts were orbiting the moon before their historic landing, *The New York Times* retracted its 1920 scoffing at Goddard's contention that rockets would one day fly through a vacuum to the moon. On the earlier occasion the *Times* snidely suggested that Goddard lacked "the knowledge ladled out daily in our high schools." "It is now definitely established," the belated postscript noted, "that a rocket can function in a vacuum. The *Times* regrets the error."

ROCKING CHAIR: Benjamin Franklin is one of several ingenious Yankees who, in the mid-1700s, are said to have come up with the notion of combining the usual stay-put chair with a device that dated back to the Middle Ages: the rocking cradle. Initially, furniture makers merely augmented ordinary chairs with curved runners so sharp that they were called "carpet cutters." The manufacture of real rockers began about 1790. After about thirty years they lost their vogue, but they attracted renewed attention when tenanted by "Mrs. Bates" in Alfred Hitchcock's 1960 thriller, *Psycho*, and by aching-back-afflicted John F. Kennedy, who brought one to the White House in January 1961.

ROCK 'N' ROLL: The emergence of rock 'n' roll in 1954 fuzzed what had previously been clear distinctions between such music record categories as pop, rhythm and blues, and country and Western. The first rock record was the original version of "Sh-Boom," by the Chords, a rhythm-and-blues number that also scored in the pop charts. Another version of the same song had impact in the country-and-Western market. Within months it was one of England's top sellers. "Sh-Boom" contained all the rock trademarks: the blending of vocal and instrumental sound; fragmentary or seemingly improvised lyrics often consisting of "oohs," "aahs," and "dip-dips"; and an insistent four-fourths beat.

One of the first rock classics, James E. Myers' 1954 "Rock Around the Clock," performed by Bill Haley and the Comets, a "cover" version of an unsuccessful Sonny Dae rhythm-and-blues disc, became the first rock disc to zoom to the number-one spot in both the American and English pop charts after the 1955 release of the movie *Blackboard Jungle*. An important difference between Haley's sound and that of other early rockers was the stress on amplified guitars.

The most important individual rock artist to emerge during the early rock years, beginning with the 1956 release of "Heartbreak Hotel," was Elvis Presley. Accompanying his singing with suggestive movements, he added a sensuous quality to the new music. Rock's rise was abetted by the ardent support of Alan Freed, who claimed that he coined the phrase "rock and roll" in 1951, and other radio disc jockeys. Many of them, including Freed, vanished from the rock scene after the "payola" scandals of 1959-60 revealed that platter spinners were often paid in cash or part ownership to play certain records. Another boost for rock music was provided by RCA's development of the 45 r.p.m. record, which could be pressed and distributed more quickly and more cheaply. It became the platter of choice for rock singles. Rock albums on 33 1/3 r.p.m. LP discs came later.

Seminal American rock stars included Chuck Berry, Little Richard, Buddy Holly, and Bob Dylan. They paved the way for overseas superstars like the Beatles and the Rolling Stones.

ROLLER COASTER: There was a popular gravity-powered version in Mauchunk, Pennsylvania, (a town later renamed Jim Thorpe, in honor of the Indian Olympics champion), before 1884; but LaMarcus Thompson's Switchback Railway, which began terrifying the timorous and exhilarating the devil-may-care riders at New York's Coney Island that year, was the first mechanically driven roller coaster. Its single passenger car started at a height of 40 feet and skimmed 480 feet on a straight track with some gentle dips and rises at six miles per hour, barely fast enough to whip a lady's bonnet from her head. People sat sideways, facing each other. Mild or not, it was considered a thriller in its time and was highly profitable.

The word got around, and soon roller coasters began to erupt everywhere—at resorts like Coney Island, which was not yet an amusement park, and at picnic groves that railroads established at the end of their lines. The parks vied to provide the highest, the longest, the scariest, the most convoluted, with pretzellike twists and turns. The coaster Thompson built for Atlantic City in 1886, which some roller coaster mavens consider the real daddy of them all, featured a tunnel. One big advance was the safety coach, with wheels that locked to the track, so that coasters could roll around curves and reach speeds of as much as sixty-six miles an hour. Later innovations included the Loop-the-Loop, which caused qualms because people feared they'd tumble out, and a version in which the train leaped across a break in the tracks. Wooden coasters on steel tracks are considered more thrilling than the newer steel-on-steel variety because wood is more flexible and produces a swaying sensation.

By the 1920s, as many as two thousand wooden coasters were in operation. Coney Island's Cyclone, built in 1928, is still going strong. The vogue passed only to return in 1970 when new coasters were built for about $3 million apiece and old ones preserved. The Philadelphia Toboggan Company in Lansdale, Pennsylvania, America's last builder of wooden roller coasters, deliberately tries to make its cars look rickety and sound creaky. Space Mountain at Tokyo Disneyland (*see* DISNEYLAND) bars small children, pregnant women, and sufferers from assorted ailments.

ROLLER SKATES: A Londoner, James Merlin, created the first recorded pair of roller skates in the early 1760s and, during a fashionable masquerade party, decided to skate around the ballroom while playing his violin. Alas, Merlin was no magician. He crashed into an expensive mirror, causing damage to the mirror, the violin, and himself. In 1819, a Frenchman, Monsieur Petitbled, received the first patent for roller skates. The modern roller skate, however, was invented in 1863 by James Leonard Plimpton of Medfield, Massachusetts. Moving to New York shortly after the start of the Civil War, he began ice skating in Central Park for his health. Eager to continue his exercising after the ice thawed, he devised a new kind of skate. Patented in 1863, his wooden skates, from which he earned $1 million, differed from previous models because they were steerable, thanks to cushioned mountings that enabled the four wheels on each skate to turn slightly when the skater shifted his weight. To popularize his invention, Plimpton opened a number of roller-skating rinks. In 1866, Everett H. Barney of Springfield, Massachusetts, patented a metal clamp that enabled skaters to fasten their shoes to metal skates. By 1870, roller-skating had become popular throughout the United States and in twenty other countries.

RONALD McDONALD HOUSE: In 1971, Fran Hill and her Philadelphia Eagles tight end husband were dismayed to learn that their three-year-old daughter, Kim, had leukemia. A despairing Fred Hill, who feared that his daughter had only weeks to live, started collecting money for the Leukemia Society of America. His teammates joined the effort, their wives netted nearly ten thousand dollars from a fashion show, and an annual "Eagles Fly for Leukemia" campaign was launched. The Eagles owner at the time, Leonard Tose, put the team and the stadium at Hill's disposal.

With huge sums accruing from fashion shows, radiothons, and one-thousand-dollar-a-couple galas, the Eagles general manager Jim Murray consulted the pediatrician Dr. Audrey Evans, head of the oncology division at Philadelphia's Children's Hospital, on how the money could be put to most beneficial use. Among her recommendations was a home-away-from-home for the parents of hospitalized children. She suggested a potential site, a dilapidated nearby building. Murray phoned an advertising executive who handled the local McDonald's account, to ask if the fast-food chain would care to participate. McDonald's top brass approved the idea, on the condition that the house bore the name of the chain's clown mascot, Ronald McDonald. McDonald's provided forty-two thousand dollars to buy the four-story, seven-bedroom row house. Major interior work was contributed by John Canuso, a New Jersey builder who had spent a miserable night at the hospital with his wife, Joan, after learning that their nine-year-old daughter, Babe, had leukemia and had been appalled to learn that one mother had spent six weeks on an old leather sofa in a hospital corridor.

The first Ronald McDonald House, providing homelike overnight accommodations for fifteen dollars or whatever a worried parent could afford to pay, opened on October 15, 1974. It later moved to more commodious quarters with accommodations for nineteen families. A decade after the project started, there were seventy Ronald McDonald Houses in the United States, Canada, and Australia supervised by a Ronald McDonald House International Advisory Board. More are planned for other countries.

P.S.: Both Kim Hill and Babe Canuso underwent successful treatment for leukemia.

ROOT BEER: American Indians were the first to brew homemade root or herb beer; but a twenty-four-year-old Philadelphia druggist, Charles E. Hires (1852-1937), was the first to capitalize on it. Unlike most newlyweds, Hires found his honeymoon a source of fortune, as well as fun. While he and his bride were in a New Jersey inn, they sampled a herb tea made by the innkeeper's wife and enjoyed it so much that Hires asked for the recipe. Back in his drugstore, with the help of two Jefferson Medical College friends, he developed a solid concentrate that could be mixed with water, sugar, and yeast to produce a delicious drink. Hires named his mixture of roots, bark, and berries Hires Herb Tea. A friend, the Reverend Dr. Russell Conwell, founder of Temple University, opined that "tea" lacked sales appeal for male buyers and suggested "beer" instead.

Hires Root Beer was first dispensed, free (as a promotional gimmick), at the 1876 Philadelphia Centennial Exposition. A believer in advertising, Hires, a devout Quaker, touted his beverage primarily as a salubrious tonic and a temperance alternative to hard liquor, "soothing to the nerves, vitalizing to the blood, refreshing to the brain." It strengthened children, he claimed, and enabled "even a cynic to see the brighter side of life." At first, he sold only a twenty-five-cent box of solid extract that made five gallons of the drink; but in 1890, he added a three-ounce bottle of liquid extract. Five years later, the thriving Charles E. Hires Company was bottling root beer at plants throughout the United States. At the time of Hires' death at eighty-five, his potion was the world's best-selling root beer. It is now one of the numerous products merchandised worldwide by Procter and Gamble.

RUBBER, CONTRACEPTIVE: No one knows when the prophylactic condom (a thin sheath for the penis, to avert venereal diseases and to retain sperm and prevent impregnation) was first used, but apparently there was an eighteenth-century British physician named Condom. The venerable contraceptive device has often been referred to as a "French letter," perhaps, because it is usually sold, tightly rolled up, inside a small envelope. However, the French dub it *une capote Anglaise*, "an English hood." Before Charles Goodyear vulcanized rubber in 1839, enabling the substance to heat up without getting sticky, condoms were made of goldbeater's skin (sheep gut). Among the first vulcanized rubber products for which Goodyear secured patents were birth control devices. The "rubber," cheap and convenient, has long been the world's most frequently used male contraceptive and continues to be a big seller despite the emergence of another American discovery: the oral contraceptive (*see* BIRTH CONTROL PILL).

RUBBER, VULCANIZED: New Haven, Connecticut-born Charles Goodyear (1800-1860) had nothing to do with Goodyear or Goodrich tires, but his discovery of vulcanization (named for Vulcan, the Roman god of fire) made them possible. Despite thirty years of rubber research, Goodyear died in abject poverty. America's early rubber industry was limited to boots, caps, and wagon covers because rubber decomposed into a smelly mess in hot weather and became hard and brittle in cold weather. Goodyear felt that an additive might lessen or overcome these drawbacks and decided to find it by trial and error. During his first experiments, while he was in debtors' prison, he combined rubber with everything handy—including ink, soup, cream cheese, witch hazel, and castor oil. A mixture of quicklime and magnesia had unexpected results: a kind of white rubber that resembled leather. Goodyear thought he had finally found a way to fame and fortune—until he discovered that any acid, even a drop of lemonade, would cause the white substance to decompose.

In 1839, he accidentally spilled a mixture of rubber and sulfur on his hot kitchen stove and discovered the secret of vulcanization, which increases rubber's durability during temperature changes. For five years he tried without success to raise financial backing for his process. In 1844, he finally received a patent, but it did not provide a windfall. Hard pressed for cash, he was forced to license the process for whatever he could get.

Meanwhile, Thomas Hancock, an English chemist, acquired a sample of Goodyear's new rubber and detected the presence of sulfur. Hancock achieved vulcanization on his own and received a provisional patent two months before Goodyear's application reached England. As a result, English manufacturers dealt only with Hancock. Litigation further diminished Goodyear's meager bankroll. For an hour's work he had to pay the lawyer Daniel Webster twenty-five thousand dollars, more than he himself ever earned in a year. When Emperor Napoleon III of France awarded him the gold medal of honor of the Paris World Exhibition and the Cross of the Legion of Honor, Goodyear was in Paris, serving a term in debtors' prison.

When he died in New York, his debts totaled two hundred thousand dollars.

RUBIK'S CUBE: The devilishly difficult wooden block made up of rotating cubes with different-colored faces frustrated puzzle buffs in several countries and made a fortune for Erno Rubik, a Hungarian teacher who patented the puzzle in his own country in 1977. American rights were purchased from Rubik by the Ideal Toy Corporation, a subsidiary of CBS, which says it netted $75 million from the cube and variations from 1980 to 1983. However, in May 1982, a $60 million patent-infringement suit was filed by Arthur S. Obermayer, president of Moleculon Research Corporation in Cambridge, Massachusetts, who claimed that his company held a 1972 U.S. patent for a similar device. In America, Obermayer contended, the Rubik's Cube™ should be called the Nichols Cube, because it was invented in 1969 by Larry D. Nichols, Moleculon's chief research scientist. For three years, Obermayer says, he tried to find someone to market the puzzle but was turned down by more than fifty toy and game manufacturers, including Ideal. In October 1984, U.S. District Judge Walter K. Stapleton sided with Moleculon, which was seeking "a reasonable royalty." CBS attacked the validity of Nichols's patent and claimed that there were marked differences between the two cubes. Recognition for his creation, however belated, was a major reason for the suit, Nichols said, because it might help him sell a dozen other games and puzzles.

Nichols had concocted the cube puzzle, he claimed, by working on it in spurts over a ten-year period. It was inspired, he said, by the Sam Lloyd 15, a flat puzzle made up of a frame containing fifteen movable numbered squares in the space for sixteen, allowing them to be shifted into numerical order. Because, when he was twenty-one, he considered the Sam Lloyd 15 too easy, Nichols said, he sought a way to make it more difficult. In 1957, while taking a summer stroll, he decided that the way to improve a flat puzzle was to make it nonflat. Later he started using the Moleculon machine shop to develop the cube. He enjoys doing the puzzle, Nichols said, but can't always manage a quick solution.

S

SACCHARIN: Approximately three hundred times sweeter than sugar and used for a multitude of food products, saccharin was synthesized in 1879 by New York City-born Ira Remsen (1847-1927), a Johns Hopkins chemistry professor who later became the university's president. Twenty-nine years later, when doubts first surfaced about saccharin's safety, President Theodore Roosevelt appointed a referee board consisting of five scientists. The chairman was Remsen. The day before, listening to Harvey W. Wiley, chief of the Department of Agriculture's Bureau of Chemistry, tell Congressmen, food processors, and lawyers what food additives he considered harmful, Roosevelt endorsed a ban on benzoate of soda in catsup but was incensed at the mention of saccharin. His own doctor prescribed saccharin, the president asserted, and anybody who claimed it was injurious to health was "an idiot!" Many T.R.-styled idiots have emerged since, but saccharin's safety remains arguable. Canners and bottlers first used saccharin, which has no nutritional value and passes through the body unchanged, only because it was cheaper than sugar; but later, more emphasis was placed on its fewer calories and its medical value to diabetics and others requiring a sugar-free diet.

In 1912, the federal government banned saccharin from general food use as a "poisonous or other added deleterious ingredient" and tried to restrict its use to those who required it for medical reasons. Products intended for medical patients were to carry a special label. However, food processors, noting the review board's ruling that more than 3/10 of a gram per day could be harmful, promptly proclaimed that their wares contained less. Wiley, who retired the same year, denounced this stratagem as a "perversion" of the law.

Questions about saccharin's relationship to cancer first rose about 1970 and have been hotly argued ever since. When a ban was proposed in 1977, Congress declared a temporary moratorium. Most present-day users of saccharin seem less concerned with health than with weight. A substitute now available for the sugar substitute (*see* ASPARTAME) has its own devotees and detractors. Sweet 'N Low, a popular saccharin sweetener, is the holder of the U.S. Patent Office's one millionth trademark.

SAFETY PIN: Late Bronze Age graves from Greece to Denmark contain safety pins that look remarkably similar to the kind that exist today, with one end hooking under a little bend in the other end. Some even contain a similar tension-producing springlike coil. However, such pins were replaced by less efficient straight pins in later civilizations—until Walter Hunt, a New York inventor and draftsman, almost casually reinvented the safety pin in 1825 in less than three hours by twisting a piece of wire into the proper shape. The kind of safety pin now in universal use is basically like Hunt's except for the hornlike piece of metal that provides added protection against finger punctures.

Because he wanted to repay an urgent fifteen dollar debt to a friend, Hunt sold the patent rights, worth millions, for a trifling sum variously placed between one hundred dollars and four hundred dollars. It was the second time in his life that Hunt missed out on a bonanza. In 1832, he invented the world's first lock-stitch sewing machine, which could sew a few inches of straight seam, but didn't apply for a patent because his daughter suggested that seamstresses might lose their jobs. In 1854, when he made a belated effort to patent his sewing machine, he was advised that he was eight years too late. A man named Elias Howe was already cashing in on a similar piece of equipment (*see* SEWING MACHINE). Other results of Hunt's hunt for new products included a repeating rifle, a nail-making machine, an ice plow, a dry dock, a paper collar, and a metal bullet with a built-in explosive charge.

SATELLITE, COMMUNICATIONS: The first transatlantic transmission of a picture via communications satellite was made on July 10, 1962, when the image of the chairman of the American Telephone and Telegraph Company, Frederick Kappel, was relayed via Bell's *Telstar* from Andover, Maine, to Goonhilly Downs, Cornwall, England. *Telstar* was preceded by the short-lived *Score* and *Courier I-B* and followed, later in 1962, by RCA's *Relay I*, which added U.S. transmissions to South America and Japan.

The first transatlantic satellite telecast was the May 2, 1965, "Out of This World," using *Early Bird*, the first commercial satellite launched by the privately owned, Congress-authorized Communications Satellite Corporation (COMSAT). The program, bounced back from twenty-three thousand miles out in space, linked 300 million viewers in nine countries. Among its features were a heart operation in progress in Houston; Dr. Martin Luther King, Jr., speaking in Philadelphia; a papal address in the Vatican; a bullfight from Barcelona; Russian sailors singing and dancing aboard a British ship; the Feast of Santa Cruz from Mexico; and scenes from Washington, Quebec, and Stockholm. "Wanted" photos of a Canadian criminal, Georges Lemay, resulted in his arrest in Fort Lauderdale, Florida.

Earth-orbiting satellites were a favorite notion of scientists long before Russia's Sputnik soared into space in 1957. Among their proponents was Dr. John R. Pierce of Bell Telephone Laboratories. When the National Aeronautics and Space Administration (NASA), responding to the Sputnik gauntlet, prepared to launch a large aluminum-coated balloon to study space phenomena, Pierce suggested using it as a communications reflector. *Echo*, launched in August 1960, bounced back the microwave beam bearing the first satellite telephone conversation. Because of distance and interference, it was barely intelligible. What was needed, Pierce decided, was signal amplification. Because of the limited launch power of the 1960 Thor-Delta rocket, *Telstar* was tiny, with only 2¼ watts of power. To compensate for its diminutiveness, a huge horn-reflector antenna was installed at Andover. Together, the horn, technicians' precision, and *Telstar*'s foot-long traveling-wave tube capable of amplifying a signal ten thousand times made history.

SCOTCH TAPE: Richard G. Drew, a chemical engineer who was working as a laboratory technician for the Minnesota Mining and Manufacturing Company in St. Paul, invented the transparent sealing tape in September 1930. His specific assignment had been to find a way to seal the cellophane wrappings of such wares as candy, baked goods, and shirts, but Scotch tape has been put to multitudinous uses. Drew's discovery made him a millionaire and made the 3M Corporation a billion-dollar enterprise. In 1944, 3M gave Drew his own lab and made him the head of its "idea department" as Products Fabrication Laboratory director. The original tape begat more than six hundred varieties of 3M stick-on tapes, earning $700 million a year worldwide.

In 1921, responding to a "blind" help-wanted ad seeking a lab assistant for sixty-five dollars per month, Drew wrote on correspondence-school stationery, "If your company needs a pretty good banjo player with three semesters of college engineering, I am your man." Selected from more than a dozen applicants, he doubled 3M's research staff. At the time, one of the company's major products was sandpaper. One of Drew's chores was to take batches of experimental waterproof sandpaper to automobile repair shops. The shops used gummed tapes when painting two-toned cars to keep a sharp edge where the colors met, but often, when a job was done, paint was stripped away with the masking tape. Because of one mechanic's complaints, Drew experimented with sticky mixtures and developed a formula that safeguarded the paint. When car painters complained that the width of two-inch-wide 3M masking tape made it too costly, the company limited the adhesive coating on the tape to a quarter-inch strip on each side, instead of coating the entire surface. However, this cost-cutting approach often defeated its purpose because the tape wouldn't stay put. When a 3M salesman called, he was told, "Take this Scotch tape back to those bosses of yours and tell them to put adhesive all over it, not just the edges." When the salesman returned, he was chidingly asked if he was still selling "that Scotch tape." Result: a product's name and its distinctive tartan.

SCRABBLE: This crossword game, Monopoly's only rival for the title of best-selling trademarked game in the world, is still selling briskly more than thirty years after becoming a 1953 coast-to-coast craze. The Selchow and Righter Company, which manufactures SCRABBLE® Brand Crossword Game in Holbrook, Long Island, insists that there's actually no contest because Scrabble tournaments are a nonstop weekend activity.

The game was invented in 1931 by Alfred M. Butts, an unemployed architect, who decided to combat the Depression by concocting a game that would require both luck and skill while combining two of his favorite avocations: crossword puzzles and anagrams. He shaped the requisite pieces with a jigsaw in his Queens, New York, apartment and glued the blueprinted playing grids on checkerboards. It was originally more Scramble than Scrabble. A hundred wooden tiles bearing letters of the alphabet were dumped in the middle of a playing area. The player was supposed to use tiles picked at random to form a word. The more tiles needed for the word, the higher the score. Butts kept adding improvements: a playing board and a point value for each letter, based on the frequency of its use. He also gave his game a name: Criss-Cross Words. Later it was redubbed Lexiko. A set made for a friend, James Brunot, so impressed Brunot and his wife that, in 1948, they offered to help market it after numerous companies, including Selchow and Righter, rejected it. They renamed the game Scrabble and assembled 180 sets in a schoolhouse workshop. Selchow and Righter, which had been manufacturing the boards, took over its marketing in 1953.

Scrabble has been translated into six other languages (French, Spanish, Italian, German, Russian, and Hebrew) plus Braille. A TV version, featuring flashing grids, video-arcade noises, and a climactic "Scrabble Sprint," became a daily daytime NBC program in July 1984. After the death of his wife, Nina, Butts, at eighty-five, created a spin-off version of Scrabble, Alfred's Other Game, that can be played solo. Butts played his own game often but, he confessed, with indifferent success.

SEARS, ROEBUCK: The largest retailing organization in the world has its headquarters in the tallest building on earth, Chicago's 110-story Sears Tower. President Franklin D. Roosevelt once opined that the best way to convince Russians of the superiority of the American life-style would be to bombard the USSR with Sears catalogs. When the Soviet premier Nikita Khrushchev visited San Francisco in 1959, Mrs. K. was waiting at a Sears store door when it opened for the day, to buy one hundred dollars' worth of nylons, toys, and baby clothes.

The chain owns or co-owns outlets in Canada, Mexico, South America, and Spain. For the first twenty years of its existence, Sears, Roebuck owned no stores at all; it was strictly a mail-order business. Each of the five annual Sears catalogs—big ones in the fall and spring, smaller ones for the summer, winter, and Christmas—gets wider distribution than any other U.S. publication except the Bible.

Richard Warren Sears was working as stationmaster and telegrapher in Redwood, Minnesota, in 1886 when he decided to moonlight as a watch peddler. The sideline was so profitable that he quit his railroad job to start the R. W. Sears Watch Company in Minneapolis. In 1887, he moved to Chicago, where he hired Alvah Roebuck, who hailed from Indiana, to assemble and repair watches. Sears added installment plan diamonds and other jewelry to his wares and opened a branch in Toronto. His first catalog, offering money-back guarantees, appeared in 1887. From the start, the catalog stressed low prices. The motto, "Cheapest Supply House on Earth," imprinted over a world globe, appeared on the cover of the 1894 edition and on a five-story Chicago building that Sears, Roebuck and Company rented in 1895. Considered too big, it quickly became too small. Overwork and worry over his partner's custom of looking for merchandise only after orders poured in caused Roebuck to sell out in 1895 for twenty-five thousand dollars. In 1933, he rejoined the firm as a clerk. Julius Rosenwald became Sears' skillful manager, but, in 1908, a disagreement over policy led to founder Sears's resignation as president. Sears has even provided a wife: when a Montana rancher "ordered" one, a Sears order clerk quit her job and headed West.

SELF-STARTER: George H. Gallup, president of the American Institute of Public Opinion, familiarly known as the Gallup Poll, once opined that the only contribution to the development of the automobile that was unequivocally American was the self-starter. That invention, first used in 1911 Cadillacs, is generally credited to

Ohio-born Charles Franklin Kettering (1876-1958), who later became president of General Motors Research Corporation. However, the self-starter's starter was Clyde Jay Coleman of New York, who invented the device in 1899. The Delco Company, later one of many absorbed by General Motors, purchased Coleman's rights. In 1915, Kettering patented his own "engine starting device." He also invented an electric motor for cash registers and improved ignition and lighting systems for automobiles. As head GM research honcho, he supervised efforts to achieve maximum engine performance and to develop such products as leaded (ethyl) gasoline, high-octane fuels, fast-drying lacquer, chromium plating, crankcase ventilators, balancing machines, engine-oil coolers, two-way shock absorbers, variable-speed transmissions, the high-speed compress engine for automobiles, and the high-speed diesel engine for trains.

SEN-SEN: The unique, and secret, flavor of the tiny packets of breath freshener that have been toted by amorous U.S. swains since the late nineteenth century is the result of an international mixture of ingredients from Bulgaria, France, Turkey, Greece, Italy, and almost inaccessible Asian areas. They were first combined by a man named Kerschner, employed as a superintendent at the T. B. Dunn and Company chewing gum plant. Shortly after 1909, when T. B. Dunn merged with four large gum-manufacturing companies to form the Sen-Sen-Chiclet Company, Sen-Sen became an international odor inhibitor. Foil has replaced the paper packets that once enclosed the product, but the formula remains unchanged. Sen-Sen is still a godsend-send for sweeter-breath seekers around the world.

SEWING MACHINE: Several kinds of sewing machines were already on the market by 1850 when Isaac Merrit Singer (1811-1875) of Oswego, New York, invented the first truly practical model. Elias Howe, Jr., whose own rather cumbersome machine introduced four years earlier had failed to attract buyers because it could sew only a few stitches at a time, promptly sued for twenty-five thousand dollars. He had grounds for complaint because Singer, a former ditchdigger and sawmill worker, had used a discarded Howe machine as the starting point for his tinkering. What was needed, Singer decided, were simply modifications that would produce a seam, straight or curved, more than six inches long. When two other sewing machine manufacturers also threatened suit, Singer hastened to enlist legal help from a young lawyer, Edward Clark, who subsequently became his partner. To end the ensuing "sewing machine war," with everyone suing everyone else, Clark suggested to the manufacturers that they pool all their patents in a single Singer Sewing Machine Corporation and divvy up the proceeds, with one-third going to Singer and Clark.

A Singer model intended for home use was introduced in 1856, but there were few takers for a one hundred dollar machine when the average annual income of an entire family was five hundred dollars. Clark got around that difficulty by devising history's first installment plan. He also inaugurated the concept of the trade-in, offering fifty dollars for old machines, which he promptly smashed. To combat the notion that Singer machines were too complex, Clark hired pretty young women to demonstrate ease of operation in store windows. He also established easily accessible service facilities. While the ingenious Clark kept clicking, Singer indulged a most unusual life-style. Married only once but, eventually, the father of twenty-four children by four different women, he drove a nine-horse yellow carriage that seated thirty-one and had room for a nursery and a small orchestra.

As early as the Civil War, Singer agents were stationed in Mexico and Uruguay, making the company America's first multinational firm. Within three decades of its debut, the Singer sewing machine was in virtually every middle-class home in America and Europe. South Pacific islanders once listed as life's three basic essentials food, shelter, and a Singer sewing machine.

SEX: Come now, of course we're not suggesting that Americans invented sex, although many individual Americans—and Russians, Hottentots, or whatever—as their mates will attest, often act as if *they*, personally, did. However, American researchers, using American respondents, have made significant contributions to the world's store of knowledge about psychological and physiological aspects of the reproductive process that makes the whole world kin and creates the kin's kin.

For instance, zoologist Alfred C. Kinsey (1894-1956), author of the 1948 *Sexual Behavior in the Human Male* (which came to be known as "the Kinsey Report") and of the 1953 *Sexual Behavior in the Human Female*, concluded after studying thousands of case histories that several so-called "perversions" were sufficiently common to be considered normal. Testimony indicating that women achieve orgasm 95 percent of the time when masturbating led him to assert that any woman with a history of masturbation would be responsive to marital intercourse.

Sexual therapists William H. Masters (1915-   ) and Virginia E. Johnson (1925-   ), authors of the 1966 *Human Sexual Response,* could find no significant difference between "clitoral" and "vaginal" orgasm. Their studies indicated that many women are multiorgasmic and that women, in general, derive their most intense orgasms from masturbation. Although sexual functioning continues for older people, they found, it is attended by changes in such areas as the time required to achieve erection and the copiousness of vaginal lubrication.

The fashion-model-turned-sex-researcher Shere Hite (1943-   ), author of the 1976 *The Hite Report,* concluded that female orgasms derived from clitoris-stimulating masturbation and cunnilingus were more pleasurable than penile penetration but that most women welcomed the intimacy of intercourse. "Intercourse," she opined, "was never meant to stimulate women to orgasm."

SHOPPING CART: Early supermarket shoppers were handed wicker baskets in which to carry their purchases. In 1937, Sylvan N. Goldman, an Oklahoma City supermarket owner, found a way to ease the housewife's food-buying chores—and to enable her to buy and tote more—by inventing the supermarket shopping cart. After noticing that women tended to stop shopping when their baskets became too full or too heavy, he sat in his office one June evening wondering how to increase per capita purchasing when he spotted two folding chairs standing against a wall. He envisioned metal baskets that could be folded and stacked on the floor to minimize storage space when not in use. With the help of a carpenter and a maintenance man, he built a two-tier folding cart with metal baskets in a frame.

Because Oklahoma City shoppers were unenthusiastic about the new gadgets, Goldman stopped advertising them as a lure for patrons. Instead, he hired men and women to blithely push the carts while pretending to be shoppers and stationed a woman at the entrance to offer carts to new arrivals. The strategems worked. He offered the carts to other store owners at seven dollars apiece but, at first, found few takers because store managers feared that the carts would knock cans and bottles off their shelves or, even worse, roll into customers and cause injuries. However, when they saw how well the carts were working at Goldman's market, they overcame their qualms and Goldman's Folding Carrier Corporation soon earned him the first million of a fortune that was later estimated at $200 million. Over the years the size of the cart expanded, confirming his thesis that shoppers would buy whatever they could haul easily.

Goldman also designed the modern-day shopping carts, costing as much as one hundred fifty dollars apiece, that stack inside each other and the luggage cart widely used at airports and at train and bus stations. At the time of Goldman's death in December 1984, the number of carts being wheeled through stores around the globe was estimated at more than twenty-five million. In 1982, Goldman was the subject of a biography titled *The Cart That Changed the World.*

SHOPPING MALL: Although a case could be made for St. Mark's Square in Venice, the first shopping mall, according to the

Guinness Book of World Records, was Suburban Square, established by architect Frederick W. Dreher in Ardmore, Pennsylvania, in 1928. Dreher's concept of a one-stop shopping center was vigorously opposed by nearby residents who subsequently became its ardent supporters. A preplanned mix, it consisted of small stores that offered personalized service.

After World War II, shopping malls proliferated throughout America and beyond. According to a 1985 estimate, the number in the United States alone exceeds forty-seven hundred. Most were dominated by large, nonlocal companies that stressed three principles in designing and managing them: enclosure, protection, and control. Most of these cathedrals of consumption looked alike, encompassed similar franchises, and sold the same nationally advertised merchandise. They were self-contained commercial communities with their own rules, their own security systems, and their own clean-up crews.

Complicated formulas have been devised to help shopping center planners achieve optimum results. One mall architect confessed, "Our biggest complaint from shoppers is getting lost in the mall, but that is our intent. We are trying to entice people to enter the mall and keep them there." Commented the humorist Erma Bombeck, "These designers aren't going to stop until every man, woman, and child in this country is milling around with glazed eyes and the egg money in their hands, wandering from shoe store to cheese shop."

SIDEWALK, MOVING: The first mechanized sidewalk was installed at the 1893 World's Columbia Exposition in Chicago. Capable of advancing one mile in ten minutes, it transported 5,510 fairgoers at once. Similar conveyor belts for humans are now common at airports at home and abroad.

SILLY PUTTY: The chemical engineer James Wright accidentally discovered this strange, sticky stuff in 1945 while working for the General Electric Corporation, but it was the ad man Peter Hodgson who figured out how to persuade people to buy it. Wright was looking for a new kind of synthetic rubber for World War II military use when he inadvertently mixed boric acid and silicone oil. The result was a peculiar-looking, peculiarly versatile blob. Tests showed that the soft, claylike chemical compound could be shattered with a hammer, snapped in half, stretched like taffy, bounced (it rebounds 25 percent higher than a rubber ball), kneaded, molded into assorted shapes, and flattened. In the latter state it could be used to take an impression off a newspaper page or a comic book. All very interesting, and all very unsaleable. Hodgson, who first saw the stuff in a New Haven toy shop in 1949, decided that the way to intrigue potential customers was to let them figure out for themselves what the goo was good for. He borrowed $147 to put his theory to the test. Labeled Silly Putty and advertised as "a toy with one moving part," one-ounce dabs in plastic eggs were dispatched to toy stores, where they promptly triggered small-fry enthusiasm. Since then, older buyers have been advised by the maker, Binney and Smith (*see* CRAYON), of more utilitarian possibilities like cleaning typewriter keys, removing lint, and stabilizing teetering tables. Silly Putty factories have been built in West Germany and Japan.

SKATEBOARD: A popular preteen toy used to be the "skatemobile" scooter fashioned from a discarded orange crate, a two-by-four board, two hunks of wood for steering handles, and roller-skate wheels. Skateboarding, or sidewalk surfing, a fad that swept the United States in the mid-1960s and then had a worldwide revival during the following decade, reduced those five ingredients to two: the wheels and the connecting board.

Skateboarding started in the late 1950s among California surfers as a way to practice during bad weather and achieved national popularity with the help of skateboarding rhapsodies by rock stars Jan and Dean; but it petered out because the steel-clay-and-rubber-composition wheels wore out fast, were easily snagged, and permitted few stunts. Frank Nasworthy, a surfing buff who dropped out of Virginia Polytechnic Institute to head for California in pursuit of the perfect wave, brought with him some of the soft, durable urethane roller-skate wheels a factory in his home state of Virginia was having trouble selling because they were too slow for skilled roller skaters. In 1973, after discovering that on asphalt or concrete surfaces they gave skateboards far better traction and maneuverability, he formed a company and, within a year, sold ten thousand sets of his Cadillac Wheels, subsequently trademarked in twelve countries. Henry Larrucea increased skateboards' flexibility by extending the wheel out beyond the axle nut. The bearings were refined, the trucks (the wheel assembly) improved (to make steering more precise), and suddenly skateboarding was converted from child's play to an intricate skill, subject of the film *That Magic Feeling* and TV specials.

Equipment, once under ten dollars, zoomed to as much as three thousand dollars for a custom-made Ermico speedboard. The first paved park designed expressly for skateboarding opened in Port Orange, Florida, in February 1976. The first World Masters Invitational took place in Uniondale, Long Island, in June 1976 and the first open World Professional Invitational in Long Beach, California, three months later. The following year contestants represented the United States, Canada, England, West Germany, Switzerland, and Japan.

SKYSCRAPER: Although New York is the city usually associated with altitudinous architecture, Chicago housed the first towering office structure—William Le Baron Jenney's 1885 Home Insurance Building. The term "skyscraper" was used as far back as the 1840s to describe a tall tale, a tall person, or a building all of four stories high.

Buildings more than five stories high were made possible by the development of the elevator in the 1850s. Even higher construction became feasible with the introduction of the steel skeleton in the 1880s. Chicago took advantage of the new technology of verticality to restore its commercial center, ravaged by the 1871 fire attributed to "Mrs. O'Leary's cow."

The profile of U.S. cities changed most dramatically, however, after the turn of the century. The motto of New York State, "Excelsior!"—onward and upward—was reflected in the completion in 1930 of the Chrysler Building, the first structure taller (by sixty-two feet) than Paris's Eiffel Tower. The following year the Empire State Building, eight blocks away, topped the 1,046-foot Chrysler Building by four feet after New York developer John Raskob asked architect William Lamb, "Bill, how high can you make it so that it won't fall down?" To safeguard the Empire State's claims to being New York's—and the world's—tallest building, Raskob added a two-hundred-foot dirigible mooring mast that has been used only once, raising the building's official height to 1,250 feet. (An additional 222 feet were added in 1950 by a TV transmitter.) In 1970, New York's World Trade Center stretched to 1,369 feet but lost its "tallest" title soon after to Chicago's 1,454-foot, 110-story Sears Tower. Donald Trump plans to bring the title back to New York with a building 1,670 feet high. Architects have proposed 180-story and mile-high, 500-story skyscrapers.

Although it is no longer the tallest, the Empire State, "the Everest of Fifth Avenue," retains a special glamor as the only skyscraper ever used as a climbing pole by a giant gorilla—King Kong.

SLINKY: A three-inch tightly coiled piece of steel ribbon that sinuously slithers down steps like a caterpillar, one half propelling the other, the Slinky is not only fascinating to watch but educative as well, demonstrating two laws of physics: the law of inertia, about continuing in the same direction; and Hooke's law, about returning to the original shape after being stretched. Richard James, a young Philadelphia engineer, was working at the Cramp Shipyard for fifty dollars a week during World War II, conducting experiments with coil springs to insulate delicate instruments from shock, when a torsion spring tumbled from a shelf above his desk, "walked" across a pile of books and bounced to the floor. "Strictly speaking," he said years later, "I didn't invent Slinky; it practically walked into my life."

His wife, Betty, leafed through a dictionary, looking for a name, and thought Slinky—"stealthy, sleek, and sinuous"—was just right. The Jameses took out a five hundred dollar loan to produce four hundred toy-size springs and, in November 1946, began demonstrating their device at one corner of a Gimbels department store toy counter. Within ninety minutes their entire stock was gone. It subsequently sold by the millions, in the United States and abroad.

Initially made of metal and sold for a dollar, it is now being manufactured in plastic as well by James Industries, in Holidaysburg, Pennsylvania. The company, now operated by Mrs. James (whose license plate reads "SLINKY"), also markets smaller "junior" Slinkys and "Crazy Eyeballs" (plastic eyeballs on springs). The only change in the Slinky design in forty years has been crimping of the ends for safety. Examples of Slinky were displayed in the Soviet Union as part of an Industrial Design U.S.A.-sponsored tour and are on exhibit in Washington at the Smithsonian Institution's National Museum of American History.

The Jameses were divorced in 1960 when Richard left his wife and their six children, aged two to eighteen, and moved to Bolivia. Before departing, he transferred all his James Industries stock to the children. He remarried, became a missionary, and died in Bolivia in 1974 at the age of fifty-six.

SNEEZING POWDER: Soren Sorensen Adams, of Asbury Park, New Jersey, was a salesman for a coal-tar product when he became aware that the stuff was more potent than pepper as a sneeze-inducer. Just for laughs, he began sprinkling it about, discombobulating various inhalers. In 1906, he decided to sell his sneeze powder to other practical jokers, charging a dollar a bottle for "Cachoo!" It infuriated its victims, but sales were brisk.

Rival sneeze powders soon became available at lower cost. Instead of getting into a sneeze snit, Adams looked about for other novelties that would appeal to hijinksers and came up with the bingo shooting device, a mousetraplike gadget that, when inadvertently moved, exploded a percussion cap. He installed the miniature noisemaker inside playing card packets, cigar boxes, and raunchy book covers. It, too, sold well until competitors converged.

Adams subsequently introduced the telegram that fluttered when opened, the snake jar, the dribble glass, the bleeding finger, the shiner (a telescope that leaves a black ring around the unsuspecting user's eye), the all-metal ink blot, the skin-dyeing soap, the iron cigar, the exploding pencil, the rubber nail, the rubber clothes hook, the imitation poached egg, the kiss-simulating rubber stamp, the stick-um door bell, the shooting pop ball box, the explosive bouquet, and the explosive package.

He was especially fond of the joy buzzer. That gadget, which he patented in 1931, converts a handshake into a handshock.

SNOOPY: The quirky comic-strip beagle (*see* "PEANUTS") who has replaced the Teddy Bear (*see* TEDDY) and Mickey Mouse (*see* MICKEY) as the world's most beloved non-human personality is based on a black-and-white non-beagle named Spike that "Peanuts'" creator Charles M. Schulz had as a pet when he was thirteen years old. Initially depicted as a relatively realistic pooch who ran about on all fours and whose cartoon-balloon thoughts were limited to "!" and "?," Snoopy has become increasingly anthropomorphic. Since 1958, he's been standing and walking on two legs when not lying atop his dog house dreaming of airborne World War I victories over the Red Baron; typing the dubious novel that begins, "It was a dark and stormy night"; swaggering about as Joe Cool; embarking on assorted adventures with his bird buddy, Woodstock; or having outrageous thoughts that are translated into 26 languages.

Snoopy, born at the Daisy Hill Puppy Farm, was part of the original "Peanuts" cast. An international celebrity, he has been accorded many honors. A versatile athlete who jogs, skis, cycles, runs in marathons, and plays basketball, tennis, and hockey, he was invited because of his figure-skating skill to participate in the 1976 Winter Olympics at Innsbruck, Austria, and was issued accreditation card Number 008. In 1969, when the United States sent a manned spacecraft within ten miles of the moon, the Apollo 10 command module was dubbed *Charle Brown* for Snoopy's alleged master, and its lunar lander bore the name *Snoopy*. A *Snoopy* musical, starring a human surrogate, was a 1983 Broadway and British West End entry. The same year, Camp Snoopy opened at Knott's Berry Farm in Buena Park, California.

Some of his more ardent fans think that Snoopy stands head, shoulders, and tail over his comic-strip colleagues and that "Peanuts" should be retitled "Snoopy," because he dominates the day-to-day doings much as Popeye did in "Thimble Theater." Aware of Snoopy's overpowering presence, Schulz deliberately avoids putting him in every strip, although he finds it easier to think up ideas for the bumptious beagle than for other "Peanuts" personnel.

SOAP OPERA, RADIO: Daytime radio serials, aimed mainly at housewives, were named "soap operas" because they were usually sponsored by manufacturers of soap products. Later, reflecting technological advances in cleansing aids and writers' addiction to alliteration, they were also dubbed "detergent dramas." The earliest were fifteen-minute broadcasts, Monday through Friday, between 10 A.M. and 4:30 P.M. Which "soap" was the first has never been clearly established, but nominees include the Blue Network's 1931 Chicago-based "Clara, Lu 'n' Em,' the first daily daytime serial to receive network exposure, initially improvised for the amusement of their sorority sisters by three Northwestern co-eds, Louise Starkey (Clara), Isobel Carothers (Lu), 'n' Helen King (Em); "Painted Dreams," on WGN, Chicago, which evolved from an even earlier program titled "Sue and Irene" and costarred its writer, Irna Phillips; "The Stolen Husband," in which at first all the parts were played by a single actor; and "Marie, the Little French Princess," about a princess who ran away to become a commoner. A case can also be made for "Henry Adams and His Book," produced in 1925 by Patt Barnes at WHT, Chicago.

During the late 1920s and early 1930s, the genre developed trademarks: highly emotional situations involving ecstatic or blighted romance, complex relationships, a "star" system, and organ music at climactic moments. Most of the serials were broadcast from Chicago or New York, and many achieved awesome longevity. In fact, some soap-opera actresses made lifelong careers of a single role. The most prolific producers of soaps were Frank and Anne Hummert, whose numerous entries included "Backstage Wife," "John's Other Wife," "Stella Dallas," and "Young Widder Brown." Irna Phillips, who was tagged "queen of the soap operas," supervised dozens of writers who kept grinding out audience-involving tales of marital difficulties, terminal illnesses, amnesia, and long-lost relatives. Among Phillips creations was "Guiding Light," which first appeared on NBC radio in 1938, made the transition to television in 1952 (identical scripts were aired on radio and TV for four years), became strictly TV in 1956, and is still going strong.

SOAP OPERA, TV: On October 2, 1946, the two-station (New York and Washington) DuMont network substituted for its usual Wednesday night quiz show a half-hour drama, "Faraway Hill," written, directed, and produced by an Omaha ad agency employee, David P. Lewis. It was telecast from DuMont's makeshift studio in the basement of the John Wanamaker department store in New York's Greenwich Village. Soap opera subsequently became one of TV's most enduring and lucrative genres. Its first impact was felt in the daytime hours occupied by radio equivalents. Many of the first successes were carryovers from the older medium, like NBC's "One Man's Family," with Bert Lytell, Marjorie Gateson and Eva Marie Saint. In more recent years, as soap operas lengthened to an hour per day, juggling several stories at once, audience favorites included ABC's "General Hospital," which ruled the roost in 1985, CBS's "The Young and the Restless," and ABC's "All My Children," which kept vying for second place.

The first soap opera to become a major hit in "prime time" (between 8 P.M. and 11 P.M.) was ABC's "Peyton Place" (1964-1969), which began with half-hour episodes Tuesdays and Thursdays at 9:30 P.M. and expanded in its second season to three nights a week. Two of its one-hundred-odd "principal" roles were played by movie-stars-to-be Ryan O'Neal and Mia Farrow. "Peyton Place" was revived as a daytime serial from 1972 to 1974 and re-revived as a two-hour prime-time special in May 1985. "Peyton Place" had impact abroad, but nothing comparable to that caused by CBS's "Dallas," with Larry Hagman as resident villain J. R. Ewing, which began its lengthy career in April 1978. After a slow start, it became America's most popular program during the 1980-81 season. A source of avid international speculation after the final 1979-80 episode was "Who shot JR?" There were rumors that because Hagman, son of the Broadway singing star Mary Martin, wanted a hefty raise, JR would die during the show's summer hiatus or undergo plastic surgery and return with another actor's face. "Dallas" spawned one spin-off, "Knots Landing," and several imitators, including ABC's "Dynasty" (1981), with John Forsythe, Linda Evans, and later, Joan Collins, which surged ahead of "Dallas" in the 1984-85 rating race.

SODA FOUNTAIN: Conflicting names and dates are linked to the invention of the soda fountain. One source says that the first mechanism "by which soda could be automatically made and dispensed" was the doghouse-sized brainchild of the British immigrant John Matthews in 1832. Another gives the nod a year later to Jacob Ebert of Cadiz, Ohio, and George Dulty of Wheeling, West Virginia. The first ornamented fountain, an eye popper constructed in white Italian marble adorned with spread eagles, is attributed to Gustavus D. Dows of Lowell, Massachusetts, in 1858. Four years later, Dows added "the double-stream draft arm and cock," which permitted regulation of the soda water's flow. Subsequent ice-cream fountain designers ran amok with cathedral spires, Doric columns, gargoyle spigots, sphinxes, and goddesses. Robert M. Green's delectable innovation (*see* ICE-CREAM SODA) was dispensed from a three-foot-square soda fountain at a Philadelphia festival in 1874. Two years later, at another Philadelphia celebration, marking the centennial of the Declaration of Independence, James W. Tufts, who had paid fifty thousand dollars for the concession, served ice-cream sodas inside a three-story soda-fountain cathedral more than thirty feet tall, which featured a fountain of perfumed waters in a sylvan setting. In 1894, the four largest soda-fountain-manufacturing firms—Tufts, Puffer, Lippincott, and Matthews—merged to become the American Soda Fountain Company.

In 1903, the first modern soda-fountain counter was installed at

Philadelphia's Broad Street Pharmacy. Similar counters were soon being manned by "soda jerks" everywhere. American soda fountains, with marble counters and banks of syrup pumps, were exported to countries as distant as Japan. U.S. drugstores began removing their soda fountains at the rate of twelve hundred per year during the early 1950s, not because of diminished ice-cream consumption, but because store owners found the space could be used more profitably to display nylon stockings, cosmetics, and other nondrug items and because much of the ice-cream "action" had moved from soda fountain to supermarket. However, numerous soda fountains continue to prosper.

SOFTBALL: Softball began on Thanksgiving Day, 1887, when one of the young men assembled in Chicago's Farragut Boat Club to learn via telegraph the outcome of the Harvard-Yale football game threw an old boxing glove at a pal who hit it with a broomstick. According to legend, George Hancock grabbed the glove, used the laces to tie it into a sphere and yelled, "Let's play ball." Hancock then went home and made a crude ball, larger than a baseball, and compiled rules for what he dubbed Indoor Baseball. With the advent of warm weather, the game was moved outdoors and renamed Indoor-Outdoor. So tame a game that it was known as "kitten ball" or "mush ball," its rules were codified in Minneapolis in 1895. It became Softball, at the suggestion of Walter Hakanson, at a 1926 meeting of the National Recreation Congress. An Amateur Softball Association (ASA) committee met in 1933 to establish standard rules. That same year the first fast-pitch national tournament for both men and women was held in Chicago.

As the game's popularity spread to other countries, the ASA committee became the International Joint Rules Committee on Softball. In 1965, five countries competed in the first worldwide women's championship tourney in Melbourne, Australia. The home team bested the United States in a 1-0 finale. A U.S. team won the first men's world championship in Mexico City in 1966. Slow-pitch softball developed as an alternative style of play, and in 1950, the International Softball Federation was formed as the world governing body for both versions. Just how widespread the game has become is underscored by the *1985 Guinness Book of World Records*, which lists male and female record holders in various fast-pitch softball categories from the United States, Canada, Puerto Rico, Guam, the Philippines, Mexico, Venezuela, Panama, Australia, New Zealand, Japan, and Taiwan. The highest batting averages, so far, are .556 for Japan's Seiichi Tanka in 1980 and .550 for Panama's Tamara Bryce in 1978. New Zealand's Basil McLean and Japan's Miyoko Naruse both had seventeen hits in a single game. In 1976, America's Ty Stofflet pitched thirty-three strikeouts in a twenty-inning 1-0 win over New Zealand.

SOLAR ENERGY: Home solar heating units, simple devices usually consisting of a sheet of glass, a metal box, and copper tubing, were offered for sale in Florida and California at the turn of the century by amateur builders and a few firms like the Day/Night Company. Although tens of thousands of solar units were in operation by the 1930s, they offered no real threat to gas heaters, so Day/-Night and other solar outfits switched. By the 1970s, solar-heated homes were virtually nonexistent. All that has changed. Using sunlight as a source of cheap, unlimited power by 1988 is the goal of the Southern California Edison Company, which in October 1980 began construction of Solar One, the world's largest solar energy plant. By the end of 1982, the $142 million installation in the Mojave Desert near Daggett, California, was generating enough power to supply the electrical needs of six thousand homes but at costs far higher than other energy sources.

Solar One, slated to be augmented by an even larger version, consists of 1,818 twenty-three-square-foot heliostats, computer-controlled mirrors, arranged in a one-hundred-acre circle around a central tower. The heliostats concentrate sunlight onto a boiler atop the tower, generating 960 degrees Fahrenheit steam that is used to drive a turbine generator. A holding tank filled with oil and crushed rock stores enough energy to operate the generator for as much as seven hours sans sunlight. An alternative approach, seen as a financially more feasible way to help in the development of the Third World, is via photoelectric cells. Scientists believe that the cells, if made cheaper and more long lasting, could produce electricity at one-fifth the cost of present sources. One approach being pursued by U.S. researchers converts sunlight directly into electricity; another uses the cells to produce fuels. When photovoltaic cells were first introduced in the 1960s, their cost per watt was about six hundred dollars compared to less than 50 cents for conventional sources. With the cost of conventional sources steadily going up and the cost of photoelectric cells going down, by the end of the 1980s, the cost per watt is expected to be about the same.

SPACE PROBE: The first man-made object to fly beyond the planets was the U.S. space probe *Pioneer X*, which left earth's solar system on June 13, 1983. Launched on March 2, 1972, *Pioneer X* was the first space probe to reach the asteroid belt and then, in 1973, Jupiter. After the Jupiter flyby, *Pioneer X* used that planet's strong gravitational field to speed it farther along in its journey toward deep space. On June 13, 1983, *Pioneer X* crossed Neptune's orbit, almost three billion miles from the sun. At the time, because Pluto has a more elliptical orbit, Neptune was farther from the sun.

Some purists contend that *Pioneer X*, in fact, will not leave earth's solar system until it passes beyond the farthest point of Pluto's orbit, an event slated to occur on June 19, 1990; it leaves the heliosphere, the area in which the sun exerts magnetic influence; or it passes the Oort cloud, where comets originate. To meet either of the last two stipulations, *Pioneer X* will have to keep going for an indeterminate number of additional years. It is expected to keep transmitting data for about a dozen years. Three other space probes *(Pioneer XI, Voyager 1,* and *Voyager 2)* are also slated to leave the solar system. In addition to scientific instruments, both *Pioneer XI* and *Voyager 2* bear messages for any extraterrestrial intelligence. In *Pioneer* it's a plaque showing a man, a woman and the earth as the third planet from the sun. Just in case E.T. and his friends can't read, *Voyager 2* substituted a gold-plated phonograph record.

SPACE SHUTTLE: The first reusable space shuttle, *Columbia,* was launched by America's Space Transportation System (STS) on April 12, 1981, and completed a successful round-trip on April 14. Designed to leave the earth like a rocket and return like a glider, it ushered in a new spaceflight era in which the shuttle is envisioned as a relatively inexpensive way to haul skyward personnel and equipment for a prospective permanently staffed space station—*Star Trek* time! *Columbia*'s pioneer flight was piloted by the spaceflight veteran Commander John Young and Robert Crippen. The shuttle went into orbit 169 miles up, circled for two days, and then glided to a perfect landing at California's Edwards Air Force Base. The trip required 2½ years of preparation at a cost of about $9 billion. The shuttle's three main engines, linked to a huge fuel tank, developed about 1 million pounds of thrust at blast-off and two booster rockets added 5 million more. The fuel tank was released sans parachutes and vanished in the Indian Ocean. The reusable booster rockets were recovered. The heat shields used on all previous manned spaceflights to prevent conflagration during reentry had to be discarded after a single trip. For *Columbia,* the National Aeronautics and Space Administration (NASA) created a reusable heat shield.

In 1985, after 17 flights, NASA was predicting a total of 165 flights—toting commercial, military and scientific payloads, at a cost of $71 million each until 1989, when the price, reflecting inflation, would rise to $87 million. The eighteenth shuttle launch on June 17, 1985, involved twenty-seven nations. The shuttle *Discovery* carried five American astronauts, a French test pilot, and a Saudi Arabian prince for a mission that included a *Star Wars* laser test and a hunt for a "black hole" in space. It deployed three commercial satellites, owned by AT&T, the Mexican government, and a consortium of twenty-two Arab nations. Also aboard were two French medical experiments, three West German technology experiments, and a Canadian-built robot arm.

The space shuttle program suffered a severe setback when *Challenger* exploded, with seven fatalities, on January 28, 1986.

SPACE SUIT: In 1934, long before cosmonauts and astronauts, though long after science-fiction fantasists like Jules Verne, the first pressurized suit was created for Grand Saline, Texas-born one-eyed aviator Wiley Post (1899-1935). Post, who flew around the world in a record-breaking 8½ days in 1931, wanted to up his speed during an October 1934 aerial race from London to Melbourne by setting a stratospheric course. That required an environmental envelope to feed oxygen to his entire body at constant pressure. The suit provided by B. F. Goodrich, made of rubberized parachute fabric and an aluminum helmet, cost about seventy-five dollars. Tested at Wright Field in Ohio, it sprang a leak and gave way at the waist. Goodrich engineer Russell Colley salvaged the helmet and made a second suit; but a plumper Post, able to get into the suit, was unable to get out of it. It had to be cut off. The first two suits had restricted movement when inflated. Colley's third try—assembled at home on his wife's sewing machine—consisted of two layers, a rubber bag inside to contain the gas under pressure, and a fabric shell outside to control the inner bag's shape. (Wily Wiley, standing by to be measured, taught Colley's eleven-year-old daughter how to shoot craps. He ended up owing her "fifty thousand" and gave her an I.O.U. A year later, he told her he meant kisses, but she never collected.)

Although the suit was restrictive and odd looking, it worked. Post tested it in the Wright Field's altitude chamber and then wore it aloft in his plane, the *Winnie Mae,* thus making it the first full-pressure suit actually tested in the air. However, the *Winnie Mae* developed problems and Post was compelled to withdraw from the race. Soon Great Britain, where a pressure suit had already been tested in a pressure chamber, plus France, Germany, Italy, the Soviet Union, and other countries were at work on pressure suits, enlisting manufacturers of items as diverse as armor, diving suits, girdles, and galoshes. Some were bizarre, like an Italian model that had to be entered through a hole in the back. Pressure suits became superfluous when airplane cabins were pressurized in the 1940s but regained importance with the first space walk in 1965.

SPECTROHELIOGRAPH: The device that makes photographs of the sun possible, showing the distribution of elemental gases in its outer regions, was invented in 1891 by the Chicago-born astronomer George Ellery Hale (1868-1938) between semesters at the Massachusetts Institute of Technology in what he called the "Kenwood Observatory" next to his family's Kenwood Avenue home. In 1895, he founded the *Astrophysical Journal,* which became the world's leading publication in its field. He was instrumental in establishing the Yerkes Observatory in Williams Bay, Wisconsin; the Mt. Wilson Observatory near Pasadena, California (where his solar research revealed the magnetic fields associated with sunspots); and five years after his supposed retirement because of ill health, the Mt. Palomar Observatory in Southern California. Ten years after his death, a huge two-hundred-inch telescope was installed at Mt. Palomar and named in his honor.

STANDARD TIME: When trains began to move passengers long distances in short periods of time, "o'clocks" that jibed at starting point and destination became essential. Before noon on Sunday, November 18, 1883, the United States encompassed fifty-six irregularly shaped time zones and each community determined its own time according to sundials. The differences were in odd numbers of minutes and seconds. Baltimore, for instance, was ten minutes twenty-seven seconds behind New York City.

In 1869, Charles E. Dowd, head of a New York private school, suggested dividing the country into four "time belts." Shortly after, Cleveland Abbe, director of the Cincinnati Observatory and the nation's first official weather forecaster, began urging adoption of standard time. An 1879 Abbe report won the railroads' support, and a provisional plan, dividing the nation by equal degrees of longitude one hour wide, was worked out two years later by William Frederick Allen, secretary of the General Time Convention, who edited a compilation of railroad timetables. His plan was revised and, in 1883, implemented.

Coordinating the world's timepieces was the subject of an international 1884 Washington conference sponsored by the U.S. Congress. Because Britain already had an extremely well-equipped observatory that was extensively used by shippers for navigational purposes, it was decided that the imaginary north-south line that passes through the naval observatory at Greenwich, England, would be used as the starting point for calculating time around the world. An hour was added to Greenwich mean time for each of twelve 15-degree-wide zones east of the prime meridian and an hour subtracted for each of the twelve 15-degree zones to the west. Where the zones meet on the other side of the world was designated the International Date Line. There, travelers moving west lost a day and those moving east gained a day. Today almost all nations subscribe to the standard-time system.

"STAR TREK": For a TV series that never drew top ratings throughout its verge-of-cancellation 1966-69 NBC existence, "Star Trek," chronicling futuristic adventures aboard the starship *Enterprise*, has enjoyed amazing longevity. That has been due to the fanatic loyalty of "Star Trek" cultists who mounted a letter-writing campaign to stave off an earlier network departure and who tune in religiously to nonstop syndicate reruns, some watching the same episode as many as forty times. Some one hundred thousand missives from "Star Trek" fans also persuaded President Gerald R. Ford to change the name of the first space shuttle orbiter from *Constitution* to *Enterprise*. Annual conventions in the United States and England have drawn hordes of "Trekkies."

Unlike other sci-fi series, "Star Trek" often dealt seriously with extraterrestrial versions of contemporary problems and imparted a sense of reality to characters as improbable as a pointed-eared, green-complexioned Vulcan-earthling half-breed, that imperturbable epitome of logic, Mr. Spock. Cast members held in reverence by worldwide "Star Trek" buffs include William Shatner as Captain James T. Kirk, Leonard Nimoy as Mr. Spock, DeForest Kelley as the starship medic Leonard ("Bones") McCoy, James Doohan as the engineer Montgomery ("Scotty") Scott, George Takei as the chief navigator Sulu, and Nichelle Nichols as the communications officer Uhura.

One reason NBC dropped the series was that too large a percentage of its dwindling audience was deemed too young demographically to suit sponsors. From 1973 to 1975 the network revived "Star Trek" as a Saturday morning animated cartoon series for even younger viewers. In 1979, in response to Trekkies' incessant pleadings and the box-office grosses for *Star Wars*, Paramount Pictures produced a movie version of *Star Trek* at a cost of $40 million. Returns were disappointing, but Paramount fared considerably better with the 1982 *Star Trek II: The Wrath of Khan*, which ended with the seeming death of Mr. Spock; and the 1984 *Star Trek III: The Search for Spock*, which was directed by the underemployed portrayer of Spock, who appeared— still very much alive—only in the final scene.

STEAMBOAT: There are so many claimants to the discovery of the steamboat that they merited an entire 1944 volume, subsequently updated, Thomas Flexner's *Steamboats Come True: American Inventors in Action*. Steam-engine pioneers included England's Marquis of Worcester, who began seeking a "water-commanding machine" to help miners in 1628; and Britain's Thomas Savery, Thomas Newcomen, and Jonathan Hulls. Hulls, a Gloucestershire clockmaker, applied Newcomen's 1705 engine (the first capable of directly converting steam into mechanical motion) to a towboat's single paddle wheel in 1736 (the year Scotland's James Watt, generally credited with the invention of the steam engine, was born). Watt was asked to repair a Newcomen engine and made major improvements in 1769. (Watt coined the word "horsepower" and subsequently was honored via "watt" as the unit of electrical power.) Steamboat pioneers included America's William Henry in 1763; France's Marquis Claude Francois Dorothee de Jouffroy d'Abbans in 1783; England's William Symington in 1788 (among the passengers for the first trial run was Scottish poet Robert Burns); and the Maryland-born blacksmith-turned-inventor James Rumsey. A protégé of George Washington, in December 1787, Rumsey demonstrated on the Potomac River a steamboat that was, in effect, the world's first jet-propelled vehicle. Far ahead of his time, Rumsey failed both at home and in England to raise the capital needed for its development.

The first commercial steamboat service was inaugurated on the Delaware River in July 1790 by Rumsey's chief rival in the field, John Fitch. The charge for passage from Philadelphia to Trenton, New Jersey, with several intermediate stops, was five shillings. Because the route was already served by stagecoaches that moved faster than his boat's seven miles per hour, the Fitch venture failed, even though he charged half the stagecoach fare. The first commercially operated passenger steamboat in the world to maintain successful regular service was Robert Fulton's *Clermont,* which began runs between New York City and Albany in 1807. The first round-trip took sixty-two hours of steaming time. The Pennsylvania-born Fulton (1765-1815), a one-time artist, is generally hailed as the inventor of the steamboat.

STENOTYPE: The Stenotype shorthand machine, widely used in the chronicling of business conferences and courtroom proceedings, was invented in 1906 by Ward Stone Ireland, a Dallas, Texas, court reporter and stenographer. Equipped with a compact keyboard of twenty-two small, light and silent keys, it enables its operator, while maintaining eye contact with a speaker, to use all his fingers and to increase "dictation" speed even more by striking several keys simultaneously. A later model was named the Stenograph. Expert stenotypists can exceed 250 words per minute. In recent years the functions of the Stenotype and Stenograph have been largely co-opted by the audiotape recorder, but that device may in turn be replaced by the voice-operated typewriter.

STETSON: The Stetson hat, the wide-brimmed, high-crowned, natural-colored headgear that became a classic symbol of Wild West cowboys and a favorite of dudes everywhere who yearned to look like dashing buckaroos, was designated "The Boss of the Plains" by John

Batterson Stetson, a Philadelphia hat manufacturer. He tailored different kinds of hats to what he considered different regional tastes, but only the B.O.P. variety were commonly referred to as "Stetsons."

The consumptive son of an Orange, New Jersey, hat maker, John Stetson headed West for his health in the late 1850s. When his brick-selling business in St. Joseph, Missouri, was destroyed by a Missouri River flood, he set out for Pike's Peak with a dozen adventurous companions, each bringing along only the clothes on his back, a shotgun, and a hatchet. Lacking anything to provide shelter, they trapped some of the abundant animal life—including rabbit, muskrat, beaver, and coyote—and sewed the pelts together; but the subsequent stench made them jettison their makeshift tents. Stetson took the discarded skins and, remembering his father's technique, converted them into felt and fashioned headgear for all his fellow derring-doers. After attaining the summit of Pike's Peak, Stetson decided to go back East and make felt hats commercially. Instead of depending on what turned out to be unprofitable local trade in Philadelphia, he designed the B.O.P. and sent free samples to clothing and hat dealers throughout the Southwest. His gamble paid off. Within two weeks he had so many orders that prospective buyers were advised that terms were strictly cash-in-advance.

Because the Stetson name was considered a guarantee of quality, by about 1900 the John B. Stetson Company was the largest hat factory in the world, employing more than three thousand workers. When its fortunes declined in the 1950s, because of new trade restrictions and duties, the Stetson company stopped exporting and began to license foreign hat manufacturers instead of building and maintaining factories abroad. By then, however, Stetson himself was long gone. In the 1960s, the Stetson Company began to license other U.S. hat manufacturers and diversified into other kinds of men's apparel.

STRAW, FLEXIBLE: In 1888, the first tubes for siphoning drinks were made of glass, inviting lip lacerations. Marvin Chester Stone, of Washington, D.C., introduced hand rolled straws made of paraffined manila paper, but they cracked easily and were often unsanitary. In 1938, Joseph B. Friedman of Santa Monica, California, observing his young daughter's exasperation when her soda straw bent over the rim of her glass, preventing successful suction, decided to free the world's small fry from similar frustration by creating a straw with a corrugated section. His disposable Flexi-Straw, made of plastic, bends to any angle.

STREPTOMYCIN: A sulfate that proved of major importance in the treatment of tuberculosis was discovered in 1944 by the microbiologist Selman Abraham Waksman (1888-1973). In 1911, less than a year after he emigrated from Russia, Waksman enrolled at Rutgers College to study agriculture. In 1918, he returned to Rutgers' New Jersey Agricultural Experiment Station with a doctorate in biochemistry from the University of California at Berkeley. His major field of study was soil bacteriology, but he recalled afterward, "Little did I dream at that time that there was gold in those ditches in the form of microbes, many of which had never been seen before by the human eye." In 1939, Waksman and his associates began a highly organized study to determine the nature of the substances by which the various soil microbes destroy each other. Because of indications that soil was able to kill tubercle bacilli, Waksman assigned study of such bacilli in soil and water to a graduate student, Chester Rhimes. The first streptomycin-producing culture was obtained by swabbing the throat of a chicken. The discovery of the new antibiotic was announced in January 1944, and the following July, Merck and Company agreed to produce it.

After successful tests on guinea pigs at the Mayo Clinic, clinical testing on human patients indicated that streptomycin adversely affected hearing and balance, a drawback that was largely eliminated by careful control of dosage. Tests on thousands of Veterans' Administration patients demonstrated that streptomycin helped and often cured pulmonary and miliary tuberculosis and tuberculous meningitis and was effective against strains of bacteria resistant to penicillin. Waksman was awarded the Nobel Prize in physiology and medicine in 1952. By the following year streptomycin was being manufactured by nine U.S. companies and by others in Great Britain, France, Sweden, Denmark, Germany, Italy, Spain, Japan, and several Iron Curtain countries. The 1946 bulk price of twenty-four dollars per gram dropped to twenty-five cents.

STROBE AND PHOTOFLASH LIGHT: The strobe light (STROB is a Graflex-registered trademark) was invented in May 1931 by Dr. Harold E. Edgerton (1904-1990) of the Massachusetts Institute of Technology. Producing fast, high-intensity flashes when a capacitor discharged high voltage into a tube of inert gas, it made possible such photos as a close-up of the moment of contact between a kicker's toe and a football. Edgerton also devised a vacuum-tube circuit for precise triggering of each flash. At the 1939 New York World's Fair, an Eastman Kodak exhibit installed by Edgerton included a speedlight that functioned at 1/100,000 of a second. Xenon and krypton proved to be the optimum gases, and the tubes underwent several changes in shape. The *Milwaukee Journal* photographic chief Frank Sherschel and two colleagues created an electronically triggered speedlight. The engineer Ed Wilcox devised the first practical battery-powered portable version.

Since 1949, electronic flash equipment has become more compact, lighter, and safer. One spectacular application of strobe principles is the laser. Among the ultraversatile flash's other exotic uses are missile tracking, nose-cone recovery, photomicrography, "stop-action" stage and discotheque effects, and landing-strip illumination. Edgerton took key aerial photos of the Normandy beach the night before World War II's D-Day invasion and helped to locate the sunken HMS *Britannic* and the Civil War USS *Monitor*.

SUBMARINE: The first submersible vessel ordered into action as a war weapon, utilized to absolutely no effect by George Washington during the American Revolution, was invented by David Bushnell, a young Saybrook, Connecticut, farmer. While a freshman at Yale College, he impressed the faculty by demonstrating, to their astonishment, the first underwater gunpowder explosion. In 1775, as sentiment for independence from England mounted, he began mulling ways to use an underwater weapon. He devised an egg-shaped, tar-smeared wooden vessel, the *American Turtle*, its six-foot interior crammed with machinery. Submersion occurred when a foot pedal filled a water tank. Resurfacing required energetic utilization of two hand pumps. The *Turtle* had an estimated underwater cruising time of thirty minutes, but the supply of oxygen was much more quickly depleted if candles were lighted to enable the pilot to see what he was doing. One hand-operated screw propeller, a Bushnell innovation, controlled up-and-down movement; a second controlled back-and-forth movement. If the operator turned the crank vigorously, the *Turtle* could achieve a speed of three miles per hour.

On September 6, 1776, after the British had ousted the Americans from Long Island, Washington ordered the *Turtle* to attack Admiral Howe's sixty-five-gun flagship, the *Eagle*, anchored off Staten Island. Bushnell pleaded illness, so the first *Turtle* strike was piloted by a volunteer, Sgt. Ezra Lee of Lyme, Connecticut. Lee had trouble locating his objective and then discovered that Plan A was impossible. He was supposed to bore a hole in the *Eagle*'s hull with a drill so that he could attach a 150-pound box of gunpowder, but the *Eagle*'s timbers were sheathed in impenetrably thick copper. Retreating, Lee again lost his bearings and surfaced a few hundred yards from Governor's Island, in full view of British soldiers, who dispatched a bargeful of men to investigate. Lee jettisoned his bomb, submerged, and fled. After floating for a half hour, the bomb exploded, causing a thunderous noise, a huge water spout, and no casualties. A second try in the Hudson River was also ineffectual.

SUBMARINE, NUCLEAR: The 319-foot USS *Nautilus*, the world's first nuclear-powered submarine, launched in 1954, could travel farther, move faster (twenty knots per hour), and stay submerged longer than any previous submarine. Its first record-breaking four-month ocean voyage began on January 17, 1955, with Commander Eugene P. Wilkinson's signaling to his superiors at the Submarine Force Command: "Under way on nuclear power." When it went into port in January 1958 for its first refueling after logging more than one hundred thousand miles, President Dwight D. Eisenhower hailed "the gallant ship which has paced a revolution in naval tactics and construction." Later that year the *Nautilus* accomplished what had been considered an impossible feat by passing under the North Pole while cruising for ninety-six hours beneath the Arctic ice cap. It was a second try. A 1957 effort had to be called off when the ship got lost. After the polar crossing, the *Nautilus* was used primarily for training exercises. One exception was its participation in the 1962 naval quarantine of Cuba.

The ship's final voyage under its own power ended in 1979. It was decommissioned at the Mare Island naval base, near San Francisco, on March 3, 1980. In the summer of 1985, it was towed through the Panama Canal to a dock at New London, Connecticut, preparatory to the April 1986 opening of the $7 million USS *Nautilus* Memorial Submarine Force Library and Museum at Groton, near the Electric Boat Yard where it was built. By 1971, the United States and the Soviet Union, between them, had more than ninety nuclear-powered submarines and an annual production rate of four for the U.S. and twelve to fourteen for the USSR. In 1985, the U.S. Navy's fleet included six Trident nuclear submarines, direct descendants of the *Nautilus,* but nearly twice its size and equipped with nuclear weapons.

The *Nautilus* was nicknamed "Lola" by its crew because the ultra-high priority accorded its every request for supplies reminded them of a song in the 1956 musical comedy *Damn Yankees,* "Whatever Lola Wants, Lola Gets."

SUGAR-COATED PILL: The huge Warner-Lambert multiproduct conglomerate stems from the pre-Civil War creation of delicious drug dosages by Philadelphia pharmacist William R. Warner. His sugar-coated pills brought him blessings and bucks galore. In 1908 Gustavus A. Pfeiffer and Company, of St. Louis, which sold patent medicines, bought out Warner's firm, retaining its name, and subsequently absorbed other companies and added other products before merging in 1955 with Lambert Pharmacal, maker of Listerine. Warner-Lambert's acquisition of Entenmann's bakeries in 1979 for $230 million extended a sweet success story from sugar-coated pills to sugar-coated pastries.

SUPERMAN: The world-famous "man of steel" made his debut in the June 1938 issue of Action Comics (*see* COMIC BOOK). Later his exploits were heralded in twelve languages in fifty-four countries, making him the best-selling comic-book character on earth. His powers—and perils—became more and more outlandish until July 1986, when D.C. Comics began toning them down. The object: to make the superhero more vulnerably "human." Syndication of the newspaper comic strip began in January 1939, and a three-times-a-week radio version with Bud Collyer—later the busy host of TV quiz shows like "Beat the Clock" and "Break the Bank"—was launched the following year. An animated cartoon produced by Hollywood's Fleischer Studios received theatrical release. Beginning in 1960, the Krypton Kid was the hero of a half-hour Kellogg's-sponsored live-action TV series in syndication and on the ABC network. CBS revived Superman in 1966 as a Saturday morning cartoon entry, with Bud Collyer again providing the title voice. Both the live-action and cartoon video versions are still being aired around the world.

Superman's international impact became explosive with Warner Brothers's 1978 release of the first of three big-budget *Superman* feature films. President Jimmy Carter took his daughter, Amy, to the Washington premiere. Queen Elizabeth II took Prince Andrew to the London premiere. Coincidentally, George Reeves starred in the live-action TV shows and a name-alike, Christopher Reeve, in the live-action feature films.

Despite Superman's supersuccess, not all the real-life humans associated with him prospered. His creators, Joe Shuster and Jerry Siegel, sold the multimillion multimedia idea in 1933 for $130. They complained that it was not until 1975, after a barrage of press protests, that they were able to get additional reimbursement via a Warner Communications pledge of twenty thousand dollars apiece annually for the rest of their lives. However, records indicated that between 1938 and 1947 they were paid more than four hundred thousand dollars, and that after 1947, Siegel was rehired as a twenty-thousand-dollar-a-year writer and Shuster, unable to work because of his poor eyesight, received an annual seventy-five hundred dollar stipend. There was no similar silver—or gold—lining for George Reeves. Typecast as Superman and unable to get other employment, he committed suicide in June 1959.

SUPERMARKET: In 1912, an independent grocery store (Ward's Grocerteria in Ocean Park, California) was the first to invite customers to pick their own foodstuff. In 1914, the Gerrard brothers, who operated several small stores, borrowed the Grocerteria system for their Pomona, California, Triangle Cash Market but found that confused customers were unable to locate the items on their shopping lists. Albert Gerrard solved the problem by displaying the merchandise in alphabetical order. It worked so well that in 1917 the store was renamed with the slogan "If your child knows the alphabet, he can shop at the Alpha Beta store." At about the same time the Bay Cities Mercantile Company launched a self-service chain, the Humpty

Dumpty Stores, throughout California, but did *not* use the slogan, "If your child knows Mother Goose, he can shop at the Humpty Dumpty store."

In 1916, Clarence Saunders cannily introduced a routing system that forced customers to file down one merchandise-packed aisle after another before being funneled into the checkout counter, at the first of his Piggly Wiggly self-service groceries in Memphis, Tennessee. By 1928, there were twenty-eight hundred Piggly Wigglies in forty-one states.

The first store to merit the "super" half of "supermarket" was the twelve-thousand-square-foot King Kullen the Price Wrecker food store opened in an abandoned Long Island garage by Michael Cullen during the Depression year of 1930. Cullen quit his job with a grocery chain because it rejected his pricing formula: 300 items at cost, 200 at plus 5 percent, 300 at plus 15 percent, and 300 at plus 20 percent. He also advocated low-rent location, night hours, and brash advertising. Although the word "supermarket" had been used previously, the first firm to make the word part of its name was Albers Super Markets, which opened its first store in November 1933. Marion Skaggs's Idaho-based chain of 428 groceries merged with southern California's Sam Seelig Stores in 1926 to form Safeway Stores, the largest supermarket chain, with 2,425 stores in the United States, Canada, the United Kingdom, Australia, and West Germany. Japan's OK supermarket chain has tested a totally computerized supermarket in Kokobunji.

SWING: Jazz has always had its dedicated devotees; but only the kind dubbed swing, performed by orchestral organizations numbering twelve or more (*see* BIG BANDS), has ever achieved anything like majority approval. Characterized by melody as well as beat, swing was the global pop-music favorite from the 1930s until the advent in the late 1950s of the four Liverpudlians known as the Beatles. It was initially performed by black bands in the Southwest (especially near Kansas City) and those led by Benny Moten, Count Basie, and Jay McShann; but it was popularized by white orchestras via sponsored network radio shows. Jelly Roll Morton titled a 1928 composition "Georgia Swing." In 1932, Duke Ellington summarized in the title of a song what quickly became a worldwide sentiment: "It Don't Mean a Thing If It Ain't Got That Swing." Red Norvo led a Swing Septet in 1934. Shortly after, swing achieved its apogee with the figurative coronation of Benny Goodman as "King of Swing." Goodman held coast-to-coast court via his "Let's Dance" radio show, with his East Coast subjects tuning in past midnight to hear the royal West Coast broadcasts. His reign continued until World War II and resumed after it, ending when younger audiences switched their allegiance to rock 'n' roll.

284

T

TABASCO: This fiery condiment, purchasable in at least a hundred countries, uses a Mexican pepper, *Capsicum frutescens,* but it isn't authentic unless the mashed pepper is mixed with salt from America's first salt mine, located on Louisiana's Avery Island. The hot stuff has been produced for more than a hundred years by the island's McIlhenny family. Mary Eliza Avery, whose New Jersey grandfather bought part of the island in 1818, married a New Orleans banker, Edmund McIlhenny. McIlhenny, who had somehow acquired capsicum peppers (bringing them from Texas after his Civil War exile, according to one story; receiving them from a prewar traveler, according to another), chopped them up, mixed them with vinegar and Avery Island salt, aged the mixture in wooden barrels, and poured the concoction into empty cologne bottles. After friends sampled and approved them, McIlhenny decided to go commercial. Seeking a name for his sauce, he decided to borrow that of a river in southern Mexico: Tabasco. In 1868, 350 bottles were distributed. A year later, several thousand were sold at a dollar apiece. In 1871, the product had become so popular in Europe that McIlhenny opened a London office. The biggest foreign user is Japan.

TALKIES: Max Faetkenheur screened a Chromophone color-and-sound film in Cleveland in 1907, the same year Hammerstein's Roof Theater in New York presented film-and-phonograph Cameraphone. Thomas Alva Edison demonstrated his Kinetophone, with a phonograph behind the movie screen, in 1913. D. W. Griffith had sound and ten minutes of dialogue in his 1921 Photokinema film, *Dream Street.* The same year Lee De Forest demonstrated his own Phonofilm sound-on-film recording. On August 6, 1926, Warner Brothers introduced the Vitaphone sound system, using synchronized discs, in New York City via *Don Juan,* a feature film enhanced by music and sound effects. Also on the bill were eight shorts containing talk as well as music. Audiences cheered when John Barrymore's sword clanged against Montagu Love's. A few snatches of dialogue, some ad libbed and others subsequently added, supplemented the five songs sung by Al Jolson in Warner Brothers' historic *The Jazz Singer*, which opened in New York on October 6, 1927. As far as the movie industry was concerned, Jolson was prophetic when he husked, "You ain't heard nothin' yet." The following year came the first all-talking picture, *Lights of New York*.

The advent of sound created new stars, many of them recruited from the stage, and destroyed old ones. "Rin Tin Tin," James Stewart once reminisced, "was the only actor in Hollywood that wasn't worried." Among stars who quickly vanished were Bronx-accented Clara Bow and German-accented Emil Jannings who returned to Europe immediately after accepting the first Best Actor Oscar. An often-cited example of sound's devastating effect on a movie career is romantic superstar John Gilbert, who supposedly plummeted because of a high-pitched voice; but his daughter, Leatrice Fountain, rebuts that legend in a 1985 biography, *Dark Star*, pointing out that her father appeared in nine talkies between 1929 and 1934. What did him in as a romantic star, she claims, was studio politics and his dialogue in a silent-film-style love scene, so naive that it caused audiences to giggle.

TAMPON: Cotton and paper tampons for internal absorption during menstruation were developed by Gertrude Kendrick for a Denver company, Tampax Sales. The firm was purchased by three partners who, in 1936, renamed it Tampax and established new headquarters in New York. Although competitive products were quickly on the market, Tampax retained a commanding lead through 1970, when Kimberly-Clark, Johnson and Johnson, Procter and Gamble, and Esmark's Playtex (which in 1975 became the first tampon advertised on TV) increasingly siphoned off sales.

A medical and legal crisis confronted one major manufacturer after its introduction of a kind of tampon in 1980. Because of its greater absorbency, due to polyester sponges and highly absorbent synthetic fibers, this product was considered especially culpable during an outbreak of often-fatal toxic shock syndrome attributed to tampons by the Center for Disease Control. Although it denied it was at fault, the company recalled the product.

TAP DANCE: Tap dancing, one of America's few native arts, is a melting-pot blend of the rhythmic dances brought from Africa by black slaves, the Irish jig, and the Lancashire clog. Minstrel shows (*see* MINSTREL SHOW) introduced it to audiences across the United States and across the Atlantic as part of blackface caricatures. By the early 1920s, tap had reached Broadway in black musicals like *Shuffle Along*.

Tap received global touting via movies starring Bill (Bojangles) Robinson, who scored not only as a skilled dancer up and down stairs but also as the genial companion and sometime tap teacher for the world's number-one moppet star, Shirley Temple. Other black tappers whose fame spread beyond black theaters, ghetto "challenge" sites, and Harlem's Hoofers Club included the Nicholas brothers (renowned for their spins, flips and splits), John Bubbles, and tall and elegant Charles "Honi" Coles (featured on Broadway in his seventies in the 1983-85 *My One and Only*).

Although most top-drawer tappers have been American, male, and black, the knack has been acquired by dancers of dissimilar nationality, sex, and race—including Fred Astaire, Gene Kelly, Donald O'Connor, Eleanor Powell, Ann Miller, and the Radio City Music Hall's peas-in-a-pod Rockettes. Tap remains viable via thousands of small dance studios, beauty and talent contests, small clubs, and an occasional major breakthrough like Broadway's *42nd Street, A Chorus Line*, and *The Tap Dance Kid*. Among current top tappers are brothers Maurice and Gregory Hines (who were taught by the legendary Henry LeTang) and Hinton Battle. The Brooklyn Academy of Music's 1980 tap festival, *Steps in Time*, showcased skilled clackety-clackers Sandman Sims, Buster Brown, Bubba Gaines, Phace Roberts, Charles Cook, Chuck Green, Leon Collins, Bunny Briggs, and the Copasetics. They performed such intricate and flashy steps as the "buck and wing," "over the top," "through the trenches," and "nerve rolls."

On August 19, 1984, 3,450 professional and nonprofessional dancers between the ages of two and seventy, waving white straw hats and tap-tap-tapping to the tune of "Give My Regards to Broadway," danced down New York's 34th Street into the *Guinness Book of World Records*, ousting the previous record holder, Australia, which had marshaled only 2,647 tap dancers.

TARZAN: The twenty-six volumes about Tarzan, alias Lord Greystoke, reared by apes in the African jungle, have been published in fifty-six languages, including Russian. Fantasy buffs have also met the King of the Apes in real-life and animated movies, radio and TV series, and comic books. This worldwide vine-swinging winner was created by a conspicuous loser, Chicago-born Edgar Rice Burroughs (1875-1950), who failed at one business venture after another before finding his niche as an author. While placing ads in pulp magazines, he decided he could write better stories himself. His first try, "A Princess of Mars," written on the backs of letterheads from his failed projects, was published in a sci-fi magazine under the pseudonym

"Normal Bean," for "average mind." "Tarzan of the Apes" was sold first to *All-Story Magazine* for seven hundred dollars in 1912 and published as a book two years later.

Sixteen actors have portrayed Tarzan in forty-two movies. The first, chunky Elmo Lincoln, who wore a band around his head to keep his toupee from falling off, got the job in the 1918 production after three earlier choices hurt themselves falling from tree limbs. Another, James H. Pierce, married Burroughs's daughter, Joan, and costarred with her in 364 Tarzan radio shows. The most famous Tarzan was the Olympic swimmer Johnny Weissmuller, who starred in twelve of the epics between 1932 and 1948 and introduced the famous Tarzan shriek. Weissmuller claimed he invented it; but Danton Burroughs, the author's grandson, asserts it was actually compounded from a camel's bleat, a soprano singing high C, violin chords, a yodel, and other ingredients. Another noteworthy Tarzan was the Olympic swimmer Buster Crabbe. Miles O'Keefe was subordinated to a nude Bo Derek in a 1981 vanity production; and the French actor Christopher Lambert played the role in the most ambitious film version, the 1984 *Greystoke: The Legend of Tarzan, Lord of the Apes.*

In 1930, Burroughs's California ranch became the town of Tarzana. In 1963, a librarian banned Tarzan on the grounds that he was living with Jane out of wedlock, but they had been married by Jane's minister father in the 1915 *The Return of Tarzan.* In no Burroughs novel does his hero say, "Me Tarzan, you Jane."

TECHNICOLOR: The first colored movies were shorts from France, laboriously tinted by hand. The development in the early 1900s of Pathecolor, an intricate stenciling system, raised hand tinting to an art. A cumbersome, "flicker" effect-producing British process, Kinemacolor, was introduced in 1908. Efforts by American, English, French, and German inventors to devise more satisfactory ways to simulate realistic color were largely ignored. A lithographylike process invented by the St. Louis engraver Max Handschiegl was used in sequences of D. W. Griffith's 1915 *The Birth of a Nation.* Most movie producers were content to follow the lead of ingenious projectionists who held colored gelatin in front of the projector lens. They used sepia-toned film stock: blue for night scenes, amber for daylight sequences, red for fires. This gave way to "toning," which converted to color only the black portions of each frame. Toning was discontinued with the advent of the talkies, but only because it affected sound tracks.

The system that first made possible mass production of color prints was invented in 1923, after five years of experimentation, by the Chelsea, Massachusetts-born chemical engineer Dr. Herbert Thomas Kalmus (1881-1963). His Technicolor process required the laminating of pairs of frames shot simultaneously—one sensitive to red, orange, and, yellow; the other to green, blue, and purple. Public enthusiasm was triggered by vivid color sequences in movies like Lon Chaney's 1925 *The Phantom of the Opera* and Douglas Fairbanks's 1926 *The Black Pirate*. Shortly after, Kalmus simplified his process by using an emulsion that eliminated the need for paired prints. Early Technicolor was beset with problems like fuzziness and peculiar color tones, but they were gradually overcome. The three-strip Technicolor camera, introduced in 1932, exposed three black-and-white negatives, each sensitive to a different primary color, through a single lens.

In 1935, Rouben Mamoulian made skillful use of the improvements in the first full-length feature involving the process, the critically acclaimed *Becky Sharp*, starring Miriam Hopkins. The stunning contrast in the 1939 *The Wizard of Oz* when Dorothy went from black-and-white Kansas to rainbow-hued Technicolor Oz provided one of that imaginative film's most magical moments.

TEDDY BEAR: In November 1902, ostentatiously macho President Theodore Roosevelt took time out from serving as a Dutch uncle in a border dispute between Mississippi and Louisiana to engage in one of his favorite sports: hunting. His hosts, imbued with the spirit of Southern hospitality, obligingly trapped a frisky bear cub as a prospective target. When he realized it was all a setup, Roosevelt declined to pull the trigger. Artist Clifford Berryman used the incident for a widely published newspaper cartoon titled "Drawing the Line in Mississsippi." It depicted Roosevelt, rifle in hand, with his back turned to a frightened bear cub. After Morris Michtom, owner of a Brooklyn candy store, saw the cartoon, he constructed a small brown-plush animal with button eyes and movable limbs. To lure customers, he placed the toy in his display window with a copy of the Berryman cartoon and a sign bearing the words "Teddy's Bear." A number of his patrons asked Michtom to make cuddlesome duplicates. A recent immigrant from Russia, Michtom wondered if he had committed *lèse-majesté* and wrote to the White House for permission to use "Teddy" as his toy's trademark. Roosevelt reputedly wrote back, "I don't think my name is worth much to the toy bear cub business, but you are welcome to use it." The letter, which supposedly became the property of Michtom's oldest son, was not found among his effects.

By 1906, the teddy bear was the nation's best-selling toy and was being pirated at home and abroad. One Michigan priest feared that children would transfer to teddy bears the affection they owed their mothers. In 1903, the Butler Brothers wholesaling firm contracted to buy all of Michtom's teddy bears. This guarantee of unlimited credit with suppliers of plush enabled Michtom to sell his candy store and launch the Ideal Novelty and Toy Company. It subsequently became the Ideal Toy Company, the world's largest doll manufacturer, which still plumps out millions of teddy bears. Ideal's principal rival in the baby bruin business is Reeves International, which uses a bear design it attributes to Margaret Steiff, a German polio victim confined to a wheelchair, who began sewing felt animals in the 1880s.

TEFLON: In 1960, when Teflon was first used to coat cookware, it posed the same problem that would plague a universal solvent: How do you package something that dissolves everything? In the case of Teflon, the question was, how do you make something "nonstickable" stick? Spatulas scraped the Teflon off the bottom of a pan as easily as they lifted what was being cooked on the pan's supersmooth surface. Du Pont scientists recogitated, added some secret ingredients, concocted a new primer for the metal, and went on to create hundreds of new uses for Roy Plunkett's accidental April 6, 1938, discovery.

Plunkett, a Du Pont research chemist, was experimenting with fluorocarbon gases while seeking a new refrigerator coolant. Some of the gas, he noticed, had polymerized into a waxy, white solid. He decided to explore the mysterious substance's characteristics and found that it melted and boiled away at near-"red hot" temperatures; burned without residue; was insoluble in hot or cold water, acetone, or ether; and most importantly, produced virtually no friction when sliding across almost any surface, so the effect was like rubbing ice cubes together. The Du Pont product namers assigned "Teflon" to the magical substance, polytetrafluorethylene, that had plunked into Plunkett's lap. Patented in 1941, it was kept secret during World War II while its military potential was being assessed. It was used for Manhattan Project gaskets to prevent leakage of uranium hexafluoride. After the war, bakeries used it to coat cookware, and glassblowing operations used it to line their chutes so that molten glass would flow uniformly.

When Teflon-lined cooking utensils were first put on sale at Macy's department store in New York City just before Christmas 1960, they were grabbed up by housewives eager to lighten kitchen chores; but the first pans were soon being panned. After Du Pont's additional improvements, however, Teflon cookware became an accoladed accessory. Teflon is also used for space suits, carpet-soil repellents, artificial body parts, and over Plunkett's protests, newsmen's references to blame-resistant Ronald Reagan as "the Teflon president." "It suggests," Plunkett complained, "that the president is slippery."

TELEGRAPH: In 1832, returning to New York after three years of European study and travel, the aspiring artist Samuel F. B. Morse had a casual conversation about electromagnetism that started him thinking about electrical transmission of data. He drafted preliminary sketches while still on the ship. Then began an unsuccessful search for financial backing. Hoping to raise seed money, Morse painted several large paintings for exhibition around the country, but they evoked little interest and less cash. (One, *The Gallery of the Louvre*, was sold 150 years later for $3.25 million.)

Telegraphic experiments were not new. In 1827, Harrison Gray Dyar operated a two-mile system at the Long Island race course, using iron wire attached to glass insulators on wooden posts to relay electrical currents that produced red marks on litmus paper. The lapse of time between sparks indicated letters. An electromagnetic telegraph was demonstrated, but never put to practical use, by the physicist Joseph Henry in Albany, New York, in 1831. Morse and Henry corresponded, and by 1838, Morse had created a working model and the dot-and-dash Morse code that is still in use. A major Morse innovation was a relay device that made long-distance messages feasible. In 1843, Congress belatedly allocated thirty thousand dollars to string telegraph wire from Washington to Baltimore. On May 1, 1844, while it was still being installed, Morse was able to announce in Washington, an hour before the news arrived by train, that the Whig Convention in Baltimore had nominated Henry Clay for president. Three weeks later, on May 24, from a sending station in the Supreme Court chamber, Morse tapped out the official "historic" first message: "What hath God wrought?" Morse and Alfred Vail, his principal aide, offered Congress all their rights to the telegraph, for use as a post office adjunct, for one hundred thousand dollars. When the offer was declined, the two partners, joined by Amos Kendall and others, began private development. Numerous patent suits followed. One was filed by Charles T. Jackson, a fellow voyager way back in 1832. Morse's claims to priority were finally validated by the Supreme Court in 1854. A patent issued to Thomas Alva Edison in 1892 made possible simultaneous transmissions on a single wire.

TELEPHONE: The inventor of the telephone, Scotland-born Alexander Graham Bell (1847-1922), was neither scientist nor engineer. Instead, like his father and his grandfather (reputedly the model for Professor Henry Higgins in George Bernard Shaw's *Pygmalion* and its musical version, *My Fair Lady*), he was a professor of elocution with great know-how about human speech. The basic principle of the telephone—a vibrating membrane—stemmed from another Bell invention designed to help deaf children speak.

The first words heard on a telephone were Bell's "Mr. Watson, come here . . . I want to see you," addressed to his assistant, Thomas A. Watson, on March 10, 1876, arguably because he had spilled acid on himself. The two men held another historic telephone conversation on January 25, 1915, to help launch transcontinental telephone service six months after completion of the coast-to-coast telephone line. Bell repeated his original message, to which Watson, in San Francisco, replied that he'd be happy to oblige, but it would take him at least a week to get there.

Bell's invention achieved instant popularity. By March 1880, thirty thousand telephones had been installed in the United States. Dial service began in Norfolk, Virginia, on November 8, 1919. Overseas service between new York and London began in 1927. Today, the number of telephones in the world is almost uncountable. Other highlights in the instrument's history include the introduction of the coaxial cable in 1941, the first telephone conversation via a communications satellite in 1960 (see SATELLITE, COMMUNICATIONS) and the start of international direct dialing in 1970. In recent years, development of new kinds of phones and new telephone capabilities has been nonstop. Bell Telephone scientists have amassed about twenty thousand patents and five Nobel Prizes. A thirteen-cent U.S. stamp showing the schematic that accompanied Bell's telephone-patent application was issued in March 1976. The title of a Bell biography by Robert V. Bruce aptly credits him with *The Conquest of Solitude. (See also* TELEPHONE BOOTH, TELEPHONE EXCHANGE, TELEPHONE OPERATOR, TELEPHONE SWITCHBOARD.)

A contemporary of Thomas Alva Edison, who accumulated patents galore, Bell displayed similar ingenuity. After sailing to Canada in 1870, he began imparting his father's "visible speech" technique to teachers at a Boston school for the deaf. His experiments in electrical production of sound resulted in the invention in 1875 of a multiplexing telegraph system. He then began to explore the possibilities of transmitting the human voice electrically and received his patent for the telephone two hours before Elisha Gray of Barnesville, Ohio, was granted a similar patent, a coincidence that subsequently triggered litigation. After establishment of the Bell Telephone Company, Bell moved to Washington, D.C., where he conducted experiments leading to the invention of the photophone, a device that transmitted speech on a beam of light; an audiometer; improvements on Edison's phonograph; and a system to detect metallic objects in the body. The latter, first used in 1881 to probe for the assassin's bullet that killed President James A. Garfield, was a useful medical aid before X-ray technology. In his later years Bell was intrigued by aviation and in 1907 founded the Aerial Experimental Association.

TELEPHONE BOOTH: The first telephone booth was made available for public use at the New Haven office of the Connecticut Telephone Company on June 1, 1880. The first coin-operated model was installed at the Hartford Bank in Hartford, Connecticut, by the Southern New England Telephone Company in 1889. Two years later, William Gray, inventor of the coin mechanism, formed the Gray Telephone Pay Station Company, which rented coin-operated telephones to storekeepers. Reportedly, the American billionaire J. Paul Getty kept a coin-operated telephone in his home in England to prevent his guests from taking advantage of his hospitality and wealth.

TELEPHONE EXCHANGE: The first telephone exchange was installed in August 1877 at the Capitol Avenue Drug Store in Hartford, Connecticut, by Isaac D. Smith, agent for the New England Telephone Company. Initially intended as a convenience for the city's "allopathic physicians," it was made available to the general public in October. Within a month there were seventeen subscribers.

The first automatic telephone exchange was patented on March 12, 1889, by the Kansas City undertaker Almon B. Strowger, who worked out its details with the help of a collar box and a number of used matches. According to legend, Strowger wanted to eliminate telephone operators like the wife of his principal business rival, who kept switching calls from his clients to her husband's office. The first Strowger automatic exchange was put into operation at La Porte, Indiana, on November 3, 1892, and was dubbed in some quarters "the girlless, cussless telephone." It used three keys, representing the numbers one to ten, multiples of ten, and multiples of one hundred. The subscriber depressed each key the number of times required to create the proper sequence.

TELEPHONE OPERATOR: The first full-time telephone operator was George Willard Coy, who began work at the District Telephone Company's New Haven, Connecticut, exchange on January 28, 1878. He manned a switchboard linking twenty-one customers. The first woman operator was Emma Nutt, a former telegraph operator, whose first day at the Boston switchboard of Edwin Holmes's Telephone Dispatch Company was September 1, 1878. She was spelled by her sister, Stella A. Nutt, also an ex-telegraph operator. By the mid-1880s, most operators were women. Young males were considered too likely to quarrel with callers. Women were also deemed preferable because of their gentler voices, more nimble fingers—and willingness to work for ten dollars per week.

Originally, calls were begun with repetitions of "ahoy! ahoy!"; but that was replaced by "hello," which had become a common greeting in the mid-1860s. An earlier version of "hello" was "holla!"—a combination of the exclamatory "ho!" (like "hey!") and the French word "la," for "there," used originally to attract attention. "Operator" was borrowed from the telegraph, which had used it since the 1840s. The "hello girl" of the mid-1880s became the "telephone girl" of 1892 and the "telephone operator" of 1894. The precisely enunciated phrase, "the li-on is busy," reportedly was first uttered about 1882 by a Brooklyn-born operator at the Nassau exchange of New York's Metropolitan Telephone and Telegraph Company.

TELEPHONE SWITCHBOARD: The first telephone switchboard linked five clients to Boston's Holmes Burglar Alarm Company. They were interconnected by the existing burglar-alarm lines. The switchboard, which began operation on May 17, 1877, was used only during the day. At night the lines reverted to their original intruder-detecting purpose. The switchboard service was a no-cost bonus. The proprietor, Edwin Holmes, later established the Telephone Despatch Company, which hired America's—and the world's —first female telephone operator.

TELEPROMPTER: The electronic device enabling heads of state and other speakers and performers to deliver colloquies without seeming to consult notes was invented, appropriately, by an actor, Fred Barton, while he was portraying Gerhart in the original cast of the Thomas Heggen-Joshua Logan 1948-51 Broadway hit, *Mr. Roberts.* Eliminating the need for hand-held scripts, hand-juggled cue cards, or human memory nudgers strategically located in the wings or under the stage, the TelePrompTer makes visible to the speaker—but out of audience sight—a printed script, in large letters, unreeled at the speaker's preferred rate of speed. After launching his acting career with the Cleveland Playhouse and Chicago's Goodman Theater, Barton acted in many radio shows, in stock, and in repertory. He first performed on Broadway in the original cast of the 1944 *A Bell for Adano.* For many years he was half owner and board chairman of the TelePrompTer Company and, shortly before his death in 1982, was supervising Q TV, a Los Angeles adjunct of TelePrompTer, which became the nation's largest owner of cable TV systems. Many seemingly glib TV personalities, most notably local and national newscasters, owe their seeming on-camera proficiency with words to Barton's instant-fluency machine.

TELEVISION: The word "television," like the medium it identifies, is a hybrid: half Greek ("tele," meaning "far") and half Latin ("videre," meaning "to see"). The word may have first appeared in print in a 1907 issue of *Scientific American,* long before it was applied to any existing mechanism.

Who sired TV is arguable. Preliminary contributions were made by Alexander Graham Bell, Samuel Morse, Guglielmo Marconi, and Lee

De Forest. In 1884, Germany's Paul Nipkow developed a mechanical scanning device, the Nipkow disc, that reproduced an image a short distance away. The cathode ray tube, an essential TV ingredient, was known as early as 1908. In London, on January 26, 1926, Britain's John Logie Baird demonstrated his "televisor," a jerrybuilt assemblage of knitting needles, tin cans, and cardboard held together by sealing wax and glue. The following June, Ohio-born Charles Francis Jenkins transmitted the first crude black-and-white pictures of an object in motion.

Electronic transmission of images, instead of systems utilizing mechanical scanners, was proposed by Russia's Boris Rosing in 1905. Inspired by Rosing, Utah-born Philo T. Farnsworth and the Russian-born immigrant Dr. Vladimir K. Zworykin perfected the all-electronic system that made TV's miraculous worldwide growth possible. Zworykin, working initially for Westinghouse (which wasn't impressed) and then for RCA (which was), patented the iconoscopic camera tube in 1923 and the kinescopic picture tube in 1924. The former, later superseded by Dr. Albert Rose's image orthicon tube, became the heart of the first practical TV camera; the latter, despite subsequent refinements and enhancements, is basically the same picture tube in use today. Farnsworth received a 1930 patent for the dissector tube (his name for a cathode ray), which provided sharp, clear electronic scanning—an element that greatly enhanced the Zworykin inventions. RCA went to court to avoid paying royalties to Farnsworth but lost. The first regularly scheduled telecast was a WGY, Schenectady, New York, farm report on May 10, 1928. In 1985, television programs were being watched by an estimated 2.5 billion people via 650 million sets in 162 countries.

TENNIS SHORTS: Until about 1920, female tennis players were expected to play while wearing rigid corsets. Tennis togs gradually became less restrictive; but a major breakthrough, permitting women racket-wielders maximal movement, occurred in 1933 when Helen Hull Jacobs appeared at Forest Hills in shorts. Later the same year, Alice Marble wore even shorter shorts at England's Wimbledon. Soon shorts or brief skirts became the ladies' costume of choice on tennis courts everywhere. Taking the trend even farther, Gussie Moran, in 1949, triggered Wimbledon whispers and witticisms by wearing lace panties. In June 1985, on an unseasonably cool summer day, Anne White startled Wimbledon spectators and, briefly, opponent Pam Shriver by donning a form-hugging white body stocking that was promptly banned by Wimbledon arbiters of "proper" attire. According to eyewitnesses, the costume included a bra but no underpants. Whither tennis court costumes? So far no participant in women's big-time tennis, however smashing, has done her lobbing in bikini, topless bathing suit, G-string, or the buff.

TEST-TUBE BABY: In 1937, Dr. John H. Rock, a Marlborough, Massachusetts-born pioneer in the field of fertilization, was the first scientist to propose in-vitro fertilization (fertilizing a human egg outside the body), four decades before the procedure resulted in the 1978 birth of the first "test-tube" baby, Louise Brown, in England. The in-vitro idea struck him while he was reading Aldous Huxley's 1932 novel, *Brave New World,* which included among pessimistic prospects for a futuristic Utopia the notion that scientific breeding and conditioning could result in a race of human robots. Rock's more optimistic outlook, first expressed in an editorial in the *New England Journal of Medicine,* was that the intervention of science could provide offspring for couples unable to conceive without help. In 1944, he became the first to demonstrate that human sperm could fertilize a human egg in the laboratory. Ironically, Rock, whose major interest as director of the Rock Reproductive Clinic in Brookline, Massachusetts, was fertility, was instrumental in securing the Food and Drug Administration's 1960 approval of the fertility-suppressing Pill (*see* BIRTH CONTROL PILL).

TEST-TUBE SKIN: A serendipitous discovery in 1974 by Dr. Howard Green of the Harvard Medical School has made possible the survival and epidermal reconstruction of many burn victims with scorched skin over as much as 97 percent of their bodies—even when the wounds are of the most serious kind, destroying both the upper and lower layers of skin and damaging the underlying tissue. While studying mouse tumors, Green, a professor of cell biology at the Massachusetts Institute of Technology with a penchant for research, noticed that unusual colonies of cells that resembled the cells in the upper layer of living skin were growing in the culture flasks. When he cultivated them in a special laboratory "broth," he discovered that, because of the presence of fibroblasts, they multiplied ten thousand-fold within a month. Green realized that this had momentous implications for burn victims because if cultured skin was derived initially from the victim himself, it would not be rejected by his body's immune system.

After experimenting with laboratory mice for several years, Green discovered that a certain bacterial enzyme made possible the transfer of the skin cultures in entire sheets. He then teamed with Dr. Nicholas O'Connor, a Boston plastic surgeon, to ascertain how his discovery could be used to repair human skin. Skin scraps the size of a postage stamp, taken from burn victims, were cultivated in laboratory flasks until they grew to playing-card size and were then sewn on muscle tissue.

When Casper, Wyoming, six-year-old Glen Selby and his five-year-old brother Jamie suffered third-degree burns over more than 80 percent of their bodies on July 1, 1983, a Boston surgical team saved their lives by taking fragments of uninjured skin from their armpits and groins for reproduction as "test-tube skin." Potential beneficiaries of Green growths also include those with congenital skin damage, ulcers, or large postoperative wounds. Although the man-made skin is shiny, pink, and smooth; without hair follicles and sweat glands; and is thinner than natural tissue because it lacks dermis (the lower skin layer), surgeons say it appears to be permanent and durable.

THEME PARK: Although Walt Disney's Disneyland in 1955 (*see* DISNEYLAND) and his Walt Disney World sixteen years later gave the theme-park concept—amusement parks with one overall motif or several themed sectors—its greatest international impact, they were not the first in what has become an ultrafertile field. That distinction goes to chock-full-of-chocolate Hershey Park, established in 1907. The Disney parks draw the biggest crowds, native and foreign, with Great Adventure, containing the world's largest drive-through safari park, a distant second.

Most theme parks use history or geography to link their assemblages of rides, shows, and shops in zealously maintained, artfully landscaped locales. The largest U.S. theme-park operator is Six Flags, with six major properties: Great Adventure, Astroworld, Magic Mountain, Six Flags Over Georgia, Six Flags Over Texas, and Six Flags Over Mid-America. Taft Broadcasting owns three: Carowinds, Kings Dominion, and Kings Island. One of the Anheuser-Busch-owned Busch Gardens, The Dark Continent, features three thousand free-roaming African animals that can be viewed from a train or monorail. The other, The Old Country, recreates seventeenth-century Europe. Busch also operates Sesame Place, a "Sesame Street"-inspired playground for children aged three to thirteen. Bugs Bunny is the official meet-and-greeter at Marriott's Great America parks in Illinois and California. Other theme parks with distinctive bents suggested by their names include the live-music-featuring Opryland USA, Lion Country Safari, Santa's Workshop, Storybook Forest, Fairyland Forest, Sea World, Circus World, Dutch Wonderland, and in 1986, Dolly Parton's Dollywood. . . . The list goes on and on. A trend that emerged in 1983 was the wedding of the theme park and the old swimming hole via operations bearing such names as White Water, Raging Waters, Water World, and Six Flags Atlantis.

Theme parks are emerging overseas, but except for Tokyo Disneyland, none displays comparable razzle-dazzle. Copenhagen's Tivoli

Gardens are nonpareil, but in the old-fashioned amusement-park tradition. In Billund, Denmark, a thriving tourist attraction is the miniworld of Legoland, "the Disneyland of Europe," created in 1968 by Godtfred Kirk Christiansen, of the LEGO toy building-bricks clan.

TIME: In 1984 *Time* magazine's weekly circulation was 4,719,343 in the United States plus 1,347,018 from various international editions, making it the world's best-read newsmagazine. When it was launched on March 3, 1923, from a fifty-five-dollar-a-month New York apartment by Briton Hadden and Henry Robinson Luce—Yale classmates who had been editors of the university's *Daily News*—several newsmagazines were already in existence. The best known, the *Literary Digest,* was wordy and weighty; and the young entrepreneurs felt that no one who led a busy life could spare the time required to wade through it.

The first issue of terse, tart *Time,* consisting mainly of reworded stories from New York newspapers, contained twenty-two pages of editorial matter and six pages of advertising. It introduced the vivid vocabular and grammatical quirks, devised by Hadden, that were subsequently referred to as "Timese." Every news story, the product of anonymous "group journalism," became a minidrama with a punch-line ending. "Loaded" adjectives and adverbs abounded. Sentences were inverted. Words were coined (for example, "cinemaddict," "GOPolitics," "socialite," "tycoon"). The result was eminently readable but far from objective, often reflecting the Yalies' prejudices. With Hadden's death from influenza in December 1928, Luce, who had been primarily concerned with the business end, assumed complete control. He promptly took sides in the pages of *Time* in numerous political and ideological disputes. The magazine gradually assembled a distinguished complement of world correspondents. Over the years, magazine spin-offs from *Time* included *Fortune, Life, Sports Illustrated,* and *People.* Diversification added to the Luce empire a prolific Time book-publishing firm and, after Luce's death in February 1967, the pioneer cable TV network, Home Box Office (HBO).

What Pepsi-Cola is to Coca-Cola, *Newsweek* magazine is to *Time*; a relentless rival and a constant goad. *Newsweek* surged ahead during the Vietnam War, and subsequently, there was constant seesawing for primacy. Charles Lindbergh, the first man to fly across the Atlantic solo, was the first choice for what has become an annual tradition: *Time*'s New Year-cover "Man of the Year."

TIMEX: Norwegian-born, U.S.-educated Joakim Lehmkuhl, who had helped publish an anti-Nazi newspaper, fled to England just before the 1940 German invasion of Norway. Because he had directed a small shipbuilding firm, the Norwegian government-in-exile asked him to proceed to America to organize a Norwegian shipping office. Looking forward to a peacetime future, he joined a group of investors who acquired a majority interest in the Waterbury Clock Company and converted it into the nation's largest producer of fuses. When sales dropped because of dwindling defense orders, Lehmkuhl felt that the precision-tooling technique used in making fuse timers could be linked to automation to produce a good but inexpensive watch. He designed the first Timex, much simpler than most costly Swiss watches and with bearings made of a hard alloy developed by wartime research instead of the jewels in Swiss movements.

For the first few years after its 1950 introduction by the United States Time Corporation of Middlebury, Connecticut, Lehmkuhl's watches received no advertising. Then an effective campaign stressed the product's unbreakability. Timex, magazine ads proclaimed, could "take a licking and keep on ticking" despite one hundred thousand rides on Ben Hogan's golf club and repeated swings of Mickey Mantle's bat. In 1954, Timex introduced an even more graphic point-of-purchase proof of the product's durability. A showcase was fitted with levers that submerged a Timex in water and then plopped it on an anvil. Beginning in 1956, Timex "torture tests" on TV made Timex famous in the United States and abroad. Sales soared. In one TV test, demonstrated "live," a Timex was fastened to an outboard engine propeller. It slipped off, not according to plan, but was later recovered, still ticking, to the company's promotional profit.

The Timex Company became the Timex Corporation in 1969 and gradually increased its wares to include seventeen- and twenty-one-jewel watches, an electric watch, digital watches, and in 1983, a personal computer.

TIN PAN ALLEY: New York's marketplace-oriented music-publishing firms that ground out songs like piece goods from about 1890 were later known, collectively and pejoratively, as Tin Pan Alley. The name was first assigned to the street where ultraprolific tune-smith Harry Von Tilzer, born Harry Gumm, could be heard producing loud, tinny sounds from a piano with paper across its strings.

Initially clustered in the Union Square area, the music manufacturers gradually moved uptown to 28th Street, between Broadway and Sixth Avenue. They competed fiercely, using song "pluggers" and outright bribes to persuade entertainers to perform their wares. Most of their product was flashy trash, hack-written rip-offs of what was momentarily in vogue, often with bizarre titles. However, whatever their quality, many succeeded in catching the fancy of America and the world. The 1910 "Let Me Call You Sweetheart" sold more than eight million copies. Ernest R. Ball scored with "When Irish Eyes Are Smiling" and "Mother Machree." Gus Edwards had a string of hits, including "School Days" and "By the Light of the Silvery Moon."

Some of America's—and the world's—most popular songs and songwriters came from musty cubicles where piano pounders and word jugglers, working for meager weekly wages, spent hour after hour trying to find combinations that would sell enough sheet music to justify their staying on the payroll. Irving Berlin, the most successful Tin Pan Alley alumnus, became an international sensation with "Alexander's Ragtime Band" four years after he had begun his career in 1907 by writing the lyrics for an ethnic potboiler, "Marie from Sunny Italy." George Gershwin graduated from staff pianist for the Remick music-publishing company to composer of works for theaters, concert halls, and opera stages. Jerome Kern, who was later to write "Old Man River" and "The Last Time I Saw Paris," served a Tin Pan Alley apprenticeship as a Shapiro-Remick song plugger. Among Tin Pan Alley classics are the Milton Ager-Jack Yellen "Happy Days Are Here Again," Con Conrad's "Ma, He's Making Eyes at Me," Harry Warren's "You Must Have Been a Beautiful Baby," and Walter Donaldson's "My Blue Heaven."

TIRES: Some two-thirds of the rubber annually used in the United States goes into the manufacture of tires. The tire industry, with Irish, Belgian, English, and French pioneers, still relies on the process discovered by Charles Goodyear (*see* RUBBER, VULCANIZED), who wore rubber hats, vests, and ties and envisioned rubber pillows, gloves, toys, and even banknotes, if not "rubber checks." However, automobile tires never entered his thoughts because automobiles had not yet been invented. The rubber now used is largely synthetic. German scientists made isoprene tires for Kaiser Wilhelm's automobile in 1912. Germany produced methyl rubber during World War I; and when World War II started, the Russians were making rubber in commercial quantities from petroleum and alcohol. "Thiokol" artificial rubber was a U.S. commodity in 1930. The following year, the Du Pont Company, using patents held by Julius Arthur Nieuwland and Wallace Hume Carothers, introduced "Neoprene," made of acetylene, salt, and sulfuric acid.

In June 1940, spurred on by the prospect of war and by the consequent loss of its sources of rubber, the B. F. Goodrich Company announced the first practical synthetic rubber tire, made from petroleum, coal tar, potatoes, and grain sugar molasses. It became the wartime standard. Goodyear, named in honor of the man who made widespread utilization of rubber possible but ended up broke, is the world's largest tire manufacturer, with plants in thirty foreign countries. Firestone, ranked second, has tire plants in twenty-five countries plus rubber plantations in the Philippines, Brazil, Ghana, and

Liberia; the latter the world's largest. Uniroyal, ranked third, sells most of its tires to General Motors.

In addition to its pioneering in the development of synthetic rubber, fourth-place Goodrich, named for the physician who founded the company in 1870, Dr. Benjamin Franklin Goodrich, made the first automobile tires (in 1896, for Cleveland bicycle manufacturer Alexander Winton, who had just built a "horseless carriage"); the first pneumatic tires, the first puncture-proof tubeless tires, and the first U.S. radial tires. The company owns tire factories in Columbia, Brazil, and the Philippines.

TOFUTTI: A non-dairy ice-cream-like product made from tofu, which is a soybean curd used in Oriental cuisine, Tofutti contains no cholesterol or lactose and provides an alternative dessert for those who have trouble digesting dairy products. Tofu can be converted into a reasonable replica of cuisine items ranging from lasagna and blintzes to pastrami. Its most successful masquerade, however, has been as Tofutti, introduced in New York City in 1982 and quickly borrowed by seven other countries. Available in numerous ice-cream flavors, it was created by the ex-caterer David Mintz, who heads Tofu Time. Although its final "i" makes it sound Italian, Tofutti is strictly kosher.

A devout Orthodox Jew, Mintz was looking for a milk substitute that he could use for sauces and desserts without violating a Jewish dietary rule that prohibits mixing meat and dairy dishes during the same meal. After reading that soybean curd, an Oriental staple, was capable of absorbing any taste, he experimented in his Brooklyn kitchen and produced such tofu combinations as kosher beef stroganoff (no cream), croissants (no butter), and egg salad (no mayonnaise). However, what his restaurant patrons wanted most was a nondairy ice cream to top off meat dinners. After nine years of testing and tasting, gaining thirty pounds in the process, Mintz perfected Tofutti in two versions—soft like frozen yogurt and hard like ice cream—and eleven flavors, including exotic varieties like wildberry and vanilla-almond bark. In late 1984, Mintz began mulling ways to pare Tofutti's forty calories per ounce (more than frozen yogurt's thirty but less than real ice cream's, which can range from slightly more than forty to as much as seventy-five). In addition to experimenting with low-fat and sugarless versions of Tofutti, Mintz tested a Tofutti yogurt and a new Tofutti flavor; strawberry-raspberry-rhubarb. *Newsweek* promptly recommended another three-word flavor: tutti-frutti Tofutti.

TOILET, PAY: The first specimen of this frequently denounced seat of capitalism was installed in 1910 at the Pennsylvania Railroad's Terre Haute, Indiana, depot—sans tariff—for the convenience of its passengers. However, when travelers rushed from the train to avail

301

themselves of unprecedentedly modern restrooms, they found the accommodations monopolized by localites bemused by the novelty of indoor plumbing. Because of passengers' complaints, coin-operated pay locks invented by Charles N. Van Cleave were put on the restroom doors to dissuade free riders who were nonriders. The stationmaster unlocked the doors for ticket holders. Others paid a nickel. That admission charge was reflected in the name of the new call-of-nature-impeding abomination: the Nik-O-Lok. The practice of charging for discharging spread, the price increased, and pay toilets became a $2 million-a-year business. However, a backside backlash developed. Women's rights groups, for instance, protested sexual discrimination because males weren't required to pay for using urinals. In response, states limited and even banned fee-to-pee facilities.

TOILET, PET: A product of American ingenuity that has not yet achieved international acceptance but is being included in this tome in the expectation that its worldwide time may come because animals everywhere have to go is the flush toilet for cats and dogs invented in 1974 by Franklin Temel of Miami. The result of eight years of experimentation and an outlay of $110,000, it consists of a stall with spray nozzles that draw water from a tank under a stainless steel floor. The unit in Temel's own home cost him ten thousand dollars, but he predicted that his pet pet product could be mass-produced for $250.

TOILET PAPER: Not everyone approves of the use of toilet paper. Hindus, for instance, are said to consider it an abomination, preferring earth and water, applied solely with the left hand. During the days of outdoor privies, Americans had reason to share such distaste because toilet paper consisted of stapled batches of sadistically rough-textured yellow sheets. In 1857, Joseph C. Gayetty of New York City made a considerable contribution to consumers' comfort and convenience when he introduced "Gayetty's Medicated Paper," described as "a perfectly pure article for the toilet and for the prevention of piles." Gayetty probably inspired global gaiety by inscribing his name on each sheet of the unbleached, pearl-colored, pure manila hemp paper. (Many years later, novelty shops sold toilet tissue similarly inscribed with the names and faces of unpopular individuals.) Gayetty charged fifty cents per hundred sheets for his bathroom boon.

In 1879, two Philadelphia brothers who sold scratch paper and paper bags from a pushcart, E. Irvin and Clarence Scott, introduced toilet paper in rolls, converted from large rolls they purchased from tissue-paper manufacturers. The Scott Paper Company subsequently sold toilet paper under some twenty-eight hundred brand names, including Foldum, Twilldu, and Kowntit. In 1905, Irvin's son, Arthur Hoyt Scott, successfully campaigned for concentration on a few top-of-the-line items. The company's "cottony softness"-featuring Cottonelle, patented by Albert L. McConnell, was decorously described in the patent application as "Bonded, Differentially Creped, Fibrous Webs." Ads for Scott's tenderer tissues included lines like "They have a pretty house, Mother, but their bathroom paper hurts." After acquiring the Charmin paper mills, Procter and Gamble developed new technology to produce a supersoft product that, helped by a supereffective "Don't Squeeze the Charmin" advertising campaign, has become the "number-two" number one. Procter and Gamble has also taken the lead in paper towels, a product that Scott introduced in 1907 when a shipment of paper was judged too abrasive for its intended use.

TOOTHBRUSH, ELECTRIC: The Broxodent electric toothbrush, the world's first dental wrist rester of its kind, was introduced in 1961 by New York-based Squibb, which also markets caries causers like candy and bubble gum. "Electric" has been a favorite advertising adjective even when utterly inappropriate. A late nineteenth-century product, Dobbins's Electric Soap, warned buyers that it was not to be confused with two inferior items, Magnetic Soap or Electro-Magic Soap. On the market at about the same time were Philadelphia Electric Soap and Dr. Scott's Electric Hairbrush. Also available in 1880 was a companion product: Dr. Scott's Electric Toothbrush.

TOOTHPASTE TUBE: The first collapsible tube, used commercially by the Devoe and Reynolds Company as a container for oil paints, was patented by the American artist John Rand on September 11, 1841. A collapsible metal tube for the dispensing of toothpaste was devised in 1892 by Dr. Washington Wentworth Sheffield, a New London, Connecticut, dentist, who had seen foreign foods packaged in that manner. Between 1892 and 1902, Dr. Sheffield's Creme Dentifrice became increasingly popular. The Sheffield Tube Corporation then began producing flexible tubes for numerous nondentifrices.

The toothpaste tube was welcomed at home and abroad as a more sanitary alternative to digging toothbrushes into porcelain jars of dental cream, and England's Beecham Tooth Paste quickly substituted tubes for its round Staffordshireware pots. The first collapsible polyethelene tubes were manufactured in 1953 for Sea and Ski, a suntanning lotion, by Delaware's Bradley Container Corporation. In 1984, the dominance of the toothpaste tube was challenged by the importation from Europe of the pump dispenser. First brought to the United States in late 1983 when Minneapolis-based Minnetonka Incorporated went national with its Checkup tooth gel, the pump was quickly adopted by such familiar brands as Colgate, Crest, and Aim, even though it was admittedly more costly than the tube. That fact was apparently outweighed in the opinion of Colgate-Palmolive, Procter and Gamble, and Lever Brothers by the pump's novelty, convenience, neatness and esthetic effect on the bathroom sink. Another possible consideration may have been corporate America's civic-minded wish to diminish domestic disharmony, since the pump presumably could halt endless family arguments about who left the cap off the tube and who persisted in squeezing it from the wrong end. In 1985, toothpaste sales were estimated to total $1 billion a year. Watching the pump's progress with much interest and some concern is a trade group; the Tube Council of America.

TOOTHPICK: The first time a human ejected a foreign object from between two teeth with a twig instead of a fingernail was probably in the Year One; but the first patent for a toothpick-manufacturing machine was granted to Silas Noble and James P. Cooley of Granville, Massachusetts, on February 20, 1872. The machine made it possible for "a block of wood, with little waste, at one operation [to] be cut up into toothpicks ready for use." As a log revolved in the machine, an array of chisels and knives sliced off toothpicks of standard size, length, and weight and sharpened them at both ends. The process continued until the log was a mere shadow of its former self, with a diameter of 2½ inches.

TOPLESS BATHING SUIT: Rudi Gernreich (1923-1984), at the age of 15, emigrated from Austria to America with his mother after the death of his hosiery-manufacturer father. He became involved in the California sportswear industry and introduced such 1960s fashion trends as miniskirts; vinyl clothing; knit tank suits; colored stockings; bold, and sometimes clashing, color combinations; and see-through blouses. In 1964, he was thrust into the international spotlight when he designed swimsuits that took the "through" out of see-through. The idea of topless bathing suits occurred to him during a 1962 *Women's Wear Daily* interview in which he predicted that within five years U.S. women would bare their breasts on the nation's beaches. He erred horologically and geographically, but in recent years, topless-ness has become an increasingly prevalent phenomenon, primarily on overseas beaches.

When the "topless" interview triggered chiding phone calls, Gernreich whomped up a prototype bathing suit for *Look* magazine and then sold three thousand copies at twenty-five dollars each. A San Francisco press agent, Davey Rosenberg, bought one for a waitress to wear onstage and made an instant celebrity of silicone-augmented Carol Doda. Gernreich's swimsuit, with suspender-like straps, evoked condemnation from the Vatican, the Kremlin, and many American clergymen. Women picketed stores carrying the topless togs; and in

St. Tropez, on the French Riviera, the mayor assigned a helicopter patrol to fly over the beach and make sure the ladies were muzzling their mammaries. St. Tropez may have won that battle but, eventually lost the war. In 1985, when breasts were on display all along the Riviera, curious tourists were causing traffic congestion with their peek-a-boo pilgrimages to St. Tropez, where tan seekers were topless all the way down to their toes.

In 1970, after a yearlong sabbatical spent in Europe and at his Hollywood home, Gernreich returned to the fashion fray with the unisex look that included—for both men and women—shaved heads and identical garb, including skirts and two-piece bathing suits that ended male toplessness.

TRACTOR: McDonald's was not the only company to create a historic Burger. That was the name assigned by Chicago's Charter Engine Company, in 1889, to the first gasoline-powered agricultural tractor. Previously, comparable farm functions had been powered first by horses, oxen, and mules and, then, by steam engines. A one-cylinder Charter engine was hitched to the running gear of a Rumely steam-traction engine. The firebox, boiler, and smokestack—which comprised the steam engine's frame—were replaced by a chassis, and a reverse gear was added. The resultant hybrid was the first gasoline-engined vehicle in North America. The prototype, sold to a South Dakota wheat grower, performed so well that Charter built six more that were also put to wheatfield use. The first gasoline-powered tractor advertised for sale was Charter's 1893 Sterling Tractor, but by then, numerous competing firms were in the field. A tractor produced by the Ohio Manufacturing Company was the first with a chassis specially designed to house a gasoline engine.

Emergence, in the 1920s, of the Farm-all tractor with multipurpose attachments heralded a new era in farm mechanization. By 1925, more than fifty thousand tractors were chugging on U.S. farms. By the end of the decade, many had been wed to cost-cutting combines. Pneumatic Firestone tires were added in 1932. Chicago-based International Harvester (now Navistar International), which was begat by the McCormick Harvesting Machine Company, which was begat by Cyrus McCormick's 1831 invention (*see* REAPER), manufactures heavy gasoline- and diesel-powered tractors and less imposing lawn and garden models, among other products, in twenty-six plants in America and sixteen in Europe and Africa. Although it still led overseas, in the 1960s, International Harvester lost its ranking as the world's number-one manufacturer of farm machinery to another Illinois tractor-plus company: Moline-based John Deere (named for its founder, the Vermont blacksmith who, in 1837, invented the first self-cleaning steel plow). Deere owns factories in Mexico, Venezuela, Europe, South Africa, Australia, and Japan.

TRAFFIC CONTROL ROAD MARKING: The white line down the center of highways, to control traffic flow, was devised by Edward Norris Hines, road commissioner of Wayne County, Michigan. The first "center-line safety stripe" was painted on River Road, near Trenton, Michigan, in 1911.

TRAFFIC LIGHT: London had the first red-for-stop, green-for-caution traffic light: a revolving lantern manually operated by a constable for the street-corner convenience of Parliament-bound members of that august body. It was installed in December 1868 but was unpopular with the general public, including a hansom-cab driver who complained that it was "another of them fakements to wex poor cabbies." After its removal in 1872, London shunned traffic lights for more than fifty years.

The first electric traffic light designed to control traffic heading in conflicting directions was a fifteen-foot-high signal installed at a Cleveland, Ohio, crossing on August 5, 1914, by the American Traffic Signal Company. Red and green lights were accompanied by a warning buzzer. The first three-color light, with amber for caution, made its debut in New York City in 1918. The modern automatic four-way traffic lights, flashing signals in red, yellow, and green, were first installed in, appropriately, Motown—the motor town, Detroit, Michigan—in the early 1920s.

TRAFFIC SAFETY: New York City-born William Phelps Eno (1858-1945), responsible for most of the regulations that promote automobile traffic safety, figured out one surefire way to avoid being the cause of collisions. He never learned how to drive. Dubbed "the father of traffic safety," he is credited with stop signs, one-way streets, taxi stands, pedestrian safety islands, traffic rotaries, and the first police manual of traffic regulations. An article he wrote in 1900, "Reform in Our Street Traffic Urgently Needed," brought him an instant reputation for expertise. He continued to write articles on the subject and served as a consultant for other countries. He recommended the circular traffic pattern around Paris's Arc de Triomphe, not one of his happier inspirations. In 1921, he established the Eno Foundation for Transportation, a nonprofit study center, in Saugatuck, Connecticut.

TRAILER: A dictionary definition of "trailer"—"an automobile-drawn highway vehicle designed to serve wherever parked as a dwelling or as a place of business"—contains no hint of the trailers' many ramifications. There's the never-truly-mobile "mobile home" ("a trailer that is used as a permanent dwelling, usually connected to utilities, designed without a permanent foundation") and "motor home" (MH) ("an automotive vehicle built on a truck or bus chassis and equipped as a self-contained traveling home"). Then there's the recreational vehicle (RV), which subdivides into tent trailers, travel trailers, pick-up campers, minihomes, vans, and fifth wheelers. According to trailer historians, the forerunner of the whole varied lot was the luggage rack attached to the rear of Henry Ford's Model T. After the exigencies of World War I, Americans yearned to hit the road. At the start, their auto-borne impedimenta was limited to a blanket and a roll of toilet paper, but it burgeoned into sleeping bags, chamber pots, kerosene lanterns, fishing gear, cameras, and tents until a box on wheels had to be attached to the car to carry it all. Then some anonymous Edison conceived the notion of bedding down in the box. The word "trailer" entered the language in 1926. ("Mobile home" didn't follow until the 1950s.)

In the 1920s, trailers were usually assembled from magazine diagrams by do-it-yourselfers and were usually used only in summer because of the absence of a safe heating system. This drawback ended with the introduction, in the early 1930s, of liquefied petroleum gas (an inexpensive fuel for heating, cooking, and refrigerating). Concurrently, trailer construction shifted from backyards to factories. Development of the self-contained unit ended dependence on electricity, water, and sewer hook-ups. Because of an urgent World War II need for housing near military bases and construction centers, the U.S. government purchased thirty-five thousand trailers that were bunched into what often became slum trailer camps. After the war, however, trailers—and trailer parks—reflected a more opulent lifestyle. By the summer of 1984, the estimated number of RVs and MHs in U.S. use, from twenty-five hundred dollar folding trailers to eighty-seven thousand dollar motor coaches, was seven million. Elkhart, Indiana is home base for more than thirty manufacturers.

TRAMPOLINE: The first trampoline-type stunts were performed by circus acrobats after someone got the idea of tightening up the landing nets that served as life savers for plummeting high-wire and trapeze performers. However, in 1926, George Nissen, working in his Cedar Rapids, Iowa, garage, designed and produced the first trampoline, a "bed" suspended by strings on a frame. The better bounce provided by his modernized version multiplied the number and kinds of tricks that could be performed. Increased popularity was inevitably attended by increased skill. From 1947 through 1964 trampolining was classified by the Amateur Athletic Union (AAU) and the National Collegiate Athletic Association (NCAA) as a gymnastics event. However, trampolining has more in common with diving; and serious divers often devote a quarter or more of their practice time to working out on a trampoline.

In 1967, because gymnasts rarely won trampoline events and divers frequently did, the AAU and the NCAA made trampolining a separate sport. Its popularity spread to other countries, and trampolining became an international competitive event. The first world trampoline championships, in London in 1964, were won by Dan Millman of California and Judy Wills of Illinois. Since 1978, World Age-Group competitions, for contestants aged even ten and under, are held every other year in a different part of the world. As in every other sport, trampolining has evolved a vocabulary all its own. A "fliffis," for instance, is a double front flip with a half twist, and other trampoline tricks are tagged with such names as the Barani, the Cody, pike, somie, tuck, layout, crash dive, ball-out, and porpoise.

TRANSATLANTIC LINER: The first ocean liner operating on a fixed schedule was the Black Ball Line's 424-ton sailing packet, the *James Monroe*. The ship's maiden voyage from New York to Liverpool, beginning January 5, 1818, required twenty-eight days. The eight passengers entered their satinwood-paneled staterooms through doors flanked by marble pillars and lounged in a large, mahogany-furnished salon. Cows, pigs, sheep, and hens were also housed aboard to provide fresh meat, milk, and eggs.

TRANSISTOR: The often shocking William Bradford Shockley (1910-), whose views on black genetic inferiority have made civil libertarians charge that he hardly merits a Noble Prize, shared the 1956 Nobel Prize in physics for his contributions to the development of the transistor. While working at Bell Telephone Laboratories after World War II research stints for the military, the London-born, American-educated Shockley conducted research in collaboration with fellow physicists John Bardeen and Walter H. Brattain, which in 1947, resulted in the invention of the transfer resistor, later dubbed the transistor. It consisted of a slim metal cylinder about an inch long, containing two hair-thin wires whose points, 1/1,000th of an inch apart, pressed on a pinhead of germanium. In 1951, Shockley improved on the original point-contact type of transistor by inventing the junction transistor. The transistor has replaced the vacuum tube in the whole spectrum of electronic equipment, including essential elements in telephones, radios, TV sets, radar, aircraft, and computers. (*See also* MICROCHIP.)

T-SHIRT: The T-shirt may originally have been the tea-shirt, worn in the seventeenth century by Annapolis, Maryland, longshoremen because a collarless, short-sleeved shirt with a round neckline prevented under-the-collar itch from loose tea leaves. A more likely explanation of the T's name, however, is that it forms a *T* when laid flat. About the time of World War I, T-type undershirts began to replace baggy union suits. Jockey International claims it made the first Ts in the early 1930s for a California football coach who wanted something soft and absorbent under shoulder pads and mass-produced them as the Sanitaire shirt in 1943. Union Underwear, which markets B.V.D. and Fruit of the Loom, counterclaims that it originated the T for the U.S. Navy during World War II as the regulation skivy shirt. Broadway producer Alexander H. Cohen opines that Charles C. (Cash and Carry) Pyle invented the T-shirt in the 1920s as a merchandising item when he was managing Football Hall of Famer Harold E. (Red) Grange.

The T became popular with men when Marlon Brando bulged a torn one over his chest in the stage and screen versions of Tennessee Williams's *A Streetcar Named Desire*, and with style-minded women when Jean Seberg dittoed in France's 1959 film classic, *Breathless*.

What had been a white, unadorned undergarment worn only by men and children became a visible, rainbow-hued and flamboyantly decorated wardrobe item in the 1960s, flaunted by members of both sexes. Once strictly utilitarian, it became high fashion, embellished with political, sexual, and anti-Establishment slogans, pop-art-style commercial products and celebrity portraits, and assorted designs both bizarre and beautiful. T-shirts became available at outlets ranging in steeply ascending price from Army-Navy surplus stores to tony boutiques supplied by international arbiters of chic. Some Ts were considered galleryworthy. The Los Angeles Institute of Contemporary Art conducted a "T-Shirt Extravaganza" in Century City. Turned On Tees changed color to reflect wearers' moods. And in 1975, New York's Smell This Shirt Company and Miami's Smell It Like It Is offered Ts that produced aromas-to-order when scratched. Even mock marijuana.

TUPPERWARE: Both the durable plastic containers known as Tupperware and the novel notion of selling them only through "parties" held in homes were created in 1954 by an American chemist, Du Pont alumnus Earl W. Tupper. Housewives who invited their neighbors, friends, and relatives to examine vari-sized Tupperware wares were rewarded by the company's demonstrators with free samples. Rigid rules controlled party proceedings. The number of allowable "icebreaker" games was specified and, to prevent accidents, hostesses were instructed to refrain from cooking while a party was in progress.

Observance of such strictures made Tupperware second only to

Avon in house-to-house sales, with an 80 percent share of the world market for plastic food containers, more than 300,000 saleswomen, and an impcsing Tupperware International headquarters in Orlando, Florida, surrounded by four hundred miniature orange trees, one apiece for each of the company's initial distributors. However, when women's changing life-styles and the availability of cheaper plastic containers at supermarkets and discount stores began adversely affecting sales of Tupperware Flavor Savers and Velveeta Keepers, the Dart and Kraft subsidiary decided to alter its traditional tactics. In 1985, $15 million was allocated to advertising that sought customers, instead of dealers, with young working women, rather than middle-aged housewives (one of whom had sighed, "I'm all Tuppered out") as the principal targets. While one competitor urged prospective customers, "Be a party pooper," Tupperware demonstrators were advised to switch from the leisurely living room get-togethers to twenty-minute sessions at health clubs or during office lunch hours. In the summer of 1985, also in keeping with new life-styles, Tupperware introduced an Ultra 21 line of plastic dishes and casseroles that can be transferred directly from the refrigerator to a microwave or conventional oven.

TUXEDO: The first "dinner jacket," although it was not identified in that way until a dozen years later, was worn by Griswold Lorillard, heir to a tobacco fortune, on October 10, 1886, at the Autumn Ball held in New York's exclusive Tuxedo Park Country Club, which is why it became known in the United States as the "tuxedo" or, more familiarly, "tux." It was reputedly designed by Pierre Lorillard, "Grizzy's" father, who abhorred white tie and tails.

A short black coat with satin lapels, it was patterned after a contemporary item of apparel, the English smoking jacket. Although it came to be considered formal attire, at the time of its introduction the dinner jacket was considered shockingly informal, and in England, where it was first worn in 1888, the dinner jacket was initially dubbed the "dress lounge." In fact, before World War I, the tux was considered proper and acceptable as evening wear only when women were not present. In 1985, Princess Diana attended a party wearing a specially remodeled version borrowed from Prince Charles's wardrobe.

"Tuxedo" was originally an Algonquin Indian word meaning "he has a round foot" and referred to wolves. The nonhuman kind.

TV DINNER: Frozen dinners and the trademarked phrase "TV dinner" were invented in 1952 by Omaha's Clarke and Gilbert Swanson. The first example, in a compartmentalized aluminum tray covered by aluminum foil, consisted of sliced turkey on cornbread, buttered peas, sweet potatoes, and gravy and was priced at $1.09.

Numerous food packagers quickly assembled competitive compartments. TV dinners became popular as a quick fix not only for TV addicts but for harassed housewives, weary or lazy loners, and kids temporarily on their own.

For two decades they stayed simple, barely palatable, and cheap; but in the 1970s, when fewer women, because of full-time jobs or other outside-the-kitchen interests, were bothering to make elaborate dinners from scratch, the TV dinner began offering lower-calorie and fancier fare at escalated cost. In 1981, Armour, the meat-packing company that began in the Chicago stockyards during the Civil War, reformulated the Continental Cuisine line it first tested in 1958. With the advent of Armour Dinner Classics, the TV dinner went gourmet. On rectangular plastic dishes that could be toted from the microwave oven to the dining-room table came seafood Newburg and teriyaki steak, served with exotic vegetable combinations. Other companies joined the rush to *hauter* cuisine and low-calorie entrées at pricier prices up to $7.50. In 1983, according to the National Frozen Foods Association, Americans spent more than $500 million on TV dinners.

TV DRAMA: Four performers—or, more accurately, two actors plus supplementary hands—were used in "The Queen's Messenger," a forty-minute pioneer drama telecast by the General Electric Company's WGY in Schenectady, New York, on September 11, 1928. While Izotta Jewell and Maurice Randall portrayed the two title characters, the hands of Joyce E. Rector and William J. Toniski appeared in close-ups of props like cigarettes, glasses, and keys. Two cameras were trained on the actors and a third on the manual manipulations. Reception was reported on the West Coast. The first regularly scheduled network drama series was NBC's live, hour-long "Kraft Television Theater," which bowed in on May 7, 1947, with "Double Door," starring John Baragrey. Before it switched to musical programs in 1958, the Kraft Foods Company sponsored 650 plays—originals, adaptations, and classics. Between October 1953 and January 1955 a second "Kraft Television Theater" was concurrently presented on ABC.

Also contributing to what was dubbed "the Golden Age of TV drama" were NBC's live, hour-long "Philco TV Playhouse," 1948-55, which during its last four seasons alternated with "Goodyear TV Playhouse," and CBS's live, hour-long "Studio One," a carryover from a year-old radio series, which made its TV debut in November 1948, one month after "Philco." From the initial opus, "The Storm," starring Margaret Sullavan, producer Worthington Miner stressed TV techniques. Early on, "Studio One" developed its own frequently cast stars: Charlton Heston, Mary Sinclair, and Maria Riva. In January 1958, the program moved to the West Coast and was retitled "Studio One in Hollywood."

During its decade on the air, East Coast and West Coast, "Studio One" aired almost five hundred plays. A multi-Emmy-winner was Reginald Rose's 1954 "Twelve Angry Men," which became a prestigious 1957 movie. "Golden Age" playwrights who were published in book form included Rose, Paddy Chayefsky, Rod Serling, Horton Foote, Tad Mosel, and Gore Vidal. The apotheosis of "Golden Age" TV drama was achieved via CBS's mostly live ninety-minute "Playhouse 90" from 1956 to 1961. Among its highlights were Serling's "Requiem for a Heavyweight" and William Gibson's "The Miracle Worker."

TV NEWSCAST: The first televised news event was the presidential nomination of Alfred E. Smith at the Democratic party convention in Albany, New York, on August 22, 1928. It was transmitted by WGY, Schenectady. The first regularly scheduled newscasts were fifteen-minute programs telecast on the same day, July 1, 1941, by the New York flagship stations of NBC and CBS. NBC's Sunoco-sponsored program, via WNBT, was anchored by Lowell Thomas. The name of the newscaster on CBS's WCBS was not recorded.

TV PERFORMER: The first time television was used as an entertainment medium anywhere in the world was April 7, 1927, on the occasion of the first U.S. demonstration of TV. An invited audience at New York's Bell Telephone Laboratories witnessed an experimental transmission from the American Telephone and Telegraph Company's station in Whippany, New Jersey, 22 miles away. An Irish-American comedian, A. Dolan, was hired to perform briefly in Irish costume and side-whiskers as singer and monologist. His head was seen approximately life-size on a 2-by-2½-foot screen and the picture was sharp enough to make clearly visible the clay pipe in his mouth. The first on-screen "talent" to be signed to a TV contract, Natalie Towers, was hired by CBS's experimental station W2XAB shortly after her graduation from Wellesley. Used as a pretty focus for TV cameras, she was introduced to the station's minuscule audience by New York's mayor, Jimmy Walker, on July 21, 1931.

TV RECEIVER: The first TV receivers, assembled or in kits, were offered for sale to the public in an ad in the July 1928 issue of *Television*, published in New York. The manufacturer was the Daven Corporation of Newark, New Jersey; the price, for an assembled model: seventy-five dollars. The sets were adjustable to 24-, 36-, or 48-line transmissions, but there was a catch. Although scheduled programs were being telecast on an experimental basis in Schenectady, transmissions of any kind were nonexistent in New York City. By August 1931, the number of sets in New York was approximately nine thousand and in the rest of the nation, thirty thousand. About a half dozen makes were available at prices ranging from $80 to $160. Do-it-yourself kits cost $36. In 1932, W. C. Rawls and Company of Norfolk, Virginia, offered a luxury set in fumed oak for $295. It featured an unprecedented "large screen," measuring 11.3 inches longitudinally and latitudinally.

TWINKIE: Supercake, the planet's most popular pastry, is the Hostess Twinkie, produced at the rate of a billion a year by International Telephone and Telegraph Corporation-owned bakeries in the United States, Mexico, Guatemala, and Japan. It was created in November 1930 by James A. Dewar (1897-1985), a manager for Chicago's Continental Bakeries, shortly after his promotion from one of Continental's horse-drawn pound-cake wagons. In the mood for a snack, he sliced a slender chunk of shortcake and spread marshmallow frosting between two halves. It tasted so good that he recommended it as a way to boost the shortcake's sales, usually slow except during the annual six-week strawberry season. While visiting Continental's St. Louis bakery, Dewar saw a billboard advertising Twinkle Toe Shoes, which immediately suggested "Twinkies" as a tag with kid appeal. Dewar, who claimed he ate three Twinkies daily, never received any direct compensation for his idea and never complained about it.

Unlike Coca-Cola, the Big Mac, and other worldwide American junk-food palate pleasers, the Twinkie contains no secret ingredient. It's made of flour, sugar, shortening, baking soda, liquid vanilla, milk, salt, and eggs with a sorbic acid preservative in the creamy filling. Its distinctive shape, which has inspired X-rated quips, was dictated by the kind of pans Continental had on hand in 1930. (One music critic likened the shape of pelvis-gyrating pop singer Tom Jones's crotch to that of a Twinkie. Others are reminded of caterpillars or foam-rubber cushions.) The confection's weight, unlike that of constant consumers, remains the same—an ounce and a half— but it is no longer sold two-for-a-nickel.

A frequent target for gags by entertainers like Johnny Carson and Carol Burnett, the Twinkie was christened "WASP soul food" in television's "All in the Family." The Twinkie may be the only unpoisoned confection ever charged with murder. When the former San Francisco supervisor Dan White (who, after his release, committed suicide) was tried for the killing of Mayor George Moscone and the gay supervisor Harvey Milk, the Marin County psychiatrist Martin Blinder testified that White's behavior had been affected, in part, by his consumption of Twinkies and other sugar-rich foods. His surprisingly light sentence was attributed to "the Twinkie defense."

TYPEWRITER: At least fifty-one inventors, including Thomas Alva Edison, tried to produce a typing machine before Christopher Latham Sholes, Carlos Glidden, and several associates, after beginning with a device designed to number the pages of a book, produced the first practical model in Milwaukee in 1867. It was patented in 1868 and, after several refinements, put on the market in 1873 by the Ilion, New York-based firm of E. Remington and Sons, manufacturers of firearms and sewing machines. The Remington "Type Writer" resembled a sewing machine. Its carriage return was operated by a foot treadle, and its black case was adorned with stenciled flowers. Improvements over the years included an attached carriage return, rearrangement of the type bars so that the typist could see what was being typed, the addition of lowercase letters, and a ribbon that reversed itself automatically. Sholes's keyboard arrangement (*see* TYPEWRITER KEYBOARD) is still the one generally used.

Not until 1909 did the typewriter begin to gain wide acceptance. Few people wanted to pay $125 to replace the penny pen point. To encourage the transition, women demonstrators, dubbed "typewriters," visited business offices, where prospective purchasers indicated that they would be interested in the typewriters if they were accompanied by the "typewriters." The machines are credited for the subsequent influx of women into the business world. The first American novelist to type a manuscript was Mark Twain. In 1920, James Smathers invented the first electric typewriter suitable for office use. Much more sophisticated machines were available by the 1940s, and numerous technological improvements were added later. "Memory" typewriters allow recall and revision of previously typed material.

During World War II, Martin Tytell, a New York typewriter expert, produced a machine for the Office of Strategic Services that could print in sixteen languages. His company currently fills orders by United Nations delegates, university professors, and others for typewriters that type in 145 languages, from Persian script to Japanese.

TYPEWRITER KEYBOARD: The first Sholes-Glidden typewriter (*see* TYPEWRITER) had a keyboard in which the letters were arranged alphabetically, but it proved impractical because the letters tapped most frequently kept jamming. To obviate the problem, James Densmore, one of Sholes's associates, asked his son-in-law, a Pennsylvania school superintendent, what letters and combinations of letters appeared most often in the English language. As a result, the virtually random QWERTY keyboard was created in 1872. QWERTY are the six keyboard letters at the left end of the top row of letters. Sholes and Densmore merely scattered the most-used vowels and consonants (E, T, O, A, N, I) and put frequent combinations like "ed" where they would require use of the same finger, thereby slowing typing speed and lessening the risk of locked keys. By the 1930s, mechanical improvements had made QWERTY's quirks unnecessary, but by then, it was too late. Although efficiency experts have been keening for decades that QWERTY is slow, wrist wearying, and error prone, a vastly better system is only slowly overcoming typists' inertia.

In 1932, Dr. August Dvorak, a University of Washington psychologist who pioneered in "ergonomics," the study of the interaction between man and machine, devised a system that put the ten most-used letters on the third row, the vowels at the left and the consonants (D, H, T, N, S) at the right. Dvorak's "home row" can produce three thousand common English words without moving the fingers up or down; QWERTY's provides less than a hundred. The Dvorak system also speeds up typing by giving right and left hands almost equal work; QWERTY makes the left hand, slower for most typists, do 60 percent. After Dvorak published *Typewriter Behavior* in 1936, the U.S. Navy ordered two thousand Dvorak typewriters for World War II use, but Smith-Corona later phased out a Dvorak model because of public disinterest. That disinterest is being overcome. The invention, just after Dvorak's death in 1975, of electronic keyboards controlled by a programmed microchip, permitting either QWERTY or Dvorak or both, has given impetus to the worldwide proselytizing efforts of the Brandon, Vermont-based International Dvorak Federation.

U

UNCLE TOM'S CABIN: This anti-slavery novel, subtitled *Life among the Lowly*, caused Abraham Lincoln to say when he met its author, Harriet Beecher Stowe (1811-1896), during the Civil War, "So, this is the little lady who made this big war." It has been printed in more versions than any book except the Bible. During its author's lifetime, three million copies were sold and the book circulated in 37 languages.

Mrs. Stowe, the daughter, sister, and wife of ministers, credited God with its authorship, saying that the book was inspired by a vision of Uncle Tom's death that came to her while she was occupying Pew 23 of the broad aisle in the First Parish Church of Brunswick, Maine. She went home and began writing, finishing the task on brown grocery wrapping paper. The sentimental saga of noble blacks—Uncle Tom, his wife Aunt Chloe, and Little Topsy, who "just growed"—and of good Southern whites like the kindly Shelby family, forced to sell their slaves because of financial difficulties, and bad Northerners like the transplanted planter Simon Legree, loosed a universal torrent of tears. (Mrs. Stowe deliberately made her arch-villain a Northerner, because she hoped the book would persuade the gently treated Southerners to free their slaves.)

Who could remain dry-eyed while reading about Eliza's dash across the frozen Ohio River with her infant child; the death of the angelic Little Eva, or the fatal flogging of Uncle Tom? However, several of these characters later evoked sneers, rather than tears, via lampoons and caricatures. Among blacks, the name of the pious, long-suffering Uncle Tom has become a pejorative synonym for servility.

Mrs. Stowe earned relatively little from the most successful of her sixteen novels, after opting for a ten percent royalty instead of the fifty percent that would have been her share if she had provided half the publication cost. From the multitudinous stage versions that cashed in on her tome she earned nothing at all.

Shortly after the book's publication, some 500 troupes were barnstorming across the country. The most elaborate was mounted by entrepreneur Al Martin, who billed his production as "Too Big for Imitators, Too Strong for Rivalry." On the assumption that bigger was better, Martin sometimes had pairs of Topsies, Simon Legrees and Uncle Toms on stage simultaneously. "'Tom' shows" continued to tour under canvas long after the Civil War. In 1853, five competing versions were in New York, one of them a burlesque by Christy's Minstrels. Six productions were presented simultaneously in London.

UNICORN: The Ringling Brothers and Barnum and Bailey Circus introduced a man-made mythological animal in Houston, Texas, in July 1984. On the circus's subsequent tour, a booming voice proclaimed "an event unparalleled in history—the Living Unicorn!" And there it was, perched on a glittering gold float: a snowy-white curly-furred critter with a single horn jutting from the middle of its forehead, tended by a blond fairy godmother. Skeptical newspapermen said it looked more like a billy goat. So did the less gullible "children of all ages" in the audience. It looked like a goat, it behaved like a goat (and presumably, it smelled like a goat); but undeniably, it had only one centrally located horn. Animal-rights activists, perhaps cheered on by Big Top publicists, charged that someone had cruelly transplanted a bull's horn. U.S. Department of Agriculture inspectors rushed backstage to check out four—count 'em—four alleged unicorns and reported that they were billy goats all right but that the horns in the center of their skulls were their own twin horn buds repositioned during infancy. The inspectors gave the circus a clean bill of goat health. Two doctors at the University of Pennsylvania's animal hospital declared the circus attraction a true unicorn—"an animal with one horn." The unicorn made headlines everywhere. The austere *New York Times* ignored it, but ran a full-page circus ad that urged "DON'T LET THE GRINCHES STEAL THE FANTASY!" The circus president Kenneth Feld convened a press conference to denounce "malicious harassment" from the American Society for the Prevention of Cruelty to Animals. Clowns and acrobats, parodying "Peter Pan's" plea for other fantastical creatures, kept yelling, "I believe in the unicorn!"

Unless Ringling Brothers has also managed to corner the world market, unicorns could become an American export item. That's because they're manufactured by an unconventional California couple, Otter and Morning Glory G'Zell. In 1980, after reading about a cow that had been metamorphosed into a unicorn almost fifty years earlier, the G-Zells founded The Living Unicorn Company. They claim that they rediscovered a "lost art" and slapped a patent on it.

U.S. OPEN: The prestigious international golf tournament that draws some five thousand contestants from as far away as Japan and Australia to try their luck with eighteen holes a day for four days, each year at a different site that has been "toughened" by the U.S. Golf Association, was first played at the Newport, Rhode Island, Golf Club in 1895 as almost a spur-of-the-moment postscript to the first U.S. Amateur Championship. Both amateurs and professionals were invited to participate in four rounds of nine holes each, to be played on a single October day. Less than two hundred spectators turned out to watch ten Britons and a Canadian compete for a small gold medal and picayune cash prizes. Horace Rawlins, the host club's new assistant pro from England, won the $150 top prize with a thirty-six-hole 173 (45-46-41-41).

The first American to win the American tourney, in 1911, was John J. McDermott, one of only five golfers ever to win the Open twice in a row. The others are Willie Anderson, Bobby Jones, Ralph Guldahl, and Ben Hogan. In 1960, seven strokes down entering the final round, Arnold Palmer carded a sixty-five to win. Palmer played in thirty-one consecutive Opens, a record he shares with Gene Sarazen, but failed to qualify in 1983 and 1984. Sam Snead, the victor in a record eighty-four tournaments, never won a U.S. Open. In 1985, the world's largest open golf competition kept nearly 100 of 156 places available to all comers, including amateurs with a handicap of two or less. To complaints that courses were being made excessively difficult for U.S. Open contestants, Sandy Tatum, a U.S.G.A. president, once replied, "Our intention is not to embarrass the greatest players in the world, merely to identify them."

V

VACUUM CLEANER: In 1901, at a time when the shooing of dust was accomplished with brooms, carpet sweepers, or compressed air devices that blew it away, an Englishman named Hubert Cecil Booth reportedly demonstrated the effectiveness of a king-size vacuum cleaner by extracting an awesome amount of dust from the plush upholstery of his seat in a posh London restaurant. However, he apparently jettisoned the idea after building a single model that utilized a heavy motor and fan. The very same year two Americans introduced variations on the same theme. Corinne Dufour's was an electrically powered cleaner that sucked dust into a wet sponge. David E. Kenney's huge suction device could be installed in a cellar and connected by pipelines to outlets in each room. The power plant could also be wheeled from house to house by a corps of cleaners.

In 1907, James Murray Spangler, working as a janitor in a Canton, Ohio, department store, decided that the carpet cleaner provided by his employer caused his hacking cough. He proceeded to improvise something more effective against dust by placing an old motor from an electric fan on top of a soap box stapled to a broom handle. A pillowcase behind the fan outlet served as a dust bag. The result, though primitive, was the first portable, electrically powered vacuum cleaner. Spangler refined his device, patented it in 1908, and formed the Electric Suction Sweeper Company; but sales were few. One buyer was a cousin. Her husband, William H. Hoover, a saddle maker, was intrigued. He became president of a new Hoover Company, with Spangler as superintendent. The original Hoover Model O resembled a bagpipe attached to a cake box, but it worked. Putting the product into hardware stores produced few sales, except when someone knowledgeable could show housewives how to use it. The offer of a free ten-day home trial often clinched a sale. The company began running national ads offering free home demonstrations by a freshly recruited corps of salesmen. This "demonstration principle," still used by the company, and aggressive sales methods initiated in the 1920s put Hoovers into dust-routing action almost everywhere.

VACUUM CLEANER, CORDLESS: The concept of the easily portable cordless vacuum cleaner, manufactured in many versions around the globe, was created by America's premier toolmaking company, Black and Decker, which first put the lightweight chore lightener on the market in the mid-1970s. The pioneer model, introduced as part of an entire Mod/4 line of household items utilizing rechargeable power handles—including drill, flashlight, hedge trimmer, and grass clipper—flopped after early interest because buyers forgot to unplug the front of the unit and recharge the power handle. The company's 1.4-pound Dustbuster, introduced in 1979, used the same technology Black and Decker had incorporated in the lunar surface drill used by the Apollo 15 astronauts in 1969 to dig moon samples. It was an instant hit—and promptly copied by so many manufacturers that Black and Decker filed thirteen suits worldwide for patent infringements. Just over a foot long, the Dustbuster can suck dirt for eight to ten minutes between rechargings and has a life span of about 150 hours.

VALIUM: The world's most widely used tranquilizer, Valium, the trademark for diazepam, came along in 1963 to displace such previous favorites as Miltown, Equanil, and Librium. It was developed for Roche Laboratory by the Polish-American scientist Leo Sternback, who three years earlier had created Librium, the brand name for chlordiazepoxide, which had proved effective in treating anxiety, tension, convulsions, and neuromuscular and cardiovascular disorders.

VARIETY: The international show-biz bible, religiously purchased by nearly fifty thousand purveyors of entertainment in ninety-eight world markets, maintains headquarters in New York, Hollywood, Chicago, Washington, Toronto, London, Paris, Rome, Madrid, Sydney and Copenhagen has considerable corps of correspondents, including seventy in other foreign cities. Published weekly out of New York, it contains reports on movies, plays, pop music, radio, and TV, including assessments of earning potential, week-to-week grosses, and pertinent news notes.

Basically a trade journal, *Variety* occasionally, though less often than it once did, injects "the spice of life" into what could be dull data via a breezy, irreverent abbreviation-filled lingo that has been dubbed Varietyese. A frequently cited headline: STICKS NIX HICK PIX (translation: Rural areas reject farm films). Among *Variety* coinages are such standard dictionary entries as baloney, brush-off, cliffhanger, corny, disc jockey, emcee, freeloader, hick, oldie, payoff, pushover, soap opera, tie-in, and whodunit, as well as scram, screwy, and nuts.

Variety was founded in December 1905 by Sime Silverman (1873-1933), after being fired as a vaudeville critic for the *New York Morning Telegraph* because an act he had panned retaliated by canceling its Christmas ad. With fifteen hundred dollars borrowed from his father-in-law, Sime set out to establish a publication that would champion performers and stagehands and would not pander to advertisers. He chose the name *Variety*, the English term for vaudeville, because it seemed to encompass all kinds of entertainment. Although *Variety* did not show a profit until 1929 (a noteworthy headline that year: WALL ST. LAYS AN EGG), it quickly achieved cachet. One New York mayor said of Times Square, "Hell, it ought to be called Sime's Square." Among obscure newcomers Silverman applauded were Buster Keaton, whose vaudeville act he reviewed in *Variety's* first issue; Charlie Chaplin; Al Jolson; and Jimmy Durante. After Sime's death in September 1933, three weeks after the start of the film-accenting Hollywood-based daily *Variety*, the editorship was assumed by Abel Green. Syd Silverman, Sime's grandson, *Variety's* third editor, made it less slangy, more profitable, and far more international minded before selling it to a British conglomerate in 1987.

VASELINE: In 1850, when the twenty-two-year-old chemist Robert Augustus Chesebrough began experimenting in his Brooklyn laboratory with rod wax, the paraffinlike residue on oil pump rods (which oil field workers told him healed cuts and burns), he was interested only in its medicinal possibilities. But after trial and error finally enabled him, in 1859, to perfect a process for extracting what he called "petroleum jelly" from crude oil, it proved much more versatile. Fishermen used it to lure trout, movie actors used it to simulate tears, housewives used it to remove white rings from mahogany furniture, lovers used it for assorted lubricant purposes. In 1916, Russian peasants discovered that as an additive for their oil-burning lamps, it reduced smoke and fumes, and because it never turned rancid, African natives swapped jars as a medium of exchange. When one of his employees was shocked to learn that in India it was being spread on bread as a butter substitute, Chesebrough revealed that he ate a spoonful every day to keep fit. He was so convinced of his product's panacean powers that when seriously ill with pleurisy in his late fifties, he had himself Vaselined from head to toe like an English Channel swimmer. He lived to the age of ninety-six.

Chesebrough's first business, kerosene, took him to Titusville, Pennsylvania—site of the world's first oil well—where he first heard about the curative powers of rod wax. To test the testimonials, he repeatedly cut, scratched, and burned himself before applying the magical balm. He began marketing petroleum jelly in 1870 and registered "Vaseline" as a trademark eight years later, deriving the name from a German word, *wasser*, for "water," and a Greek word, *elaion*, for "olive oil." Instead of spending large sums on advertising, he went on the road in a horse and buggy, distributing thousands of sample jars. Soon he had twelve salesmen finding buyers galore at a penny an ounce. In 1881, a year after he created the Chesebrough Manufacturing Company in New York, Standard Oil, which supplied his petroleum, bought the firm; but he regained it in 1911 after the dissolution of the Standard Oil Trust. In 1955, a merger created Chesebrough-Pond's, which also produces products as varied as cold cream and spaghetti sauce.

VENDING MACHINE: Coin-operated dispensers have been around a long time. As early as the first century, worshipers in some Greek temples could use a coin to activate a mechanism that provided a few drops of purifying water. The mass-marketing potential of vending machines was demonstrated most dramatically in 1888 when Thomas Adams, founder of the Adams chewing gum company, installed tutti-frutti gum machines on New York subway station platforms. Vendors around the world took note and followed suit.

VIBRATOR: The vibrating massager is manufactured by many highly respectable firms and sold in many highly respectable outlets, ostensibly for nonsexual uses; but it was sexual uses that twenty-year-old Gershon Legman had in mind in 1938, when he invited an inventor to help him adapt the principles of the battery-operated scalp vibrator. "I wanted to prove," Legman said years later, "there was no such thing as frigidity." To make the same point, he also wrote a book for the guidance of timid couples, *Oragenitality*. It was the first of several sex-linked volumes he signed "G. Legman." Among them were an encyclopedic two-volume tome, *The Rationale of the Dirty Joke;* a collection of X-rated limericks; and scholarly studies of various aspects of human sensuality.

He made his first public impact in 1949 with the privately printed *Love and Death*, subtitled *A Study in Censorship*, consisting of four essays in which he posed such questions as why a nude breast was considered more reprehensible on a movie screen than a gory murder. A deft dig at hypocrisy was a reference to one of "Alfred Hitchc——k's" films. Views expressed in the book later surfaced in *Neurotica*, a magazine he edited in the early 1950s. The book and the magazine helped make him an international cult figure. In 1953, when the U.S. Post Office halted delivery of his mail, he emigrated to France.

Born in Scranton, Pennsylvania, and groomed as a prospective rabbi, he was detoured at the age of eleven when he discovered erotica. His father was outraged, his mother tolerant. With her blessing, he left home at sixteen and went to New York, where in his late teens he began delivering lectures for the Birth Control League. The fact that questions from women in the audience often reflected disappointment in sex spurred him to develop a satisfaction-guaranteed surrogate penis. Manufacturers, retailers, and lonely or frustrated females profited from the project; Legman himself never earned a penny. His principal accomplishments, he once opined, were the vibrator and another Legman invention: the phrase "Make love, not war."

VICHYSOISSE: The delectable cold soup made of pureed leeks or onions and potatoes, cream, and chicken stock is considered one of the delicacies of French cuisine; but it was invented by Louis Diat, a chef at New York's Ritz Carlton Hotel, in 1910 in response to requests for a cool, refreshing summer dish. It is served in France only at hotels and restaurants catering to U.S. tourists. When they first began getting requests for vichyssoise in the late 1940s, French restaurateurs ladled up a potage that stressed carrots, the vegetable usually associated with dishes of Vichy origin. It must be conceded, however, that Diat was French and that he based his creation on a recipe used by his mother, who frequently fed him a hot potato soup at night and whatever was left over, cold, for lunch the next day.

VICK'S VAPORUB: In the 1890s cold sufferers relied on poultices or plasters and sometimes vapor lamps, but the former left blisters and the latter were costly and complicated. Lunsford Richardson, a Selma, North Carolina, druggist, decided that what was needed was an elixir that combined the benefits of the other methods and omitted their drawbacks. Combining cooling menthol, which effectively opened clogged nasal passages, with other medications in a petroleum base, he produced an effective chest rub that he christened Richardson's Croup and Pneumonia Cure Salve. He later devised eighteen other Richardson's Home Remedies.

Although his products were known only locally, Richardson vowed to sell them both nationally and internationally. To accomplish that ambitious goal, he summoned from New York his college-graduate son, H.S., whose business background was limited to jobs as a streetcar conductor, department store clerk, and blanket salesman. H.S. organized a sales force and began canvassing all of North Carolina's drugstores and general stores. Discovering that only his father's initial nostrum had sales appeal, he discarded the rest.

Pressed to come up with a shorter, snappier name, Papa Richardson suggested Vick's Salve because it was in the drugstore owned by his brother-in-law, Dr. Joshua Vick, that he had first concocted his formula. Dozens of nostrums being peddled at the time, useful or not, were labeled "salve." H.S. coined "VapoRub," a word that suggested the two treatments his father had set out to combine: vapor lamps and blood-flow-stimulating plasters. H.S. also inaugurated several high-pressure sales techniques. One was the "spoon test." Lighting a match under a tin spoonful of VapoRub that was then waved under the storekeeper's nose resulted in persuasive inhalation of pungent vapor. Because newspaper ads contained coupons entitling the bearer to a free trial jar, shopkeepers were soon being inundated with requests for samples of a product previously unheard of. VapoRub's debut in Great Britain in 1918 began worldwide distribution. In 1960 Vick Chemical Company became a division of Richardson-Merrell.

VIDEOCASSETTE RECORDER: Technology has both unified and divided the world, as many an American traveler abroad has discovered, sadly or furiously, when trying to plug a hair dryer or razor into an inhospitable outlet. Like TV sets in different countries, videocassette recorders (VCRs), which enable viewers to watch what and when they like, use different standards. Not only are the two VCR types prevalent in America, VHS (for Video Home System) and Beta (for Betamax), incompatible; but neither system can be used universally. Equipment and software made for the United States will not function in many foreign markets and vice versa. The VCR technology was created in America, but virtually every VCR, whatever the brand name, is of Japanese manufacture.

In 1956, during a National Association of Broadcasters convention in Chicago, the Ampex Corporation, which had already introduced the audiotape recorder, demonstrated the first practical method of storing video images on magnetic tape. The price of the black-and-white recorder, about the size of a rolltop desk, was fifty thousand dollars. TV stations promptly ordered $4 million worth. Each hour of tape required a fourteen-inch reel. In 1961, Dr. Peter C. Goldmark, CBS's resident inventive genius, began long and eventually futile efforts to persuade the network to support his electronic video recording (EVR) scheme for putting miniaturized film in cassettes for home viewing on TV sets. In 1963, the British came up with Telcan, which provided eleven minutes of fuzzy black-and-white pictures on an 11½-inch reel. *Television Digest*'s curt critique of Telcan: "Telcan't." In 1965 Ampex, Sony, and Panasonic produced improved black-and-white video recorders that were simpler and cheaper but evoked public apathy. A Sony color unit marketed in 1972, not entirely suitable for home use, was priced at a prohibitive thirteen hundred dollars. That same year, Cartridge Television supplied the first true home VCR, Cartrivision, but only in costly twenty-five-inch color TV consoles. Only six thousand units were produced before the company went bankrupt. In 1975, Sony introduced Betamax, offering one hour of recording time on half-inch-wide tape. VHS, with two-hour tapes, bowed in a year later. In October 1984, Eastman Kodak compounded VCR incompatability via a video camera requiring 8mm tape cassettes.

VIDEO GAME, ARCADE: The world's first coin-operated video game, Computer Space, was invented in 1969 by Utah-born Nolan K. Bushnell. The idea occurred to him while he was still an engineering student at the University of Utah, but he did nothing about it until he was working in Santa Clara, California, as a research engineer for Ampex, which manufactured recording tape and other products.

"I started designing a game in my daughter's bedroom," Bushnell recalled. "I kicked her out, doubled her up with my other daughter." He completed the game, which pitted spaceships against flying saucers, days later at four in the morning. Marketed by Nutting Associates, its sales totaled a disappointing 2,000 units. Bushnell decided that Computer Space was too intricate for nonengineers and tried again. This time, he formed his own company, which he named Atari, borrowing the word (which means "Prepare to be attacked!") from the Japanese game of Go.

The first Atari entry was the Ping-Pong-like Pong, now considered the great-granddaddy of all arcade video games. Bushnell put the prototype in Andy Capp's Tavern in Sunnyvale, California, and went home to await a report on its customer appeal. A couple of days later, he was advised that the machine wasn't working. It had been put out of commission by an overflow of quarters in the gallon-bucket coin repository. An estimated one hundred thousand Pong games were sold, but only about 10 percent were Atari-made. The rest were rip-offs by other companies, mostly Japanese. Several Atari race-driving games did moderately well; but it was 1976 before Atari had another biggie, Breakout, a video jailbreak, which sold fifteen thousand machines.

Warner Brothers Communication then purchased Atari, which had been started a decade earlier on a $500 shoestring, for $28 million. It seemed a good buy—until sales began to drop. One reason was the Bally Manufacturing Company's Japanese-invented Space Invaders, which set a world record by selling more than 350,000 machines. Atari countered with Asteroids, which outsold Space Invaders in the United States, and with Battle Zone but was routed by Bally's next Japanese import, the 1980 blockbuster Pac-Man, renamed from Puck-Man to avoid a raunchy rhyme.

VIDEO GAME, HOME: In 1965, engineer Ralph Baer was working in the equipment design studio at Sanders Associates in Nashua, New Hampshire, arranging tubes and circuits, when he was struck by the idea that TV sets and TV viewers should have more interaction. "It was bugging me," he recalled, "that the television sits there and does nothing." With two colleagues, he set up a makeshift lab and, using little moving dots on a TV screen, created a hockey game. Additional experimentation resulted in volleyball and target games. Baer tried to sell the idea of living-room video games to RCA, Zenith, and other firms but was repeatedly rebuffed. He finally found a sympathetic ear at Magnavox.

Baer's Magnavox-made games all worked the same way: When wired to TV antenna terminals, an electronic brain the size of a quarter with tiny, printed circuits made possible on-screen competitions between two players while displaying a running score. The first games were test marketed with selected dealers who unanimously approved; and in May 1972, Magnavox, with much fanfare, introduced its one hundred Odyssey video games at a New York press conference. Other companies quickly concocted games of their own, several of them far more imaginative. Atari (*see* **VIDEO GAME, ARCADE**) entered the list with a home version of its arcade hit, Pong, and a four-player Super-Pong.

All the early games were extremely simple variations on catch, hockey, tennis, handball, target shooting, and racing; but they became increasingly intricate. Fairchild pioneered microprocessor-driven programmable games via its Video Entertainment System, which utilized videocassettes. Among its cassette choices were tic-tac-toe, turkey shoot, doodle, quadra-doodle, a tank warfare game with sound effects, and blackjack. Predating both arcade and home video games was Spacewar, a computer game devised in 1962 by students and assistants at Harvard's Littauer Statistical Laboratory. It was played on a large, room-sized computer.

VIEW-MASTER: In 1984 Michael Jackson's "Thriller" became the first Talking View-Master. Because of the added built-in soundtrack, as well as the traditional seven pairs of pictures for three-dimensional effect, it was quickly View-Master's all-time best-seller, spurting past scenes from Steven Spielberg's 1982 movie, *E.T.* View-Master reels are sold in more than 116 countries and their succinct captions are printed in 17 languages.

Since this distant descendant of the stereoscopic slide-holder made its debut just before Christmas 1938, more than a billion picture reels and 100 million viewers have been sold worldwide. The View-Master was first manufactured by the nation's leading supplier of scenic postcards, Sawyer's Inc., in Portland, Oregon. It was acquired in 1981 by a limited partnership headed by Arnold Thaler, who promptly decreed that the way to boost sales was to choose more contemporary subjects. He then proceeded to purchase the 3-D rights to movies like *Close Encounters of the Third Kind,* TV series like "The A-Team," and rock groups like Culture Club.

VOLLEYBALL: Although some sources claim that volleyball is a steal from *faustball,* a sport introduced to Germany in 1893, most authorities credit as its originator William George Morgan, physical director of the Holyoke, Massachusetts, YMCA, who initially (in 1895) called it "mintonette." Morgan was a student of James B. Naismith, an instructor for the International YMCA Training School in Springfield, Massachusetts, who in 1891, at the request of the school's director, invented basketball. Morgan decided that basketball was too strenuous for middle-aged businessmen and set about devising something more suited to their age and avoirdupois. *Faustball* called for bouncing a large ball over a rope, with two bounces permissible each time. Volleyball began with a basketball bladder and a rope, but the ball had to be kept in the air. Later, a lightweight leather-covered ball and an eight-foot-high tennis net were substituted. Rules varied in different communities until 1900, when a YMCA Physical Directors' Association committee established guidelines. Soldiers and missionaries spread the volleyball gospel and, worldwide, the game became second only to soccer in popularity.

Skilled athletes, male and female, made contests so rousing, with over-the-net "spikes" topping one hundred miles per hour, that in 1964 volleyball was added to the Olympic roster. While the game continued to be mainly a backyard, beach, and school playground source of fun on its home heath, international volleyball superstars surfaced in Japan, the Soviet Union, China, Cuba, and East Germany. Americans belatedly took up the gauntlet; and in the 1984 Olympic Games in Los Angeles, the U.S. men's team won the gold medal, and the U.S. women's team won the silver. Meanwhile, back in Holyoke, Mayor Ernest E. Proulx ordered the posting of signs proclaiming, "Welcome to Holyoke, the Birthplace of Volleyball and the Home of the Volleyball Hall of Fame." The signs were somewhat premature. The closest thing to a Hall of Fame was a couple of trophy cases in city hall.

WASHING MACHINE: A 1780 machine called a "laundry" by its English inventor, Rodger Rodgerson, predates American Nathaniel Briggs's 1797 device for "washing cloaths," but no description remains of how it worked. Automatic washing machines were being assembled in the United States as early as 1851. By 1875, about two thousand patents had been granted, but the models most frequently used continued to leave housewives' hands red and chapped. Those hands were not spared until the invention of the first self-contained electric machine by Howard Snyder in 1922. Snyder placed a circular plate studded with four vertical fins at the bottom of a tub and attached it to a drive shaft, producing an agitator-type washer. Although most home washing machines still use agitators, they have been augmented by devices that automatically wash, rinse, and dry.

Foreign buyers of American washing machines have put them to unorthodox uses. During the Nazi occupation of the Netherlands, for instance, Dutch farmers, deprived of their butter churns because their captors wanted to centralize the industry, substituted washing machines. On Johnston Island, seven hundred miles southwest of Honolulu, women welcomed the arrival of a laundromat because the washing machines facilitated the tenderizing of a favorite dish: octopus.

WASH 'N DRY: Because Ross Williams was uncomfortable when water shortages aboard the ship on which he served during World War II caused him to forego nightly prebedtime washups, in 1953 he devised a way to eliminate such dirty dilemmas. His antisoiling solution was a paper towel soaked in liquid soap and sealed in foil. A single packet of Wash 'n Dry reputedly provides as much cleansing power as a quart of water. The product is now manufactured and sold worldwide by Colgate-Palmolive, second in the soap and detergent departments only to Procter and Gamble. The company—which does more than half its business outside the United States, marketing directly to 1.5 billion people in fifty-eight countries and exporting to 641 million more in seventy other countries—was formed after World War I by three soap-making firms. One was launched in 1806 by New York's William Colgate; another in 1864 by Milwaukee's B. J. Johnson, who in 1898 introduced Palmolive, once the world's best-selling toilet soap; and the third in 1872 by Kansas City's Peet brothers. The combine's name, Colgate-Palmolive-Peet, was shortened in 1953.

WATER BED: The sci-fi writer Robert A. Heinlein conceived the idea of the water bed in his 1961 cult novel, *Stranger in a Strange Land,* but it was just one of many offbeat Heinlein notions that never got off the printed page. Practical application, however, was not long in coming. The relief of paraplegics and patients suffering from bed sores, not the comfort of insomniacs and lovers, was what prompted Dr. James Weinstein and Dr. Barry Davidson, while at Tufts University, to devise a water-filled medical mattress for hospital use some time before 1965. The mattresses were manufactured first by the Scott Paper Company and, later, under license, by the De Puy Company of Warsaw, Indiana.

Charles Prior Hall claims that he devised the first heated water bed in 1967 while he was a graduate student in design at San Francisco State College. (He filled his first effort with starch and Jell-O.) Touted as a source of better sleep and better sex and a boon for aching backs, water beds, heated and unheated, first sprouted in California hippies' pads and then spread into suburban bedrooms and posh or raunchy hotels in the United States and abroad. Playboy publisher Hugh Hefner covered his king-size model with Tasmanian opossum.

Basically a vinyl bag filled with water inside a wooden frame, the water bed was faulted by city safety bureaus and other detractors as a potential source of hazard as well as happiness. The weight (nearly a ton when filled with two hundred gallons of water) could collapse floors, leakage could flood rooms, the combining of water and heating units could cause electrocution. Water-bed manufacturers countered by guaranteeing their products for periods ranging from ninety days to fifty years. In 1984 sales of water beds in the United States alone totaled 3.4 million. To snare future generations, many manufacturers also offer water bed cribs.

WILD WEST: The entire concept of the "Wild West," chock-full of cowboys and Indians, ranchers and rustlers, train robberies and shoot-outs, which has so intrigued fantasy fans in many countries (*see* COWBOY), is attributed to writers from the effete East.

The Virginian, written in 1902 by a native Philadelphian, Owen

Wister (1860-1938), grandson of famed English actress Fanny Kemble, was the first novel of literary quality to introduce the cowboy to the general public as a folk hero. "When you call me that, *smile!*" a line uttered with laconic menace by the eponymous hero, has echoed through the years. The book, which first used such terms as "cow-puncher" and "sons of the sagebrush," was translated into at least six other languages. It sparked four movies, the first in 1914 and the most noteworthy a 1929 opus starring Gary Cooper in the title role, and was revived as recently as NBC's 1962-71 "The Virginian," television's first ninety-minute Western series.

What Wister did for the "good guys," Stamford, New York-born Edward Zane Carroll Judson, alias "Ned Buntline" (1823-1886), did for the bad—including gunfighters, train robbers, and other rapscallions—in some four hundred adventure-crammed "dime novels." Also a prolific source of glamorizations of the Wild West was Pearl Grey (1875-1939), of Zanesville, Ohio, who later adopted his mother's maiden name and became Zane Grey. Beginning with *The Heritage of the Desert* in 1910 and the ultrapopular *Riders of the Purple Sage* in 1912, he produced a spate of Westerns, many of them romanticizing the lone-wolf gunfighter. Grey authored a Western best-seller every year between 1917 and 1926 and left twenty-four novels for posthumous publication.

Among more recent Western novelists, the most prolific has been Louis L'Amour, who has written ninety-two books with worldwide sales totaling 160 million. More than thirty of his stories and novels, beginning with his very first Western, *Hondo*, have been sold to movies and television. In 1985, he reportedly had thirty more books in the planning stage.

Romantic notions of cowboys-and-Indians were reinforced in the United States and throughout Europe for three decades by "Buffalo Bill's Wild West Show," created in 1883 by Scott County, Iowa-born William Frederick Cody (1846-1917). Cody, dubbed "Pahaska" ("Longhair") by Indians and "Buffalo Bill" after he killed 4,280 buffalo as an 1867-1868 supplier of meat for Kansas Pacific Railroad construction crews, was the hero of about 3,000 dime novels by Ned Buntline and almost 20 other writers. He was later portrayed in 35 movies by, among others, Paul Newman, Charlton Heston, Joel McCrea, Richard Arlen, and Roy Rogers. From the age of eleven Cody held jobs as varied as horse wrangler, mounted messenger, prospector, Pony Express rider, army scout, actor (on stage in Buntline/Judson's *Scouts of the Plain* and on screen in ten silent films), rancher and impresario. His "Wild West Show" co-stars included supersharp-shooter Annie Oakley and Indian chief Sitting Bull. The trio was reunited, via surrogates, in the long-running 1946 Irving Berlin-

Herbert and Dorothy Fields musical, *Annie Get Your Gun,* and its 1950 movie version.

WIRE COAT HANGER: The wire coat hanger has been gratefully used and intemperately abused. A cheap, convenient way to hang clothes, it was also, until automobile manufacturers made design changes, a most efficient instrument for opening locked car doors. However, according to *Mommy Dearest,* the memoir of her adopted daughter, Christina Crawford, movie star Joan Crawford was catapulted into paroxysms of rage by the sight of costly garb draped over a bent-out-of-shape wire hanger.

Boon or bane, the hanger is a descendant of the clothes hook patented in 1869 by O. A. North of New Britain, Connecticut. It resembled today's hanger but had hooks underneath, from which other garments could be hung. According to Barbara Mussell of Woodland Hills, California, her grandfather, Albert J. Parkhouse, invented the wire coat hanger about 1903 while working for the Timberlake Wire and Novelty Company in Jackson, Michigan. Timberlake's employees were constantly irked, she claims, because there were never enough hooks for their coats and hats, and the coats kept getting wrinkled. Finally, Parkhouse bent a piece of wire into two large oblong hoops, twisted both ends at the center where a hook had been formed, and raised the outside of the hoops to fit the shape of his coat. Timberlake patented the idea, but his granddaughter doubts that Parkhouse profited.

By the 1930s, wire hangers were being made in a triangular shape, to facilitate their use on overhead rods at cleaning establishments or in clothes closets. To eliminate the creases that formed when freshly cleaned garments dried on wire hangers, Schuyler C. Hulett, of Spokane, Washington, devised a cardboard tube with a spiral slit that could be screwed around both the upper and lower parts of a hanger. He was granted a patent in 1932. Three years later, Elmer Donald Rogers of Detroit created a hanger with a loosely fitting cardboard tube around the lower bar—a design in common use today.

WITCH HAZEL: Indian medicine men found many uses for the liquid produced by boiling the bark of the witch hazel shrub. It was credited with soothing skin, alleviating internal bleeding, and staving off dimming of the eyes. The potion's witchcraftlike powers presumably were imparted to the Pilgrims, who may have misnamed the shrub, mistaking it because of superficial resemblances for the hazel tree they knew back home. The hazel, too, was supposed to have eerie capabilities. Hazel rods could point out water, gold, thieves, and murderers. Hazel nuts tucked into a pocket were a toothache preventive. According to Indian legend, the braves first began to suspect that the shrub had special powers because it sprouted golden flowers late in autumn after its leaves had fallen. In compliance with what they considered the Great Spirit's wish, they boiled some of the bush's twigs in a huge pot, and lo! the image of a beautiful maiden shimmered in the steam. Somehow this luminous lass was metamorphosed, perhaps by the witch-wary colonists, into a witch named Hazel; and the shrub in which she allegedly made her debut was named the witch hazel bush.

Early in the nineteenth century a man named Hawes, a missionary to the Indians, studied witch hazel's medicinal properties; but it wasn't until a few years later that Thomas Newton Dickinson, a clergyman, decided to cash in on them. Devising a formula that remains largely the same, he established a plant in Essex, Connecticut, in an area generously endowed with witch hazel shrubs. Dickinson's witch hazel went on the market in 1866 and is still being produced at the same site by the E. E. Dickinson Company. At first, druggists filled bottles from kegs bearing Dickinson's bull's-eye trademark and the slogan "Double Distilled—Not Double Diluted." The distribution method changed as women discovered added uses for the pain assuager. Witch hazel serves as a cleanser, an astringent, a "dry" shampoo for corn-row hairdos, and an ingredient in facial masks, toners, hand lotions, and many costly cosmetics marketed by other manufacturers.

XEROX: The first photocopier, the Rectigraph, was conceived in 1903 by George C. Beidler, working in an Oklahoma City land-claim office, as a way to eliminate laborious rewriting or retyping of legal documents. His early experiments, made with an ordinary dry-plate camera, led to the 1906 patenting of equipment marketed a year later by the Rectigraph Company of Rochester, New York. However, photocopying did not become a worldwide preoccupation until the dry, electrostatic Xerox copying process was devised in October 1938 by Seattle-born Chester Floyd Carlson (1906-1968), who conducted his experiments in a one-room lab behind his mother-in-law's beauty parlor in the Astoria, Queen's, section of New York City.

After inking "10-22-38 Astoria" on a transparent celluloid ruler, Carlson. working with an assistant in a darkened room, rubbed a sulfur-coated zinc plate with a handkerchief to impart static electricity, placed it over the ruler, exposed ruler and plate to light, then dusted the plate with lycopodium powder and pressed a sheet of paper against it. When the paper was stripped away, it contained an éxact duplicate of the ruler and Carlson's notation.

Although Carlson's process worked in only a fraction of the time required by other duplicating machines and could be operated without special training, some thirty companies—including IBM, RCA, GE, and Remington Rand—rejected it. Finally, in 1947, the Haloid Company in Rochester acquired production rights. Now the Xerox Corporation, it sold its first copier in 1950 and, currently, dominates the market. The company's trademark, Xerox, comes from a Greek word, *xeros*, meaning "dry."

Xerox copying machines have proliferated everywhere, even in the USSR, where Gosplan, the state planning committee, uses them to reproduce many of its official documents. Annual Xerox revenues from sales and rentals are in the billions. The ease with which copyrighted material can be duplicated by Xerox and other photo-copiers, without payment of royalties, has triggered protests from authors and publishers. Canadian pundit Marshall McLuhan observed, "Whereas Caxton and Gutenberg enabled all men to become readers, Xerox has enabled all men to become publishers."

Y

YALE LOCK: The cylinder lock, which revolutionized lock making, was patented in 1861 by Salisbury, New York-born Linus Yale, Jr. (1821-1868) and became the world's first unidentical mass-produced product. A failed artist, Linus decided to forget about painting and follow his father's trade of locksmithing. In 1848, the senior Linus had already made improvements in venerable pin-tumbler design.

In the 1840s, Linus Junior began making bank locks in a small factory at Shelburne Falls, Massachusetts, devising a series of increasingly effective key-operated mechanisms, a dial-operated combination lock, and in 1863, the first double-dial bank lock. His cylinder lock—with pin tumblers of varying heights operated by a key, making lock picking almost impossible—was intended for use in house and store doors. In 1865, he patented an improved model, which is basically the same Yale lock in use 120 years later. Although Yale's cylinder lock was based on the oldest type known: the pin tumbler or Egyptian lock depicted in bas-reliefs dating back to 2000 B.C., it could be used on a door of any thickness, eliminating the need for massive keys.

When it came to competitors' products, Yale was a chronic lock mocker. He especially enjoyed indulging a pixyish penchant for demonstrating the ease with which he could pick various models of the highly regarded Parautopic Lock. After unlocking them, he would relock them in such a way that they could not be reopened even with the correct key. Because his own shop was busy making bank locks, Yale formed a partnership with Henry R. Towne of Philadelphia, under the name of the Yale Lock Manufacturing Company, to manufacture the cylinder safeguard. Towne persuaded his father to build a factory in Stamford, Connecticut. Yale died three months after its completion in 1868, but Towne made the company a flourishing enterprise. Although Yale locks are still in wide use for everything from school lockers to shop doors, they have acquired formidable rivals in lever locks (popular for protecting houses) and combination locks (with tumblers that are activated by turning a numbered dial).

YO-YO: The name, if not the object, is of American origin. The returning top, an offshoot of the spinning top, has been traced back to ancient Greece, early France and England, and less convincingly, China. Centuries ago, Philippine Island hunters used stone discs on a leather thong as a bolo-type weapon to ensnare animals' legs. The device was a favorite toy of Filipino children, who sometimes became spectacularly adept. Several Americans spotted the commercial possibilities of two round pieces of wood linked by an axle and manipulated by a string. In 1866, a pair of Ohioans patented "an improved bandolore." The following year, a German immigrant, Charles Kirchof, later the inventor of the pop gun, patented and sold a moderately popular "return wheel."

But it was Donald F. Duncan who made the toy an international fad. After seeing a demonstration in California by Pedro Flores, who ran a small company manufacturing the toy, Duncan paid Flores twenty-five thousand dollars for the rights to his Filipino-style version, with the string looped around the axle, instead of tied to it, permitting a far more varied repertoire of tricks. In 1928, Duncan registered the name "yo-yo" (possibly a variation on the French word *joujou* used to identify that and other playthings) with the U.S. Patent Office and coined the motto, "If it's not a Duncan, it's not a Yo-Yo." He made "yo-yo" a national and international catchword by building intensive promotional campaigns around demonstrations, contests, and prizes. One contest attracted entrants from thirty-five nations. It was won by Nemo Concepcion, who ended his routine by flipping his yo-yo into the air and then snaring it in his inside coat pocket.

The world's largest yo-yo, created by M.I.T. professor James H. Williams in 1974, weighed thirty pounds, had a 265-foot cord, and was equipped with a 1½ horse power motor. When it was dropped from a height of twenty-one stories, it rewound for fifteen.

"Yo-yo" has become a pejorative description for individuals who seem unable to make up their minds or who otherwise fail to behave rationally.

Z

ZAMBONI: No culinary cousin to warm-or-cold zabaglione, the "Zamboni" invariably makes its appearance on ice—resurfacing skate-skewered rinks in thirty-three countries. A formidable chunk of equipment, it picks up debris, squeegees off dirty water, and substitutes the clean water needed for a smooth, unmarred surface.

The versatile machine was concocted by Eureka, Utah-born Frank J. Zamboni to pare work hours at the family-owned Iceland Skating Rink in Paramount, California. Before he started experimenting in 1942, five men had to work from ten to as late as eleven-thirty each night to restore the Iceland ice to pristine smoothness. The fourth version of the Zamboni, completed in 1949, did the same job in fifteen minutes. In 1950, Olympic skating star Sonja Henie, who used Iceland as a rehearsal rink for her touring troupe, paid $10,000 for a pair of Zambonis to accompany her coast-to-coast. Another national skating show, the IceCapades, also became a buyer.

The Zamboni earned international accolades when six machines were utilized during the 1960 Winter Olympics in Squaw Valley. Distributorships were arranged in Switzerland and Japan and a secondary plant was established in Brantford, Ontario. In 1986, Zambonis sweeping ice throughout the world numbered about 38 hundred, including more than two hundred in Japan and about nine hundred in Europe. Their cost ranges from six thousand dollars for tractor-towed models to fifty thousand dollars for self-propelled versions with four-wheel drive and skidproof tires.

Because Zambonis are the cynosure of audience eyes during breaks in ice shows and ice hockey games, they have become a popular advertising medium. At the Los Angeles Forum Zambonis publicize Toyotas, and in St. Louis a Zamboni has been gussied up to resemble a king-size six-pack of Budweiser beer.

ZIP CODE: Zip, a word that seems eminently suitable for a system intended to hasten mail delivery—it imitates the sound of a speeding object and one of its dictionary definitions is "to transport with speed"—in this instance is an acronym for Zone Improvement Plan. The first postal zone plan tested by the U.S. Post Office was a two-digit system initiated in Pittsburgh, Pennsylvania, on May 1, 1943, and later installed at 125 of the nation's largest-volume post offices.

The five-digit ZIP code, in which the first two numbers designate a large geographical area and the last three a local delivery area, was inaugurated in July 1963. The practice of pinpointing addresses by adding numerals, letters, or both is now worldwide.

In 1976, a post office task force headed by the present postmaster general, William F. Bolger, mulled zoning changes to speed even more the sorting and delivery of mail. The Canadian system, which utilizes three letters and three numbers that can be combined in myriad ways, was considered and rejected because it would have meant jettisoning all existing ZIPs. Moreover, envelope-scanning optical readers cannot differentiate between the letter *O* and the numeral *0*. In September 1978, the Post Office Department announced a nine-digit system, using a hyphen and four additional numbers after existing ZIPs that can provide enough combinations to suffice until the U.S. population passes the 400 million mark.

From the start it was stressed that the new nine-digit system was entirely voluntary and intended for volume mailers. In late 1983, businesses that made mass mailings were offered a cost-per-item reduction from 18 cents to 17.5 cents if they used the newer system for 85 percent of their presorted mail. Response was so lukewarm that in April 1985 the Post Office revoked the 85 percent requirement, offering the discount for any bundle of presorted mail that contained at least five hundred nine-digit items. Under the five-digit ZIP system, the Post Office was delivering some seventy billion pieces of mail annually to about forty thousand ZIP-designated locales. With nine digits the potential number of ZIP codes soars to forty million.

ZIPPER: The metallic "locker-unlocker" was originally intended to replace shoelaces. In 1893, Whitcomb L. Judson of Chicago invented the mechanism, consisting of two metal chains that could be meshed or unmeshed by using a slide fastener. In his application for the patent granted three years later, he referred to his hookless fastener as a "clasp locker or unlocker for shoes."

When the hootchie-cootchie dancer Little Egypt used one at the 1893 Chicago World's Fair for quick skirt shedding, the device attracted the attention of Col. Lewis Walker, a Meadville, Pennsylvania, lawyer, who subsequently devoted a million dollars to its development. Early models kept coming apart. An improved version, dubbed C-Curity, was marketed in 1902 by Walker's Universal Fastener Company, but that, too, had design flaws. A more reliable product, "separable fasteners," the first to use identical units on parallel tracks, was invented about 1906 by Dr. Gideon Sundback, a young Swedish electrical engineer from Hoboken, New Jersey, but not patented until April 29, 1913. Sundback's Plako slide fastener was the forerunner of the modern zipper. Even better was the Hookless 2, which the Hookless Fastener Company put to profitable use as a way to open and close money belts and tobacco pouches.

In general, however, public acceptance was slow until America entered World War I, when the fasteners were ordered in huge quantities for windproof navy flying suits. In 1922, noticing how well his slide-fastened tobacco pouch worked, the pipe smoker Frederick H. Martin suggested using sliders on B. F. Goodrich galoshes. Because of their z-z-zipping- sound, Goodrich's Mystik Boots became "zipper boots." In 1928, the Hookless Fastener Company adopted Talon as the new name for its product, awarding a share of stock to the suggester.

The use of zippers in clothing received a boost when the fashion-setting Prince of Wales visited the United States wearing zippered trousers. Paris couturier Mme. Schiaparelli's 1938 spring collection arrived in New York with zippers galore. During World War II the U.S. military made extensive use of the device, and in 1959, Nikita Khrushchev urged Soviet farm workers to swap their buttons for zippers.

ZIPPO LIGHTER: The Zippo windproof liquid lighter is perhaps the only product in the world that is guaranteed to remain operative *forever*. In case of any malfunction, the Zippo Manufacturing Company's Bradford, Pennsylvania, factory is pledged to repair, replace, or rejuvenate the offending item without charge. What's more, Zippo won't even accept return postage. Compounding the what's more, the company accompanies its shipped-back merchandise, usually en route within forty-eight hours, with a note thanking the customer for the opportunity to live up to its guaranty. This cheerful dedication to indestructibility reportedly costs the firm more than two hundred thousand dollars a year. The reputation for reliability shared by the company and its product may explain why the Zippo, which comes in forty styles, is the world's best-selling lighter, purchased by the millions each year, usually as a gift or as a promotional giveaway.

George G. Blaisdell, known as "the Zippo man," created the phenomenal flicker in 1932 by redesigning an Austrian army lighter. Zippo zealots claim that the wicks of their prized lighters possess almost awesome longevity and that the cases are effective for multitudinous uses, including bottle opening, hammering, and screw driving. The company declines to put reasonable limits on reclaimability and has repaired or replaced lighters submerged in water for long periods of time, frozen in snow, and run over by trucks.

In 1985, Zippo began marketing a second kind of lighter, a costlier refillable butane model tagged Contempo, with a qualified lifetime warranty and a four-dollar handling charge for repairs.

ZOOT SUIT: Perhaps the most abominable male wardrobe item ever foisted on the world by America's so-called "hepcats" was the zoot suit, which has been blamed on Clyde Duncan, a Gainesville, Georgia, busboy, who in February 1941 ordered "a coat four sizes too long; pant cuffs so tight that a shoehorn had to be used to get the foot through: and 'reat,' or exaggerated, pleats." The bizarre costume may have been inspired by the authentic Civil War-era garb worn by Clark Gable as Rhett Butler in the 1939 movie version of *Gone with the Wind*, the best-selling 1936 novel by another Georgian, Margaret Mitchell (*see GONE WITH THE WIND*). The approved accessories for the zoot suit included a wide, flat hat and a watch chain that dangled almost to the ground. The style found immediate and enthusiastic acceptance in Harlem and the Los Angeles slums and was copied, perhaps mockingly, by convention-scorning youths elsewhere.